Financial Management for Int

Financial Management for International Business

Dr Istemi Demirag

*Reader in Accounting and Finance
in the School of Management at the University of Sheffield*

Scott Goddard

*Senior Lecturer in Finance in the School of Management
and Finance at the University of Nottingham*

McGRAW-HILL BOOK COMPANY

London · New York · St Louis · San Francisco · Auckland · Bogotá · Caracas
Lisbon · Madrid · Mexico · Milan · Montreal · New Delhi · Panama
Paris · San Juan · São Paulo · Singapore · Sydney · Tokyo · Toronto

Published by
McGRAW-HILL Book Company Europe
Shoppenhangers Road, Maidenhead, Berkshire, SL6 2QL, England
Telephone 01628 23432
Fax 01628 770224

British Library Cataloguing in Publication Data

Demirag, Istemi
 Financial Management for International Business
 I. Title   II. Goddard, Scott
 332

ISBN 0–07–707869–1

Library of Congress Cataloging-in-Publication Data

Demirag, Istemi
  Financial management for international business / Istemi Demirag,
Scott Goddard.
    p. cm.
  Includes bibliographical references and index.
  ISBN 0–07–707869–1
  1. International business enterprises—Finance. 2. International
finance. I. Goddard, Scott, 1949– . II. Title.
HG4027.5.D46 1994
658.15'99—dc20   94–14167
                                                     CIP

McGraw-Hill

A Division of The McGraw-Hill Companies

345BP976

Typeset by Datix International Limited, Bungay, Suffolk
and printed and bound in Great Britain by The Bath Press, Avon

Printed on permanent paper in compliance with ISO Standard 9706

To my father: Muhterem Demirag and to my mother: Hayrinusa Akinci

Istemi Demirag

To my wife: Fiona

Scott Goddard

CONTENTS

FOREWORD

With the increasing internationalization of business, volatility of exchange rates and deregulation of financial markets the development and enhancement of effective international management skills is becoming ever more important. Accordingly, this text on the financial aspects of international business is a welcome contribution to meeting the many new challenges of financial and treasury management today.

The scope of *Financial Management for International Business* is wide-ranging and reflects the authors' extensive experience in teaching this subject at many levels over the years. The three parts of the book, international financial markets and institutions, international risk management, and international asset management provide a useful framework for analysing a variety of key issues. In tackling these issues, the authors adopt a decision-oriented approach drawing on relevant theories and empirical studies of company practices. While the analysis and exposition is primarily from a European and especially UK perspective, use is made of a wide range of sources and comparisons made with the US and elsewhere. The clearly written and approachable text is supplemented by a large number of worked examples and solutions to illustrate, as appropriate, relevant concepts and practices.

All concerned should find this book an invaluable asset to improving their understanding of an increasingly important set of financial management issues relating to international business.

Sidney J. Gray
Professor of International Business
Warwick Business School

PREFACE

This book examines financial management and treasury management decisions for international business operations. While theoretical framework is provided to give an essential underpinning to sensible international financial decisions, the book concentrates on modern financial practice and incorporates frequent worked examples, with solutions, which illustrate the complexities and specific problems of the international environment. Worked solutions provide an excellent means of gaining a deeper understanding of the practical elements of international financial management, and readers are strongly advised to use these examples as an important part of the learning process.

The book draws upon many years' experience of the authors in devising and running international financial management courses at both undergraduate and postgraduate levels, and was written to fill a perceived gap in international financial management texts. Although there are several admirable US texts on the subject, much of their content relates specifically to the institutional, accounting and tax framework of the USA, which is not directly relevant to the UK and Europe. The selection of UK-based texts is very limited, and some of their content is incomplete. The current text concentrates on the UK, with many examples incorporating a European dimension.

The text is written to satisfy the needs of a wide market, including:

- MBA and MSc courses in international business and finance
- Undergraduate courses in international business and international finance
- Professional courses, especially relating to the finance papers of the professional accounting, financial and banking bodies, in particular the Financial Strategy paper of the ACCA
- Managers and professional advisers concerned with business operations

Although some prior knowledge of accounting and finance would assist the reader of the book, much of the content has been devised to be comprehensible to the non-specialist. Complex mathematics and econometrics have been avoided, but quantitative techniques have been incorporated whenever they are valuable to the international decision-making process.

The authors would like to thank the many people who provided information for the production of this book, especially Grant Thornton for assistance in the preparation of Chapter 17 on International Taxation, the Chartered Association of Certified Accountants for permission to reproduce past examination questions relating to international finance, and to an anonymous referee for his or her helpful suggestions.

Any remaining errors are entirely the responsibility of the authors.

Istemi Demirag and Scott Goddard

INTRODUCTION
THE GLOBAL FINANCIAL ENVIRONMENT AND MULTINATIONAL COMPANIES

INTRODUCTION

The 1980s and early 1990s were a period of substantial change and development in the international financial environment. Volatile interest rate and exchange rate movements existed in many countries, the international debt burden still crippled numerous developing countries (and some Western banks), the Cold War was, hopefully, assigned to the history books and European integration stuttered forwards. Interspersed with these events were periods of international instability such as the Gulf War, crises in Eastern Europe and the former Soviet Union, and economic recession in many major Western nations, including the United Kingdom. Although these events might seem quite dramatic, it is likely that subsequent decades will experience events that are equally dramatic and have equally important effects on the development of international trade and investment. This is the environment in which companies must now operate and must take decisions affecting their future growth and prosperity.

This book examines the financial bases of such decisions, and illustrates how companies might react to protect themselves from very uncertain future events. The emphasis of this book is financial; however, it must be stressed that many international business decisions are taken for political, cultural or other non-financial reasons. It is the function of the decision-maker to incorporate into the decision process both relevant financial and non-financial data.

Globalization

In recent years financial markets have become increasingly international, a process sometimes referred to as globalization. Globalization has been facilitated by widespread deregulation of financial and capital markets during the 1980s, which has allowed banks and other financial institutions to offer a global service to their clients. Deregulation has taken a number of forms:

1. *Foreign exchange controls* International trade and investment can only expand if there are no significant restrictions on currency movements. The UK removed all of its exchange controls as long ago as 1979, and most other major Western trading nations have done so since, although a few restrictions still exist.
2. *Capital markets and controls* Access by foreign companies to many domestic capital markets has been improved during the last decade, especially Japan, Germany and Switzerland and the range and type of financial instruments that can be issued have been increased.

3. *Taxation*   Many countries have scrapped the at source withholding tax that was payable by foreigners on investment income, leaving income receivable gross of tax. This has made markets such as the USA much more attractive to foreign investors.
4. *Interest rates*   Some countries, including Japan and the USA, have often imposed restrictions on the amount of interest that could be paid on bank or other deposits. Many of these restrictions have now been removed.
5. *Geographical restrictions*   Many countries imposed barriers which prevented foreign companies operating as banks, or members of local stock exchanges. These rules have been relaxed, usually by reciprocal agreements between individual countries.

While deregulation was a necessary stimulus to the process of globalization it was by no means the only one. The information technology revolution has provided banks, foreign exchange dealers and money managers with instant access to information all around the world. Dealing in shares, fixed interest securities and currencies now takes place on a 24-hour basis with trading moving from one major financial centre to another, and the massive growth of new risk protection techniques such as options, swaps and futures (discussed in later chapters) has stimulated international securities issues.

The results of increased internationalization have been dramatic. Flows of funds between countries have substantially increased to the extent that foreign exchange trading now totals approximately US$500 billion per day, mostly for the purchase and sale of financial assets. International investment has increased, both in real assets such as foreign subsidiaries owned by multinational companies, and financial investments. International investment in shares and bonds is today easy for both institutional investors, such as pension funds and life assurance companies, and individual investors through the vast array of international unit trusts (mutual funds) and investment trusts that have been established as exchange controls, and other barriers to the international movement of capital have been removed.

There has also been a fundamental change in the role of banks with a shift from traditional deposit taking and lending to fee-earning business. This is known as the process of disintermediation.

Disintermediation

Disintermediation involves companies raising funds directly from investors rather than borrowing from a financial institution such as a bank. This is achieved by their issuing securities, sometimes referred to as securitization, mostly in the form of marketable debt, which is purchased by investors. There is an alternative meaning of securitization, which is the raising of funds through the issue of marketable debt that is secured against the company's existing assets or future earnings.

The advantage of disintermediation to borrowers is that by eliminating the bank as the middle man funds may be raised at a lower cost, often more quickly and in a more flexible form. Investors can also benefit from receiving a higher rate of interest than from a bank deposit (taking into account the relative risk of banks and issuers of corporate debt), and in most cases hold a marketable security which can be sold, if the investor wishes, prior to its maturity date. Banks often have a role to play in the securitization process in that they act as fee earning advisers rather than playing their traditional role as direct lenders.

Securitization, as an alternative to bank borrowing, is only available to relatively large companies with good credit ratings.

Multinational companies in international business

Companies which issue securitized debt are often multinational companies, which today dominate the trade and production of many countries. There are several definitions of multinational companies, but the essential feature is that they are engaged in manufacturing or other operations abroad as well as in a domestic economy. Alternative definitions include:

1. The ratio of foreign to total operations, usually measured by turnover or assets. Companies with greater than 25 per cent or 30 per cent foreign activities are considered to be multinational. Such measures are somewhat arbitrary in their selection of the percentage that constitutes a multinational company.
2. Companies with operations in six or more foreign countries.
3. Multinationality depends upon the style of management of the company (Perlmutter, 1969). Only companies with a geocentric style, which take decisions based upon their implications for worldwide operations and engage in integrated global planning, are regarded as multinational companies.
4. Any company with production or other operations in at least one foreign country.

Table 1 The world's largest multinational companies, 1989

Company	Country	Turnover ($US million)
Sumitomo Corporation	Japan	158,221
C. Itoh & Co. Ltd	Japan	147,106
Mitsui & Co. Ltd	Japan	136,578
Marubeni Corporation	Japan	131,419
Mitsubishi Corporation	Japan	129,689
General Motors	USA	126,932
Nissho Iwai Corporation	Japan	108,118
Ford Motor	USA	96,146
Exxon	USA	86,656
Royal Dutch/Shell	Netherlands/UK	85,536
IBM	USA	62,710
Selected European multinationals:		
British Petroleum	UK	48,602
Daimler-Benz	Germany	40,633
Fiat Group	Italy	38,044
Volkswagen	Germany	34,760
Siemens	Germany	32,676
Unilever	Netherlands	31,256
Nestlé	Switzerland	29,341
Philips	Netherlands	26,972
Peugeot Group	France	23,981
ICI	UK	21,595

Reprinted by permission of FORBES Magazine © Forbes Incorporated 1990

Statements about multinational companies and data showing the size and significance of such companies will be influenced by the definition selected. However, there is little doubt that no matter what definition is used, more than half of the world's direct investment abroad is undertaken by multinational companies, and the turnover of the largest multinational companies is in excess of the gross national product of many countries.

By comparison, the gross national product in the same year (1989) was:

	$US million
Mexico	126,000
South Africa	59,900
Ireland	28,600
Israel	25,900

Such league tables can be produced in many ways, for example, based upon turnover, profit, assets values, and stock market capitalization. Relative positions can vary significantly from year to year, partly because of physical growth of the multinationals, but mainly because of fluctuations in the value of the US dollar against the yen and other major currencies. In some years Japanese companies dominate the table, in other years US multinationals form a higher proportion of the top ten.

The influence of multinational companies on the economies of individual countries is substantial. Direct investment by multinationals is seen as a major means of economic development by many nations. Multinationals provide the capital that is not available domestically in a host country and can stimulate employment, exports, and transfer a higher level of technology to the country than previously existed. There may, however, be a price for the host country to pay. Multinationals seek to maximize profits or shareholder wealth on a global basis. This involves shifting large amounts of funds between the major money and capital markets to take advantage of high interest rates produced by temporary market imperfections. Such actions can significantly affect a country's monetary policies and balance of payments position. Potential conflicts between multinational and host nations are discussed in Chapter 13.

The 1980s and early 1990s saw many fundamental changes in the international financial environment, a rapid growth in international markets and in the complexity and sophistication of techniques that are available to companies to manage their international trade and investment operations. In the remainder of this book the implications of these changes for efficient corporate management will be examined.

REFERENCE

Perlmutter H. V. (1969) 'The tortuous evolution of the multinational corporation', *Columbia Journal of World Business*, Jan–Feb.

ADDITIONAL READING

Zenoff D. B. (1987) (ed), 'Corporate finance in multinational companies', *Euromoney Publications*.

ONE

INTERNATIONAL FINANCIAL MARKETS AND INSTITUTIONS

THE INTERNATIONAL MONETARY SYSTEM

INTRODUCTION

The international monetary system is a general term for the institutions, laws and procedures that exist to facilitate international payments. This chapter examines the development of the international monetary system from its early years to the 1990s and the entry of the UK into the European Monetary System (EMS). International monetary relations have periodically been subject to dramatic changes which have had a significant influence on the international financial decisions of the corporate sector. Today's managers must work within the environment dictated by international monetary relationships and require an understanding of the nature and function of the current system.

The early years

An international monetary system has been in existence since the time that goods were first traded internationally for money. It is, however, since the widespread adoption of the gold standard in the late nineteenth century that the major developments have occurred. The UK entered the gold standard as long ago as 1816, but it was not until the 1870s that most major European countries and the USA adopted the system, and the 1890s for Russia and Japan. A country is on the gold standard when its central bank is obliged, on demand, to exchange the country's currency for gold. The gold standard valued currencies in terms of a gold equivalent; for example, for many years one ounce of gold was valued at US$20.67. As most major currencies had a fixed value in terms of gold this meant that the values of such currencies were effectively linked together in a system of fixed exchange rates.

In order for the gold standard to exist, the governments of the participating countries had to undertake to buy or sell gold at the agreed price for their currency. Gold was selected as it is a scarce commodity which is produced in a standard and verifiable quality, is easy to transport and can be divided into convenient units of a standard weight and known value. Another useful attribute is that supplies of gold cannot quickly be increased. As currency values were linked to gold, the supply of money within an economy was constrained by the supply of gold.

Although the supply of gold fluctuated historically, such fluctuations were relatively small and for much of the period that the gold standard existed the link between currency values and gold helped to promote long-term price stability. Gold effectively became a form of world money which was part of the mechanism to remedy any balance of payments disequilibria between countries. If, for example, France experienced a balance of payments deficit there would be net outflows of gold from France, effectively reducing the French money supply and ultimately French prices. A country experiencing a balance of payments surplus, on the other hand, would see an increase in its money supply and prices. These changes in relative prices would lead to an increase in French exports and a decrease in the exports of the country where prices had increased and would tend to restore the balance of payments of both countries to an equilibrium position. Although this is a somewhat simplified representation of economic relationships, the period of the gold standard between the 1880s and the start of the First World War was one of unprecedented price stability and growth in international trade.

Gold was not the only form of international money at this time. Foreign traders and central banks made settlements with either gold or one of the two reserve currencies—sterling, or, to a lesser extent, the US dollar. Both the UK and the USA could create international money by increasing the supply of their currencies. The gold standard effectively ended with the outbreak of the First World War when most governments encouraged or forced private holdings of gold to be sold to them, and were reluctant to use gold to settle international payments.

Much of Europe experienced very rapid inflation during and immediately after the First World War, which made it impossible to return to a gold standard for several years and, when a return was contemplated, the gold standard could not be restored for most countries at the old exchange values that had existed before the war. The USA, which suffered relatively little inflation at this time, returned to the gold standard in 1919. West Germany eventually controlled the post-war hyperinflation which saw the value of the Deutschmark plummet to 4 trillion to the US dollar and rejoined in 1924. The UK did not rejoin until 1925 and, despite the inflation that had occurred, rejoined at the pre-war rate. From 1925 the UK actually participated in a modified form of the gold standard, the gold bullion standard, whereby it was no longer possible to convert individual bank notes into gold, but gold bars of 400 ounces were bought and sold by the Bank of England. Returning at the pre-war value despite inflation in the intervening years meant that sterling was overvalued, and this led to deflationary effects on British wages and prices and a reduction in exports. Eventually a run on UK gold reserves caused by substantial foreign demands to convert sterling into gold forced the UK to abandon the gold standard in 1931. Two other notable events of this time contributed to the decision to leave the gold standard: the Great Depression which began in the late 1920s, and an international financial crisis in 1931 precipitated by the collapse of the Kredit-Anstalt bank in Austria.

The 1930s saw many countries engaging in competitive devaluations in order to stimulate their economies after the depression, and the widespread use of protective exchange controls. These exchange controls remained in force during the Second World War in order to facilitate the war effort of the countries involved.

The eras of the gold standard and gold bullion standard are often cited as golden periods of economic progress, and there have been some advocates of a return to the gold standard as a possible remedy for today's economic problems. Such suggestions ignore the limitations of the gold standard and its relevance to the 1990s, where interest rates, exchange rates, prices and economic growth are far less stable than when the gold standard existed.

Like all commodity monies gold has its shortcomings, namely:

1. High cost of production.
2. Use of gold provides benefits to those countries where it is produced, and the world's largest gold producers, South Africa and the former USSR, are countries which, until recently, have not enjoyed good political relations with the major Western nations.

3. The increase in the supply of gold may not reflect the world's need for extra liquidity or its demand.

Bretton Woods

In 1944 the leaders of 21 countries gathered together at Bretton Woods, New Hampshire, for an International Monetary and Financial Conference. The aims of this meeting were:

1. To promote international monetary cooperation.
2. To enable and encourage the expansion and balanced growth of international trade, thus maintaining high levels of employment and real income and the development of productive resources of all members.
3. To stabilize the exchange rates in order to minimize the exchange risks of international trade and avoid competitive exchange depreciation.
4. To establish a multinational system of payments and eliminate foreign exchange restrictions which hamper growth.
5. To enable member countries to temporarily borrow funds under adequate safeguards in order to correct any balance of payments deficits without having to take measures which could damage national or international prosperity (thus shortening or lessening the degree of any disequilibrium in balance of payments).

The meeting resulted in the agreement upon and implementation of what has become known as the Bretton Woods system and also the establishment of the International Monetary Fund and the World Bank Group.

The Bretton Woods system involved each participating country fixing the value of its currency in terms of gold, but not being required to exchange its currency into gold, as was the case under the gold standard. Only the US dollar remained convertible into gold. By this time the US dollar was easily the world's most important currency and one ounce of gold was set at the equivalent of US$35. As each other currency was also fixed in terms of gold, all participating currencies were effectively linked in a system of fixed exchange rates. Each country was committed to keeping the value of its currency within + or − 1 per cent of the central parity value. In order to maintain this relationship central banks had to buy or sell their own currency, usually against the US dollar (by using or building up the country's foreign currency reserves) to maintain the currency's value at the agreed level. The Bretton Woods conference appreciated that countries periodically experience balance of payments difficulties which create problems for the maintenance of the agreed currency parities, and to assist countries in these circumstances a new international organization was created: the International Monetary Fund (IMF).

The IMF was established to encourage communication and collaboration concerning international monetary problems and, through a system of loans, to provide member countries with the necessary short-term funds to try to eliminate any balance of payments deficits.

When a balance of payments disequilibrium was considered to be insoluble at the prevailing exchange rate a devaluation of a country's currency was allowed by up to 10 per cent without any formal IMF approval. Approval for changes greater than 10 per cent would only be given by the IMF if there was sufficient evidence to suggest that the country was suffering from a fundamental disequilibrium, i.e. a long and continuing loss of reserves due to an overvalued exchange rate.

Each country paid a subscription or quota into a pool of funds managed by the IMF, the amount of the quota being proportionate to the economic size of the country. Originally quotas were paid 25 per cent in gold or US dollars and 75 per cent in the member's own currency. Any member country was then able to borrow back its 25 per cent in gold plus 100 per cent of the total quota so that in any 12-month period a member country could borrow 125 per cent of its quota in convertible currencies or gold. (Under present guidelines each member could annually borrow 150 per cent of its quota or up to 450 per cent during a three-year period.)

During its early years the Bretton Woods system (the gold exchange standard) achieved its objectives and facilitated a large increase in international trade. However, the system contained no automatic mechanism to increase international reserves in line with the rapidly expanding world trade. The demand for increased international reserves was largely filled by the US dollar in its role as a reserve currency, but increased reserves and liquidity required a continual increase in the international supply of dollars largely through the USA experiencing substantial balance of payments deficits. As US liabilities to foreign central banks increased, the stock of US gold holdings became an ever smaller percentage of US foreign liabilities. This situation could only exist as long as countries retained confidence in the dollar and did not choose to convert their holdings of dollars into gold, as they were allowed to do under the terms of the Bretton Woods agreement. Some alleviation of the problem of international reserves occurred during the 1960s through a system of official currency swaps between the central banks of the 'Group of Ten' most industrialized countries. If the pound was relatively weak, the Bank of England could, for example, make pounds available to a foreign central bank, in return for which an equivalent amount of a foreign currency would be made available to the Bank of England. The foreign currency could then be used to buy pounds on the foreign exchange market to increase its value. The foreign central bank would make no use of the pounds it had available under the swap agreement, and when the pressure on the pound disappeared the swap would be reversed. However, concern about the international role of the dollar led to the creation in 1969 of a new international reserve asset, the Special Drawing Rights (SDR).

SDRs were a new kind of reserve which the IMF would distribute to member countries in proportion to their quotas. These reserves were created to maintain the proportion of international reserves to world trade. (By mid-1988 a total of more than SDR 19 billion or US$22 billion was outstanding, or 4 per cent of the world international reserves other than gold.) They were originally valued at US$1, the weighted average of 16 currencies at the time of introduction, but are now valued at the weighted average of a basket of five major currencies, the US dollar, Japanese yen, French franc, Deutschmark and pound sterling. SDRs could be used by the holder to acquire foreign currency from another country by depositing them via the IMF special drawing account.

During the 1960s there were also significant developments relating to gold. The opening of a gold market in London led to an upward pressure on the price of gold, and in 1962 a central gold pool of US$80 million was set up by eight countries in order to stabilize the price at US$35 an ounce. Both central banks and private speculators were able to convert dollars into gold at this price, but by 1968 it was apparent that the free market price of gold would be well in excess of this price. Speculative buying of gold forced the central banks to abandon the gold price to market forces for commercial transactions while maintaining the price at US$35 an ounce for international settlements between themselves. The increasing gap between the gold prices and the fact that countries were unwilling to revalue their currencies even in the face of massive disequilibrium led to mounting pressure on the system. Speculation against the dollar increased as President Nixon pursued an expansionist policy which forced European and Japanese banks to buy dollars to maintain their exchange rates. The market price of gold rose sharply and many countries demanded the conversion of their dollar reserves into gold, but the USA, having a reserves to liability ratio of only 1:5, decided to suspend convertibility and allow the dollar to float freely.

The Smithsonian agreement and post-1972 developments

The Smithsonian agreement of December 1971 increased the permitted exchange rate variation from 1 to 4.5 per cent, revalued currencies against the dollar and devalued the dollar against gold from US$35 to US$38. This was further devalued to US$42.22 per ounce in February 1973, but a further exchange rate crisis in March led to the final collapse of the Bretton Woods system when European central banks refused to buy dollars.

In 1972, the members and prospective members of the EC all entered into the European Joint Float Agreement, known as the Snake. Under this agreement the member countries pledged to keep their exchange rates within a 2.25 per cent trading band of each other and also within a 4.5 per cent band of the US dollar (the Dutch and the Belgians maintaining a still narrower band of 1 per cent), but within two months market pressure had forced the UK and Denmark to leave, followed by Italy in February 1973.

The same market pressures were also forcing changes in the exchange rates set down by the less than a year old Smithsonian agreement, and it was recognized that changes had to be made to the international monetary system. In Jamaica, in January 1976, the members finally came to an agreement on the changes which are the basis for the system today. The main points were:

1. Floating exchange rates were accepted and member countries were no longer required to maintain their par values.
2. Gold was demonetized as a reserve asset and members could now trade gold at the market price.
3. IMF quotas were increased to US$41 billion and less developed countries were given greater access to IMF funds.
4. Voting rights were adjusted to reflect new trade and reserve distributions, leaving the OPEC countries with 10 per cent of the voting shares.

THE UK AND THE EUROPEAN MONETARY SYSTEM

The European Monetary System

In March 1979 the EC countries formed the European Monetary System (EMS) in order to stabilize the volatility in the foreign exchange markets and to give impetus to the movement towards economic union within Europe. The EMS agreement involved the creation of a new reserve, the European Currency Unit (ECU), which operates in much the same way as SDRs, i.e. it is valued on the weighted average of the member countries' currencies, the weights being based on the members' shares of intra-European trade. Full members of the EMS agreed, under the Exchange Rate Mechanism (ERM), to maintain their exchange rates within 2.25 per cent of a central parity (originally with the exception of Italy). If a member's currency deviated by more than 1.69 per cent from the central rate then steps would be taken by that country to correct it (if the currency was weak, by buying its own currency to support its value) or the currency would be devalued. Devaluation is considered to be a last resort and can only take place with the agreement of all EMS members.

Member countries are able to intervene in the foreign exchange markets to support their currency because of an almost unlimited borrowing facility made available as part of the system. This is known as the VSTF (very short-term financing facility) and must be repaid within three months. Additionally, short-term (up to nine months) and medium-term financial support (up to five years) are available to EMS members.

The European Monetary Cooperation Fund (EMCF) was established in 1982 with the aim of administering the credit facilities open to members and to issue ECUs in the same way as the IMF issue SDRs.

The UK did not become a full participating member of the EMS until October 1990, when it joined the ERM with permitted fluctuations of + or − 6 per cent of agreed central parities. The central rates, upper limits and lower limits for sterling against the other member countries of the ERM in 1990 are shown in Table 1.1 below. Greece and Portugal were not participating in the ERM.

Table 1.1 (Currency values are per £ on 22 October 1990)

	+ 6%	*Central rate*	− 6%
French franc	10.5055	9.89389	9.31800
Belgian/Lux. franc	64.6050	60.8451	57.3035
Italian lira	2343.62	2207.25	2078.79
Dutch florin	3.52950	3.32389	3.13050
Deutschmark	3.13200	2.95000	2.77800
Irish punt	1.16920	1.10118	1.03710
Danish krone	11.9479	11.2526	10.5976
Spanish peseta	203.600	191.750	180.590

Source: Bank of England factsheet, 'The European Monetary System'

In theory, the pound could have fluctuated against the French franc from 9.31800/£ to 10.5055/£, but it is unlikely that this full range of fluctuation would have been possible as the pound would probably have reached its limit against one of the other ERM currencies, necessitating corrective action, before it reached both extreme values against the French franc.

In September 1992, in the midst of an economic recession, an international currency crisis, poor UK export performance and widespread calls for the reduction in UK interest rates, sterling reached its ERM floor against the Deutschmark. The UK government used substantial sums from the country's foreign currency reserves to support sterling, raised interest rates by 2 per cent and then announced a further unprecedented 3 per cent rise. None of these measures proved adequate to maintain the level of sterling and on 15 September, a date better known as 'Black Wednesday', the UK's membership of the ERM was suspended and sterling was allowed to float against other currencies. Italy also suspended its membership of the ERM around the same time. Subsequently the value of sterling has fallen against most major currencies, and in mid-1993 was approximately 15 per cent lower against the Deutschmark than its ERM mid-rate.

The ERM came under further pressure during the summer of 1993, with the French franc in particular facing the threat of devaluation. The pressure on the franc finally became unsustainable during the weekend of 31 July–1 August 1993, when speculative pressures forced the abandonment of the old ERM currency limits and the adoption of much broader trading bands for all members. Currency values of ERM member countries were allowed to fluctuate within a 15 per cent band, with the exception of the Deutschmark, Dutch guilder and Belgian franc which agreed a 6 per cent band. These new broader bands were a severe blow to the objective of convergence in currency values and ultimately a single European currency. It is the declared policy of the UK government to resume membership of the ERM when economic circumstances permit; whether there is an ERM for the UK to eventually rejoin remains to be seen.

Different forms of exchange rate mechanism The EMS is one example of exchange rate relationships that exist between different countries. There are several mechanisms by which the relationships between exchange rates are determined.

There has been considerable debate as to whether exchange rate systems that are fixed, or almost fixed, are better than flexible exchange rate systems which react quickly to market forces (see, for example, Friedman (1953) or Sohmen (1969)). Flexible rates offer a more direct adjustment process to changes in the economic relationships between nations. As a country moves into a situation of balance of payments deficit, exchange rates will react to reflect this, with the country's currency falling in value on the foreign exchange markets. The process is one of gradual movement, rather than the one-off substantial movement through devaluation or revaluation that might be necessary with a fixed rate regime. An extension of this argument is that flexible rates should prevent persistent balance of payments deficits and lead to greater confidence in the international monetary system and less speculative international movements of funds.

Flexible exchange rates also mean that the need for countries to hold large amounts of foreign currency reserves is reduced. With a fixed rate regime (or a system where rates are constrained within a narrow band), when a country experiences balance of payments difficulties and pressure on its currency it will usually require large amounts of foreign currency reserves to support the currency until the pressure recedes, or devaluation is forced. Government intervention to influence exchange rates is not so necessary with floating rates since the market rate changes themselves are reflecting the changes in economic relationships. Intervention in fixed rate regimes does not only take the form of buying and selling foreign currency reserves: tariffs, quotas, exchange controls and other restrictions may be imposed to support a currency which stifle the development of free trade and international capital movements. Such restrictions should not be necessary with floating rates.

Fixed exchange rates inevitably mean that domestic economic policies are influenced by the policies of other countries, especially where there is a dominant economic force within the fixed rate block. Many countries link their exchange rates to the US dollar: if the USA increases its money supply, and therefore inflation, similar effects are likely to be felt in other countries which have their currencies tied to the dollar, especially if the USA is also the dominant trading partner with such countries. A floating rate regime would mean that inflation in the USA should result in a fall in the value of the dollar without significant inflationary effects in other countries.

The exchange rate mechanisms of most of the world's nations are summarized in Table 1.2.

The future for Europe

The Delors committee report of 1989 proposed a three-stage approach to economic and monetary union.

Stage 1 (from July 1990) is a convergence stage which involves:

Table 1.2 International monetary agreements as at March 1993

Currency pegged to					Flexibility limited in terms of a single currency or group of currencies			More flexible		
US dollar	French franc	Russian ruble	Other currency	SDR	Other composite[2]	Single currency[3]	Cooperative arrangements[4]	Adjusted according to a set of indicators[5]	Other managed floating[5]	Independently floating
Angola	Benin	Armenia	Bhutan (Indian rupee)	Libya	Algeria	Bahrain	Belgium	Chile	China, P.R.	Afghanistan, Islamic State of
Antigua & Barbuda	Burkina Faso	Azerbaijan	Estonia (Deutsch-mark)	Myanmar	Austria	Qatar	Denmark	Colombia	Ecuador	Albania
Argentina	Cameroon	Belarus		Rwanda	Bangladesh	Saudi Arabia	France	Madagascar	Egypt	Australia
Bahamas, The	C. African Rep.	Georgia		Seychelles	Botswana	United Arab Emirates	Germany		Greece	Bolivia
Barbados	Chad	Kazakhstan			Burundi		Ireland		Guinea	Brazil
	Comoros	Kyrgyzstan	Kiribati (Australian dollar)		Cape Verde		Luxembourg		Guinea-Bissau	Bulgaria
Belize	Congo	Moldova			Cyprus		Netherlands		Indonesia	Canada
Djibouti	Côte d'Ivoire				Fiji		Portugal		Israel	Costa Rica
Dominica	Equatorial Guinea		Lesotho (South African rand)		Hungary		Spain		Korea	Dominican Rep.
Ethiopia	Gabon				Iceland				Lao P.D. Rep.	El Salvador
Grenada			(South African rand)		Jordan				Maldives	Finland
Iraq	Mali		Namibia (South African rand)		Kenya				Mexico	Gambia, The
Liberia	Niger				Kuwait				Pakistan	Ghana
Marshall Islands	Senegal				Malawi				Poland	Guatemala
Mongolia	Togo				Malaysia				Sao Tome & Principe	Guyana
Nicaragua			Swaziland (South African rand)		Malta				Singapore	Haiti
Oman					Mauritania				Somalia	Honduras
Panama					Mauritius				Sri Lanka	India
St. Kitts & Nevis					Morocco				Tunisia	Iran, I.R. of
St. Lucia					Papua New Guinea				Turkey	Italy
St. Vincent and the Grenadines					Solomon Islands				Uruguay	Jamaica
Suriname					Tanzania				Vietnam	Japan
Syrian Arab Rep.					Thailand					Latvia
Yemen, Republic of					Tonga					Lebanon
					Vanuatu					Lithuania
					Western Samoa					Mozambique
					Zimbabwe					New Zealand
										Nepal
										Nigeria
										Norway
										Paraguay
										Peru
										Philippines
										Romania
										Russia

Sierra Leone
South Africa
Sudan
Sweden
Switzerland
Trinidad and Tobago
Uganda
Ukraine
United Kingdom
United States
Venezuela
Zaïre
Zambia

Classification status[1]	1986	1987	1988	1989	End of Period 1990		1991				1992				1993
					QIII	QIV	QI	QII	QIII	QIV	QI	QII	QIII	QIV	QI
Currency pegged to															
US dollar	32	38	36	32	25	25	27	26	25	24	23	24	26	24	23
French franc	14	14	14	14	14	14	14	14	14	14	14	14	14	14	14
Russian ruble	—	—	—	—	—	—	—	—	—	4	4	—	5	6	7
Other currency	5	5	5	5	5	5	5	5	5	6	6	5	6	6	6
SDR	10	8	8	7	7	6	6	6	6	6	6	5	5	5	4
Other currency composite[2]	30	27	31	35	35	35	35	35	34	33	32	32	31	29	27
Flexibility limited vis-à-vis a single currency[3]	5	4	4	4	4	4	4	4	4	4	4	4	4	4	4
Cooperative arrangements[4]	8	8	8	9	9	10	10	10	10	10	10	11	9	9	9
Adjusted according to a set of indicators[5]	6	5	5	5	4	3	5	5	5	5	5	4	4	3	3
Managed floating	21	23	22	21	23	23	22	22	23	27	25	23	22	23	22
Independently floating	19	18	17	20	26	25	27	28	29	29	33	36	41	44	48
Total[6]	151	151	151	152	154	154	155	155	155	156	156	158	167	167	167

[1] For members with dual or multiple exchange markets, the arrangement shown is that in the major market.

[2] Comprises currencies which are pegged to various 'baskets' of currencies of the members' own choice, as distinct from the SDR basket.

[3] Exchange rates of all currencies have shown limited flexibility in terms of the US dollar.

[4] Refers to the cooperative arrangement maintained under the European Monetary System.

[5] Includes exchange arrangements under which the exchange rate is adjusted at relatively frequent intervals, on the basis of indicators determined by the respective member countries.

[6] Excluding the following eight countries which as of end-March 1993 have not yet formally notified the Fund of their exchange rate arrangements: Cambodia, Croatia, Czech Republic, San Marino, Slovak Republic, Slovenia, Turkmenistan, and Uzbekistan.

Source: International Monetary Fund

1. Continuing the single market programme
2. Removal of physical, technical and fiscal barriers
3. Reform of EC structural funds
4. Deregulation of financial markets, a single financial market
5. Reduced subsidies and stronger competition policy
6. All EC currencies join the ERM
7. Greater convergence of economic and monetary policies

Stage 2, the 'institutional' stage, was seen as a transitional phase where further convergence occurred, a European system of central banks was established, and progress was to be made towards a common monetary policy.

Stage 3 is economic and monetary union (EMU). This final stage involves:

1. Irrevocable fixing of exchange rates and a single currency within the European community
2. Constraints on national budgets
3. Monetary policy under the control of a European central bank
4. Common international policy between community members

The Delors report was by no means universally welcomed, but the process of integration stuttered forwards until the next major milestone, the Maastricht summit of December 1991. This summit proposed that Stage 2 of the Delors plan should commence in 1994 and the members of the European community, with the possible exception of the UK, would introduce a common European currency, probably based on the ECU, by 1999 at the latest. An autonomous European central bank , with national central banks as shareholders, is to form an integral part of monetary union. However, the events of 1993 make monetary union by 1999 very unlikely.

This form of EMU is strongly advocated by most EC members. Its advantages include:

1. The elimination of transactions costs between currencies. The European Commission has attempted to quantify the benefits from the removal of transactions costs and the spread between the exchange rates when buying and selling a currency (Commission of the European Communities (1990)). The range of savings was estimated to be very substantial, at between 8.2 and 13.1 billion ECU.
2. The removal of uncertainty with respect to exchange rates for managers wishing to trade with or invest in European Community countries.
3. The introduction of a single European central bank. This should lead to greater price stability within the EC, and lower interest and exchange rates. Additionally managers, when making their investment and other decisions, would only need to be concerned with the actions of one central bank rather than the varied and often conflicting policies of 12 individual central banks.
4. A single currency would encourage competition and cross-border investment.
5. The need for foreign exchange reserves is reduced, being necessary only for dealings with countries outside the union.
6. Lower interest rates resulting from lower sustainable levels of inflation.

However, there is a growing body of opinion that these advantages may not all be realized or the cost of achieving them may be too high. Among the arguments against EMU are:

1. Loss of sovereignty.
2. A reduction in the ability of a national government to control demand in its own economy,

especially through influencing the money supply (and, to a certain extent, by artificially manipulating exchange rates). Considerable latitude in fiscal policy is, however, likely to remain with individual governments.

3. The need for policy agreement and coordination between members of the union. Historically this has proved very difficult to achieve as individual governments have pushed for policies and agreements which favour their own country.

4. A much larger EC central budget is needed in order to provide for substantial transfers of funds from the richer to the poorer parts of the community.

In the 1990s the international financial environment in which UK companies must operate comprises the UK in a managed float situation relative to most major currencies, and a flexibly linked exchange rate block within the majority of the European union countries. (Since the ratification of the Maastricht Treaty the European community, EC, became the European Union, EU.) Both interest rates and exchange rates are volatile in comparison with earlier parts of this century, and pose significant risks for companies engaged in international trade and investment.

REFERENCES

Commission of the European Communities (1990) 'One Market, One Money: An evaluation of the potential benefits and costs of forming an economic and monetary union', *European Economy*, No. 44, October.

Friedman M. (1953) 'The case for flexible exchange rates', in *Essays in Positive Economics*, University of Chicago Press, Chicago.

Sohmen, E. (1969) *Flexible Exchange Rates: Theory and Controversy*, University of Chicago Press, Chicago.

ADDITIONAL READING

Coffey, P. (1987) *The European Monetary System—Past, Present and Future*, Kluwer, England.

Goodhart, C. (1991) 'An Assessment of EMU', *The Royal Bank of Scotland Review*, No. 170, June.

TWO

INTERNATIONAL FINANCIAL MARKETS

INTRODUCTION

International money and capital markets are markets in which borrowers from one country may seek lenders in another country to conduct transactions which need not take place in the currency of either the borrower or the lender.

The 1980s were a decade of dramatic change for international financial markets. Increasingly, financial barriers between countries have been dismantled and international transactions have become less subject to restrictions. This chapter examines the international financial markets which exist today, concentrating on the money and capital markets. Money markets are those in which transactions are normally for periods of less than one year, and capital markets for periods of greater than one year. Banks are active participants in both money and capital markets, and their international role is considered in both this chapter and the next. Other international markets, such as the foreign exchange and options and futures markets, are discussed extensively in later chapters.

THE EUROMARKETS

The Euromarkets consist of the banking and financial markets which are located outside the country which has the jurisdiction to issue the particular currency. The prefix 'Euro' really means 'external' and implies that the funds in the market are outside the control of the central bank of the country which issues the currency. Hence one of the most important aspects of Euromarkets is the absence of government regulation.

Banks in Euromarkets tend to concentrate on currencies for which 'deep' markets exist. The US dollar is the predominant currency in the Euromarkets, but there are many other Euro currencies including the Deutschmark, sterling, yen and ECU. Although the term 'Euromarkets' is used, these markets are not confined to Europe.

Euromarkets have grown tremendously in size and influence over the last three decades (some indication of the size of the main Euromarkets is given in Table 2.1). Thus, given their relative importance, much of this chapter is devoted to examining the mechanisms and trends of Euromarkets.

The gross size of the Eurocurrency market is measured as total deposits held in all Eurobanks. The net size is found by subtracting interbank deposits and is a measure of the actual credit extended to non-bank borrowers.

Table 2.1   The size of the Euromarkets (US$ billion)

	Gross market size	By denomination US$	By denomination Others	Net market size	Growth of net market size
1977	740	76%	24%	379	21%
1978	949	74%	26%	478	26%
1979	1,233	72%	28%	578	21%
1980	1,524	75%	25%	705	22%
1981	1,861	78%	22%	859	22%
1982	2,168	80%	20%	1,285	50%
1983	2,278	81%	19%	1,382	8%
1984	2,386	82%	18%	1,430	3%
1985	2,846	75%	25%	1,676	17%
1986	3,579	71%	29%	1,979	18%
1987	4,461	66%	34%	2,377	20%

Source: World Financial Markets, Morgan Guarantee Trust Co.

Origins of the Euromarkets

A combination of factors resulted in the rapid development and expansion of Euromarkets during the last 30 years:

1. A somewhat surprising stimulus for the rise of Eurocurrency markets occurred as a result of the actions of the major socialist nations of the world, especially the former USSR. During the Cold War period of the late 1950s such nations were reluctant to invest their reserves of US dollars in the USA because of the threat of possible confiscation of their investments by the US government. These reserves had been built up through trade and the sale of gold. Instead they transferred their dollar deposits into banks in European financial centres, especially London and Paris.
2. In the late 1950s confidence in the US dollar as the major world currency was restored. Additionally the reopening of the US money markets provided investors with greater opportunities to acquire and transfer funds, thus inspiring the growth of Euromarkets.
3. The imposition of four restrictions in the USA in the 1960s had a marked impact upon the Euromarkets:
    (a) The interest equalization tax of 1963 imposed a penalty on foreign debt sold in the USA; thus borrowers, who had for so long acquired funds from US capital markets, had to seek alternative markets for their sources of funds. The Eurocurrency markets proved to be an obvious choice.
    (b) In 1965 'voluntary' restrictions were imposed on direct foreign investment by US corporations. Consequently US companies had to raise most of the finance for their overseas subsidiaries outside the USA, often via the Euromarkets.
    (c) The Federal Reserve Bank's foreign credit restraint programme restricted the opportunities available for foreign borrowers to borrow medium-term debt in the USA.
    (d) Regulation Q was first imposed in 1966. This limited the amount of interest US banks

could pay on time deposits and led to large sums of capital moving out of the USA and into external markets such as Euromarkets where higher rates of interest were available on dollar deposits.

4. Recurrent US balance of payments deficits in the 1960s led to massive amounts of dollars moving out of the USA. These often found their way into Euromarkets attracted by the higher returns than were available in the USA. Similarly, much of the large surpluses earned by OPEC (oil and petroleum exporting countries) during the 1970s were deposited in Euromarkets.

These factors had the effect of increasing the net size of the market from US$21 billion in 1966 to US$225 billion in 1975.

By far the most important reason for the continuing prosperity of Euromarkets is the absence of government regulation. By operating outside the borders of the country which issues the currency the players in the market are able to circumvent many regulations which are imposed on domestic banking.

The Euromarkets are often divided into four components: the Eurocurrency and Eurocredit which are associated with international bank borrowing and lending; and the Euronote and Eurobond markets which are international securitized debt instruments.

The Eurocurrency market   The Eurocurrency market is essentially a wholesale market where funds negotiated are not for less than US$1 million. Banks form the institutional core of the business, and borrowers and lenders are usually large, well established, 'blue-chip' companies and governments. However, because of the large sums available recently, less renowned companies have entered the market. London is the main centre of business, with New York, Paris, Frankfurt and Tokyo also engaged in large amounts of Eurocurrency business.

Incentives to deal in Eurocurrency markets   The primary incentive to deal in Eurocurrency markets is the absence of government regulation. In order to attract investors to the Eurocurrency market the returns have to be higher than domestic returns, otherwise investors would have no incentive to invest their funds in the market. Similarly, charges on loans have to be lower than domestic costs, otherwise borrowers would raise funds from the home market.

The Eurocurrency market forms the short-term to medium-term part of the Euromarkets and is by far the largest part of the market. Lenders can deposit their funds for any period from overnight to about five years. Borrowers can acquire funds for periods of up to several years although most borrowing is for less than one year.

Eurocurrency is created when a currency is deposited in a bank outside its own country of origin, e.g. a US dollar deposited with a UK clearing bank in London. This would be termed a Eurodollar. It is no different from an 'ordinary' dollar except that the deposit is outside the control of the institution that issued the dollar. An important distinction between the Eurocurrency market and domestic banking is that the Eurocurrency market is not subject to any formal reserve requirements imposed by a country's central bank or other regulatory body, or any domestic banking regulations. This allows banks operating in the Eurocurrency market to lend out 100 per cent of their deposits (if they wish to do so) and to offer slightly better interest rates to both borrowers and lenders than are available in domestic markets.

The rate of interest charged on a Euroloan is usually quoted at a rate above the London interbank offered rate (LIBOR), which is the rate at which six big London clearing banks would borrow from or lend to each other each morning. The US prime rate is also another threshold determining the rates in Eurocurrency markets, but LIBOR is the rate most often quoted.

How Eurodeposits are made   To illustrate how a Eurodeposit is made, consider the following example: suppose a UK company has £3 million in a domestic bank. Attracted by the higher rates in the Euromarket, it decides to transfer its deposits of £3 million to a Eurobank outside the UK. In turn the Eurobank will lend this sum of money to a potential borrower, but in the absence of a borrower it will simply redeposit this sum in another Eurobank. Here it will earn a fraction of a per cent greater than it must pay the UK company for the £3 million deposit. This process of interbank transfers will continue until a non-bank borrower is found and is lent the money.

Deposits in Euromarkets tend to be time deposits of short maturity (usually less than three months) at fixed interest rates. Many of these deposits are on call, i.e. they can be withdrawn at any time. Banks, governments and multinational corporations hold most of the deposits although some wealthy individuals hold Eurodeposits as well.

Eurocurrency loans and deposits are attractive to both borrowers and lenders because:

1. They offer much greater flexibility and freedom from controls than domestic markets. There are no reserve requirements or ceilings on interest rates as those existing in many domestic capital markets.
2. Borrowing costs are often lower than in domestic markets.
3. Interest is paid gross without any deduction of tax.
4. Very large loans can be arranged much more quickly than in domestic markets.

The Eurocredit market   Eurocredits are medium- to long-term international bank loans extended by banks in countries other than the country in whose currency the loan is denominated. Large multinational corporations, governments and other banks are the major borrowers. Loans are usually made on a floating rate basis at some percentage above LIBOR. The interest rate is reviewed at regular intervals, usually three months or six months. The average maturity for a loan is eight years, and managers charge the borrower a commission of 0.25 per cent to 1 per cent of the loan value. Smaller sized loans are made directly by a bank to a borrower, but where large sums of money are involved (and an individual loan can be US$1 billion or more) loans are almost always syndicated, whereby a syndicate of banks join together on an *ad hoc* basis to share the risk.

The syndicate normally comprises:

- Lead banks which negotiate the terms of the loan.
- Managing banks which try to raise the amount of funds required for the loan by contacting a large number of other banks. The latter are known as the participating banks.

Syndicated loans also exist for large short-term Eurocurrency loans. Details of the total syndicated loan and Euronotes (discussed later) are shown in Tables 2.2 and 2.3. As can be seen from these tables, there has been a significant increase in such loans since mid 1975, and over US$222 billion of syndicated loans were arranged in 1992.

Eurocurrency rates compared to domestic rates   Due to the existence of arbitrage (the seeking of riskless profits by moving from unfavourable to favourable interest rates relating to the

Table 2.2 Syndicated credits and Euronotes

Year	Total no. of loans	Amount US$ million	Average size of loan (US$ million)
1975	—	20,553	—
1976	391	27,825	71.2
1977	460	34,859	75.8
1978	1,019	81,763	80.2
1979	1,077	101,612	94.3
1980	1,044	87,981	84.3
1981	1,524	181,248	118.9
1982	1,663	159,458	95.9
1983	1,215	101,659	83.7
1984	1,758	199,236	113.3
1985	1,486	231,500	155.8
1986	1,371	216,664	158.0
1987	1,846	337,421	182.8
1988	2,257	459,043	202.5
1989 (1st quarter)	442	99,772	225.7

Source: Euromoney Supplement, June 1989

Table 2.3 Syndicated loans and Euronotes (borrowers by economic area in US$ million 1974–1989)

Year	OECD	Non-OPEC LCDs	OPEC	COMECON	Supranational
1975	5,069	12,463	6	2,515	65
1976	9,923	11,168	4,012	2,370	352
1977	12,841	12,943	5,898	3,030	147
1978	34,096	28,065	13,470	5,449	683
1979	34,213	43,833	13,727	8,300	1,539
1980	42,417	28,333	11,228	5,037	966
1981	111,794	49,347	14,494	4,324	1,290
1982	83,054	43,475	16,448	7,953	1,945
1983	63,991	22,309	8,293	1,222	2,815
1984	161,673	27,981	5,752	3,478	2,609
1985	175,975	41,867	3,930	5,651	4,077
1986	162,928	37,319	3,207	5,970	1,240
1987	278,448	46,431	4,999	4,626	2,917
1988	383,002	63,520	2,137	7,313	3,071
1989 (1st quarter)	82,237	15,180	1,048	297	1,010

Source: Euromoney Supplement, June 1989

same country), interest rates in Euromarkets tend to be closely related to interest rates in domestic markets. Arbitrageurs would buy from cheaper markets and invest in markets with higher returns when interest differentials exist. Hence the process of arbitrage would ensure that any potential gains from interest rate differentials will be short-lived.

However, the imposition of exchange controls can inhibit the arbitrage process and this creates interest rate differentials between the domestic country and the Euromarket. Furthermore, Eurocurrency spreads (the difference between the banks' lending and deposit rates) are narrower than domestic spreads, and Eurocurrency deposit rates are higher than domestic rates. The reasons for these discrepancies are:

1. Absence of regulation leads to a lack of reserve requirements, thus increasing a bank's earning asset base, allowing it to lend a larger percentage of deposits held and offer higher deposit rates.
2. Eurocurrency markets are characterized by high volume transactions involving large well known companies. This creates a process of standardization, and costs such as transaction and information gathering are reduced, thus allowing Eurobanks to offer preferential rates.
3. The use of tax-haven countries in many transactions allows for higher after-tax returns.
4. Eurocurrency deposits and their commensurate returns are perceived to be riskier than domestic deposits and returns, therefore Eurocurrency markets must offer better terms in order to attract potential investors and borrowers.

The Euronote market The Euronote market comprises a variety of short- to medium-term debt instruments issued on the Euromarkets. These include Eurocommercial paper, Euro medium-term notes (EMTNs), note issuance facilities (NIFs), revolving underwriting facilities (RUFs), and several more variations on these themes.

Eurocommercial paper Eurocommercial paper is securitized borrowing which involves a company writing a short-term promissory note that promises to pay the holder of the note a certain sum of money at a set future date. Only very highly rated companies can issue such paper. The banks and other dealers who help to place (sell) the paper have created a secondary market by being willing to purchase such paper before its maturity date.

The market for Eurocommercial paper was introduced in June 1970. However, its size and influence remained small until the early 1980s. Approximately US$48 billion of Eurocommercial paper was issued in 1990, but this decreased to US$17.5 billion in 1992.

The reasons behind the creation and expansion of the Eurocommercial paper market are analysed below:

1. Eurobanks instigated (as a fee-earning exercise) this note issuance facility (i.e. Eurocommercial paper) in response to increasing competition from the Eurobond market.
2. During the early part of the 1980s many banks reported bad loans due to events such as Third World debt crises, and banks' financial ratios depicted poor performance and results. Because of such circumstances banks could not provide large amounts in loans since this would lead to a deterioration of their capital to asset ratios. The participation in Eurocommercial paper markets provided banks with the opportunity of earning money from fees charged for the issuance facilities but without having to disclose a loan in the balance sheet.

How the system works There are several alternative strategies of issuing Eurocommercial paper; the basic issuance facility will be described here. A syndicate of banks operate together in underwriting an amount of money, say, US$100 million, for a period of five to seven years. The borrower, who has to be a large reputable corporation, draws on this money by the issue of short-term notes, with maturities of one to 12 months. Non-bank investors usually bid to buy these notes, but when there are no bids for a company's Euronotes, or where the bids are lower than the borrower's original prearranged price, the bank syndicate will be prepared to buy the paper at a specific price. In this manner banks are able to transfer money from lenders to borrowers without affecting their balance sheets.

The advantages of this market are numerous, and include: the drawdown facility allows the borrower to acquire funds as and when needed; borrowers can issue notes when interest rates are fairly stable; and borrowers have the choice of selecting the period of maturity for their debt.

Euro medium-term notes (EMTNs) The EMTN market commenced as recently as 1986 to fill a perceived gap between the issue of primarily shorter term Eurocommercial paper and long-term international bonds. They range in maturity from about nine months to 10 years. The attractiveness of EMTNs to issuers includes:

1. They may be sold continually over a period of time, in contrast to a Eurobond issue where the entire issue is made at once.
2. They may be issued in relatively small denominations, commonly less than US$5 million, which provides much greater flexibility to raise small amounts of debt to meet specific needs, in contrast to the much larger international bond issues.
3. Interest is paid on set dates no matter when the issue is made.

From modest beginnings this sector of the market has grown rapidly, and more than US$100 billion of EMTNs were issued in 1992.

Note issuance facilities (NIFs) Note issuance facilities are a form of medium-term commercial paper which are issued by companies under their own name, but where banks, for a fee, guarantee availability of funds to the issuers of the notes by either:

1. Purchasing any unsold notes
2. Providing standby credits

Such issues are normally by tender from investors, with banks managing the issues.

Revolving underwriting facilities An associated form of issue is the revolving underwriting facility (RUF), which is effectively a medium-term commercial paper programme backed by a term-syndicated credit, usually in standby facility rather than an actual loan. The borrower has the advantage of raising funds at the short-term interest rate (through the issue of a series of separate short-term commercial paper issues over time), plus a committed medium-term borrowing facility through the standby credit. Varieties of RUF include the GRUF (global revolving underwriting facility) which gives the borrower the option of borrowing in either the Euromarket or the US commercial paper market, to take advantage of wherever interest rates are perceived to be more favourable; and the CRUF (collateralized revolving underwriting facility) where the issuer provides security against the commercial paper issues, this security being increased when further issues of commercial paper are made.

The Eurobond market A Eurobond is an international bond underwritten by an international syndicate and sold in countries other than the country of the currency in which the issue is denominated. An example of a Eurobond would be a bond sold by a US company which is only available for sale outside the USA. The main parties in the Eurobond market are international banks, large multinational corporations and governments. A multinational company that wishes to issue a Eurobond first contacts an international bank whose task it will be to arrange the issue.

Eurobonds may be fixed or floating rate. Floating rate notes (FRNs) are bonds which have interest payments paid at the end of each six-month period. These notes sometimes have a guaranteed minimum rate of interest. Thus, suppose such a bond has an interest rate of LIBOR plus 1.5 per cent with a guaranteed minimum interest rate of 9 per cent. If LIBOR were to fall below 7.5 per cent the interest paid would be maintained at 9 per cent, which reduces the risk to lenders.

About 70 per cent of Eurobond issues are 'swap-driven', that is, the reason for their issue was the intention of using the Eurobond in an interest rate and/or currency swap. A swap is defined as a transaction in which two parties agree to exchange streams of payments over time. With swaps, borrowers are able to raise money and then swap one interest rate structure for another. For example, a bond yielding a fixed rate of interest can be converted into one yielding a floating rate of interest.

Many swaps have a multicurrency clause where borrowers have the potential of swapping principal and interest from one currency to another. Swaps with multicurrency clauses have proved to be very useful in fulfilling the issuer of the bond's financial objective, which is to raise the issue in the cheapest manner possible. For instance, an issuer might find that the most economical way to raise a bond in sterling would initially be via an issuance of a Eurobond in Deutschmarks, later swapping this for a bond in sterling. (Swaps are discussed in depth in Chapter 8.)

A convertible Eurobond includes an option to allow the holder to convert his or her bond into shares of the company that issued the bond at a price which had been fixed at the time of issue.

Eurobonds are popular because:

1. The Eurobond market is an offshore operation; it is not subjected to national regulations and controls.
2. Issue costs are relatively low.
3. Eurobonds are issued in bearer form and are not registered with the regulatory authorities of the country of the currency in which the funds are raised. This enables the investor to evade income tax.
4. Eurobonds can be issued for very large amounts very quickly.
5. Interest is paid gross, without any withholding tax at source which exists in many domestic bond markets.
6. There is an active secondary market in Eurobonds whereby they can be bought and sold prior to their maturity date, mainly via CEDEL and EUROCLEAR, two international secondary markets for Eurobonds.

Origins The origins of the Eurobond market are quite similar to the origins of the Eurocurrency market. The restrictions imposed in the US financial sector in the 1960s greatly stimulated the Eurobond markets. The continual US balance of payments deficits of the 1960s led to large amounts of dollars flowing out of the USA. Furthermore, since foreign borrowers were not keen on acquiring dollars from the USA owing to the existing capital restrictions of the time, investors had to turn elsewhere in order to satisfy their dollar requirements. Thus, the Eurobond market appeared to be a more attractive and viable alternative. The absence of government regulations further enhanced the appeal of Eurobond markets.

The impact of the above factors was to increase the size of the Eurobond market from US$ 164 million in 1963 to nearly US$3 billion in 1970. In 1992 new issues of Eurobonds totalled almost US$350 billion. Issues of Eurobonds in recent years are shown in Table 2.4.

Table 2.4   Eurobond issues (in US$ billion)

Year	
1985	137.1
1986	185.0
1987	141.6
1988	183.7
1989	223.7
1990	210.2

Source: Bank of England Quarterly Bulletin, May 1991

Mechanisms   The main players in the Eurobond market are international banks, large multinational corporations and governments. Wealthy individuals have an insignificant role in the market. Suppose a borrower, such as a multinational company, wishes to raise finance through the Eurobond market. First, it will approach an international bank whose task is to arrange the issue. This lead bank will organize a managing syndicate which is composed of four or five other leading banks and in addition the syndicate will also include a bank established in the borrower's country. The total cost of issuing Eurobonds, in the form of underwriting and fee costs, usually ranges between 2 and 2.5 per cent of the issue.

Terms of the transaction, which are referred to as a 'tombstone', are published in the financial press. There are different types of conditions and terms attached to Eurobond issues; the major types of Eurobonds will be discussed here. A straight bond is one which is issued at a fixed rate of interest. The interest rate on floating rate Eurobonds is usually fixed at an interval of six months at a certain margin over the LIBOR (or its equivalent) for time deposits in the domestic currency of the bond. For example, with a Eurosterling bond the interest rate will probably be based upon the LIBOR for Eurosterling deposits. Table 2.5 shows the relative importance of Eurobonds and other forms of international debt in global finance.

Eurobond v Eurocurrency loans   When should companies use Eurobonds rather than Eurocurrency loans? The contrasts between these financing sources include:

1. Interest rates on Eurobonds are issued on both fixed rate and floating rate terms, but interest rates on Eurocurrency loans are normally floating.
2. Eurobonds tend to have longer maturities than Eurocurrency loans.
3. The size of issues in Eurocurrency markets tend to be greater than in the Eurobond market, but the gap between the two has recently been narrowing.
4. In the Eurobond market the funds are borrowed and lent in a regimented manner, i.e. on

Table 2.5   International debt issues

	US$ billion	
	1991	1992
International bond issues		
Straights (fixed interest)	263.1	279.5
Equity related	43.8	23.6
of which:		
Warrants	31.8	18.3
Convertibles	12.0	5.3
FRNs	21.8	43.0
Others	1.0	1.2
Total	329.7	347.3
Credit facilities		
Euronote facilities	73.0	118.6
of which:		
Commercial paper	26.9	17.3
MTNs	45.8	100.6
NIFs/RUFs, etc.	0.3	0.7
Syndicated credits	136.7	222.0
Total	209.7	340.6

Source: Bank of England Quarterly Bulletin, May 1993

fixed dates at certain rates. A Eurocurrency loan can be adjusted to satisfy the needs of the borrower as and when they arise.

5. It is easier to switch currencies with a Eurocurrency loan than with a Eurobond.
6. Raising finance in the Eurocurrency market is often a more rapid process than in the Eurobond market.

Foreign domestic markets

An increasing number of domestic markets are available for foreign companies to raise finance in the currency of that domestic market. For example, a UK company could raise Swiss francs by borrowing in the Swiss domestic bond market, or a foreign company could borrow sterling in the UK by issuing a 'bulldog bond'. Large markets also exist in Germany and Luxembourg.

Global bonds

There has also been growth in what may be termed global bonds: bonds which are issued simultaneously in the Euromarket, US and Far East domestic markets, and are traded globally through both international and domestic clearing systems.

International equity issues

Many companies find it useful for raising cash and for purposes of publicity and prestige to have their shares quoted on at least one stock exchange outside their home country. More than 500 foreign companies are quoted on the International Stock Exchange in London.

International deregulation has greatly stimulated the growth of the world's equity markets during the last decade. It is now relatively easy for multinational companies to access equity capital in many different parts of the world. Table 2.6 illustrates the size of some of the leading equity markets.

Table 2.6   Domestic and overseas equities 1992

	No. of companies listed	Turnover value (£m)	Market value of listed companies (£m)
Stock exchange **domestic equities:**			
New York	1,969	1,085,852	2,585,120
NASDAQ	3,850	567,330	410,723
Tokyo	1,651	318,044	1,531,874
Germany (all exchanges)	425	254,674	217,935
UK	1,878	216,929	624,393
Taiwan	256	81,664	67,335
Korea	688	76,074	71,111
Paris	515	73,272	216,947
Switzerland (all exchanges)	180	69,530	129,209
Hong Kong	386	54,727	115,639
Overseas equities:			
UK	514	164,745	
New York	120	77,792	
NASDAQ	261	20,890	
Switzerland	240	6,959	
Germany	240	4,044	
Paris	217	1,776	

Source: The Stock Exchange Factbook 1993

Domestic equity markets are dominated by the American and Japanese exchanges, but the SEAQ international trading system of the International Stock Exchange in the UK is easily the market leader in international equity trading.

Euroequity

If an equity issue is made simultaneously on more than one stock market outside the country of the company making the issue it is known as a Euroequity issue. This market is still relatively small, and has suffered a series of setbacks with unsuccessful issues in recent years.

WHY DON'T ALL INVESTORS INVEST IN EUROCURRENCY MARKETS?

Given the apparent superiority of Euromarkets over their domestic counterparts in terms of higher interest rates and cheaper borrowing, why don't all investors invest in Euromarkets?
The main reasons are market imperfections and restrictions including:

1. Existence of exchange controls prevents the unrestricted flows of money into and out of some countries. Therefore, potential investors are unable to make transactions freely in Euromarkets.
2. Transferring balances into and out of the Eurocurrency market can prove to be inconvenient and costly.
3. The Eurocurrency market only deals with large sums of money (usually greater than US$1 million). Thus, this aspect of Euromarkets prevents many smaller investors from participating in the market.
4. Borrowers in Euromarkets have to be large well established institutions, hence eliminating smaller organizations from the markets.

Developments in the Euromarkets

During the 1980s and early 1990s there were significant fluctuations in the financial instruments used to raise finance in the Euromarkets. The role of the syndicated loan market first fell dramatically, but more recently has recovered as indicated in Table 2.3. Three factors effectively explain this trend:

1. High inflation rates in the early 1980s precipitated inflation-adjusted interest rates for Eurocurrency loans. The instability of interest rates in the market deterred many borrowers from using the market as a source of funds.
2. The Eurobond market started to grow in size and stature during the 1980s. FRNs started to become very popular instruments of finance. Increasing competition from Eurobond markets, which appeared to be a good substitute for the Eurocurrency market, led to a substantial fall in the syndicated loan sector of the Eurocurrency market.
3. Problems with Third World debts were at their most prominent in the early to mid-1980s. Many loans had to be written off. A recent trend in the market has been the vast reduction in the amount of loans issued to Third World countries.

Increasing competition in the Eurocurrency market has led to very low spreads in recent times. In many situations figures reveal that Eurobanks are not making a profit on certain deals. The emphasis has been on preserving market share from the threat of competition. Given the apparent lack of profitability in the Eurocurrency loan market, why do Eurobanks still compete for Eurocurrency loans? Keller (1989) outlines three reasons explaining why Eurobanks are not pulling out of the Euroloan market:

1. The Eurocurrency loan market, especially the syndicated loan market, is still a growth sector of the market—future prosperity is predicted ahead.
2. Increasing merger and acquisition activity at present and in the near future has created a demand for Euroloans.
3. The abolition in 1992 of trade and exchange barriers in the EU countries stimulates the use of Eurocurrency markets for international transactions.

In some circumstances, borrowers of a very high pedigree, such as the government of Denmark, have been granted loans below the rate determined by LIBOR. This gives a sure indication of the growing independence of the Euromarket in establishing its own interest rates.

Should offshore banking be regulated?

The increasing importance of the liberated Euromarket in the financial markets has triggered off calls for Eurobanks to be regulated in line with domestic banks. Some of the arguments for and against regulation of offshore banking practices are discussed below (Aliber (1979)).

Advantages of regulation

1. It can reduce the possibility of the failure of a Eurobank which might then precipitate a major collapse of the international banking system.
2. It can eliminate the competitive advantage which Eurobanks have over their domestic counterparts.
3. It may facilitate the domestic government's monetary policies. The unregulated Euromarket has been deemed to have exacerbated the domestic government's problem of controlling the money supply via the banking system.

Disadvantages of regulation

1. Attempts by a government for regulation will prove futile since Eurobanks will simply move to other unregulated countries. Effective regulation of Euromarkets is contingent upon international cooperation and harmonization on regulation policies.
2. The Euromarkets operate efficiently at the present time anyway so there does not seem to be any apparent need to regulate them.

Even if it was ascertained that the Eurobanks must be regulated there is the problem of what measures to use to regulate them. Wallich (1979) suggested two possible alternatives. The first is to require Eurobanks to maintain liquidity or other forms of reserves, as is the case with domestic banks. The second would be to impose limits on the amount of credit that Eurobanks can extend to borrowers. However, past experience of these policies being implemented in domestic markets implies that the success of these restrictive measures is not guaranteed.

Recent developments suggest that the Euromarkets will probably not be regulated in the near future. The introduction of the international banking facilities (IBF) in the USA in 1981 permitted US banks to participate in the Eurocurrency market. Measures like this reinforce the recognition that Euromarkets are here to stay.

FUTURE PROSPECTS

What is the likely future role and structure of the Euromarkets? The significance of the Euromarkets in the financial world is enormous and their capacity for growth and prosperity in the future should not be underestimated. 1992 has seen the removal of trade barriers between member nations in the European Union; this includes the removal of extensive regulations existing in the banking sector of the Union.

This has implications not only for European banks, but also for international banks outside the community. For non-EU banks to take full advantage of 1992 they will have to establish a firm foothold in the European banking industry. An obvious way in which international banks may try to impose their authority in EU banking will be by taking over banks which are currently operating in the EU. A Price Waterhouse study, cited by Crabbe (1989), claimed that the removal of trade barriers could lead to overall gains in financial markets of between Ecu 11 billion and Ecu 33 billion. London and Frankfurt will probably benefit most, with places like Madrid and Lyons also developing rapidly.

The Euromarket, like any other market, will probably continue to go through its periods of booms and slumps. Currently the Eurobond market is going through a minor slump, but no doubt it will soon recover. The Euromarket is dynamic in nature in the sense that the composition of institutions and investors making up the market is always changing. There has recently been a move towards a better class of borrower, especially those with the highest quality AAA credit ratings. The large houses in the market, especially the Japanese, will continue to assert their influence on the market, and if prevailing circumstances continue, the Japanese will rapidly become the most dominant force in the Euromarket. Furthermore, the continuation of the oligopolistic trend in the market will exacerbate the problems for smaller houses and banks entering the market.

Predicting the future is fraught with danger, and this is especially true when dynamic financial markets such as the Euromarket are considered. There is, however, little doubt that the Euromarket will continue to play a primary role in the world of finance.

REFERENCES

Abdullah, F. (1987) *Financial Management for the Multinational Firm*, Prentice-Hall, London.
Aliber, R. (1979) 'Monetary aspects of offshore markets', *Columbia Journal of World Business*, Fall.
Burgess, R. (1985) 'The competition intensifies as the Euromarket expands', *Euromoney*, February, p. 117–19.
Crabbe, M. (1987) 'Crash of '87', *Euromoney*, December.
Crabbe, M. (1989) 'EC law shapes the pattern of European banking', *Euromoney*, June.
Duffy, G. and I. H. Giddy, (1978) *The International Money Market*, Prentice-Hall, Englewood Cliffs, New Jersey.
Fidler, S. (1988) 'The welcoming arms of commercial banks', *Financial Times*, 29 June.
Fidler, S. (1988) 'Great leap forward', *ibid.*
Freeman, A. (1989) 'Sharper competitive edge', *Financial Times*, 13 July.
Honeygold, D. (1989) *International Financial Markets*, Woodhead-Faulkner Ltd, Cambridge.
Jackson, D. (1988) 'Attractive Rates', *Financial Times Supplement*, 29 June.
Jones, R. (1988) 'ECP—shake-out or weed-out', *Euromoney*, June, p. 173.
Keller, P. (1989) 'Lend the money then sell the debt', *Euromoney*, August p. 99.
McKinnon, S. (1979) *Money In International Exchange*, Oxford University Press, Oxford.
Osborn, N. (1989) 'No investors mean no market', *Euromoney*, September, p. 5.
Pavey, N. (1988) 'Razor-thin returns on cheap standbys', *Euromoney Supplement*, May.
Pearson, C. (1988) 'Eurosterling euphoria', *Financial Times*, 29 June.
Putnam, B. (1979) 'Controlling the Euromarkets: a policy perspective', *Columbia Journal Of World Business*, Fall.
Riley, B. (1988) 'Reciprocity worries London', *Financial Times*, 29 June.
Wallich, H. (1979) 'Why the Euromarket needs restraint', *Columbia Journal Of World Business*, Fall.

THREE

INTERNATIONAL BANKING

INTRODUCTION

This chapter examines the nature and development of international banking, and its importance to the international activities of companies. A major area of concern to international bankers is the Third World debt crisis. The reasons for the debt crisis are discussed, along with strategies to reduce or eliminate the problems caused by excessive lending to sovereign states.

THE NEED FOR INTERNATIONAL BANKING

Why has international banking developed and how do multinational companies gain from its existence?

The importance of international banking to multinational companies may be illustrated by the case of a hypothetical company which is situated in a country where the domestic capital market is limited or perhaps even non-existent. To be competitive in world markets this company may need to make large investments. If it could not borrow enough capital to finance these investments then it would suffer restricted growth, loss of competitiveness or even contraction.

To overcome this problem the company must borrow from international capital markets. Capital restrictions are not very significant for companies operating in the UK or USA, but are still of considerable importance in many other countries, particularly the developing or Third World states. Capital-intensive firms, for example, in heavy industry with large machinery costs or in the chemical industry with large research and development costs, will especially benefit from access to large capital markets. Organizations in all countries may benefit from a lower cost of borrowing if they have access to international markets as well as domestic ones. This is because, although in the long-term real interest rates around the world should be equal (as suggested by the Fisher effect, to be discussed in Chapter 5), market imperfections may create short-term differences between countries. Companies can take advantage of these differences and lower their cost of borrowing. These advantages of international borrowing may be used both by companies based wholly within their domestic economies (subject to exchange control and other government constraints on capital movements), and by multinational firms with many foreign subsidiaries.

However, there are risks associated with borrowing and investing internationally. The three ways of international financing are:

1. Raising capital in the currency in which the cash flows are expected.

2. Raising capital in a different currency to that in which cash flows are expected, but with forward market cover or some other protective hedge against adverse foreign exchange movements.
3. Raising capital in a different currency to that in which cash flows are expected, but without foreign exchange hedge.

Foreign exchange risk is avoided or controlled by methods 1 and 2 but not by 3. If exchange rate markets and interest rates were always in equilibrium then there would be no exchange rate risk. However, in the real world this is not the case, and exchange rate risk must be recognized.

Multinational firms face two different risks with investing abroad quite separate from foreign exchange risk. These are political risk and commercial risk. Political risk is a result of government interference in the national economy of the country of investment. The ways in which a government can affect the multinational investor include production regulations (limits), changes in tax regulations, discrimination against foreign controlled companies, restrictions on access to the domestic capital markets and even expropriation. However, the effects of government action can be positive as well as negative. Multinational firms are increasingly realizing the importance of formal assessment of political risk and its implications. One government action, mentioned above, gives added impetus to a need for international banking. This is the restriction of access to domestic capital markets for foreign controlled businesses. If these businesses have access to large international capital markets then this action may not be a great handicap.

Global financial markets

The multinational firm is faced with opportunities to increase its volume of borrowing and to lower its cost by tapping international capital markets.

The global capital market consists of a number of different sources of capital, Eurocurrency and Eurobonds being the most important. Other sources are international equity markets and long-term debt as well as the markets in the proposed country of investment.

The main international capital markets are London, Tokyo and New York. Other regional centres include Paris, Zurich, Singapore and Hong Kong. Singapore, Hong Kong and Switzerland are examples of financial centres where the domestic markets are relatively small, but they act as markets for non-resident lenders and borrowers.

The functions provided by a major financial centre are:

1. A link between domestic borrowers and domestic investors
2. A link between foreign borrowers and domestic investors
3. A link between domestic borrowers and foreign investors
4. A link between foreign borrowers and foreign investors, i.e. an offshore market

In order to be able to provide all four services a major financial centre must have:

1. A stable economy and political framework, giving confidence to foreign investors and borrowers that there will be no capital market restrictions.
2. The necessary know-how and financial skills to provide the services efficiently.
3. Excellent technical and support services to provide good communication both within and between the markets.
4. Regulations that do not restrict activity, but do protect the investor when needed.

THE NEED FOR INTERNATIONAL MONETARY AGREEMENTS

International transactions obviously have effects on the participating countries' balance of payments. These effects and the problems they cause must be solved so that international commerce can prosper. In other words, finance or liquidity must be available to countries and firms so that they can take advantage of the markets for foreign goods and services. In addition, there will be imbalances between the countries' currencies according to the strength of their respective economies. These monetary problems and imbalances will restrict international trade unless they are overcome. Over the years there have been various international agreements and institutions set up for this purpose. The commercial and central banking functions of countries have also been adapted in order to minimize these problems and promote international trade.

The World Bank Group

The World Bank Group is a multinational institution, consisting of three arms, which aims to provide long-term capital for the reconstruction of its member countries.

The International Bank for Reconstruction and Development (IBRD) makes loans for projects of high economic priority on nearly market terms apart from needing a government guarantee and a willingness to adopt economic policies encouraging free trade, investment and increased activity in the private sector. Longer term loans are mainly for large infrastructure projects such as education, agriculture, power stations, roads and railways. Additionally, short-term loans have been used to pay off balance of payment deficits.

The International Finance Corporation (IFC) makes loans and provides risk capital to private sector firms in manufacturing that have a reasonable chance of earning a required rate of return for investors and benefits for the nation.

The International Development Association (IDA) was founded in 1960 to concentrate not necessarily upon opportunities with a high probability of profitability, but more on the benefits from financing a project that would accrue to the host country. Although any loans need a government guarantee, they may be given at special concessionary rates.

The Bank for International Settlements (BIS)

The Bank for International Settlements, based in Basle, is responsible for monitoring the international banking system. In some respects it is effectively a supervisory body for central banks, and provides and coordinates assistance to countries experiencing financial difficulties. The BIS's major success of the 1980s was to enhance the international risk profile of commercial banks by improving capital adequacy standards of commercial banks, through increasing the requirements of bank reserves relative to loans. However, the role and powers of the BIS are limited, and it cannot be considered to be a form of a world central bank.

THE HISTORY AND WORKINGS OF THE COMMERCIAL BANKING INDUSTRY

Functions of international banking

The commercial side of the international monetary system is represented by the international banking industry. The industry provides the liquid capital needed by the countries and firms engaging in multinational trade. Another important contribution is that the industry helps finance the imbalances between countries that inevitably occur when they participate in international trade. Functions performed by international banking are:

1. The traditional function of financing imports and exports
2. Dealing in ever increasing amounts of foreign exchange
3. Borrowing and lending Eurocurrencies
4. Underwriting issues of Eurobonds, Euronotes and foreign bonds
5. Setting up or joining syndicated loan schemes
6. Providing capital for projects
7. International fund management and rapid transfer of funds
8. Accepting and competing for local currency deposits and advancing local currency loans
9. Providing, for a fee, advice and information to other customers, for example, multinational companies

Only the major international banks will offer all of these services, while most others will tend to specialize according to their expertise, size and their perceived demand.

The evolution of international banking

International banking has developed alongside world trade expansion since the Second World War. However, its origins date from centuries earlier. In those days traders relied on trust that goods would be delivered and that payment would be received. The largest and best known merchants were considered the most trustworthy and so had an advantage in international trade over smaller competitors. In order to cover the risk of not being paid these smaller traders would draw a bill of exchange which would have a value approaching the value of the goods being exported. These bills were sold to local bankers for slightly less than their value. Thus, they would receive a large sum in advance of the delivery of the goods. The discount on the price would represent an interest charge by the bank plus an amount thought necessary by the banker to cover the risk of non-payment.

Banks tended to charge very high discounts to small merchants, and so these traders started to ask larger established merchants to guarantee or accept their bills. Therefore, if payment was not received and the smaller trader did not repay to the bank the full sum owed, then the larger trader would be liable. As this practice increased, some of the larger merchants found the acceptance of bills of exchange to be more profitable than their original trading activity, and started to act as acceptance houses or merchant banks. Over the years they specialized in the finance of international trade but gradually moved into corporate finance and other specialized areas such as investment management.

Post–Second World War developments

Since the Second World War, international banking has expanded rapidly to keep up with the expansion of multinational trade. The clearing banks of the UK have set up international banking divisions in order to defend their market share against competition from home and abroad. These clearing banks are much larger than the still successful merchant banks; this is because they have access to a much larger deposit market, i.e. private deposits through their large retail branch networks. However, merchant banks still thrive either by acquiring other specialist banks and investment firms to broaden their commercial base or by staying very small and specializing in certain areas.

However, the largest international banks are Japanese owned. Japanese banks occupied six out of the top ten places in the June 1993 *Euromoney* survey of the leading 500 banks (measured by shareholders' equity), with France, the USA, Switzerland, the UK and Hong Kong also represented. Most UK banks are relatively small in comparison (Barclays was seventeenth) and none of the merchant banks are even in the table of the world's 100 largest banks.

Changes in international banking over the last 20 years

At the end of 1992 the total amount of international bank lending in the world's financial centres was an estimated US$7,350 billion, although about half of this sum was interbank lending. Since the Second World War, the expansion of world trade and the growing number of multinational companies have greatly increased the demand for the types of services provided by international financial markets and institutions. This demand has led to the creation of new financial instruments and techniques which have revolutionized international banking; for example, the growth of international banking was brought about by the quadrupling of oil prices in the 1970s. The first oil shock in 1973 triggered off the process. The OPEC countries had massive surpluses which, in order to restore world trade imbalances, needed to be recycled around the globe. These OPEC countries, looking for places to deposit their new-found wealth, placed large amounts with the international banks, such that these banks' OPEC deposits rose from US$16 billion in 1973 to US$117 billion in 1979.

International banks already had the experience and infrastructure necessary to perform the task of global financial intermediation, and so, mostly backed by the regulatory authorities, they started to lend huge amounts. In the competition to expand their market share these banks did not always lend wisely and tended, too often, to lend without giving any thought as to whether the repayments would be met in the future given the instability of the world economy. By the end of 1979 the banks had claims totalling US$665 billion as compared to US$155 billion in 1973. Only US$300 billion of this had been lent to the banks' domestic borrowers and US$157 billion had been lent to developing or Third World countries. The consequences of this have been beneficial in some cases and detrimental in others, as we shall see later.

Methods of expansion

International banks have expanded in a number of different ways.

The traditional correspondent system When goods and services are purchased from a foreign country, hard money is seldom transferred to the vendor directly from the buyer. What normally happens is that the amount owed is drawn from banks situated in the exporting country. The banks hold deposits from the buyer and these deposits can be transferred between banks of different countries. Thus, banks can provide the liquidity needed for international trade to exist via the international transfer of funds between them.

In this system banks keep deposits in domestic currencies. Transfers take place between them, but they are governed, and in some cases restricted, by the domestic countries' banking and exchange regulations relating to deposits.

An example of a transfer of funds in this traditional banking system is as follows.

A British-made refrigerator is to be exported to an American company, UFA Inc., by the British company, NBG plc. The fridge can be priced in either sterling or dollars. In this example we will use sterling. UFA Inc. will have to convert its dollars to sterling through its American bank, Citicorp. Thus, dollar deposits held by UFA at Citicorp will reduce by the price of the fridge in dollars. Then Citicorp draws on its sterling deposits held in a British bank, say, the National Westminster. An amount equal to the price of the fridge in sterling changes ownership from Citicorp to NBG. Thus, NBG holds a sterling deposit at the National Westminster equal to the price of the fridge.

The advantages of the correspondent system for banks are that costs of entering a foreign market are limited to the service costs. There are no overheads of setting up a branch in terms of building, equipment or staff. Furthermore, entry into the market is not directly competing with local banks and other such institutions. Another benefit is that the bank's correspondent in a country will have local contacts and experience.

The disadvantages of the correspondent system is that the correspondent may not be able or willing to raise the finance required by the bank. In other words, the correspondent may not consider the international bank's needs as important as some other activity and so may not devote the amount of resources that the international bank would deem necessary. A scarcity of funds owing to a small local capital market or local legal restrictions to the correspondence activity may compound such problems.

One way of tackling the above issues is for an international bank to open representative offices in foreign countries where they operate a correspondence system. These offices do not directly offer banking services; they are representatives of the international bank whose capacity it is to advise other banks and customers and to form a working link with the parent bank's correspondent. The circumstances which would prompt an international bank to open a representative office in a country are usually as follows:

1. The market is too small to require the setting up of a bank.
2. More local information is needed by the bank before it can decide upon its strategy in that country.
3. Larger investment is prohibited by local regulations.
4. The large benefits of the proposed market are offset by a large amount of political risk in that country.
5. The main activity of the bank in this market does not require other facilities, such as a branch.

The benefits to a bank of this sort of expansion is that it costs less than setting up a branch, and provides a way of getting to know the local market and serving the bank's interests in that country.

The drawbacks are that these offices are unable to exploit opportunities if they arise and so, in some cases, may not be able to justify monetarily the cost of setting them up. Another problem is that the most able and experienced staff will be attracted to mainline banking activities and not these small offices.

The opening of a foreign branch may be required where a large market cannot be penetrated by the above methods to the extent that the international bank would like. These branches offer extensive banking services, most importantly the lending of money. However, they find it difficult to attract deposits for they do not have the extensive branch network that local banks may have. The opening of foreign branches is regulated by many governments, but despite this, in the last two decades this activity has expanded rapidly. For example, in 1960 only seven US banks had 132 foreign branches; by 1980 this had increased to 130 banks having 800 foreign branches. The reasons for this explosion centre mainly on the profits made by the banks lending to foreign businesses. As multinational companies have expanded overseas, their domestic banks have followed them so as not to lose their clients' business. This provides banks with more diversified earnings so they do not rely so heavily on one market. Obviously international banks need branches in the world's financial centres so that they can tap these sources of funds—hence the huge number of foreign branches existing in London (currently more than 400 different banks!).

Other advantages to a bank of foreign branches are that through them a bank has complete control of its foreign activities and a network of them allows rapid transfer of funds. The disadvantages are the costs of setting them up, maintaining them and the possibility that relations with local correspondents will be seriously damaged.

International banks are faced with an alternative to opening foreign branches. This is the acquisition of foreign banks. The benefits of this are that it provides the bank with deposit-taking facilities, local contacts and also existing clients. However, the disadvantages of this are backed up by the statistics showing many ill-fated acquisitions. A good example is that of the UK Midland bank's acquisition of a 57 per cent stake in the Californian bank, Crocker-National. It cost Midland US$820 million in 1981 and in 1985 it was valued at US$300 million. The massive losses sustained by Crocker-National in these years forced the Midland bank to make further huge investments in it, until eventually Midland sold it in 1986, with huge losses. Unless an acquiror is bringing new strategies and successful solutions to the problems of an ailing acquired bank, it is a very risky venture.

Risks faced by international banks

International banks are multinational companies and face similar risks to those of other multinationals. International lending exposes the banks to commercial risk as always, but also to country risk which can be split up into political and currency risk.

Commercial risk to an international bank is the risk of debts held by foreign-based clients not being paid because of business reasons. This differs from domestic commercial risk as it can be a great deal more difficult and expensive to assess and predict business results in a foreign country. This can be due to a number of reasons, for example, different regulations, different culture, lack of information and a differing economic background and cycle. Thus, a bank lending internationally faces a much more complex risk assessment procedure than its domestic counterpart.

Country risk is the chance that an unexpected economic or political change in a country may affect the likelihood of its government or companies repaying loans to international banks.

Political risk (see Chapter 13) is the chance that the government of this indebted country may, in a number of ways, either directly not pay its debts or prevent its domestic companies from paying theirs.

Currency risk is a change in exchange rates that will alter the value of a loan and its repayments either in favour of the bank or against it.

Benefits of international lending

International lending by banks performs an essential service and some of the benefits are as follows:

1. International lending has, overall, been a very profitable business and has been instrumental in the growth of major banks.
2. Syndication of loans helps to diversify risk, as does lending to many countries.
3. The largest international lenders are those banks with the most experience and hopefully the best ability to assess country risk.
4. The majority of loans extended to Third World countries do go to projects which, if successful, generate income needed to repay the debt. This is necessary for the developing countries to experience growth. Also, it means that international development funds from world institutions can be concentrated on the poorest uncreditworthy nations.

HOW DO COMPANIES RAISE FINANCE?

Markets or intermediaries?

Companies can raise capital directly from the financial markets or via the use of financial intermediaries, for example, bank borrowing. As a generalization, British and US firms tend to raise a great deal of their capital from the financial market by issuing negotiable securities. On the other hand, firms in West Germany and Japan rely to a far greater extent on bank borrowing. However, the worldwide general trend is that bank borrowing is declining and security issues are increasing. This securitization is clearly shown in Japan where, in a two-year period from 1982 to 1984, the percentage of external corporate funds coming from bank lending had decreased from 60 per cent to 35 per cent. Deregulation, which has occurred in all major financial centres, has opened up the competition for low-cost funds, and banks now have to compete directly with other financial institutions. The result of this is that companies can raise capital by, for instance, issuing commercial paper more cheaply than they can borrow from banks.

Given this, then, why do companies borrow from banks at all? A widely accepted theory for this is that banks specialize in credit analysis and in monitoring debtors. Thus, a firm which can show in its accounts that it borrowed from banks will gain access to the cheapest funds on the financial markets as they are seen to be creditworthy. On the other hand, a company showing no bank borrowing is difficult to assess in terms of creditworthiness and so will incur higher costs of borrowing from the financial markets to make up for the higher risk involved in lending to them.

Recently, however, access to computers and improved communications have made credit analysis easier and cheaper for the market analyst, and so the future may see an even higher proportion of external corporate capital being raised on the public markets. This raises an interesting question as to the future of financial intermediaries, such as commercial banks, in corporate financing, especially for large multinational companies; only time will tell.

THE THIRD WORLD DEBT CRISIS: WHAT IS IT AND WHAT CAUSED IT?

The circumstances leading up to the crisis

The growth of bank lending to developing countries during the 1970s gave rise to a number of concerns about the stability of the world economy. If major countries were to default on their interest or principal payments, the stability of the international financial system would be under threat. A default would be likely to produce failures in individual banks, the theoretical bankruptcy of the country concerned, and a general loss in confidence in the international banking system. Growth in the developing world could virtually come to a standstill, and the volume of international trade and investment would be likely to fall. Concern was particularly centred upon huge loans granted to Latin American countries, especially Mexico, Brazil and Argentina.

The causes of the crisis may be traced largely to a number of developments which took place at the end of the 1970s. The massive expansion of lending to developing countries during the 1970s has been criticized on several grounds:

1. International banks did not fully realize the complexity of risk assessment, commercial and country risk when making the loans.
2. International banks have a poor record in the prediction of political upheavals including revolutions, wars, etc.
3. International loans were extended without proper risk assessment because of low domestic demand for capital.
4. Most bank debt is based on variable interest rates, and the effects of a change to high interest rates around the world was not properly considered by banks when extending the loans. Medium-term bank lending is usually funded by short-term Eurocurrency borrowing which partially protects these loans. However, a change in the term structure of interest rates can result in reduced profits or even losses for banks as the maturities of these Eurocurrency borrowings and the extended loans are mismatched.
5. Many loans were extended by international banks to governments in order that they can finance their balance of payments deficits. Such loans are not going to increase the income-earning capacities of these countries. Therefore, they do not generate earnings to finance their debt. Another similar problem is where loans are extended in order to finance existing debt on projects. These lending policies only store up more problems for the future.

The trend for international banks to use floating interest rates for overseas loans made borrowers more vulnerable to changes in the real rate of interest. A rising nominal rate of interest caused by increases in inflation works to the advantage of the borrower by reducing the real cost of the loan repayments. The US dollar had fallen in value almost continuously throughout the 1970s, and this was obviously to the advantage of the debtor countries whose international loans were in dollars.

Then came the second oil price shock in 1979. Non-OPEC countries had great difficulty in adjusting to the oil price increases, and large balance of payments deficits ensued. The developing countries suffered worst, and by 1981 their total deficits had risen sharply to US$67 billion. Obviously this level of deficit greatly increased the developing countries' need for external financing.

Given all these factors, the last thing developing countries wanted was the deflationary economic policies adopted by the leading industrial countries, particularly the USA, in order to reduce their domestic inflation. These led to large increases in interest rates in the USA, and in the Euromarket. Loan repayments of developing countries grew in response to the increase in real interest rates made possible by the floating rate loans. They also grew as developing countries' debt increased to finance their balance of payments deficits. In the early 1980s the decline in the value of the dollar dramatically turned around and sharp rises in its real value were experienced. This had the effect of increasing the real cost of loan repayments to debtor countries, since most loans were denominated in dollars. This would have caused a crisis without further adverse developments, but was made much more severe by the world recession of 1982 which reduced demand for developing countries' exports.

Developing countries' net interest payments to banks had increased from US$11 billion in 1978 to US$44 billion by 1982. By this time developing countries faced a situation whereby half of the income they earned from exports was used in paying interest payments, i.e. they faced a 50 per cent interest payment/export ratio. This left little for the purchase of necessary imports and repayment of the principal of the bank loans.

Given these circumstances it is no surprise that in August 1982 Mexico officially announced that it could not continue to meet its international loan repayments. This was followed by similar announcements from Brazil and Argentina, and by April 1983 25 developing countries, accounting for two-thirds of developing country debt, were in this situation.

Rescheduling

The response of the affected international banks was to try to reschedule these loans. This seemed the only practical way of avoiding writing off the debts and facing their losses. However, the rescheduling of these debts led to the over-exposure of some banks to particular countries. For instance in 1982 the total debt or exposure of the nine largest US banks to developing countries amounted to about 275 per cent of these banks' primary capital.

Since 1981 international banks have reduced lending to developing countries. Loans fell from US$40 billion in 1981 to US$20 billion in 1982 and US$12 billion in 1983. Considering the fact that most of these new loans were made to reschedule other loans, these figures represent almost a complete halt of voluntary new lending to developing countries.

What was responsible for the crisis and why?

International banks must take some blame for the debt crisis, as they pumped huge amounts of capital into developing countries without proper regard for the risks of this activity. However, at this point it is necessary to recognize a fact which is sometimes overlooked: namely, a country with a large amount of debt does not, as a direct result, face a crisis. In other words, a large amount of debt is not necessarily a bad thing. The important factor, which is the crux of the debt crisis, is whether the borrowed funds are used efficiently to promote development and growth. If a country uses its debt purely to finance consumption and inefficient investments then it will face a problem as no extra income will be earned to pay back the debt and its interest.

Therefore, the fact that there is a debt problem shows us that in part these funds have not been efficiently used. We can identify a number of broad areas, which have affected the way in which debt has been used and the terms in which it has been granted.

1. *Current trade balance*—A deficit or surplus in this account has a direct bearing on a country's requirement for external finance. Factors that influence this account are split into two groups, those within and those outside a country's control. In the former group factors include exchange rate, export promotion, import dependence and substitution, industrial and other economic performance policies. Those factors outside control include a change in the terms of trade and climatic conditions.
2. *Domestic savings, consumption and fiscal performance*—As discussed earlier, if debt is used for consumption then problems will arise. These factors are very much geared to economic policies, but can be affected by events outside domestic government control, such as wars, droughts and world shocks.
3. *Efficiency of investment*—The efficient investment of debt is imperative if the income needed to repay the debt is to be generated. Obviously this is affected by all internal economic policies, but is also susceptible to world economic shocks.
4. *Terms of borrowing*—As we have seen, changes in interest rates have had serious effects on the debt burdens of developing countries. Also, different countries face different terms for their debt, depending on their perceived risk.
5. *Role of creditors*—Creditors do have a strong hand in influencing the type of project invested in, and some creditors have backed failures. Given this, then, obviously some responsibility rests on them for the choice of projects invested in.

The situation in the late 1980s and early 1990s

Bank lending has picked up since 1983, but most of the increase is represented by interbank lending and so new lending to developing countries is still much lower than the peaks reached in the 1970s. Exposure as a percentage of primary capital of the major banks has decreased significantly, but nevertheless many individual banks continue to face serious losses.

As well as the rescheduling of debt, which in itself does little to alleviate the underlying problems faced by many heavily indebted less developed countries (LDCs), several other methods have been used to try to resolve the debt crisis. Almost all rescheduling agreements are now linked to economic adjustment programmes imposed and monitored by the IMF, known as IMF conditionality agreements. Such programmes typically require the government concerned to impose strict monetary policy, reduce levels of domestic inflation, and liberalize trade and foreign currency regulations. As a local currency is often heavily devalued in order to improve international competitiveness, and local employment levels and the standard of living often suffer.

By 1987 some large US and British banks still faced a situation where loan loss reserves amounted to only a small proportion of their exposure. This is illustrated in Table 3.1.

The economic position of the major debtor countries at the same date is shown in Table 3.2.

Aggregating these results, we can see that for these 17 countries 17.3 per cent of their export earnings were taken up by interest payments on debt. The three most indebted countries, Brazil, Mexico and Argentina, all showed percentages over 30 per cent for this ratio. Given that the terms of their loans required them to pay back the principal on a schedule, it is evident that they were in an impossible situation.

A good example of this is Brazil. From 1987 to 1989 inclusive Brazil's total debt repayment obligations were approximately US$20.5 billion annually. Against this, Brazil's total annual export earnings were US$26.4 billion. An indicator of the size of the problem is that in the years 1983–87 Brazil's net earnings after imports amounted to an annual average of US$8.6 billion. Clearly, an annual debt repayment of US$20.5 billion is impossible.

Table 3.1   Bank reserves and LDC exposure

	Latin American loans ($ billion)	Per cent of total equity	Reserves per cent exposure
Commercial banks			
American			
(Latin American exposure only)			
Citicorp	11.6	80	25
Bank of America	7.3	178	29
Chase Manhattan	7.0	190	15
Morgan Guaranty	4.6	88	20
Chemical	5.3	168	20
Manufacturers Hanover	7.6	202	13
British			
(Latin American exposure only)			
Barclays	4.0	65	7
Lloyds	8.7	193	7
Midland	7.1	210	8
National Westminster	4.2	54	13
Japanese			
(Exposure to 31 developing countries)			
The Bank of Tokyo	5.2	128.3	> 5
Dai-Ichi Kangyo	3.4	57	> 5
Fuji Bank	2.6	41.2	> 5
Industrial Bank of Japan	2.6	57.5	> 5
West German			
(Exposure to 31 developing countries)			
Deutsche	3.4	40	70
Commerzbank	3.2	115	n.a.
Dresdner	3.4	n.a.	50

Source: The Economist, 30 May 1987

This was clearly far from an ideal situation, and in the late 1980s banks in most countries increased their reserves by methods such as share issues. By as early as the end of 1987 the large US and British banks had increased these reserves by a total of US$23 billion. This was a strategic decision by the banks with the purpose of giving themselves a much tougher negotiating position against the debtor nations. The main reason for this was that the banks did not believe the debtor countries were trying hard enough to follow the Baker plan of 1985.

This plan, initiated by the US Treasury Secretary, James Baker, in October 1985, called for growth promoting economic reforms by 15 of the major middle-income, debtor, developing countries. Such reforms were to be financed by World Bank lending, boosted by the opening

Table 3.2   17 highly indebted countries 1987

| Country | Debt outstanding | | | Average annual growth rates 1980–87 (%) | | | |
	Total ($ billion)	of which private Source (%)	GDP	Exports	Imports	per capita consumption
Argentina	49.4	85.8	0.0	1.4	− 11.0	1.2
Bolivia	4.6	26.7	− 3.5	− 0.3	− 2.4	5.1
Brazil	114.5	75.5	3.4	3.2	− 4.4	1.1
Chile	20.5	83.2	0.9	4.1	− 6.8	2.2
Colombia	15.1	49.4	2.8	8.0	− 3.3	0.2
Costa Rica	4.5	50.8	1.5	2.1	− 2.4	1.4
Côte d'Ivoire	9.1	60.5	− 0.6	3.8	− 2.8	4.3
Ecuador	9.0	70.2	1.4	5.9	− 2.6	2.2
Jamaica	3.8	17.4	0.2	− 5.4	− 2.2	1.4
Mexico	105.0	86.2	0.3	6.4	− 7.7	2.7
Morocco	17.3	32.0	3.4	2.9	1.6	0.8
Nigeria	27.0	55.1	− 3.4	− 5.9	− 19.2	6.5
Peru	16.7	53.2	0.7	− 0.6	− 5.7	0.2
Philippines	29.0	60.6	− 0.5	− 0.5	− 4.9	1.0
Uruguay	3.8	80.1	− 1.4	− 0.1	− 8.1	2.4
Venezuela	33.9	99.3	− 0.7	− 0.9	− 5.7	4.6
Yugoslavia	21.8	69.6	1.1	0.5	− 0.6	0.5
TOTAL	485.0	74.3	1.0	1.4	− 6.2	1.6

Source: World Debt Tables, The World Bank, 1987–1988 edition

up of markets by major industrial nations to developing countries' exports. Commercial bank lending was expected to increase to these 15 countries. If successful, these measures would boost the economic growth and thus export earnings of the developing countries, and lead to a restoration of their creditworthiness among the various international capital markets.

This plan was, however, unsuccessful, and did not generate significant additional economic growth. Commercial banks did not lend large amounts as had been hoped and they were reluctant to further increase their exposure to developing countries.

Developing countries have tried to solve the problem in a number of ways. Some, following the Baker plan, have attempted to decrease demands for imports and so give more capacity to export production. This has been facilitated by tighter fiscal and monetary policies, which have resulted in a reduction in growth rates and consumption. Obviously, this is unpopular with ordinary voters in developing countries; however, much of it is blamed on the world and commercial banks. Because of this there is a limit to the extent that these policies can be carried out.

The exchange rate mechanism has also been used by developing countries to combat the debt problem. Many have over-devalued their currencies in an effort to boost export competitiveness and encourage traditional export growth. The industrial nations have gone along with this as they accept its value in tackling the debt crisis.

Another step taken by many debtor countries is to encourage domestic investment and investment from abroad. This was in response to the problem of capital flight experienced throughout the 1980s. Capital flight is a term meaning the outflow of capital from a country. This has occurred in massive proportions in developing countries. As a whole, capital flight has been estimated to be, in the period of 1977–87, in the region of US$50 billion–US$200 billion or even higher. It is extremely difficult to measure this accurately, but there is no doubt that developing countries have suffered from its consequences. Obviously they suffer because this capital is urgently needed by their domestic economies, but developing countries also suffer because major banks have used it as a reason for the clamp-down on lending to them.

As well as increasing their loan loss reserves banks have also made very substantial provisions against LDC bad debts. This involves banks placing reserves in almost risk-free assets, effectively to offset loans which are not expected to be repaid. A consequence of making provisions is that the reported profits of banks fall dramatically. This led in the early 1990s to some major UK banks announcing substantial losses. The extent of provisions relative to LDC debt varies with individual banks, but for UK and European banks has generally been between 50 per cent and 75 per cent of the outstanding debt.

A further move has been the attempts by banks to sell off their loans at discounts to investors who do not mind the big risks. The price of debt differs depending on the country it is held by. For example, in May 1988, Peruvian debt was nearly worthless since Peru had defaulted on virtually all of its debt. In contrast, Brazilian debt was selling for about 54 cents on the dollar. However, the market has noticed the worsening position of the banks and this has been reflected in the large falls in the banks' credit ratings. This has made banks reluctant to lend more money to developing countries, so compounding their problem.

In 1988 at a conference in Basle, Switzerland, the international banking authorities met to prevent a worsening of the situation and in particular to prevent any large bank failures resulting from it. They set standards for the banks to follow: these included a requirement for international banks to keep, by 1992, a minimum of an 8 per cent ratio of capital to weighted risk assets; at least 50 per cent of this capital must be core capital, which is made up of equity, disclosed reserves and non-cumulative preference shares.

By the early 1990s the debt crisis had disappeared from the headlines, but the problem still remains. Table 3.3 shows the external debt position for less developed countries for selected years between 1980 and 1990.

In 1990 LDC debt still totalled more than US$1,300 billion. Although official debt (debt from the IMF, the International Bank for Reconstruction and Development, the European Bank for Reconstruction and Development and various regional development banks) has now overtaken bank debt, the proportion of loans with payments difficulties remains very high at 62 per cent. This is an improvement from the 69 per cent figure of 1982, but clearly illustrates that there is some way to go before the debt problem can be considered to be solved.

THE PRESENT DEBT STRATEGY

Debt relief

After the Baker plan had been seen to fall well short of its economic objectives there was pressure from the US government to actually relieve certain developing countries, for example, Mexico, of their debt burdens by interest and principal concessions forced on the banks. This,

Table 3.3   LDC external debt 1980–1990 ($ billion)

	1980	1982	1984	1986	1988	1990
All LDCs of which:	636	836	930	1,096	1,224	1,306
Short-term	136	184	174	176	206	225
Long-term	500	652	756	920	1,017	1,082
Debt source:						
Official	191	250	304	409	497	576
Banks	n.a.	428	472	507	532	518
Other private	n.a.	158	155	180	195	213
Percentage of debts with payment difficulties	n.a.	69	67	64	63	62

Source: Bank of England Quarterly Bulletin, November 1991

it was argued, would only be given to countries who committed themselves to economic policies that promoted faster economic growth. One of the reasons behind this argument was that the supposed increased purchasing power of the relieved debtor nations would reduce the alarming size of the US trade deficit as these countries purchased US exports. This idea did not receive much support then or now, particularly from the banks.

In a joint declaration by the governments of Argentina, Brazil, Colombia, Mexico, Peru, Uruguay and Venezuela in October 1988, they stated that they realized that the onus to pull out of the crisis rested on themselves. They declared that, to this end, very far-reaching reforms had been introduced both to improve their productive structures and to bring their economies more in line with the world markets. However, they complained that all this was being put at risk by the continued developments in international trade outside their control. They claimed that this was where the developed countries should, but do not, help. Specifically they target protectionism and other obstacles to international trade, the burden of debt repayments and the lack of development finance in the quantities needed as the factors threatening their social and economic development. They emphasize the point that it is in the interests of the industrialized nations to assist developing countries as they will all gain from the resulting increases in international trade.

In March 1988 economic growth for these debtor countries as a whole stood at 3 per cent per annum, far below what was needed to pull them out of the crisis. On 10 March 1989 the US Secretary of State, Nicholas Brady, introduced an enhanced international debt strategy which asked commercial banks to offer to debtor countries 'a broader range of alternatives for financial support'. He advocated both principal and debt interest reductions. This was supported by the World Bank. The main thrust of this initiative was to stick to the broad outline of the Baker plan described earlier with the addition of several new elements:

1. The strategy must differentiate between countries of differing performance. In other words, the reduction of debt must go hand in hand with changes in the policies which caused it. The IMF and the World Bank were to make substantial funds available to countries adopting such policies.

2. The debt reduction strategy must be available to all countries which accept and implement the reforms necessary.
3. Poverty must be reduced so that developing countries can regain their creditworthiness in international financial markets.
4. The strategy must be flexible to reflect the differing needs and problems of developing countries. Also, it must be large enough to make real visible reductions in the debt burdens of developing countries.
5. The strategy must be managed by experienced people. Early applications of the strategy to countries with the best chance of success will increase these people's experience so that they are better able to cope with the more difficult situations.
6. The application of this strategy must not bankrupt the international institutions or commercial banks, as any detrimental effect on the international financial system would affect the world economy.

On 23 May 1989, the IMF backed approved new guidelines for debt strategy. These were:

1. Increasing emphasis on medium-term strategy and policy reforms to go hand in hand with debt and debt interest reductions. The reversal of capital flight by increasing domestic and foreign investment is given great importance.
2. About 25 per cent of a country's total access to IMF capital can be used for activities involving the reduction of debt principal.
3. 40 per cent of a country's access may, if approved, be used to reduce the debt interest payments.
4. Individual countries may, on occasions, receive IMF backing before negotiations with its creditors have been completed if it is essential for the success of the project and where creditor backing is expected to be granted.

The role of international banks in this process was particularly important. They were to be effectively given four options:

1. To provide their share of new finance to LDCs, along with new official financing. We have noted above reasons why many banks might be unwilling to do this
2. If banks felt unable to provide new loans they could sell existing debt back to their creditors at substantial discounts on the face value of the debt. The amount of the discount would be based upon the existing secondary market value of the debt
3. The exchange of old debt at a discount for new secured bonds
4. The exchange of old debt at par for new debt at much lower interest rates

It is too early to judge the success of the Brady plan, although there are encouraging signs that arrangements made with some countries, and especially Mexico, have been successful. By mid-1991 an estimated US$13 billion of Mexican debt had been relieved.

In addition to the Brady plan, innovations that began prior to the plan, such as debt–equity swaps, were to continue. A debt–equity swap involves the sale of LDC debt by banks, at a discount to its face value to a third party, possibly a potential investor in the country which originally issued the debt. The investor may then exchange the debt for *local* currency in that country in order to purchase equity capital in local companies. The exchange into local currency will often be at a smaller discount, so that both the country and the investor show a gain, at the expense of the bank. The bank, however, may be content to reduce its LDC exposure and to receive repayment of some proportion of the debt, rather than risk a total write-off. Debt–equity swaps effectively bring new foreign direct investment into the country, stimulating economic growth and employment. Although these schemes appear to be very attractive they have had limited success, partly owing to the unwillingness of some countries to see a major increase in the foreign ownership of local companies.

There have been various other moves to help the poorest and most illiquid countries, who would benefit little by mere debt rescheduling as they were virtually insolvent. Under the Toronto and Trinidad terms of 1987 and 1990 respectively, substantial amounts of debt forgiveness, or write-offs, were proposed. After the forgiveness, remaining debt would be rescheduled over 14 years, with a substantial period of grace when interest payments would not be due. Other options agreed were much longer repayment periods, or a grace period for repayment followed by concessionary interest rates. African countries would gain most from these moves.

Prospects for the future

The debt strategies to date have achieved some important results. These are:

1. First and foremost a collapse in the international financial system has been avoided. The significance of this cannot be overstated.
2. An increase in real terms in gross domestic product of the heavily indebted countries; between 1982 and 1988 this improved by about 8 per cent. This is after accounting for a terms of trade reduction of 3 per cent of GDP.
3. The world financial system has been protected and strengthened. The large commercial banks of the world are now healthier than in 1982.

However, in other areas the debt strategy up to now has not achieved its aims. These are:

1. The heavily indebted countries' economic growth has been slow.
2. The improvement in these countries' trade accounts has been achieved at the expense of serious reductions in the ratio of investment to GDP. This will drastically limit the ability of these countries to grow and reform further. This is due to a number of factors:
   (a) Some of these countries have not devoted enough effort to internal reforms.
   (b) International financing for these countries has been inadequate to support high growth and reforms.
   (c) The ratio of debt to export income has not significantly improved for many heavily indebted countries.

In order for debt strategy to work, the most urgent requirement is to strengthen the ability and the willingness of debt troubled countries to sustain and, as necessary, reinforce efforts to grow out of their debt burdens. There is no one-off solution applicable to all countries. Each country must be looked at and aided according to their particular problems as they arise. This will involve new flows of capital to facilitate the economic adjustments which are necessary for any solution to the debt problem.

Although the reasons behind the commercial banks' reluctance to lend is understandable, increased lending by these banks to developing countries is essential. The success of the present debt strategy is relying on the commercial banks to support and back fully the reforms that most developing countries are trying hard to implement.

ADDITIONAL READING

AMEX Bank Review (1984) *International Debt: Banks and the LDCs*, Special Paper No.10, March.

AMEX Bank Review (1988) *A Comprehensive Agenda for LDC Debt and World Trade Growth*, Special Paper No.13.

Bank of England (1991) 'The LDC Debt Crisis', *Bank of England Quarterly Bulletin*, November.

Bayard, T. and Young, S. (1989) *Economic Relations between US and Korea, Conflict or Cooperation?*, Institute for International Economics Special Report, 8 January.

Bergston, C. and Cline, W. (1985) *Bank Lending to Developing Countries: the Policy Alternatives*, Institute for International Economics, Policy Analysis 10, Washington DC, April.

Coggan, P. (1986) *The Money Machine: How the City Works*, Penguin, Harmondsworth.

IMF Survey (1988) 'Camdessus reaffirms debt strategy: rejects radical solutions', Vol. 17, March.

IMF Survey (1989) 'U.S. calls for wider range of options for financing developing country debt', Vol. 18, March.

Killick, T. (1982) *Adjustment and Financing in the Developing World: the Role of the IMF*, IMF and Overseas Development Institute, London.

Lancaster, C. and Williamson, J. (1986) *African Debt and Financing*, Institute for International Economics, Special Report No. 5, Washington DC.

Lessard, D. and Williamson, J. (1985) *Capital Flight and Third World Debt*, Institute for International Economics, Washington DC.

Macesich, G. (1984) *World Banking and Finance*, Praeger, New York.

Payer, C. (1974) *The Debt Trap: The IMF and the Third World*, Monthly Review Press, New York.

World Financial Markets (1986) LDC Debt: Debt Relief or Market Solutions, September, pp. 1–13

INTERNATIONAL RISK MANAGEMENT

THE FOREIGN EXCHANGE MARKET

INTRODUCTION

All companies which engage in foreign trade or investment require an understanding of the purpose and function of the foreign exchange market. This chapter explains how the market operates, the different methods of quoting exchange rates and the various types of exchange rate available to the corporate financial manager. The case study at the end of the chapter provides further discussion and illustration of the issues outlined in the chapter.

THE FOREIGN EXCHANGE MARKET

International financial deals normally involve transactions denominated in more than one currency. The foreign exchange market exists to facilitate the exchange of one currency into another. From the viewpoint of a UK company this is essential, as the pound sterling is not accepted as a means of settling financial transactions in most foreign countries. For example, an English company importing goods from Japan, with the price of those goods denominated in Japanese yen, will need to buy yen in order to pay the Japanese supplier. Similarly, an English company exporting goods to Japan, again with the price denominated in yen, receives yen which it will have to sell in the foreign exchange market to finally receive sterling.

A sound understanding of international financial management requires knowledge of the mechanics and operations of the foreign exchange market. Rodriguez and Carter (1984) provide a succinct definition of the foreign exchange market as:

A place where money denominated in one currency is bought and sold with money denominated in another currency.

The foreign exchange market spans the globe, with trading taking place every hour of the working week. In a typical day trading may be considered to start each morning in Wellington and Sydney, then move west to Tokyo, Hong Kong and Singapore. Next it moves to Bahrain, followed by the main European markets of London, Frankfurt and Zurich. Finally it moves across the Atlantic to New York and then San Francisco and Los Angeles. Most trading takes place when both the European and US East Coast markets are open, which occur in the early afternoon (UK time). The overlapping of time zones means that there is always one centre which is open, apart from at weekends (Figure 4.1).

The foreign exchange market is easily the largest market in the world, with estimated world-wide daily foreign exchange transactions approaching US$1 trillion (million million US$) or

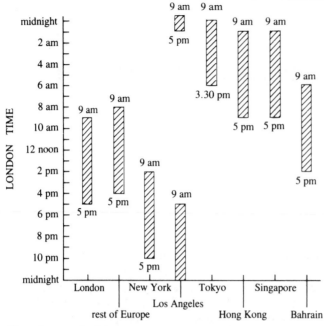

Times shown are local times.

Figure 4.1 Global foreign exchange dealing

US$250 trillion a year. As a comparison, the US gross national product was approximately US$4.5 trillion in 1987. The relative importance of foreign currencies traded in the UK according to the 1992 survey by the Bank of England is set out in Table 4.1.

It can be seen from this table that the US dollar is the most actively traded currency in the UK, with trading not only against the pound, but also against other major currencies. London is the world's leading centre today for foreign exchange trading, with an estimated turnover of US$300 billion per day, well ahead of the USA and Japan with daily trading volumes of US$192 billion and US$128 billion respectively.

The participants in the foreign exchange markets

The foreign exchange markets can be divided into two sections:

1. The interbank or wholesale market in which transactions usually involve large sums of money, usually several million US dollars or the equivalent value in other currencies
2. The smaller client or retail market

The major participants in the foreign exchange market are the large commercial banks, the brokers who operate in the interbank market, and the central banks. Individuals and companies obtain their foreign currencies from the commercial banks. The central banks' role is to smooth out exchange rate fluctuations, that is, to keep the exchange rate in a desired range by intervening in the market. This intervention, which involves the buying and selling of their own countries' currency, is often indistinguishable from the foreign dealings of commercial banks, or from the other traders' dealings. Foreign exchange brokers are specialists in bringing buyers and sellers together, and receive a commission on all trades. They handle all the major currencies,

Table 4.1   The importance of foreign currencies traded in the UK in April 1992 (% of the total)

	Spot	Forwards	Total
£/US$	6.4	10.1	17
US$/DM	13.8	9.1	24
US$/yen	4.9	6.9	12
US$/Swiss franc	2.8	3.0	6
US$/French franc	0.9	2.0	3
US$/Canadian $	0.6	1.6	2
US$/Australian $	0.5	0.7	1
US$/Lire plus other ERM currencies	2.2	6.0	8
US$/other currencies	0.9	2.5	3
£/DM	4.3	0.9	6
£/other	0.7	0.6	1
DM/yen	2.0	0.3	3
DM/other ERM	3.8	0.3	4
Other cross-currencies	3.0	0.8	4
ECU denominated	2.3	2.6	6

N.B. Totals include options and futures business.

Source: Bank of England Quarterly Bulletin, November 1992

but some specialize in particular currencies. The use of these independent brokers permits banks to trade without revealing their name until an agreement is reached, so the name of the other party cannot influence the price quoted. A survey, by the Federal Bank of New York, of 119 banking institutions and 10 foreign exchange brokers in the USA, showed that 56 per cent of interbank transactions in foreign currencies for immediate delivery were handled by brokers.

There are also many speculative participants who buy and sell currency they do not need without even having the total funds to complete the deal in the hope that they can sell or buy for a profit before the delivery date. These kinds of transactions usually take place over the telephone, by telex or by some other means of communication. The deals are usually first agreed verbally and then followed up by some written form of confirmation.

The foreign exchange rate

Honeygold (1989) describes the foreign exchange rate as the relative price between two countries' currencies, that is, the price of one currency expressed in terms of another currency. This rate can either be the result of supply and demand in the unrestricted market, or at the other extreme it can be fixed firmly by the government of a country. The value of currencies is usually influenced by some form of intervention by the monetary authorities to ensure that their currencies do not appreciate or depreciate excessively. Intervention can range from the 'dirty float' mechanism, where a freely floating system is partially controlled by government foreign currency sales and purchases, to agreed exchange rate mechanisms which permit floating within defined exchange rate bands (e.g. the European Exchange Rate Mechanism) or are totally fixed and can only change through a devaluation or revaluation.

Eiteman and Stonehill (1989) describe a foreign exchange quotation as an announcement of willingness to trade at an announced rate. There are two ways of quoting exchange rates, the direct quote and the indirect quote.

A *direct quote* gives the home currency price of a unit of foreign currency. Quotations in most foreign exchange markets are made in this way; for example, in the USA exchange rates are mostly quoted in terms of dollars per foreign monetary unit:

US$0.1683/FF (i.e. 1 French franc costs 0.1683 US dollars)

In France the quotation would be the other way round with French francs per unit of foreign exchange, e.g.:

FF5.9418/US$

An *indirect quote* gives the number of units of foreign currency that can be bought with one unit of home currency. If the above quotation was made in the USA then it would be an example of an indirect quote. In that example one dollar buys 5.9418 French francs. The UK is relatively unusual in that it uses the indirect method of quotation with the foreign currency expressed in terms of £1, e.g.:

US$1.5000/£ FF8.9115/£

European markets usually adopt the direct quotations method, whereas in the USA both quotation methods are used; direct quotations are used for local customers (home), but when a US bank is dealing with foreign banks (except UK banks) indirect quotations are used.

With direct and indirect quotations being used inconsistently around the world, foreign exchange quotations can be confusing. It is useful to be sure which currency in the quotation is the unit of account and which currency is the unit for which the price is being quoted. A quotation can be made clearer by placing the unit of account before the quoted price and the unit of currency being priced after the quotation, for example:

US$0.5708/DM

Unit of account (local currency if direct quote)	Unit of currency being priced

Appreciation and depreciation of currencies If the price of French francs against the US dollar moves from FF4.9667/US$ to FF5.0000/US$ we can say that the French franc has *depreciated* against the dollar by FF0.0333 (5.0000 − 4.9667 = 0.033) (i.e. 1 US$ costs more FFs), or that the dollar has *appreciated* against the French franc by the same amount. If we wish to translate the quote of FF4.9667/US$ from French terms to US terms, we only have to take the *reciprocal* of 4.9667, i.e.:

if FF/US$ = 4.9667 then US$/FF = 1/4.9667 = US$0.2013/FF

This example shows that direct and indirect quotations are reciprocals since FF4.9667/US$ is a direct quote in France and US$0.2013/FF is an indirect quote.

Bid and offer rates Foreign exchange dealers will usually quote two numbers: the rate at which they are prepared to sell a currency and the rate at which they are willing to buy a currency. The first price is the *offer* or *ask price* and the second is the *bid price*. The difference between the bid price and the offer price is called the *spread* and is one of the potential sources of profit for dealers.

The quotations used earlier were middle rates between the bid and offer prices. An example of how a French dealer quotes the dollar–franc rate might be FF4.9032–4.9059/US$. This means that the dealer is willing to buy dollars at FF4.9032/US$ and is willing to sell dollars at FF4.9059/US$. In transactions between dealers usually only the last digits of the bid and offer rates are quoted. These last digits are referred to as 'points'. The bid rate of DM per £ may be given in full as 2.8875, but the offer rate may be expressed only as the digits which differ from the bid rate. Hence the bid and offer rate for Deutschmarks would be printed 2.8875–85. If the first digits are assumed to be known the quotation may be even shorter, i.e.:

75–85, in the example above.

The 'depth' of the foreign exchange market The size of the spread between the bid and offer quotations varies according to the depth of the market, and the market's stability at a certain point in time. The term depth refers to the volume of transactions in a particular currency. Deep markets are those which have many dealers whereas shallow markets have few dealers. Large spreads are related to high uncertainty, i.e. impending devaluation and a low number of transactions, while smaller spreads are associated with a stable currency which is traded regularly. Deep markets usually have narrower spreads than shallow ones. In the example above, DM2.8875–85/£.

The spread is equal to 0.001 = 2.8885–2.8875.

Transactions in third currencies and cross-rates

As the US dollar is the base currency for most transactions, competitive quotations for a minor currency against another one, or against a major currency, are not easily obtained. Most of the dealings are in sterling/dollars, dollars/Deutschmarks, dollars/Swiss francs, dollars/French francs, etc.; if a dealer wants a realistic price for Deutschmarks against French francs, he might find there are not many specialists in the market offering this kind of service, and they may charge extra fees for offering it.

The exchange rate between any two currencies can be obtained from the exchange rates of these currencies expressed in terms of a third currency. The rate obtained is known as the *cross-rate*.

How cross-rates are calculated Suppose an English trader gave the following quotes in London for the dollar and the Deutschmark against the pound:

US$1.9090/£   DM2.9585/£

If we require a quote for the dollar against the Deutschmark it can be worked out using the formula below:

$$US\$/DM = US\$/£ \times £/DM$$

Thus, from the information given:

$$US\$/DM = 1.9090 \times 1/2.9585 = US\$0.6452/DM$$

A quote for the Deutschmark against the dollar can also be obtained, by applying the formula below:

$$DM/US\$ = DM/£ × £/US\$$$

Thus, from the information given:

$$DM/US\$ = 2.9585 × 1/1.9090 = DM1.5498*/US\$$$

The exchange rates computed, DM1.5498/US\$ and US\$0.6452/DM, are the cross-rates of the quotes given by the English trader in London.

Note: 1.5498 is the reciprocal of 0.6452, which is what one would expect.

A more realistic example is where the trader gives both a bid and offer rate.

Cross-rate calculation using bid and offer rates   Suppose the English trader gave us the following spot quotations against the pound:

SF/£	SF2.5880/915
FF/£	FF10.0480/705

These quotes mean that sterling can be bought and sold in Paris and Zurich for the amounts set out below.

	Bid	*Offer*
Zurich	SF2.5880/£	2.5915/£
Paris	FF10.0480/£	10.0705/£

Suppose that a direct quote for the Swiss franc against French francs is required. This can be found by using sterling to estimate the cross-rates.

The offer rate for the Swiss franc in Paris can be computed by recognizing that selling Swiss francs for French francs is equivalent to combining the two transactions set out below:

1. Selling Swiss francs for sterling at the rate SF2.5915/£.
   (*Note*: 2.5915 is the offer rate, i.e. the rate at which the dealer is willing to sell sterling.)
2. Converting the sterling into French francs at the rate FF10.0480/£.
   (*Note*: 10.0480 is the bid rate, i.e. the rate at which the dealer is prepared to buy sterling.)

So the Swiss franc/French franc offer rate is:

$$SF2.5915/10.0480 = SF0.2579/FF$$

Similarly, the French franc cost of buying one Swiss franc (the bid rate) in Paris can be found. This is done by first selling French francs against sterling (i.e. buying sterling) at FF10.0705/£ and then converting those pounds into Swiss francs (i.e. selling sterling) at SF2.5880/£.

So the Swiss franc/French franc bid rate is:

$$SF2.5880/10.0705 = SF0.2570/FF$$

Thus, the direct quotes for the Swiss franc in Paris are:

$$SF0.2570/79FF$$

Spot and forward exchange rates

The *spot exchange rate* for currency is the price quoted, for the nearest settlement day, for the purchase or sale of that currency against another currency. Honeygold (1989) states that the spot rate reflects the external value of a currency at the time of dealing, and that the emphasis is on the immediacy of the transaction, although in practice delivery will actually take place two working days later.

In contrast, a *forward exchange rate* is the price at which a currency can be bought or sold for delivery at some future date, which is generally one, three or six months or one year later. The forward rate is determined by adding a premium to an existing spot rate between two currencies, making it more expensive; or by subtracting a discount from an existing spot rate, making the currency cheaper in the future. In the unlikely event of the spot rate equalling the forward rate, traders say the forward price is 'flat'.

Forward transactions represent about half of all foreign exchange deals.

How spot and forward exchange rates work To show how forward and spot exchange markets work, consider the following example:

A foreign exchange dealer offers the following exchange rates:

Spot rate	FF9.955/£
3 months forward	FF9.973/£

If the dealer buys sterling against French francs (i.e. sells francs) for spot delivery and then sells sterling against francs (i.e. buys francs) for delivery in two months' time, and both transactions are for £1,000,000, the cash flows now and in three months' time will be:

		Currencies	
Date	*Transactions*	*FF*	*£*
Day 1	Buy sterling against franc spot	− 9,955,000	+ 1,000,000
	Sell sterling against francs for delivery in 3 months	No cash flow	
3 months	Sell sterling against francs as per contract on day 1	+ 9,973,000	− 1,000,000

In the transaction outlined above, the exchange rates and the amounts of each currency were all determined on day 1 when the transaction took place. The cash flows occur on the delivery date or 'value date'. Once a forward transaction has occurred at a given rate, the cash flows at the delivery date will take place at that rate. Forward contracts are legally binding and must be fulfilled.

The relationship between forward and spot rates The relationship between the forward rate (the rate for deliveries on a forward value date) and the spot rate (the rate for spot delivery) can be expressed in terms of a percentage per annum. This percentage is either at a premium or a discount to the existing spot rate. A foreign currency is said to be at a forward premium against another currency if the forward price of the foreign currency is higher than its spot price. When the forward price is lower than the spot price, then the currency is said to be at forward discount. The following formula may be used to estimate the percentage annual discount (−) or premium (+) in a forward quote.

$$\text{Forward premium (discount)} = \frac{[\text{forward rate–spot rate}]}{\text{spot rate}} \times \frac{12}{\text{no. of months forward}}$$

To show how this works in practice, suppose we received the following quotes for the Deutschmark against the pound:

Spot rate	DM2.96025/£
3 months forward rate	DM2.95005/£

This quote shows a premium in the forward rate of the Deutschmark against the pound, since in three months' time to buy one pound sterling less Deutschmarks are required than today. The forward premium of Deutschmarks against sterling is:

$$\text{Forward premium} = \frac{2.95005 - 2.96025}{2.96025} \times \frac{12}{3}$$

$$= \frac{-0.0102}{2.96025} \times \frac{12}{3}$$

$$= -0.0138$$

$$= -1.38\% \text{ p.a.}$$

Spot transactions   A spot transaction is the purchase of a foreign currency in the interbank market, with delivery and payment between banks to be completed on the second following day of business.

Suppose an American importer requires SF100,000 for payment to his Swiss supplier. First the importer will get a verbal quote from a US bank, after which he will have to specify two accounts: his account in a US bank which he wants debited for the equivalent dollar amount at the agreed spot exchange rate; and the account of the Swiss supplier that is to be credited with SF100,000.

The trader will contact the US bank on the Monday for the transfer equivalent to SF100,000 to the account of the Swiss bank. If the spot exchange rate were SF1.6115/US$, the US bank would transfer US$62,053.98 (i.e. 100,000/1.6115) from the trader's account on the Wednesday, and transfer SF100,000 to the Swiss bank at the same time.

Spot transactions such as this dominate the interbank market. According to a survey carried out by the Federal Reserve Bank of New York, they accounted for 63 per cent of the transactions undertaken by US banks in April 1983.

Forward transactions   Forward transactions are contracts which require delivery, at a future date, of a specified amount of one currency for a specified amount of another currency. The exchange rate is determined at the time the contract is agreed on, and is thus a forward exchange rate. When dealing with forward transactions there are considerable exchange risks involved; forward transactions using currencies of developing countries are either limited or non-existent. Payment in a forward transaction occurs on the second business day after the even month anniversary of the trade. For example, a one-month forward transaction entered into on 18 March will be for a value date of 20 April, or the next business day if 20 April falls on a weekend or a holiday.

Most forward contracts have specific maturity dates, but option forward contracts allow delivery at the beginning of the month, in the middle or at the end. The option in this case only relates to the date that the contract is fulfilled. An option forward contract must be fulfilled sometime during the agreed option period, unlike foreign currency options which are discussed in Chapter 9.

Forward contracts are very important to company treasurers, since they permit the cost of imports or exports to be fixed in terms of the company's desired currency well in advance of the time that payments have to be made. This facilitates cash flow planning and can ensure that profit margins are not eroded by severe fluctuations in exchange rates. An example of a typical forward transaction could be a German company buying chemicals from England with payment of £1 million due in 60 days. If the spot rate price of the pound is DM2.85, then over the next two months the pound could rise against the Deutschmark, causing the Deutschmark cost of the chemicals to increase. The importer can guard against this exchange rate risk by means of a forward contract with a bank at a price of, say, DM2.90/£. In two months' time the bank will give the German company £1,000,000 in exchange for the agreed DM2,900,000 at the forward rate of DM2.90/£.

Forward contracts permit the home currency cash flow to be fixed in advance, but they do not necessarily lead to companies obtaining the best possible exchange rate. With hindsight, a company might have been better not to undertake a forward market hedge. This depends on the spot rate that exists when the forward contract is fulfilled. In the above example, if the spot rate in two months' time was above DM2.90/£ the German company has made an opportunity gain from using a forward contract as it is acquiring the £1,000,000 cheaper through the forward contract than it could have done in the spot market. If the spot exchange rate in two months' time was less than DM2.90/£ then the company will experience an opportunity loss in that it would have been cheaper to acquire the £1,000,000 through the spot market (in two months' time) than to take out a forward contract.

Forward foreign exchange markets are also useful in that they facilitate trade and capital movements, encourage potential borrowers and lenders to engage in foreign currency contracts, improve the access of residents to foreign financing, and expand the choice of portfolio investment for individuals.

How the Financial Times quotes currencies

Many newspapers have specialized business sections which include coverage of foreign exchange rates. The rates quoted in the newspapers are not up-to-the-minute rates because of the time lag which is inherent in printing a paper, whereas the foreign exchange market operates 24 hours a day. The rates quoted act as a record of the previous day's market activities. Table 4.2 below shows the pound's spot and forward rates against some major currencies.

In Table 4.2 the pound is quoted in terms of the number of dollars, Deutschmarks, etc., which is an indirect quote in London. The table gives details of the previous day's spread and also shows prices for immediate delivery and for contracts involving settlement in one or three months ahead.

The forward rates give the premium (pm) or the discount (dis) to the spot rates. These premiums or discounts are shown in two ways: as an absolute difference, and as an annual percentage from the spot rate.

Table 4.2 Pound spot–forward against the pound

23 January	*Day's spread*	*Close*	*One month*	% *p.a.*	*Three months*	% *p.a.*
US	1.9380 – 1.9575	1.9545 – 1.9555	1.18–1.16cpm	7.18	3.18–3.15pm	6.48
Canada	2.2460 – 2.2715	2.2685 – 2.2695	0.61–0.52cpm	2.99	1.73–1.59pm	2.93
Netherlands	3.2775 – 3.2875	3.2775 – 3.2875	$1\frac{1}{2}$–$1\frac{1}{4}$cpm	5.03	$3\frac{3}{4}$–$3\frac{1}{2}$pm	4.42
Belgium	59.80 – 60.20	59.95 – 60.05	23–20cpm	4.30	62–55pm	3.90
Denmark	11.1830 – 11.2425	11.2325 – 11.2425	$3\frac{1}{2}$–$3\frac{1}{8}$orepm	3.54	$9\frac{3}{4}$–$8\frac{7}{8}$pm	3.31
Ireland	1.0870 – 1.1020	1.0910 – 1.0920	0.34–0.27ppm	3.35	0.80–0.65pm	2.66
Germany	2.9070 – 2.9155	2.9075 – 2.9125	$1\frac{3}{8}$–$1\frac{1}{8}$pfpm	5.15	$3\frac{1}{4}$–$3\frac{1}{8}$pm	4.38
Portugal	257.40 – 259.90	258.90 – 259.90	30cpm–par	0.69	7–58dis	−0.50
Spain	182.35 – 183.40	182.50 – 182.80	5–13cdis	−0.59	22–33dis	−0.60
Italy	2183.30 – 2192.10	2186.75 – 2187.75	3–2lirepm	1.37	9–7pm	1.46
Norway	11.3615 – 11.4375	11.4275 – 11.4375	$3\frac{1}{8}$–$2\frac{5}{8}$orepm	3.02	$7\frac{1}{2}$–$6\frac{7}{8}$pm	2.51
France	9.8875 – 9.9220	9.8875 – 9.8975	$3\frac{3}{8}$–$3\frac{1}{4}$cpm	4.02	$8\frac{7}{8}$–$8\frac{1}{2}$pm	3.51
Sweden	10.8565 – 10.9100	10.9000 – 10.9100	$1\frac{1}{8}$–$\frac{3}{4}$orepm	1.03	$2\frac{7}{8}$–$2\frac{3}{8}$pm	0.96
Japan	257.55 – 259.00	258.00 – 259.00	$1\frac{3}{8}$–$1\frac{1}{4}$ypm	6.09	$3\frac{3}{4}$–$3\frac{1}{2}$pm	5.61
Austria	20.4400 – 20.5500	20.5200 – 20.5500	9–$7\frac{3}{4}$gropm	4.89	$23\frac{1}{4}$–21pm	4.31
Switzerland	2.4425 – 2.4565	2.4425 – 2.4525	$1\frac{3}{8}$–$1\frac{1}{4}$cpm	6.44	$3\frac{3}{8}$–$3\frac{1}{4}$pm	5.41
Ecu	1.4105 – 1.4155	1.4115 – 1.4125	0.48–0.44cpm	3.91	1.22–1.16pm	3.37

Commercial rates taken towards the end of London trading. Six-month forward dollar 5.72–5.67cpm. 12 month 9.75–9.65cpm.

Source: Financial Times, 24 January 1991

If Table 4.2 is examined for sterling against the Swiss franc the quotations under spot and one month forward are given as:

Switzerland close:	2.4425 – 2.4525
One month:	$1\frac{3}{8}$–$1\frac{1}{4}$ cpm
% p.a.:	6.44

If we wish to obtain the full forward quote the spot figure must be built upon. The pm refers to the fact that the Swiss franc is at a premium in the one month forward market. Therefore, less francs will be required to buy one pound sterling in one month's time than are needed today (i.e. the franc is appreciating against the pound).

The outright forward rate is calculated as follows:

	Bid Offer	*Difference*
Spot	2.44250–2.4525	1c = 100pips
One month premium	0.01375–0.0125	$\frac{1}{8}$c = 12.5pips
Outright forward quote	2.42875–2.4400	$1\frac{1}{8}$c = 112.5pips

The annual forward premium of 6.44 per cent is calculated using the middle market quotations, halfway between bid and offer. The one month premium of the Swiss franc on sterling in our example is $[1\frac{3}{8} + 1\frac{1}{4}]/2 = 1.3125$ centimes, whereas the middle market close is $(2.4425 + 2.4525)/2 = 2.4475$ francs. The annual forward premium is calculated as follows:

$$\frac{1.3125 \text{ centimes}}{2.4475} \times \frac{12 \text{ months}}{1 \text{ month}} \times 100\%$$

$$= 6.44\% \text{ p.a.}$$

Table 4.3 Dollar spot–forward against the dollar

23 January	Day's spread	Close	One month	% p.a.	Three months	% p.a.
UK†	1.9380 – 1.9575	1.9545 – 1.9555	1.18–1.16cpm	7.18	3.18–3.15pm	6.48
Ireland†	1.7760 – 1.7850	1.7840 – 1.7850	0.22–0.27cdis	– 1.65	0.58–0.68dis	– 1.41
Canada	1.1560 – 1.1610	1.1585 – 1.1595	0.39–0.42cdis	– 4.19	1.02–1.07dis	– 3.61
Netherlands	1.6770 – 1.6930	1.6785 – 1.6795	0.29–0.33cdis	– 2.22	0.88–0.93dis	– 2.16
Belgium	30.65 – 30.95	30.65 – 30.75	6.00–9.00cdis	– 2.93	15.00–25.00dis	– 2.61
Denmark	5.7450 – 5.7860	5.7450 – 5.7500	1.60–1.80oredis	– 3.55	4.35–4.95dis	– 3.24
Germany	1.4850 – 1.5020	1.4885 – 1.4895	0.24–0.26ofdis	– 2.01	0.77–0.80dis	– 2.11
Portugal	132.00 – 133.40	132.05 – 132.15	65–80cdis	– 6.59	230–255dis	– 7.34
Spain	93.70 – 94.40	93.70 – 93.80	59–64cdis	– 7.87	169–179dis	– 7.42
Italy	1117.50 – 1129.00	1118.50 – 1119.00	5.00–5.70liredis	– 5.74	14.00–15.00dis	– 5.18
Norway	5.8400 – 5.8800	5.8450 – 5.8500	1.95–2.20oredis	– 4.26	5.75–6.35dis	– 3.45
France	5.0560 – 5.1120	5.0575 – 5.0625	1.32–1.37cdis	– 3.19	3.79–3.89dis	– 3.04
Sweden	5.5640 – 5.6090	5.5750 – 5.5800	2.80–3.00oredis	– 6.24	7.70–8.05dis	– 5.65
Japan	131.85 – 132.95	132.20 – 132.30	0.12–0.14ydis	– 1.18	0.30–0.33dis	– 0.95
Austria	10.5200 – 10.5600	10.5250 – 10.5300	1.90–2.35grodis	– 2.42	5.40–6.80dis	– 2.32
Switzerland	1.2500 – 1.2665	1.2520 – 1.2530	0.13–0.16cdis	– 1.39	0.36–0.41dis	– 1.23
Ecu†	1.3715 – 1.3845	1.3835 – 1.3845	0.41–0.38cpm	3.42	1.14–1.08pm	3.21

Commercial rates taken towards the end of London grading, † UK, Ireland and Ecu are quoted in US currency. Forward premiums and discounts apply to the US dollar and not to the individual currency.

Source: Financial Times, 24 January 1991

Table 4.3 shows the dollar spot and forward rates against the major currencies. It is the same as Table 4.2 except that sterling is quoted on the New York direct convention, so the premium or discount quoted applies to the US dollar and not to the pound. Apart from this, the outright forward rate against the dollar is calculated in the same way.

In the next section the possibility of making a profit from differences in exchange rate quotations in different countries is examined. This process is known as international arbitrage.

Arbitrage

Foreign exchange arbitrage occurs when discrepancies arise in quotations of two or more traders. There is an opportunity to profit by buying from one trader at a low price and selling immediately to another trader at a higher price. For example, if the SF/£ rate in London is 2.4560–63 and at the same time a dealer in Zurich is quoting a rate of SF2.4555–58 then an instant arbitrage profit is possible by buying Swiss francs in London at 2.4560/£ and immediately selling them back for sterling in Zurich at the rate of SF2.4558/£. Starting with £1,000,000 this would yield profit of £81.44. Arbitrage opportunities in the spot market are usually extremely short-lived and only available to dealers in the market.

Another form of arbitrage is covered interest arbitrage. This occurs in the financial markets when interest rates and exchange rates are not in equilibrium.

If the arbitrageur (person who undertakes the arbitrage operation) can be assured of the rates and knows they are fixed it is possible to carry out these transactions with no risk involved and even with no investment required. Funds can be borrowed in the certain knowledge that the amount received will more than compensate for the amount borrowed plus any accrued interest.

The theory of covered interest rate arbitrage According to Coninx (1980), covered interest arbitrage in its purest form consists of borrowing one currency and converting it into another one, placing the proceeds in an investment for the period of the hedge and the borrowing. After taking out forward cover to protect the interest and swap differentials, showing a profit on the overall transaction.

The processes of spot arbitrage and covered interest arbitrage are illustrated below.

Assume that you have just been appointed the financial adviser to Mrs Sheila Ramsey, a wealthy Australian widow. To test your ability, Mrs Ramsey has lent you A$1,000,000 and arranged for you to have access to the foreign exchange markets in Australia and New Zealand. With the current spot rates of:

Australia	*New Zealand*
A$0.7415/NZ$	NZ$1.3488/A$
A$1.2601/US$	NZ$1.6695/US$

how can you use your skills to make an immediate profit and impress your employer?

By calculation it is easy to see that there is a disequilibrium in the markets, as the cross-rates will show.

In Australia, the NZ$/US$ rate will be $1/0.7415 \times 1.2601$, giving:

$$NZ\$1.6994/US\$$$

In New Zealand, the A$/US$ rate will be $1/1.3488 \times 1.6695$, giving:

$$A\$1.2378/US\$$$

These rates are different from the ones set in the other country's market so an opportunity for arbitrage has arisen.

To exploit this, you could buy US$ in New Zealand, giving:

$$US\$807,885$$

Then, sell back in the Australian market for:

$$A\$1,018,016$$

This means you have earned an immediate risk-free profit of A$18,016.

Alternatively, you could have bought New Zealand dollars in Australia, then used these to buy US dollars in New Zealand and finally converted back to Australian dollars in Australia. Here, the profit would be A$17,906.

Having impressed Mrs Ramsey, she entrusts you with a new total of A$5,000,000 for a period of one year. She asks you to try to earn more than the Australian rate of interest. Looking at the forward market in Sydney, you observe the following:

	Spot	*12 months forward*
	A$0.7415/NZ$	A$0.7106/NZ$
	A$1.2601/US$	A$1.3163/US$

The relevant interest rates for one-year investments are:

Australia	15%
New Zealand	20%
USA	12%

First, calculate the amount that would be earned in Australia if the money were invested for one year. This is:

$$A\$5,000,000 \times 1.15 = A\$5,750,000$$

Now see if you can do better elsewhere.
1. In New Zealand

Transfer funds to NZ$ at spot	NZ$6,743,088
Invest for one year at 20 per cent	NZ$8,091,706
Sell this amount forward for	A$5,749,966

This is almost identical to the amount earned in Australia because there is no disequilibrium here.
2. In the USA

Transfer funds to US$ at spot	US$3,967,939
Invest for one year at 12 per cent	US$4,444,092
Sell this amount forward for	A$5,849,758

In this case, there is a disequilibrium which you can exploit, and because the interest and forward rates are fixed the profit is a safe, guaranteed amount.

The rate of return is 17 per cent here, better than the 15 per cent possible in Australia. The gain made is:

$$A\$5,849,758 - A\$5,750,000$$
$$= A\$99,758$$

The disequilibrium in the forward markets would have been found easily using interest and exchange rate agios as shown in section on interest rate and exchange rate differentials later in the chapter.

The above example is a very simple illustration of how to earn risk-free profits from arbitrage. The figures found by the arbitrageurs in practice are unlikely to be so generous. Additionally, they will have to deal with a variety of interest rates and also different exchange rates depending on whether they are buying or selling the currencies, but the principles involved are the same.

Obviously, this is an ideal opportunity for banks and companies. They are able to ensure totally risk-free profits, with no investment required.

Opportunities for covered interest rate arbitrage As mentioned earlier, opportunities for covered interest rate arbitrage are rare and pass quickly, but they are real. They arise when the interest and exchange rates are in a state of disequilibrium.

If the markets are in equilibrium then country A with a low interest rate would find its currency at a forward premium of x per cent in terms of the currency of country B, where the interest rates are proportionately (i.e. x per cent) higher.

To identify the oportunities for arbitrage the arbitrageurs must have perfect knowledge of the market rates and be able to immediately identify and act upon any disequilibria. The scope for arbitrage is limited as the opportunities are sometimes illusory, especially when transactions costs are taken into account, and always short-lived. When the opportunities do occur, only the most alert dealers will have the chance to act on them. The market-makers themselves (i.e. the banks) will take advantage of the situation and their actions will exert market forces which will quickly restore the equilibrium.

To help them, arbitrageurs do have available the latest computer technology. This enables them to stay in touch with the very latest interest and exchange rates around the world, to locate arbitrage opportunities and to respond immediately to them. However, they do face a serious problem in coping with constraints imposed on the foreign exchange markets by various governments which restrict free movements of funds in certain currencies. The least restricted markets at present are the Eurocurrency markets, which have unrestricted lending and borrowing rates. In the other currency markets, the central banks manipulate the markets to try to impose some control on the interest and exchange rates.

The situation of market equilibrium described above is known as interest parity. Branson (1969) uses a linear approximation to interest parity first developed by Keynes. This is a useful tool in explaining why opportunities for arbitrage are short lived.

The approximation used was:

$$\frac{rt}{ro} - 1 = d = Id - If = i$$

where:

   rt is the price of one unit of foreign currency in terms of domestic currency at delivery time, t

   ro is the same price today (i.e. spot rate)

   d is the forward discount on the domestic currency

   Id is domestic interest rate over time o to t

   If is foreign interest rate over the same time span

   i is the interest rate differential

If d exceeds i then arbitrage will take place with the arbitrageur borrowing at home at rate Id and buying foreign currency at rate ro. This amount is then deposited abroad at rate If, and the principal plus interest can be sold forward at rate rt. The total received will be more than sufficient to repay the domestic loan plus accrued interest.

The impact of arbitrage will result in rt being depressed and ro being raised. This happens because more people want to buy foreign currency now, forcing up the current price ro, and they also want to sell forward, thus the forward rate, rt, will fall. The interest differential, Id − If, will increase as there is a flow of funds abroad. Overall, the effect is to reduce d and increase i until the equilibrium is regained.

Suppose an investor wished to undertake covered interest rate arbitrage when the markets were in equilibrium. What would happen?

Consider an investor with £1m to invest for three months. He decides to invest in a West German bank and hopes to profit from arbitrage.

The spot rate is: DM2.7912/£1
The 3-month forward rate is: DM2.7445/£1
Interest rates are: UK   15%
                           Germany   8.0625%

1. The investor converts £ to DM at the spot rate giving DM2,791,200
2. This is invested in Germany.
   The effective interest rate was calculated to be:

$$0.25 \ (3 \text{ months}) \times 8.0625\% = 2.015625\%$$

The investor calculates he would receive from the bank $1.02015625 \times 2,791,200 =$ DM2,847,460

3. In anticipation of this the investor sells this amount 3 months forward at the rate of DM2.7445/£1 and receives 3 months later DM2,847,460/2.7445 = £1,037,515

The alternative was to invest in the UK at an effective rate of:

$$0.25 \times 15\% = 3.75\%$$

This would have yielded:

$$1.0375 \times 1,000,000 = £1,037,000$$

The amounts are almost identical because the markets are in equilibrium. However, the investor in our example would have lost out because of the transaction costs involved in the foreign exchange transactions.

Interest and exchange rate differentials The investor in the above example could have tested whether or not arbitrage was worth while by comparing the interest and exchange rate differentials or agios.
The interest rate agio can be found using the following formula:

$$\frac{If - Id}{1 + Id}$$

In our example this would be:

$$\frac{0.02016 - 0.0375}{1.0375} = -1.67\%$$

The exchange rate agio can be calculated using the formula:

$$\frac{rt - ro}{ro}$$

In our example this would be:

$$\frac{2.7445 - 2.7912}{2.7912} = -1.67\%$$

If, as in this case, the two agios are equal then there is no opportunity to profit from arbitrage. Only when the two agios are significantly different is there scope for profitable arbitrage. Consider our earlier example of the Australian adviser. There, a profit was available because of a disequilibrium in the interest and forward exchange rates between Australia and the USA.

$$\text{The interest rate agio was } \frac{0.12 - 0.15}{1.15} = -2.61\%$$

$$\text{The exchange rate agio was } \frac{1.3163 - 1.2601}{1.2601} = 4.46\%$$

If the arbitrageur found such a significant difference in the two agios, he would act quickly to exploit the situation before market forces brought about a change to restore the equilibrium. Arbitrageurs must overcome constraints imposed upon them and also other problems before they are able to undertake the arbitrage transactions.

Arbitrage in practice: locations and problems   The world in which the arbitrageurs must deal is not the perfect theoretical world of the textbooks. Their task is complicated by a number of problems, the most common of which are outlined below:

1. *Creditworthiness*   Banks and other firms who try to profit from arbitrage will usually borrow the amounts required to finance their operations. The smaller arbitrageurs will often find that they are at a disadvantage because banks and their larger competitors can borrow at favourable rates. As well as resulting in more profit for the bigger arbitrageurs, it also means they can find more opportunities for arbitrage and respond more quickly to these. Thus, the smaller arbitrageurs are competing at a disadvantage and will have great difficulty in finding suitable opportunities for arbitrage.

2. *Selection*   Some countries, usually the ones with exotic currencies, only permit certain banks to deal in their currencies. This reduces the scope for arbitrage to most of the market.

Covered interest rate arbitrage occurs in many countries around the world. However, the volume of arbitrage transactions is greater in North America and Western Europe than elsewhere. New York is the largest centre of arbitrage trading in the world, with a small number of specialist firms offering their services solely as arbitrage brokers to the commercial banks and multinational corporations in the market for foreign exchange.

Studies have shown that arbitrage is particularly profitable between relatively small countries and any large neighbouring economy. Perhaps the best example of this is arbitrage between the USA and Canada. This is because the Canadian economy is reliant on trade with the USA. Not surprisingly, therefore, arbitrage between the two countries is very common. Elsewhere, arbitrage generally takes place between the major free market countries, especially between the USA and the UK, West Germany, Switzerland or Japan.

The reason that the less developed countries' currencies do not play a large role in the arbitrage market is that their economies are not as stable as those of the countries mentioned above. As a result they lack the quoted forward currencies and safe government securities that are necessary for covered interest rate arbitrage.

To make a profit on covered interest rate arbitrage the gain must be a significant amount because the arbitrageur will be subject to transaction costs, such as brokerage fees and taxation. In addition to these, Einzig (1966) points out that some foreign exchange departments within commercial banks are required to achieve results that compare well with the domestic trading results of these banks. The departments are charged high interest if they have to borrow extra funds to invest abroad, and if they have surplus funds they earn only a low rate of interest through holding the funds at the bank.

Branson (1969) tried to determine the minimum profit margin required before arbitrageurs are attracted into arbitrage transactions. He studied transactions in Treasury Bills between the USA and both the UK and Canada. He concentrated the study on the New York banks, as they are the major arbitrageurs in these countries. The results showed that in both cases a gross profit of 0.18 per cent was required before arbitrage occurred. This figure is similar to earlier estimates made by Keynes and Einzig. However, it should be noted that the data used in the study were from the early 1960s and it is possible that a change may have occurred since, not least because of the advent of the floating exchange rate system in 1973.

The recent evidence suggests that transaction costs may have risen. Eiteman and Stonehill (1989) suggest that in periods of stability the costs average around 0.13 per cent, although in the mid-1970s they reached over 1 per cent. Recently, the average transaction costs were estimated at 0.18 per cent–0.25 per cent.

Two reasons for the high costs over the years 1973–75 were suggested by Frenkel and Levich (1977). First, a wider spread in buying and selling forward exchange rates emerged, as banks were concerned that the markets might change significantly and suddenly. Thus, they did not want to be caught out by offering too generous forward rates. Secondly, there were fewer and smaller transactions occurring. Therefore, the transaction costs were a higher proportion of the total amounts traded. Later, as the world's exchange markets began to accept the new floating rate system, a more tranquil period returned and transaction costs have fallen as a percentage of the total transaction.

Variations of arbitrage

Uncovered interest rate arbitrage   With covered interest rate arbitrage the rates are all fixed in advance, and the proceeds are hedged by selling forward. Thus, the total gain is known in advance and there is no risk involved.

It is possible, however, to carry out a similar set of transactions but not to cover the deal, and therefore risk that the future spot rate will be more favourable than the present forward rate. This could result in better profits, but it does have an element of risk. This uncovered arbitrage is speculating in the hope of achieving a larger gain. In fact, uncovered arbitrage is not, strictly speaking, arbitrage at all.

Arbitrage and the time factor   Covered interest rate arbitrage is usually only a short-term operation. Periods of one, three or six months are the usual length for such transactions. However, using the forward market it is possible to carry out long-term arbitrage for periods up to and in excess of one year. For example, when the UK had tight foreign exchange controls, some UK local authorities, keen to borrow funds, asked to borrow US dollars and other Eurocurrencies for quite long loans and guaranteed the exchange rate paid back at the end of the loan.

What are the implications of long-term arbitrage operations for those arbitrageurs who enter into them? The main difference is a greater degree of complexity in calculating all the transaction costs. Not all relevant factors are readily quantifiable. These factors include compounding of interest, the tax effects, the remittance of funds to any parent company or dividends to shareholders, and the future strength of the currency in which earnings will be generated, as suggested by Coninx (1980). All these could distort the expected profit from the operation, and so careful thought must be given to them before entering into a long-term arbitrage deal.

THE FOREIGN EXCHANGE DECISIONS OF COMMERCIAL ORGANIZATIONS

Under the Bretton Woods system of foreign exchange, currency transactions and transaction losses or gains had only marginal effects on investment results. As the rates were fixed within a small range the only opportunity for arbitrage was where a fundamental imbalance could be identified and profits made until the rates were fixed at a more equitable level.

Hedging foreign exchange risk was only necessary if a realignment of either currency was imminent. Even then the hedge was only undertaken by the organization if the cost of forward cover was expected to be less than the anticipated devaluation effect. Foreign exchange skills were actually developed faster in the smaller countries, while the two leading economies of the inter-war and immediate post-war periods, the UK and the USA, were largely ignorant of these techniques. UK firms felt they were protected from foreign exchange risk by dealing principally with the Commonwealth countries, and in the USA companies relied on the strength of the dollar. Indeed, many US companies got into financial difficulties by ignoring currency risk when they expanded into the overseas markets during the 1950s and 1960s.

Many companies even today would prefer only to deal in their own national currencies, as it is so much easier for them to do so. However, they could miss out on markets to sell to and cheaper sources of supply and labour if they did so. Firms must take consideration of their size and aims. If they wish to continue to expand, then at some point they will have to enter into foreign trade and, inevitably, become involved in foreign exchange. Recently, the trend has been for multinational corporations to begin production in many foreign countries to take advantage of the benefits offered there. These might include lower transportation costs, government grants and even a way around some of the official constraints on currency movements that are always an obstacle for those involved in foreign exchange and arbitrage.

Foreign exchange constraints

The constraints facing arbitrageurs and others involved in foreign exchange markets are imposed both by the central banks or governments of countries and also by the prudent philosophies of the brokers and commercial banks themselves.

The official constraints are usually limits on the capital or liquidity ratios of exchange transactions, but can be more severe, such as government permission being required for any dealings in a country's currency. Unofficial constraints that the banks impose on themselves include total, overnight and daylight limits.

The total limit is a pre-set maximum exposure of foreign currency against the national currency. This is usually a very large limit and is unlikely ever to be approached by the banks' dealings. The overnight limits are set for all major foreign currencies. They are the maximum allowable exposures that the bank is willing to maintain overnight. Daylight limits are similar, but will be set slightly higher. The banks allow the overnight limits to be exceeded if necessary during dealing hours, as long as the exposure is brought back within the overnight limit by the end of each day's trading. In exceptional circumstances, the dealers may agree to dispense with limits altogether for a very large transaction if required to do so by a large and secure client.

Additionally, dealers are strict about time limits they impose, with heavy penalties for clients who do not meet deadlines. This is not surprising since exchange rates can move suddenly and have significant effects on the profitability of a transaction.

These unofficial constraints were unheard of before the Second World War, and for many years after the war. However, after a series of bank failures in the 1960s and 1970s and large foreign exchange losses by several major banks (e.g. Lloyds Bank in Lugano, Switzerland), the banks decided to carefully monitor their own actions to limit their exposure. The initial result of this was unreasonably tight limits being imposed which greatly reduced the size and number of foreign exchange and arbitrage deals. Eventually, however, the banks have regained their confidence and the limits they impose now are higher and more flexible.

REFERENCES

Branson, W. H. (1969) 'The minimum covered interest differential needed for international arbitrage activity', *Journal of Political Economy*, Vol. 77, pp.1028–38.

Coninx, R. (1980) *Foreign Exchange Today*, Woodhead-Faulkner, Cambridge.

Einzig, P. (1966) *A Textbook on Foreign Exchange*, Macmillan, London.

Eiteman, D. and A. I. Stonehill (1989) *Multinational Business Finance*, Addison-Wesley, Reading, Mass.

Frenkel, J. A. and R. M. Levich (1977) 'Transactions costs and interest arbitrage', *Journal of Political Economy*, Vol. 85, pp.1209–29.

Honeygold, D. (1989) *International Financial Markets*, Woodhead-Faulkner Ltd, Cambridge, England.

ADDITIONAL READING

Gold, Sir Joseph (1989) 'Exchange rate law', IMF survey, 15 May.

Rodriguez, R. and E. E. Carter (1984) *International Financial Management*, Prentice-Hall, Englewood Cliffs, New Jersey.

CASE STUDY

The case study shows how to apply the technique of covered interest rate arbitrage to an example problem. It illustrates the uses of the technique compared with other foreign exchange management techniques.

Albion Ltd

Albion Ltd is expanding into France and is due to pay the final instalment of FF5,000,000 for the cost of building its new factory in three months' time. Albion only possesses sufficient liquid funds to finance normal working capital requirements, although a payment of £500,000 is due to the company in three months' time.

Market information:

	FF/£	
Spot	11.121–11.150	
1 month forward	11.198–11.224	
2 months forward	11.035–11.065	
3 months forward	10.948–10.976	

Money Markets	*Borrowing*	*Lending*
UK clearing bank	16%	11%
French Banque de Depots	11%	8%
Eurodollar	17%	13%
Eurofranc	11%	9%
Eurosterling	15.5%	12%
UK treasury bill	—	12%
1-year French bond	—	9.5%

What alternatives does Albion have for making the payment? Which should Albion choose? At the current spot rate the bill is equivalent to:

$$FF5,000,000/11.121 = £449,600$$

1. Accept the foreign exchange rate, do nothing. This is a simple but not a good solution to the payment problem. The forward rate is only a rough guide to the future spot rate and its accuracy should not be relied upon. This strategy would leave Albion open to face foreign exchange risk.
2. Hedge on forward market.
   Contract to buy French francs three months forward. The relevant rate is FF10.948/£. Therefore, the cost of this hedging is:

$$FF5,000,000/10.948 = £456,704$$

Albion can be certain of this price if the company hedges now before the rates change.
3. Lead payment.
   Borrow Eurosterling to make a lead payment (pay early).
   This requires £449,600 at 15.5 per cent interest. Therefore, total cost =

$$£449,600 \times 1.03875 = £467,022$$

Note the interest is only 3.875% because the money is borrowed for only three months.

It is clear that this is a more expensive alternative for Albion. It might be worth waiting a month and then leading the payment. This is because the pound is getting stronger according to the forward rate figures, and less sterling will be needed to pay the cost in francs. Also, because the money would be borrowed for a shorter time, the interest charge would be less.

If francs were borrowed instead, the required amount would be FF5,000,000 at 11 per cent for three months. The cost would be

$$FF5,000,000 \times 1.0275 = FF5,137,500$$

Albion would have to use the bank's selling rate of FF10.948/£ to convert to sterling three months forward. The cost would therefore be £469,264.

Thus, it can be seen that in this case leading the payment is not an economically viable alternative.

4. Money market cover.

Borrow £449,600 in the UK for three months at 15.5 per cent. Convert at the spot rate to FF5,000,000 and invest in Eurofrancs at 9 per cent for three months.

The cost of borrowing in the UK is:

$$£449,600 \times 3.875\% = £17,422$$

The interest earned in France is:

$$FF5,000,000 \times 2.25\% = FF112,500 \text{ which, selling forward at FF10.976/£, yields £10,250}$$

The total cost of this alternative is therefore:

$$£449,600 + £17,422 - £10,250 = £456,772$$

Another alternative would be to determine exactly how much needs to be invested in France today to yield FF5,000,000 in three months' time. The amount required is:

$$FF5,000,000/1.0225 = FF4,889,976$$

Converting at the spot rate equates to £439,706.

The cost of this option is therefore the cost of borrowing £439,706 for three months at 15.5 per cent. This is:

$$£439,706 \times 1.03875 = £456,745$$

From the above calculations it would appear that hedging in the forward market is the best strategy for Albion to undertake. Notice how the alternatives above show arbitrage techniques and manipulation of interest rates and spot and forward exchange rates to try to find the best possible deal for Albion. In reality, Albion would also consider other methods to minimize the risk of its foreign trade, such as interest rate swaps and parallel loans, and the different level of transaction costs of the alternatives.

FIVE

FORECASTING EXCHANGE RATES

INTRODUCTION

This chapter examines the factors that influence the movements in foreign exchange rates and whether or not it is possible to forecast future exchange rates. These are important questions for any company engaged in foreign operations as they have implications for the amount of foreign exchange risk experienced by the company. We first discuss parity conditions in international finance. This involves purchasing power parity, the Fisher effect, the interest rate parity theory and the expectations theory which provide the essential framework for forecasting exchange rates. Empirical evidence is provided to support or refute these theories. We then discuss forecasting exchange rates and outline the significance of the efficient markets hypothesis to currency forecasting, and the alternative techniques that are used to forecast currency rates.

PARITY CONDITIONS IN INTERNATIONAL FINANCE

Parity conditions examine the relationships that exist between exchange rates and a number of important economic factors. They are the set of equilibrium relationships which should hold between product prices, interest rates, and spot and forward exchange rates assuming a freely floating exchange system.

These relationships can be seen in Figure 5.1.

Purchasing power parity

When the inflation rate of one country rises relative to that of another country, the demand for the high inflation country's exports will fall as its prices become relatively high, and the demand for imported goods from the low inflation country will rise as its prices become relatively low. The effect of these changes in demand will be to exert downward pressure on the value of the currency of the relatively high inflation country. Purchasing power parity examines exactly how inflation rate differentials between countries might influence exchange rates. There are two versions of the purchasing power parity theory (PPP)—the absolute and the relative.

Absolute purchasing power parity The absolute PPP relies on the 'law of one price'. This states that 'the general level of prices, when converted to a common currency, will be the same in every country'; in other words, price changes owing to inflation in one country are compensated for by a change in the exchange rate. The exchange rate is the ratio between the domestic prices and foreign prices of internationally traded goods, i.e.:

$$e_o = \frac{P_h}{P_f}$$

where e_o is the current equilibrium exchange rate, P_h is the home country price level and P_f is the foreign price level. However, the major problem arising from the use of price indices to measure the level of inflation in the two countries is that the indices of the countries concerned may not be comparable owing to the inclusion of different types of goods and services and the choice of base year.

A further problem with using price indices is that real economic events can have an effect on exchange rates, even with inflation constant. For example, a bad harvest will alter the price of wheat relative to other prices, even though it has negligible effect on average prices. This could result in deviations from absolute PPP because there is likely to be a change in the value of the currency of major wheat producers relative to countries not producing wheat. Absolute PPP may also not hold owing to the existence of non-traded goods (mainly services). Isard (1977) shows that empirically the law of one price frequently does not hold. Absolute PPP also makes strong assumptions about capital mobility, transactions costs and the efficient and cheap dissemination of information which are violated by the existence of tariffs, quotas, different tax regimes and other restrictions on free trade. An alternative form of the PPP which does not require such strong assumptions is the relative PPP.

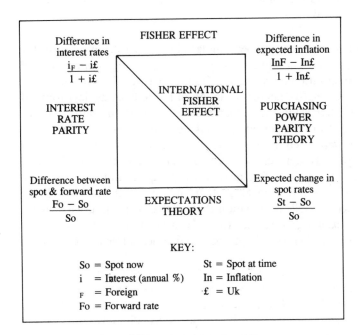

Figure 5.1   Parity conditions in international finance

Relative purchasing power parity   The relative PPP view states that any necessary adjustment in the exchange rate between two countries can be found by comparing the change in the ratio of domestic and foreign prices from a time when exchange rates were in equilibrium, i.e.:

$$\frac{e_t}{e_0} = \frac{P_h(t)/P_h(0)}{P_f(t)/P_f(0)}$$

where $P_h(t)$ and $P_f(t)$ are the home and foreign price levels respectively, and e_t is the home currency value of one unit of foreign currency, at time t. $P_h(0)$, $P_f(0)$ and e_0 are the base period equilibrium price levels and exchange rate. This can be transformed into the more commonly used equation

$$\frac{e_t - e_0}{e_0} = \frac{i_{f,t} - i_{h,t}}{1 + i_{h,t}}$$

where $i_{h,t}$ and $i_{f,t}$ are the expected rates of inflation between time 0 and time t for the home country and the foreign country respectively.

If the base price level is 100 and the current US price level is at 115, compared with the UK price level of 110, then the dollar value of the pound sterling would have to appreciate by 4.55 per cent $[(0.15 - 0.10)/1.10]$ in order for PPP to be maintained.

Relative PPP considers percentage changes in the exchange rate and the ratio of the price indices, not the absolute figures. By doing this, the problems of having to choose a base for the price index is removed.

Melvin (1985) indicates that, PPP is really not a theory of exchange rate determination. He argues that it is an equilibrium relationship between two endogenous variables. Thus to really explain prices and exchange rates, we must explain how they are affected by changes in the exogenous elements, which PPP does not do.

Empirical evidence   A vast amount of research has been undertaken into PPP, mostly on the relative version. Balassa's work (1964) and Gailliot's study (1970) lend strong support to PPP as a significant long-term theory in international economics. Gailliot reached this conclusion by examining the relationship between the relative degrees of inflation in the USA against some of its trading partners, and the relative changes in the exchange rates between the same nations. The average prices and exchange rates from the period 1900–04 were compared with the period 1963–67; the trading partners that were used were Canada, Japan, the UK, France, Italy, Switzerland and Germany. These periods were chosen because they were preceded by long periods of peace, were characterized by relatively free movement of capital and trade, and the gold standard existed. Thus, it was hoped that factors other than price changes would be eliminated. Gailliot's results supported Cassel's proposition that, in the long run, price changes are the major determinants of the exchange rate, i.e. they are more important than other factors such as barriers to trade (e.g. tariffs), transport costs and other influences on capital mobility.

Gailliot also examined PPP when non-monetary factors had experienced significant changes from period to period. This was done by studying 1900–67 on a decade-to-decade basis for the same countries. The results proved to be better than those obtained in the previous investigation and show that non-monetary factors can have an effect, but these are usually only temporary— even when the observations were influenced by two wars and a great depression.

Frenkel's tests of PPP (1981) incorporate tests of two basic properties: symmetry between the domestic and foreign currencies, and proportionality between relative prices and the exchange rate (e.g. the long-run coefficient on relative prices). However, Edison (1987) tested a third property: namely, exclusiveness. Exclusiveness is said to exist if relative prices are the only variable to affect the long-run exchange rate. Edison's survey of the dollar/pound exchange rate for the period 1890–1978 showed that the properties of symmetry and proportionality could not be rejected. The exclusiveness property could be rejected, however, so permanent deviations from PPP could not be discounted. She concluded that the results of her paper support a qualified interpretation of the PPP doctrine. The proportionality between the exchange rates and relative price level emerges in the long-run, after taking into account changes in structural factors.

Both these studies support the view that PPP is valid in the medium to long term, but fails in the short term.

Rogalski and Vinso (1977) found, in their studies of the foreign exchange market, that currency values reacted more or less immediately to changes in inflation rates. They tested a period of floating exchange rates (1920–24) and a dirty float period (the Canada–US exchange rate between 1953 and 1957). The results revealed that changes in relative price levels determine exchange rates and that increasing relative prices lead to a devaluation of a currency. In addition, the foreign exchange market appeared to be efficient with respect to inflation rates: that is to say, contrary to previous studies, no information lag was detected so that changes in price levels depended on changes in exchange rates, but information conveyed to market participants was used immediately. So according to these results it appears that changes in relative inflation rates between countries are an important determinant of changes in currency exchange rates, supporting the PPP hypothesis. However, it appears that changes in relative price levels are not the only determinant of exchange rates. Furthermore, exchange rates under a floating exchange rate regime adjust to changes in relative price levels as soon as the information is available. Therefore, using past values of relative inflation rates does not provide any more accurate forecasts of future spot rates than not using them in the information set. In addition, from the data for Canada in the 1950s it seems that intervention reduces the impact of relative price changes on exchange rates and induces inefficiency in the foreign exchange market.

Roll (1979) examined the possibility that PPP might not be valid in dirty floating exchange rate periods. He used a dynamic intertemporal theory of PPP, assuming an efficient market. From this study, he concluded that one cannot expect PPP to hold in all periods as arbitrageurs face uncertainty regarding the prices at which they will be able to sell their goods. Using 20 years of monthly observations for 23 countries, he found that the efficient markets hypothesis was relevant: With a few significant exceptions, there is little evidence of disequilibria or of slow adjustment of prices to a long-run parity. Indeed, the general impression for most countries and for all of the largest trading nations, is a very rapid adjustment of less than one month's duration.

According to the Henley Forecasting Centre, almost all serious approaches to medium- and long-term forecasting of exchange rates are based (at least in part) on some variant of the PPP approach. Research by the Henley Centre has indicated that even though deviations from PPP can be large and persistent, relative inflation rates are usually a determinant of exchange rates on a quarterly basis. However, research has shown that short-term deviations in the PPP increased in the late 1970s so that PPP became an even poorer guide to short-term (3–9 months) exchange rate movements. Isard (1977), Milore (1988) and Webster (1987) have also produced negative results and rejected PPP in the short run.

Balassa (1964) put forward the proposition that there was a relationship between purchasing power parities, exchange rates and income levels. There exist two types of goods: those which are traded internationally and those which are not; the exchange rate will reflect only the prices of internationally traded goods. Productivity differences occur among countries, especially with traded goods; whereas methods of production are similar worldwide for non-traded goods (mainly services). Higher wages which result in higher prices in the service sector generally exist in the more productive countries rather than in the less productive ones. These services are used in the calculation of price indices and so affect the PPP. However, because they are non-traded goods they do not affect the exchange rates directly. This will result in the PPP being lower than the equilibrium rate of exchange if the PPP is expressed in the currency of that country with the greater productivity level. From this, Balassa concluded that:

the greater are productivity differentials in the production of traded goods between two countries, the larger will be the difference in wages and in the prices of services and, correspondingly, the greater will be the gap between PPP and the equilibrium exchange rate.

To test this hypothesis Balassa compared the ratio of PPPs to the rate of exchange, and the ratio of PPPs to the per capita GNP for 12 industrialized countries (Belgium, Canada, Denmark, France, Germany, Italy, Japan, Netherlands, Norway, Sweden, UK, USA). The result proved that his suggestion of a relationship between PPPs, exchange rates and per capita income levels was valid.

Thus, his paper showed the need for the inclusion of non-traded goods in international trade models in order to make these models more realistic.

Frenkel (1981) looked at the nature of the two sides of the PPP equation: namely, exchange rates and price indices (i.e. inflation). Exchange rates are the relative prices of two durable assets (i.e. currencies), and future expectations are the main characteristic of asset prices. According to the efficient markets hypothesis new information concerning the future is reflected immediately in current prices resulting in a change in expectations followed by a fluctuation in the price of the asset (i.e. the currency). Because exchange rates are seen as asset prices, and new information, by definition, cannot be predicted, it follows that fluctuations of exchange rates are unpredictable. Aggregate price indices reflecting the prices of goods and services are less durable than exchange rates, and so are less likely to react quickly to new information.

Frenkel's study was devoted to discovering the reason for the failure of PPP in the 1970s. Exchange rates adjust due to them reflecting future conditions while commodity prices do not as they reflect present and past conditions. Therefore, large exchange rate fluctuations are likely to result in large deviations from PPP.

In conclusion, Frenkel states that PPP doesn't provide a guide for day-to-day or month-to-month fluctuations of exchange rates. In his opinion, PPP is not valid in the short to medium term and might not even hold in the long term owing to real structural changes which need relative price adjustments.

More recently, long-run relationships of PPP have been tested using time series properties of the real exchange rates to see if they follow a random walk. (See Alder and Lehman (1983), Hakkio (1986), Mark (1990) and Whitt (1992).) Other researchers used regression analysis (Frenkel 1978, 1981), or cointegration analysis (Taylor (1988), Kim (1990)). The outcome of these studies on the long-run validity of PPP has not been clear-cut, the outcome varying with the testing methodologies used. Favourable evidence for PPP has been found by Taylor and McMahon (1988) McNowa and Wallace (1989), Kim (1990), Johnson (1990), Choudry *et al.* (1991), Phylaktis (1992), Bleaney (1992) and Tronzano (1992). Layton and Stark (1990) and Lane (1991) have rejected the empirical validity of long-run PPP.

Even though some studies show that there are large deviations from PPP: 'Generally speaking, international finance experts nowadays accept that the key determinant of long-run exchange rate movement is relative purchasing power' (Buckley 1986)), PPP is found to hold up well in the medium to long term, but substantial deviations occur in the short term. It also appears to hold better in countries with high rates of inflation where price changes are almost continuous, and so the cost of deviating from PPP is high and acts as an incentive to maintain it.

The Fisher Effect

Fisher (1930) put forward the idea that there was a relationship between the nominal interest rates and the inflation rates: the so-called Fisher Effect. This was deemed necessary because the majority of financial contracts are stated using nominal interest rates; thus, expected inflation must be taken into account when assessing the real interest rate. The Fisher Effect states that the nominal interest rate, r, is made up of two components:

1. A real required rate of return, a, and
2. An inflation premium equal to the expected amount of inflation, i, i.e.:

$$1 + \text{nominal rate} = (1 + \text{real rate})(1 + \text{expected inflation rate})$$
$$1 + r = (1 + a)(1 + i)$$

As with the PPP theory, the Fisher Effect relies on the activities of arbitrageurs. If expected returns are higher in one country than in another, then arbitrage will force these returns to equality because capital will move from the country with the lower return to the one with the higher. This will be especially true in Eurocurrency markets where constraints on internal capital mobility are minimal.

The previous equation can now be restated as:

$$\frac{1 + r_{h,t}}{1 + r_{f,t}} = \frac{1 + i_{h,t}}{1 + i_{f,t}}$$

where $r_{h,t}$ and $r_{f,t}$ are the nominal home and foreign currencies respectively.

The main importance of the Fisher Effect is in its corollary, the International Fisher Effect, which is examined later. The majority of empirical tests have been directed at this International Fisher Effect; however, one notable study on the Fisher Effect was carried out by Fama (1975). Fama stated that:

with perfect foresight and a well-functioning capital market, the one period nominal rate of interest is the equilibrium real return plus the fully anticipated rate of inflation. In a world of uncertainty where foresight is imperfect, the nominal rate of interest can be thought of as the equilibrium expected real return plus the market's assessment of the expected rate of inflation.

Most studies, including Fisher's initial work, found no relationship between interest rates and expected inflation rates; in fact the market was not a particularly good predictor of inflation. However, there was found to be a relationship between current interest rates and past inflation rates, and this is often interpreted as evidence in favour of the Fisher Effect. As Fisher found, 'price changes do generally and perceptibly affect the interest rate in the direction indicated by a priori theory'.

At this point we need to consider the efficient markets hypothesis, which states that in an efficient market all relevant information will be used in price determination. If changes in the expected rate of inflation are not offset by a change in the expected real return, then a relationship will exist between the future rate of inflation and the observed nominal interest rate. This is only true in an efficient market, assuming that the inflation rate is to some extent predictable. Thus, Fisher's, and others', empirical evidence is contra to the efficient markets hypothesis, as there is no such relationship. This means the market is inefficient because it overlooks relevant information about future inflation.

Fama studied the efficiency in the market for one- to six-month US Treasury Bills from 1953 to 1971. His results showed that there was a relationship between nominal interest rates and the rate of inflation subsequently observed, unlike Fisher and most others; thus, his results supported the Fisher Effect. In addition, the market appeared to be efficient in that it included information about future inflation rates in the nominal interest rates.

As a possible explanation as to why most earlier studies failed to find a relationship, Fama suggested that they may have used poor commodity data (pre-1953), whereas the relationship he discovered may be due to the availability of good data beginning in 1953.

The International Fisher Effect

The International Fisher Effect holds that interest rate differentials should reflect the expected movement in the spot rate of exchange. This parity condition is derived from the two already discussed: namely, the PPP theory and the generalized Fisher Effect. PPP states that inflation differentials will be offset by changes in the exchange rates. Therefore, a rise in the home country's inflation rate will also be accompanied by a devaluation of the home country's currency, i.e. PPP. However, an increase in the home country's interest rate relative to the foreign interest rates will also take place.

This can be shown in equation form as

$$\frac{r_{h,t} - r_{f,t}}{1 + r_{f,t}} = \frac{e_t - e_0}{e_0}$$

If $r_{f,t}$ is relatively small, this is normally approximated to:

$$r_{h,t} - r_{f,t} = \frac{e_t - e_0}{e_0}$$

Central to the International Fisher Effect is the process of uncovered interest arbitrage (see Chapter 4). If investors speculating on the future spot rate expect to make a profit they will move capital from countries with low interest rates to countries with high interest rates. This action will force a movement in the exchange rate so as to eliminate this profit opportunity. Thus, the International Fisher Effect means that the interest differential between any two countries is an unbiased predictor of the future changes in the spot rate of exchange. This does not mean, however, that the interest differential is an accurate predictor; it simply means that prediction errors tend to cancel out over time.

Empirical evidence   A study by Aliber and Stickney (1975) sought to establish whether the International Fisher Effect held. This was done by calculating the percentage deviations from the Fisher Effect for seven developed countries (Belgium, Canada, France, Germany, Netherlands, Switzerland and the UK) for the period 1960–71; and six developing countries (Argentina, Brazil, Chile, Colombia, Mexico and Venezuela) for the period 1966–71. They determined that the average annual deviation could be used as a measure of long-term validity, and the maximum annual deviation could be used as a measure of short-term validity.

The results suggested that the International Fisher Effect was valid in the long term because the average annual deviation tended to be zero. Although the developing countries had larger deviations this was especially true for the developed countries. However, the maximum annual deviation was so large that they considered the theory to be invalid in the short term.

A study by Robinson and Warburton (1980) challenged this view. They noted that, according to the Fisher Effect, the possibility of earning a higher interest return would be eroded in the medium term by the appreciation of the currency of the country with the lower rate of interest relative to the currency of the country with the higher interest rate. They formulated four filter rules for placing and switching money in three-month treasury bills or three-month Eurocurrency deposits from 1972–79, and concluded that superior returns could be earned, thereby disputing the validity of the International Fisher Effect.

It has been shown that there is conflicting evidence for the International Fisher Effect; in fact evidence for this parity condition is least conclusive of all the theories on the four-way equivalence model.

The interest rate parity theory

The interest rate parity theory occurs when the interest differential between investments in two currencies is (approximately) equal to the difference between the spot and forward exchange rates. The difference between the spot and forward exchange rates is termed the premium (discount) which can be defined as 'the proportion by which a country's foreign exchange rate exceeds (falls below) its spot rate'. (Copeland, 1989 p. 91). It then follows that the forward premium or discount is equal to the interest differential.

According to interest rate parity theory, a country which has a lower interest rate than another should value its currency at a premium in terms of the other country's currency. The key to this parity condition is covered interest arbitrage. Opportunities for profitable covered interest arbitrage exist owing to differing effective rates of interest in different currencies, after taking transaction costs into account. The effective interest rate on a foreign deposit is said to equal the nominal interest rate plus the cost of forward cover (i.e. the forward premium (positive) or discount (negative)). For example, if the pound sterling interest rate is 10 per cent in London, but 15 per cent on a similar dollar investment in New York, and the forward premium on sterling is 3 per cent, then the effective interest rate is equal to 13 per cent (i.e. 10% + 3%). In this case there will be a flow of funds from London to New York because the covered interest differential is in New York's favour. This movement of funds will increase the British interest rate and decrease the US interest rate, so closing the interest rate differential. These dollar funds will be obtained by buying spot and selling forward, thus increasing the spot price and decreasing the forward price, and so the forward premium will broaden. This will continue until interest rate parity is reached.

Because the investment is 'covered' the transaction is risk-free; this makes it even less likely that disequilibrium could exist for any length of time.

Transaction costs must be taken into account when assessing whether there are opportunities for arbitrage profits or not. This is one reason why interest rate parity may not hold exactly. A further reason is government intervention in the form of controls on the movement of currencies between national markets. Again, as with the Fisher Effect, this parity condition should hold better in the Eurocurrency markets where the flow of funds is less restricted than in other money markets.

When there are no covered interest arbitrage opportunities, i.e. when the interest differential (or interest agio) equals the forward premium/discount (or exchange agio), interest rate parity is said to hold; this can be shown by the following equation:

$$\frac{1 + r_{h,t}}{1 + r_{f,t}} = \frac{f_t}{e_0}$$

where e_0 is the current spot rate, f_t is the forward rate at time t, and $r_{h,t}$ and $r_{f,t}$ are the interest rates for the home countries respectively at time t.

This is often approximated to:

$$r_{f,t} - r_{h,t} = \frac{e_0 - f_t}{e_0}$$

As with the preceding parity conditions, the next section deals with some of the empirical research carried out on this parity condition.

Empirical evidence Interest rate parity is one of the best documented relationships in international finance. In fact, in the Eurocurrency markets, the forward rate is calculated from the interest differential between the two currencies using the no-arbitrage condition. (Shapiro, 1986 p.176.)

However, deviations do occur, mainly due to government intervention or sometimes even the risk of government intervention is enough to cause deviations.

Richard Marston (1976) tested the relationship between dollar and non-dollar rates, and measured the deviations of non-dollar rates from interest rate parity. To do this, the regression of the non-dollar Eurocurrency rate on the Eurodollar rate, and the forward rate associated with these, was estimated. Two sets of equations, weekly and monthly, were also estimated for each non-dollar Eurocurrency rate over the six-year period 1965–70. The non-dollar Eurocurrencies used were Euro-pound, Euro-DM and Euro-SF. The results for the weekly equations showed that deviations from parity were limited for all three non-dollar Eurocurrencies. The results from the monthly equations were even more convincing of the fact that the non-dollar Eurocurrencies rates are determined almost entirely by interest arbitrage operations between the dollar and non-dollar markets.

The main reason suggested by Marston for this close adherence of non-dollar rates to interest parity is the lack of capital controls between these Eurocurrency markets. This point was raised in the explanation of interest rate parity.

Aliber (1973) examined the effect of different types of risk on the interest rate parity theory. The two types of risk considered were exchange risk due to the possibility that the exchange rate will change, and political risk due to the possibility of restrictions being implemented that will influence capital mobility.

The study involved predicting the exchange agio using the interest rate on dollar deposits in London and sterling deposits in Paris. The predicted exchange agio was then compared with the interest rates on US and UK Treasury Bills. The differences between the predicted forward rate and the actual forward rate were then calculated.

The results showed that the deviations are much smaller when the external dollar and sterling deposits are used to predict the forward rate than when US and UK treasury bills are used. Consequently, a major source of the difference between predicted and observed forward rates is that the securities used to predict the forward rate are not identical in terms of political risk.

Thus, Aliber concluded that political risk is borne while exchange risk is avoided by buying foreign currency spot and selling forward, i.e. covered interest arbitrage.

There is some evidence (Kohlhagen 1978) to suggest that the theory works well in the

Eurocurrency market, but not in national markets. Some of the reasons for significant deviations from the equilibrium conditions include: transactions costs (Frenkel and Levich 1981), less than infinite interest elasticities, capital market imperfections (Frenkel 1973), political risk (Aliber 1973), capital controls (Otani and Tiwari 1981), data imperfections (Committeri *et al.* 1993), speculation, taxes (Levi 1977) and default risk (Alder and Dumas 1976). The literature, however, do not seem to have a widespread agreement on the relative importance of these factors. It is expected that the trend towards more perfect markets which has existed in recent years will lead to the possibility of the Fisher Effect working even in national markets.

The final parity condition to be considered is the relationship between the forward rate and the future spot rate—or, as it is sometimes known, expectations theory.

The expectations theory

The first point to make about this theory is that a necessary prerequisite is the existence of free floating rates rather than fixed rates. Central to this relationship between forward rates and future spot rates is the efficient markets hypothesis. The major assumption here is that all relevant information should be reflected rapidly and accurately in both the spot and forward rates. In addition, investments in different currencies should be perfect substitutes for one another, and transaction costs should be low. Thus, changes in expectations will cause movements in the same direction of both the spot and forward rates. The link between them is based on interest differentials.

Those people who are receiving pounds sterling will sell them forward if they expect sterling to depreciate; while at the same time those people earning dollars in sterling areas will stop (or at least slow down) selling dollars in the forward market. This will result in the price of sterling decreasing. It is likely that banks will sell sterling spot in order to even out their long position in the forward market. Sterling earners will sell sterling and sterling area recipients of dollars will stop converting dollars to sterling. These activities will result in pressure from the forward market being placed on the spot market.

The equation representing this parity condition is:

$$\frac{f_t - e_0}{e_0} = \frac{e_t - e_0}{e_0}$$

where f_t is the forward rate for settlement at time t, and e_t is the expected future exchange rate at time t.

The argument above is just one of three major views of the extent to which the forward exchange rate represents the market's forecast of the future spot exchange rate. These three views are summarized in Dufey and Giddy (1978).

1. Speculation always creates movement in the forward rate until it equals the expected spot rate; thus, the forward rate is an unbiased predictor of the future spot rate, as above.
2. Transaction costs play an important part, because unless these are less than the expected gains there will be no real profit opportunities in the forward market. The reaction of the forward rate to changes in the expected spot rate will not always be instantaneous, which may result in the forward rate under- or over-estimating the expected spot rate. Thus, the forward rate may be a biased predictor of the future spot rate due to the existence of transaction costs.
3. Speculation will only occur if the profit opportunities are sufficient to compensate for the

risk associated with the transaction. This requires the existence of a risk premium which renders the forward rate a biased predictor of the future spot rate.

One view against the need for a risk premium is that foreign exchange risk is diversifiable (as discussed by Aliber (1973) above); therefore, the unbiased nature of forward rates is an empirical and not a theoretical issue.

Empirical evidence Cornell (1977) attempted to discover whether the forward market is efficient with respect to exchange rates or not, and also whether there was evidence to prove the existence of a liquidity premium on foreign exchange.

To test the existence of a liquidity premium he used monthly observations of spot and one-month forward exchange rates for the period April 1973 to January 1977 (except for the French franc—July 1974 to January 1977). This period was chosen because floating exchange rates were in operation. The other currencies used were the British pound, Canadian dollar, German mark, Swiss franc, Dutch guilder and Japanese yen. All the exchange rates were stated in terms of the US dollar price of foreign exchange.

After this test Cornell came to the conclusion that 'the results reveal that for none of the 7 currencies is there evidence of a liquidity premium', and 'this indicates that the forward rate can be used as a proxy for the market's expectation of the future spot rate'.

Giddy and Dufey (1975) used daily exchange rate data to analyse the flexible exchange rate periods for three currencies: namely, the Canadian dollar (1919–24, 1971–74), the French franc (1919–26, 1973–74) and the pound sterling (1919–25, 1972–74). They used various methods for predicting future spot rates (these are discussed later in this book) and found that the forward rate was the poorest predictor.

In general, the empirical evidence suggests that the forward exchange rate is an unbiased predictor of the future spot rate but more recent evidence (see Bilson (1981)) casts some doubts on this view. The bias tends to increase as the length of the forward period is increased.

FORECASTING EXCHANGE RATE CHANGES

The forecasting of exchange rate changes may be analysed with the assumption of a fixed or floating exchange rate system. In theory, the exchange rate system for many major currencies since the early 1970s has been a floating system. However, experience has shown that a 'dirty floating' or managed float system has prevailed in most cases which shares the attributes of a clean float (exchange rates determined by the interaction of currency supplies and demands) and of a fixed rate system with government intervention.

The existence of a managed float system creates problems for forecasters. In fact some recent theoretical analyses seem to imply 'a radical implication for exchange rate forecasting which is in essence that it cannot be done' (Henley Forecasting Centre (1981)). Nevertheless, commercial banks provide effective means of forward cover for short-term transactions exposure.

Furthermore, there is a large corporate demand for foreign exchange forecasts (particularly medium-term) as a basis for

- Medium-term pricing policy
- International investment and diversification policies
- Purchasing and sourcing policies
- Competitive assessment, etc.

The longer the time horizon of the exchange rate forecast, the more inaccurate and less critical the forecast is likely to be. The long-term forecast will typically be used, for example, for a direct foreign investment, and for such a forecast the forecaster will use annual data to display long-term trends in such economic fundamentals as inflation, growth and the balance of payments. Such variables will be used for medium-term forecasts. Short-term forecasts are used in the case of hedging a receivable, payable or dividend of, say, three months. Here, technical factors are more important than long-term economic fundamentals. Such technical factors include government intervention, news and passing whims of traders and investors. Contrary to long-term forecasting, accuracy of the short-term forecast is critical as most of the exchange rate changes are relatively small.

The profitability and consistency of exchange rate forecasting depends on market efficiency, a concept which is discussed later in this chapter. The less efficient the foreign exchange market is, the greater the chance that forecasters will find a relationship that will hold at least in the short run.

Before discussing the different ways of forecasting exchange rates, it is important to consider the theories of exchange rate determination, namely:

1. Inflation and interest rate differentials (four-way equivalence model)
2. Balance of payments approach
3. Monetary approach
4. Chartism (technical analysis)

The inflation and interest rate differential approach was discussed earlier. The balance of payments approach (or current account theory) can be best explained by analysing it under a fixed and floating system. Let us assume, first, a fixed exchange rate system. The balance of payments model suggests that as national income rises, the current account deteriorates. The domestic currency should then weaken (to pay for increased imports) and as it is a fixed system, the exchange rate should fall beyond certain limits, and the government intervene to counter the effect. According to this theory, the current account deficit is automatically corrected. Under a floating currency regime, when national income rises the current account deteriorates. The increase in income leads to an increase in demand for foreign currency at the expense of the home currency. Local currency is weakened, making exports more competitive and consequently this improves the current account.

The monetary approach assumes that a growing national income will induce a growing demand for money for transactions purposes. This can be met either through domestic credit creation or through a balance of payments surplus. An economy with a relatively high money supply growth, either through the PPP theorem or the mechanism explained previously, will experience a weakening exchange rate. Thus, a high money supply growth would lead to high interest rates and weakening currencies.

Chartism (sometimes referred to as technical analysis) involves the study of past price movements to seek out potential future trends. Chartism will be dealt with in greater detail under the technical analysis section later.

Forecasting floating exchange rates

In a world of floating currencies, exchange rates are determined by the interaction of demand and supply of currencies. The supply and demand are in turn determined, among other things, by relative rates of economic growth. As previously mentioned, most of the major currencies are characterized by a managed float (i.e. a combination of clean float and government intervention). In this section, the two main techniques of exchange rate forecasting will be discussed: market-based forecasts (including forward and interest rate models) and model-based forecasts which may be divided into fundamental analysis (including PPP, traditional flow model (or balance of payments approach)) and technical analysis or chartism. For both theories, the assumption of a floating exchange rate system will be made. The forecasting method under a fixed rate system is outlined later.

Currency forecasting and market efficiency

There has been accumulating evidence in recent years that the foreign exchange market has the characteristics of an efficient market. Such a market consists of numerous well-informed participants with ready and cheap access to new information and whose trading activities cause prices to rapidly adjust to available information (Shapiro 1986, p. 198). As new information arrives randomly, price changes follow what is known as a 'random walk'. Under such a theory, the best prediction of tomorrow's price is the price today, so that price changes from one period to the next are independent of past price changes and are only predictable as new information arrives. In the context of the foreign exchange market this means that exchange rates will quickly adjust to any new information. In an efficient market, the forward rate would only differ from the expected future spot rate by a risk premium. If this were not the case then an excess of the forward rate over the expected future spot rate would lead the investor to realize profits by selling foreign currency and buying it in the future at a lower price than the forward rate. In the real world, forward exchange rates adjust to the changing economic picture based on revisions of what the future spot rate will be as well as changes in the risk attached to the currencies involved. This process of price adjustments in response to new information in the efficient market rules out any certain profits from speculation.

There are in fact three gradations of the efficient markets hypothesis:

1. Weak form
2. Semi-strong form
3. Strong form

Weak form of the efficient markets hypothesis   Assumes that current prices reflect all market information, including the historical sequence of prices, price changes and any volume information. As current prices already reflect all past price changes and any other information, there can be no relationship between past price changes and future price changes. Thus, past market data cannot be of any use in predicting future prices.

Semi-strong form of the efficient markets hypothesis   Prices fully reflect all publicly available information data, i.e. market data and non-market data. The implication of this hypothesis is that investors acting on new information once it is public cannot derive above-average profits because the price already reflects the effects of the new public information.

Strong form of efficient markets hypothesis   Prices reflect all information, whether public or otherwise. Thus, no group has a monopolistic access to information and no group should be able to consistently earn above-average profits. The premiss of an efficient market is that there are a large number of profit-maximizing participants. That is true for foreign exchange markets, but there are also very large non-profit maximizers (i.e. central banks). The question is whether this intervention stops currency markets from displaying market efficiency. This is discussed by Kohlhagen (1978).

Evidence supporting the efficient markets hypothesis

A study by Giddy and Dufey (1975) which tested the random walk models compared with three alternative forecasting models for a database of a 1920s and 1970s series proved that the random walk models displayed a superior forecasting accuracy.

The alternative forecasting models (forward rate hypothesis, Box-Jenkins analysis and exponential smoothing) were compared with the two random walk models in Giddy and Dufey's analysis. These alternative models produced a better fit than the random walk model to the 1970s data. However, once tested on the basis of the mean squared predictive error (MSPE) in order to measure their level of accuracy the three alternative models fared poorly. The two time series models (the Box-Jenkins and adaptive exponential smoothing forecasts) did, however, show some extent of accuracy in the very short term, suggesting that exchange rate changes have a short-lived and weak memory. Therefore, according to this analysis, there may be a low degree of market inefficiency in the foreign exchange market, but as the forecasting horizon lengthens, the time series forecasting of exchange rates becomes more inaccurate. Thus, these results support the idea that trading rules (assumed by the time series models) are of no use in forecasting exchange rates. Giddy and Dufey stated two situations in which it would be worth while to seek to profit from exchange rate forecasting:

1. If one had better information and exclusive use of that information.
2. When the other participant in the foreign exchange market is the central bank or another trader who is dominant, whose behaviour is not determined by profit maximization, and is non-random.

Evidence against the hypothesis

Poole (1967) performed a study of the behaviour of currencies in the post-First World War period and the Canadian float from 1950 to 1962 using both filter rules and tests of serial dependence. He concluded that the strong evidence of serial correlation implied that the random walk hypothesis could be rejected. The three tests used (serial correlation, variance-time function and Alexander filter analysis) showed a statistically significant serial dependence, therefore providing evidence against the random walk hypothesis. However, Poole discovered how some of the positive serial dependence found in the series can be explained by transactions costs, e.g. brokerage fees, transfer of assets, time and trouble of buying and selling. One cannot expect the random walk hypothesis to hold with rational expectations when there are positive transactions costs.

Levich (1981), in a series of surveys, identified large profit opportunities in forward speculation. Results showed that several foreign exchange rate forecasting services, but not all, achieved significant excess profits for users from 1977 to 1980. Data were received from 13 advisory services, and overall, they suggested that the advisory services have not forecast as accurately as the forward rate. The results did not prove, however, that the foreign market is inefficient because the forward rate may contain a risk premium. If so, exchange rate forecasters ought to be able to forecast better than the forward rate. Results show that services have a record of the percentage correct forecasts that is not explained by chance; in fact if you take the track records pooled across currencies for each of the services, there are too many track records to be explained by chance. Thus, Levich's studies prove that foreign exchange advisory services can beat the market and that they have made profits. But he is careful not to reject market efficiency as the evidence that some advisory services can consistently beat the forward rate is not necessarily evidence as a lack of market efficiency. The conflicting evidence on market efficiency is due to the fact that central banks do not intervene all of the time. Therefore, in times of non-intervention we should expect the foreign exchange market to be efficient. However, when central banks intervene it can be expected that the foreign exchange market will be inefficient.

Market-based forecasts

This type of forecasting is based on the assumption that there should be a series of equilibrium relationships existing between spot rates, forward rates and interest rates (as illustrated earlier by the four-way equivalence model). Therefore, according to this theory, it is unlikely that a currency forecasting model can outperform the prediction embodied in interest and forward differentials.

To summarize the market-based forecasts, it is important to note that forward rates and interest differentials are predictors, but not necessarily accurate estimators of future currency changes. There is some evidence that the forward rate is a good predictor of spot market trends over relatively long periods of time, however, some recent evidence disputes this view.

Model-based forecasts

The two main model-based approaches to forecasting exchange rates are technical analysis and fundamental analysis. The first approach which we will be discussing is the fundamental approach, which relies to a large extent on econometric modelling techniques.

Fundamental analysis   Fundamental analysis is the most common approach to exchange rate forecasting. It is based on an analysis of the macroeconomic variables and policies that are likely to have an influence on a currency. Such variables include relative inflation rates, national income growth and changes in the level of the money supply. There are various models within the fundamental approach, with differing interpretations of the effects of the macro variables.

The traditional flow model   This approach is otherwise known as the balance of payments approach, and as such it focuses on the effects of macroeconomic variables on the balance of payments. The forecaster tries to foresee the imbalances which may occur in the current account and capital account as well as in the overall balance. In so doing, the forecaster may determine the demand and supply of the currency and therefore its future value. The estimation of such an equilibrium position between the demand and supply of the currency will correspond to where the current account imbalance is matched by a capital flow.

The current account depends on the business cycle and relative inflation rates between countries. If domestic prices rise relative to foreign prices, this is assumed to have a negative effect on the current account and therefore, according to PPP, there will be a depreciation of the domestic currency. Another variable affecting the current account is the relative growth rate of domestic real income. When there is an increase in real income, imports will also increase. Thus, according to the traditional model, an increase in real income will have an adverse effect on the trade balance and will lead to currency depreciation.

As far as the capital account is concerned, real interest differentials are an important factor.

A higher real domestic interest rate is assumed to lead to capital inflows and a stronger currency.

The asset market model   According to the asset market model, the exchange rate is the relative price of two assets, i.e. one country's currency in the terms of another's. The exchange rate is thus determined in the same way as prices of other financial assets, e.g. stocks and bonds.

The desire to hold a currency depends on the expectations of factors which affect the future supply and demand of a currency. Thus, currency values in the asset market model are determined by expectations of future economic prospects. In order to understand which factors affect the currency values one must look at the character of money and factors which affect demand for money, such as purchasing power and liquidity, demand for assets denominated in that currency, etc. Thus, the economic factors affecting the value of a currency are:

1. The currency's usefulness as a store of value determined by the expected rate of inflation.
2. The demand for liquidity determined by the volume of transactions in the currency.
3. The demand for assets denominated in that currency which is determined by the risk return pattern on investment and by wealth

All three of these factors are dependent on the nation's economic policies. The sounder the policies, the more valuable the currency.

According to the asset market model, a growing economy should lead to a stronger currency as an increase in GNP should cause an increase in the demand for money. Furthermore, contrary to the traditional flow model, the asset market model predicts the non-existence of a relationship between exchange rates and movements in the current account balance. These arguments are supported by data relating to the US dollar from 1976 to 1980 where the dollar value declined when the US current account worsened and then improved.

If one assumes that the foreign market is efficient then the asset market model approach would imply unpredictable exchange rate movements. This is due to the fact that exchange rates would move in a random fashion as participants assessed and reacted to new information. This implies that it would be impossible to earn arbitrage profits.

As stated by the Henley Forecasting Centre (1981) most of the theoretical work on floating exchange rates during the 1970s concentrated on the requirements for stock equilibrium in the markets for domestic money, domestic securities and foreign assets.

All portfolio balance models are based on the idea that asset holders seek an optimal composition of their wealth dependent upon the relative expected yield of each of their portfolio items. Therefore, changes in interest differentials can, *ceteris paribus*, be expected to induce capital flows and short-term movements in exchange rates.

Roll and Solnik (1977) are supporters of the asset market model. In Solnik's approach to the theory (Solnik, 1974) an equilibrium relationship was assumed to exist among interest rates, exchange rates and inflation in an efficient international capital market. It is assumed that traders and investors are risk-averse and price takers. The expected returns of investors on a currency is the interest rate for the currency and the period considered plus the expected exchange rate variation.

Solnik (1974) derived an equilibrium condition for international asset pricing. The equation explains the difference between riskless nominal interest rates in two countries by 'the expected change of parities between the 2 countries plus a term depending on exchange risk covariance'. This means that generally the interest rate differential (or forward exchange discount or premium) will be a biased predictor of the subsequent change in the spot exchange rate.

Exchange risk causes there to be a bias between the expected exchange rate and the forward rate and it depends on covariances between the domestic spot rate and those of other countries.

The following are important assumptions of this asset pricing model:

1. Different consumption preferences across countries
2. Perfect capital markets and capital mobility
3. No differential taxes or transactions costs
4. Continuous expectations
5. Constant equilibrium

Roll and Solnik performed tests with eight different countries using data for 43 months (July 1971–January 1975). The asset pricing model of foreign exchange was presented and fitted to the data. The equation used relates the extraordinary exchange return to an index of such return. These returns are the unhedged parts of the relative rates of change in exchange rates between two countries.

Bilson (1978) investigated the role of asset markets in the determination of the exchange rate. The model analysed is 'monetary' because it is based on two assumptions associated with the monetary approach to the balance of payments:

1. Demand for money is a stable function of a limited number of aggregate economic variables.
2. In the absence of transportation costs and restrictions upon trade, the law of one price will hold in international markets.

The asset market model was tested using monthly data for the Federal Republic of Germany and the UK from April 1970 to May 1977. It was estimated that relative money supply growth caused a 30 per cent depreciation of the pound over the period January 1972 to May 1975, but an appreciation in the following period. It appeared that during the period relative real income growth played a more important role than monetary policy in the depreciation of the pound relative to the Deutschmark. The results of the survey also showed that most of the short-term fluctuations could be attributed to the interest rate differential. Assuming an interpretation of this differential as a market estimate of the expected rate of depreciation, the results offer strong support for the view that the short-term instability of the exchange rate was due to foreign speculation. This may be explained by the uncertainty of speculators concerning the fundamental determinants of the exchange rate so that small shifts in opinion lead to dramatic changes in the expected rate of depreciation which in turn lead to dramatic changes in the actual exchange rate, justifying the diffuse expectations of speculators. Hence, even though speculators may provide forecasts which are as accurate as other forecasts, a speculative 'vicious circle' exists where varying expectations lead to erratic exchange rate movements which subsequently give rise to more diffuse expectations.

Bilson then compared the monetary model and a dynamic PPP model for the sample period, and found that the predictive accuracy was not greatly inferior to that of the dynamic PPP model:

The main advantage of the monetary model is that it expresses the relationship between the exchange rate and the underlying instruments of government policy.

Using a rational expectations variant of the monetary model, in which the expected rate of depreciation was set equal to the rate predicted by the model, the model remained fairly consistent with sample evidence. Therefore, if this model could be accepted as valid, it would be an extremely useful tool for exchange rate forecasting.

Econometric model development   Fundamental analysis now relies mainly on computer-based econometric models to generate currency forecasts. The task of the econometrician is to measure and quantify the relationships that exist among a set of variables. Exogenous variables such as the inflation differential and interest differential are used, and the nature of the functional relationship is determined such as lagged or current values, linear or exponential which best predicts the endogenous variable—in this case, the exchange rate. The actual and predicted values may differ, but econometricians expect that the difference will average out to zero over time.

An example of an econometric forecasting model would be the relation of a percentage change in the exchange rate of dollars to sterling as a linear function of the anticipated inflation differential plus the current GNP growth rate differential, including a random error with a mean value of zero, allowing statements to be made about the likely range of values for the forecasted exchange rate.

Usually, in choosing the variables to use and the functional form of the relationship, the econometrician will combine economic theory, intuition and experience. Such a model relies on the historical relationship between exogenous and endogenous variables obtained by regression analysis of past data, so that if there was a change in the framework of the international monetary system, this could destroy the validity of the econometric model.

A number of banks and private economic consulting firms sell forecasting services based on econometric models. Levich, in an analysis of a Eurocurrency survey performed in 1981, found that the best forecasting records were found among the econometric firms.

Technical analysis   Technical analysis focuses on past price and volume movements, ignoring economic and political factors. The technical analysts try to discover forecastable price trends. The main method of technical analysis is chartism, this may encompass charting (use of bar charts) or trend analysis (various mathematical computations).

Chartism   This method of technical analysis involves the examination of bar charts or the use of sophisticated computer-based extrapolation techniques to find recurring price patterns, issuing buy or sell recommendations if prices divert from their price patterns.

As stated by Rosenberg (1981), 'Technical models generate exchange rate forecasts by extrapolating the past sequences of currency movements into the future'. For example, if a currency begins to increase above a critical value the technical analyst will issue a buy recommendation, assuming that the exchange rate will continue to rise until a reversal (sell recommendation) is signalled. Thus, a trend is assumed to exist until a reverse is signalled.

One popular method used by the chartists is the filter rule which uses buy recommendations if exchange rates are x per cent above their most recent trough and sell recommendations if exchange rates fall x per cent below their most recent peak.

Modern financial theory which is based upon efficient markets has little time for chartist techniques in 'deep markets'. However, there is evidence to suggest that in foreign exchange markets chartism is more financially rewarding than econometric models for forecasting exchange rates. Criticism of technical analysis lies in the fact that it uses past price trends to forecast exchange rates, and this contradicts the finding that exchange rates generally follow a random walk consistent with a weakly efficient foreign exchange market (discussed earlier). Nevertheless, in recent years technical analysis has become a very popular and, in some cases, rewarding method of forecasting exchange rates.

In the case of forecasting exchange rates, the question of which model is the best is relative; a 'good' forecasting model is one whose predictions will lead to better decisions.

To evaluate the performance of exchange rate forecasts one may use two criteria:

1. Accuracy
2. Correctness

Accuracy emphasizes the deviations between actual and forecasted rates, whereas correctness measures whether the forecast predicts the right direction of the exchange rate change. Therefore, one can say that an accurate forecast may be incorrect in predicting the direction change and, similarly, a correct forecast may not be very accurate.

In the context of hedging with forward contracts, relative predictive abilities of forecasting services may be measured by the use of the following rule:

$$\text{When } f_1 > e_1 \quad \text{sell forward}$$
$$f_1 < e_1 \quad \text{buy forward}$$

$$\text{Where } f_1 = \text{forward rate}$$
$$e_1 = \text{forecasted spot rate}$$

The aforementioned decisions rule may also be applied to evaluating investment opportunities, e.g. plant location, or in developing market strategies, e.g. new product introduction. In the case of hedging decisions, accuracy is not important, it is profitability which is the main factor. However, for new investment or pricing decisions accuracy is a very crucial factor.

Studies by Levich and Goodman seem to suggest that profits achieved using technical forecasts seem too good to be explained by chance. The conclusion of Euromoney articles by Stephen Goodman (1980, 1981, 1982) is that technical forecasting services allow the user to do remarkably well in comparison with the poor results if the user follows a passive strategy or recommendations of an econometric service. Furthermore, Goodman found in studies of exchange rate forecasting for the late 1970s and early 1980s that a stronger performance could be obtained by combining the forecasts from more than one technical service. Therefore, it would be better to use two technical models and only act when they were in agreement. Results showed that for those using such a combination, the average annual return was 27.6 per cent, whereas for those using a single technical model the average annual adjusted return was 16.7 per cent.

To evaluate the performance of the technical forecasting services (as well as the econometric ones) the criteria used included return on capital at risk for the speculator, return on selective hedging (relevant for the corporate treasurer) and return on capital employed. In all three areas, technical forecasting services performed very well. A study of data from the late 1970s revealed that the return on capital at risk for technical services averaged between 7.4 per cent and 16 per cent annually before transactions costs, while return on capital employed for speculators averaged 243 per cent annually.

Goodman (1980, 1981, 1982) and Levich (1981) proved forecasting services can enable users to earn profits. However, there is the possibility that structural changes may affect the efficiency of their forecasts. Furthermore, profits made by forecasting services may be just enough to cover the extra risks of currency speculation.

Composite forecasts Composite forecasts may be used to improve forecasting accuracy. Bilson (1981) and Levich (1981) provide strong evidence that composite forecasts are more accurate and more reliable than the best individual forecasts.

Levich stated that:

if the overall results are similar across models the composite forecasts can increase accuracy if the correlation of error terms across models is less than 1.

The composite models provide a framework for analysing a prospective forecasting technique. If the new forecast reflects information not reflected in the existing models, it will lead to a large reduction in the mean squared error (MSE) in the composite model.

Even in the situation of costless information and efficient markets, composite forecasting may still improve forecasting. This is because, owing to uncertainty, it may take various prices to summarize the current state of the world. Regression analysis is used to construct a composite forecast. The ratio of the composite forecast MSE may be compared to that of a single forecasting model. If the ratio is less than 1 this means that the MSE has been reduced in the composite model.

Levich has found that composite forecasting has a greater impact during a floating period and when the forecasting horizon is longer. From his studies of data for nine major currencies for the period 1967–75 he found that even in cases where the currencies appeared to follow a random walk, e.g. Swiss franc and Italian lira, a six-month composite forecast reduced the MSE by 52 per cent and 24 per cent respectively during the floating period.

The general conclusion of Levich's analysis is that 'composite forecasting can lead to substantial reductions in MSE especially as the forecast horizon lengthens'. The gain from composite forecasting may be the result of information costs, search costs or government intervention which lead to separate financial markets.

Forecasting real exchange rates

Changes in the real exchange rate have important consequences for production goods and the demand for goods and services. The implication of this is that the expected profitability of plant location, product sources and marketing decisions depends on forecasts of real rather than nominal exchange rates. Currency forecasting services usually provide forecasts of nominal exchange rates. To assess and manage longer term exchange risk companies need forecasts of real exchange rates.

Real exchange rates in a floating exchange rate system follow a random walk, as analysed in the PPP theorem. This means that the best forecast of the future real exchange rate is today's spot rate and that the expected change in the real exchange rate is zero. Hence, changes in real exchange rates in a floating system are unexpected, and therefore this causes an exchange rate risk.

In a fixed rate system the differentiation between real and nominal exchange rates no longer exists, so in that situation the companies should concentrate on forecasts of nominal exchange rates.

Forecasting in a fixed rate system and the implications of government intervention

Forecasters in a fixed rate environment must determine whether or not the government will stick to its announced policies. A five-step forecasting procedure is suggested. First, the forecaster calculates an equilibrium exchange rate. Then a forecast of the balance of payments is made (step 2). Step 2 is then combined with a forecast of the central banks' level of owned and borrowed reserves. From there, the forecaster is able to estimate the country's 'grace' period. The 'grace' period is the length of time the country can afford to maintain its current policies. If R is the level of reserves and B is the annual balance of payments deficit, then the government may delay policy changes for a maximum of R/B years. In effect, the shorter the grace period, the greater the pressure on the currency to devalue. The fourth stage in the procedure is to predict which of the limited policy options the government will choose (devaluation, currency controls, deflation or borrowing abroad). The implication of the policy for future exchange rate changes will then be recycled through the model (step 5).

Taylor (1982), in evaluating official foreign intervention during the 1970s, has shown that banks failed to stabilize the exchange markets and lost billions of dollars. As US\$12 billion was lost by the central banks of Canada, France, Germany, Italy, Japan, Spain, Switzerland, the UK and the USA, exchange intervention proved to be a costly nationalized industry. Taylor's study found that not one of the central banks, apart from France, managed to stabilize the exchange rate of its currency and some of them in fact adversely affected exchange rate movements.

One major problem faced by forecasters is the fact that intervention is often cancelled to prevent it from showing up in the official international reserve figures. Central banks, by following a policy of 'leaning against the wind' (trying to moderate the speed of exchange rate movements), create a distortion of the exchange rate and a misallocation of resources. As Taylor (1982) argues, the objective of the government should be to promote economic efficiency, not to slow down exchange rate movements.

Forecasting in a fixed rate system can be quite profitable. There are two main reasons for this. First, forecasting is easier under this system because the direction and often the magnitude of an exchange rate change is known in advance. However, as the foreign exchange market is a zero-sum game, with gains of some traders offset by losses of others, without a superior model currency forecasting will only consistently be profitable if at least one market participant is willing and able to consistently make losses. Secondly, with government intervention, such a zero-sum game becomes in fact a positive-sum game. When a speculator bets against the government's ability to maintain a fixed rate in the foreign exchange market, this speculator will win, on average. This was especially true during the Bretton Woods system; Robert Aliber estimated that between 1967 and 1973 speculators earned about US\$12 billion at the expense of central banks. Due to the increased chances of profitability, exchange rate forecasters prefer a fixed rate system by a margin of greater than 2 to 1 over other exchange rate systems. In a fixed rate system it is not necessary to outguess the market in order to win. However, as stated before, a superior forecasting model will not consistently achieve profits unless there is a willing loser, and in a competitive market situation other speculators will quickly discover the efficacy of a forecasting model and imitate it.

Giddy and Dufey (1975) considered the fixed rate period of the Bretton Woods system. They argue that the crucial step of forecasting exchange rates under a fixed rate system is predicting which policy option the government will resort to in a crisis, and the success or failure of the forecasting process depends on this step. It was found that some forecasters did very well; certain banks and corporations spent a large amount on analysing government behaviour in order to achieve successful forecasts, in fact, during the Bretton Woods system it can be said that the downside risk of actions taken was quite limited; the exchange rate either remained steady or moved in the direction it was expected to take.

In the 1970s, with the breakdown of Bretton Woods and the start of a dirty float system, the forecasting environment changed considerably. It is now much more uncertain what action the government will take and its objectives are rather ambiguous. Governments must deal with the conflicting problem of a balance of payments deficit and inflation. Where the government abstains from buying or selling in the foreign exchange market or only intervenes to improve the technical condition, there is a speculative market where opportunities for monetary gain require a superior forecasting model and the exclusive use of such a model.

Forecasting controlled exchange rates

Exchange controls and restrictions on imports and capital flows create a problem for the currency forecasters, and these restrictions mask the pressures on a currency to devalue. In such an environment, interest and forward rate differentials are of little use as market-based forecasts of exchange rates. In order to solve this problem, one may use black market exchange rates as indicators of the pressure on a currency to devalue.

Black market exchange rates usually appear when there is a divergence between the equilibrium exchange rate and the official exchange rate. The black market exchange rate is usually determined by the difference between official and equilibrium exchange rates as well as penalties for illegal transactions. Therefore, economists usually assume that in the case of an overvalued exchange rate the equilibrium rate lies between the official and the black market rate.

The main source of a foreign exchange supply to the black market are receipts from the over-invoicing and under-invoicing of exports as well as receipts from tourism. The differential between the official and black market exchange rates provides an incentive for engaging in over- and under-invoicing. The greater the differential, the larger the profit possibilities.

The black market rate is a good indicator of where the official rate is likely to move to if the monetary authorities give in to market pressure. However, one cannot expect a coincidence of the black market rate and the official rate owing to government sanctions.

There has been empirical evidence, including that of Giddy (1978) that changes in the black market rate are closely linked to changes in the hypothetical equilibrium rate and the official rate. Giddy found that the black market rate appears to be an accurate forecasting tool for the official rate one month ahead, and its efficacy as a forecaster of the official rate declines as the time horizon lengthens.

Gupta (1981) performed efficiency tests on the black market exchange rates in India, Taiwan and South Korea, where E_{bt} was the black market exchange rate (US dollar in domestic currency). By using autocorrelation functions, runs analysis, filter rules and cross-correlations, Gupta found that the foreign exchange black markets were efficient. He examined the statistical significance of non-negative lags to see whether movements in the official rate are predicted by black market exchange rates and his results indicated that coefficients were statistically significant in the monthly series. This suggested that the black market rate responds immediately to changes in the official rate. For South Korea and Taiwan, the significance at lags other than zero indicated that changes in the official rate of these countries were predicted by the black market rate. In South Korea, the black market rate was shown to anticipate changes in the official rate three months before and for Taiwan official rates were forecasted 13 months ahead.

SUMMARY

In the first part of this chapter, the parity conditions of international finance were analysed, using the four-way equivalence model. In the second part it was shown how these parity conditions are used by forecasters with the important assumption of floating exchange rates.

Without this, the parity conditions would not hold. The parity conditions hypothesis, however, is only one theory used in currency predictions. The other competing hypotheses include fundamental analysis and technical analysis. As recent surveys have revealed, technical analysis has become very popular in recent years, even though it does not correspond with the finding that the foreign exchange market displays a weak form of efficiency. In terms of profitability some technical forecasts have proved very successful.

An important point to note is that in forecasting exchange rates it is not a question of which forecast is correct, but rather which is better. As revealed in the second part of the chapter, there is no single model to predict exchange rates. None of the models developed, whether market-based or model-based, can be relied on with any certainty.

Giddy and Dufey suggest that the requirements for achieving successful forecasting models are the following.

The forecaster:

1. Has exclusive use of a superior forecasting model
2. Has consistent access to information before other investors
3. Exploits small temporary deviations from equilibrium
4. Can predict the nature of government intervention in the foreign exchange market

It is essential that the currency forecaster meets at least one of these four criteria in order to achieve consistent profits. Of course, luck also plays a part.

REFERENCES

Adler, M. and B. Dumas (1976) 'Portfolio choice and the demand for forward exchange', *American Economic Review*, Vol. 66, pp. 332–339.

Adler, M. and B. Lehman (1983) 'Deviations from purchasing power parity in the long run', *Journal of Finance*, Vol. 38, pp. 1471–1487.

Aliber, R. Z. (1973) 'The interest parity theory: a reinterpretation', *Journal of Political Economy*, December, pp. 1451–59

Aliber, R. Z. and C. P. Stickney (1975) 'Accounting measures of foreign exchange exposure: the long and short of it', *Accounting Review*, January, pp. 44–57.

Balassa, B. (1964) 'The purchasing power doctrine: a reappraisal', *Journal of Political Economy*, **72**, pp. 584–96.

Bilson, J. F. O. (1978) 'The monetary approach to the exchange rate: some empirical evidence', IMF Staff Papers.

Bilson, J. F. O. (1981) 'The speculative efficiency hypothesis', *Journal of Business*, Vol. 54, July.

Bleaney, M. (1992) 'A test of long-run puchasing power parity using annual data from seven countries. 1900–88', *Economica Internazionale*, XLV, pp. 1980–195.

Buckley, A. (1986) *Multinational Finance*, Philip Allan, Oxford, England.

Choudry, T., R. McNawn and M. Wallace (1991) 'Purchasing power parity and the Canadian float in the 1950s', *Review of Economics and Statistics*, Vol. 73, pp. 558–563.

Committeri, M., S. Rossi and A. Santorelli (1993) 'Tests of covered interest parity on the Euromarket with high quality data', *Applied Financial Economics*, Vol. 3, pp. 89–93.

Copeland, L. (1989) *Exchange Rates and International Finance*, Addison-Wesley, Wokingham, England.

Cornell, B. (1977) 'Spot rates, forward rates and market efficiency', *Journal of Financial Economics*, **5**.

Dufey, G. and I. H. Giddy (1978) *The International Money Market*, Prentice-Hall, Englewood Cliffs, New Jersey.

Edison, H. J. (1987) 'Purchasing power parity in the long-run: a test of the $/£ exchange rate (1890–1978)', *Journal of Money Credit and Banking*, August, pp. 376–87.

Fama, E. F. (1975) 'Short-term interest rates as predictors of inflation', *American Economic Review*, June, pp. 269–82.

Fisher, I. (1930) *The Theory of Interest*, Macmillan, New York.

Frenkel, J. A. (1973) 'Elasticities and the interest parity theory', *Journal of Political Economy*, Vol. 81, pp. 741–747.

Frenkel, J. A. (1978) 'Purchasing power parity: doctrinal perspective and evidence from the 1920s', *Journal of International Economics*, Vol. 8, pp. 169–191.

Frenkel, J. A. (1981) 'The collapse of PPP during the 1970s', *European Economic Review*, **16**, pp. 145–65.

Frenkel, J. A. and R. M. Levich (1981) 'Covered interest arbitrage in the 1970s', *Economics Letters*, Vol. 8, pp. 267–274.

Gailliot, H. J. (1970) 'PPP as an explanation of long-term changes in exchange rates', *Journal of Money, Credit and Banking*, August, pp. 348–57

Giddy, I. H. (1978) 'Black market exchange rates as a forecasting tool', Working paper, Columbia University, May.

Giddy, I. H. and G. Dufey (1975) 'The random behaviour of flexible exchange rates', *Journal of International Business Studies*, Spring, pp. 1–32.

Goodman, S. (1980) 'Who's better than a toss of the coin?', *Euromoney*, September.

Goodman, S. (1981) 'Technical analysis still beats econometrics', *Euromoney*, August.

Goodman, S. (1982) 'Two technical analysts are even better than one', *Euromoney*, August.

Gupta, S. (1981) 'A note on the efficiency of black markets in foreign currencies', *Journal of Finance*, June, pp. 705–10.

Hakkio, C. S. (1986) 'Does the flexible exchange rate follow a random walk? A Monte Carlo study of four tests for random walk', *Journal of International Money and Finance*, Vol. 4, pp. 221–229.

Henley Forecasting Centre (1981) *Exchange Rate Movements*.

Isard, P. (1977) 'How far can we push the "law of one price"?' *American Economic Review*, December, pp. 942–48.

Johnson, D. R. (1990) 'Cointegration, error correction and purchasing power parity between Canada and the United States', *Canadian Journal of Economics*, Vol. XXIII, pp. 840–855.

Kim, Y. (1990) 'Purchasing power parity in the long-run: a cointegration approach', *Journal of Money, Credit and Banking*, Vol. 22, pp. 491–503.

Kohlhagen, S. W. (1978) *The Behaviour of Foreign Exchange Markets—A Critical Survey of the Empirical Literature*, New York University Press, New York.

Lane, T. D. (1991) 'Empirical models of exchange rate determination: picking up the pieces', *Economica Internazionale*, Vol. 44, pp. 210–226.

Layton, A. P. and J. P. Stark (1990) 'Cointegration of an empirical test of purchasing power parity', *Journal of Macroeconomics*, Vol. 12, pp. 125–136.

Levi, M. D. (1977) 'Taxation and "abnormal" international capital flows', *Journal of Political Economy*, Vol. 85, pp. 635–646.

Levich, R. M. (1981) 'How to compare chance with forecasting expertise', *Euromoney*, August, pp. 61–78.

Mark, N. C. (1990) 'Real and nominal exchange rates in the long-run: an empirical examination', *Journal of International Economics*, Vol. 28, pp. 115–136.

Marston, R. (1976) 'Interest arbitrage in the eurocurrency markets', *European Economic Review*.

McNown, R. and M. S. Wallace (1989) 'National price levels, purchasing power parity and cointegration: a test of four high inflation countries', *Journal of International Money and Finance*, Vol. 8, pp. 533–545.

Melvin, M. (1985) *International Money And Finance*, Harper and Row, New York.

Milone, M. (1986) 'Law of one price: further empirical evidence concerning Italy and the UK', *Applied Economics*, Vol. 18, pp. 645–661.

Otani, I. and S. Tiurari (1981) 'Capital controls and interest parity: the Japanese experience 1978–1981', *IMF Staff Papers*, Vol. 28, pp. 793–815.

Phylaktis, K. (1992) 'Purchasing power parity and cointegration: the Greek evidence from the 1920s', *Journal of International Money and Finance*, Vol. 11, pp. 502–503.

Poole, William (1967) 'Speculative prices as random walks: an analysis of 10 time series of flexible exchange rates', *Southern Economic Review*, April, pp. 468–78.

Robinson, W. and Warburton, P. (1980) 'Managing currency holdings: lessons from the floating period', London Business School, *Economic Outlook*, February, pp. 18–27.

Rogalski, R. J. and J. D. Vinso (1977) 'Price variations as predictors of exchange rates', *Journal of International Business Studies*, Spring–Summer, pp. 71–83.

Roll, R. W. and B. H Solnik (1977) 'A pure foreign exchange asset pricing model', *Journal of International Economics*, May, pp. 161–79.

Roll, R. W. (1979) 'Violations of the law of one price and their implications for differentially denominated assets', in M. Sarnat and G. Szego (eds), *International Finance and Trade*, Vol. 1, Ballinger, Cambridge, Mass.

Rosenberg, M. R. (1981) 'Is technical analysis right for currency forecasting?', *Euromoney*, June, pp. 125–31.

Shapiro, A. C. (1986) *Multinational Financial Management*, Allyn and Bacon, 2nd edition.

Solnik, B. (1974) 'An equilibrium model of the international capital market', *Journal of Economic Theory*, August.

Eiteman, D. and A. Stonehill (1986, 1989, 1992) *Multinational Business Finance*, Addison-Wesley, 4th, 5th and 6th editions, Reading, Mass.

Taylor, D. (1982) 'Official intervention in the foreign exchange market, or, bet against the central bank', *Journal Of Political Economy*, April, pp. 356–68.

Taylor, M. P. (1988) 'An empirical examination of long-run purchasing power parity using cointegration techniques', *Applied Economics*, Vol. 20, pp. 1369–1381.

Taylor, M. P. and P. C. McMahon (1988) 'Long-run purchasing power parity in the 1920s', *European Economic Review*, Vol. 32, pp. 179–197.

Tronzano, M. (1992) 'Long-run purhasing power parity and mean-reversion in real exchange rates: a further assessment', *Economica Internazionale*, Vol. XLV, pp. 77–99.

Webster, A. (1987) 'Purchasing power parity as a theory of international arbitrage in manufactured foods: an empirical view of UK/USA prices in the 1970s', *Applied Economics*, pp. 1433–1456.

Whitt, J. A. (1992) 'The long-run behaviour of the real exchange rate: a reconsideration', *Journal of Money, Credit and Banking*, Vol. 24, pp. 72–82.

ADDITIONAL READING

Baillier, R.T., Lippens, R.E. and McMahon, P.C. (1983) 'Testing rational expectations and efficiency in the foreign exchange market', *Econometrica*, Vol. 53, No. 3, pp. 553–63.

Isard, P. (1977) 'The process of exchange rate determination: a survey of important models and major issues', mimeo, Federal Reserve Board, January.

Officer, L. H. (1976) 'The PPP theory of exchange rates: a review article', IMF Staff Papers, March, pp. 1–60.

Stein, J. L. (1965) 'The forward rate and interest parity', *Review Of Economic Studies*, April.

MEASUREMENT OF FOREIGN CURRENCY EXPOSURE

INTRODUCTION

The general concept of exposure refers to the degree to which foreign operations are at risk from exchange rate changes. Traditionally exposure measurement has been divided into three areas: transaction, translation and economic exposure. Each will be discussed separately, but they are all, to a certain extent, measuring the same thing, but in varying detail and from different perspectives.

TRANSACTION EXPOSURE

Transaction exposure can be thought of as a short-term component of economic exposure. Ankrom (1974) defines transaction exposure as 'the exposure arising from future actions that are contained in sales and profit plan assumptions rather than in balance sheet accounts'. While translation exposure measures the effect of currency value changes on balance sheet accounts, transaction exposure measures the effect of these same changes on the operating performance of the firm. Transaction exposure is difficult to quantify as it relates to the possible consequences of future actions.

Sources of transaction exposure

Transaction exposure arises out of the various types of transactions that require settlement in a foreign currency. Ankrom (1974) points out that transaction exposure can arise, for example, on future product sales in a foreign currency. If that currency should devalue then the parent currency received when converting that currency will be reduced in amount.

Shapiro (1986) adds the following examples of sources of transaction exposure: cross border trade, borrowing and lending in foreign currencies, and the local purchasing and sales activities of foreign subsidiaries.

Measuring transaction exposure

Open and closed exchanges Shank (1976) divides transaction exposure into two categories, depending upon the type of transaction which can generate an exchange gain or loss: closed exchanges and open exchanges. A closed exchange is one in which a company settles a transaction in a foreign currency at an exchange rate different from the exchange rate used to compute the carrying value of the items on the company's books (Shank, 1976).

For example, suppose that a company borrows 2 million French francs when the exchange rate is FF4/£1. The company records the liability on its books at the pound equivalent of the amount borrowed, £500,000. If the loan is repaid at an exchange rate of FF3/£1 the company must spend £666,667 to acquire the 2 million French francs necessary to liquidate the debt. The additional £166,667 necessary to repay the loan is an exchange loss on a closed, or completed, transaction. An open exchange is a transaction across two currencies that has not yet been completed. To illustrate, suppose that the loan of 2 million French francs recorded on the borrower's books at £500,000 is not to be repaid until next year. However, by the end of this year, the rate is FF3/£1. At this point in time it is not known what the actual settlement amount of the loan will be. Should the £166,667 be recorded as a loss now on the open exchange?

If the company is committed to a receivable denominated in a foreign currency the transaction exchange gain or loss would be equal to the value of accounts receivable when payment is made less the value of accounts receivable when the export transaction was initiated. If the company is committed to a liability denominated in a foreign currency the transaction exchange gain or loss would be equal to the value of the liability when payment falls due less the value of the liability when first incurred.

Accounting policies

The recognition of transaction exposure in the UK is governed by Statement of Standard Accounting Practice (SSAP) No. 20. Basically, the foreign currency transaction is recognized at the exchange rate prevailing at the date of the transaction, then revalued at each subsequent balance sheet date until it is settled. Strictly speaking, of course, the items already on a company's balance sheet, such as loans and receivables, capture some of these transactions. However, if we wish to obtain a more detailed measure of transaction exposure we must also consider a number of off-balance sheet items as well. Such an example of transaction exposure measurement including many off-balance sheet items is shown in the following exposure report based on an example by Shapiro (1986).

Example 6.1 presents the balance sheet for Lille Construction, the French subsidiary of a UK-based multinational. In its present format, however, this balance sheet is rather uninformative; it is impossible, for example, to calculate the firm's accounting exposure without knowing the breakdown by currency of the various assets and liabilities. This breakdown is shown in Example 6.2, the exposure report for Lille Construction. Included in this report is a £10 million forward purchase of Deutschmarks to cover Lille Construction's 10 million in Deutschmark denominated payments. Also included is £15.8 million in fixed assets that involve no future obligations. Several balance sheet items which will have an impact on future financial statements also appear: these are orders to deliver £7 million of bricks to a German company (to be paid in Deutschmarks), £5 million worth of cement to a French company, purchases of £1 million worth of girders from a French company, and £2 million worth of timber from a British company.

Transaction exposure goes some way towards measuring the financial reality of a company's foreign operations. However, such exposure is but a fraction of a company's full exposure. Clearly there are many indirect consequences of exchange rate changes, consequences which cannot be measured by transaction and translation exposure alone. The wider concept of

Example 6.1   Balance sheet for Lille Construction (£000s)

	French francs	*Pounds equivalent (at FF8/£1)*
Assets		
Cash	8,760	1,095
Accounts receivable	62,000	7,750
Stock	44,800	5,600
Prepaid expenses	5,360	670
Total current assets	120,920	15,115
Fixed assets	126,400	15,800
Total assets	247,320	30,915
Liabilities		
Creditors	36,760	4,595
Long-term debt	152,000	19,000
Total liabilities	188,760	23,595
Equity	58,560	7,320
Total liabilities and equity	247,320	30,915

economic exposure measurement is an attempt to incorporate abstract effects of exchange rate movements, and extends beyond transaction exposure measurement by incorporating a component of real operating exposure.

TRANSLATION EXPOSURE

Translation exposure exists owing to the need to periodically consolidate or aggregate parents' and foreign subsidiaries' financial statements. Overseas subsidiaries' financial statements have to be translated into the home currency before being consolidated with the parents' financial statements. To prepare statements expressed in terms of home currency units, the amounts expressed in foreign currency must be changed to the home currency. The process of changing the amounts from foreign currency to home currency is commonly referred to as translation. It is important not to confuse translation with conversion; translation is simply a change in monetary expression and not a physical exchange of one currency for another. The traditional medium for translating foreign currency amounts is the foreign exchange rate: this denotes the price of a unit of foreign currency in terms of the domestic or reporting currency. If foreign exchange rates were relatively stable, the translation process would be straightforward and no more difficult than, say, translating inches into their metric equivalents. Exchange rates, however, are seldom stable as their values tend to vary in response to rather complex forces of supply and demand. If exchange rates have changed since the previous reporting period, this translation or restatement of those assets, liabilities, revenues and expenses that are represented

Example 6.2   Transaction exposure report for Lille Construction (£000s)

	French franc	Deutschmark	Sterling (unexposed)
Assets			
Cash	1,095		
Debtors	4,400	1,200	2,150
Prepaid expenses	670		
Foreign purchase contract		10,000	
Sales commitments	5,000	7,000	
Exposed assets	11,165	18,200	—
Liabilities			
Creditors	3,370	175	1,050
Long-term debt	2,000	5,000	12,000
Future purchases, commitments and leases	1,000		2,000
Exposed liabilities	6,370	5,175	—
Net position	4,795	13,025	(12,900)

in foreign currencies will result in foreign exchange gains or losses. Such gains and losses may be thought of as unrealized since no cash flows are necessarily involved. One may ask why, if gains and losses owing to translation are only book values and are primarily unrealized, are translated figures considered important?

Foreign currency translations

The National Association of Accountants (USA) states that translation to the parent's home currency may be necessary for any of the following reasons for US multinational corporations (MNCs) (the reasons are applicable for any MNCs):

1. The operations of the foreign subsidiary must be expressed in dollars in order to evaluate the return produced by the dollar investment of the US parent company.
2. Management in the USA is accustomed to thinking in terms of dollars rather than in foreign currency units.
3. Translation of local currency to dollars is a prerequisite to determining the periodic loss or gain sustained by the US parent company from movements in the exchange rates. This figure is necessary to measure the degree of success which management has had in protecting the US company's dollar investment against erosion from currency devaluation. Lorensen (1972) has suggested the following additional reasons:
   (a) To evaluate the foreign subsidiary's performance
   (b) To evaluate the performance of the foreign subsidiary's manager
   (c) To evaluate capital budgeting decisions

Measuring the exposure of a firm to the risk of losses from changes in the exchange rate is an important issue since this exposure is often the basis for the decision on whether such risk should be avoided, neutralized or carried. A study by the National Association of Accountants (1960) concluded that 'accounting reports constitute the primary source of such information received by management'.

The Committee on International Accounting (1975, p. 92) emphasized the significance of translated financial statements from a management perspective and stated that

In common with all financial statements, the main purpose of translated financial statements is to provide a means for evaluation and control of the operations and entity being reported upon. While the users of published financial statements are usually conceived to be investors in the enterprise, translated statements are of particular use to management of both foreign and domestic operations. Managements have achieved some considerable skills in controlling domestic operations, independent of conventional financial statements, whereas control and evaluation of foreign operations is substantially less well developed. Thus, there is a much larger management purpose in translated financial statements.

This issue of management of translated financial statements introduces an important consideration into the determination of which translation process should be adopted. Owing to the emphasis placed on the translated figures, it follows that accounting methodology for translating foreign financial statement items should be empirically justifiable and logically consistent with economic reality.

Foreign currency translation methodologies: an overview

Alternative currency translation methodologies are centred around the question of when to use historic, current or an appropriate average exchange rate. Prior to discussing the alternative translation methods it is perhaps appropriate to outline the major differences, in terms of reported exposure, which arise from using current and historic exchange rates. If the historic exchange rate is used (the rate on the date when the asset was acquired or the liability was incurred), the item is stated at historic cost. No gain or loss is recognized if the exchange rate changes subsequent to the acquisition date. If instead the current exchange rate is used, a gain or loss is reported if the exchange rate changes between the acquisition date and the balance sheet date. The implications of using these two exchange rates is that items translated at the historic exchange rate are not exposed to exchange gains and losses; their book values are unaffected by changes in the exchange rate. Those items translated at the current exchange rate are exposed to exchange gains and losses because their book values vary when the exchange rate changes. Ideally the chosen exchange rates should be such that the balance sheet exposure is consistent with economic reality. However, what is actually exposed in reality is an area of continuing controversy, hence the development of many alternative currency translation methods. Four methods have dominated the development of accounting standards both in the UK and the USA.

Current–non-current method This method translates the current assets and liabilities of the foreign subsidiary at the current exchange rate. The current rate is the foreign exchange rate in effect at the balance sheet date. The non-current assets and liabilities of the subsidiary are then translated at the rate in effect when the assets and liabilities were acquired or incurred; in other words, the non-current assets and liabilities are translated using a historic rate. Revenue and expense items, with the exception of those relating to non-current assets and liabilities, are translated using the average exchange rate for the time period being reported. Those items relating to non-current assets or liabilities are translated at the same rate used to translate that particular non-current asset or liability on the balance sheet.

Monetary–non-monetary method The monetary/non-monetary method differentiates between monetary assets and liabilities (those items which represent a claim to receive, or an obligation to pay, a fixed amount of foreign currency units) and non-monetary, or physical, assets and liabilities. Monetary items are translated at the current rate and non-monetary items are translated at historical rates. Income statement items are translated at the average exchange rate during the period, except for revenue and expense items related to non-monetary assets and liabilities. The latter items, primarily depreciation expense and cost of goods sold, are translated at the same rate as the corresponding balance sheet items.

Temporal method Under the temporal method the rates of exchange to be used for translation are determined by the basis of measurement used for the various items in the accounts of the overseas subsidiary. In the balance sheet, assets which are shown at a figure based on historical cost are translated at the relevant historical rate; assets which are shown on the basis of a revalued amount at some past date are translated at the rate of exchange ruling when the revalued amount was established. Assets and liabilities which are shown at a current value, which includes all monetary assets and liabilities, are translated at the current rate. In the profit and loss account, the rate of exchange used is similarly determined by the underlying basis of measurement; depreciation based on historical costs is translated at the relevant historical rate. Revenues and expenses which have occurred over the year are translated at an average rate while revenues and expenses which relate to amounts established in previous years or to a part of the current year are translated at a specific rate or an appropriate average rate.

Current rate method This approach to the translation process, as the name implies, translates assets, liabilities, revenues and expenses at the current rate of exchange, using the historical rate only in circumstances where the foreign currency is more unstable than the home currency. All profit and loss account items are to be translated at either the average rate or the current rate. Under the current method a devaluation of the foreign currency results in a translation loss and a revaluation in a translation gain. Unique to this method is the fact that operating relationships and income statement ratios remain intact throughout the translation process.

The concept of translation exposure

Translation exposure is measured by taking the difference between a firm's exposed foreign currency assets and liabilities. An excess of exposed assets over exposed liabilities (i.e. those foreign currency items translated at current exchange rates) gives rise to a net exposed asset position, referred to as a 'positive exposure'. Devaluation of the foreign currency relative to the home currency produces a translation loss as the domestic currency equivalent of the foreign currency net assets is less after devaluation than before. Revaluation of the foreign currency would produce a translation gain. Conversely, a company experiences a net exposed liability position or 'negative exposure' whenever exposed liabilities exceed exposed assets. In this instance devaluation of the foreign currency gives rise to a translation gain as the home currency equivalent of the net foreign currency liabilities decreases following the devaluation. Revaluation of the foreign currency gives rise to a translation loss.

This process is summarized below:

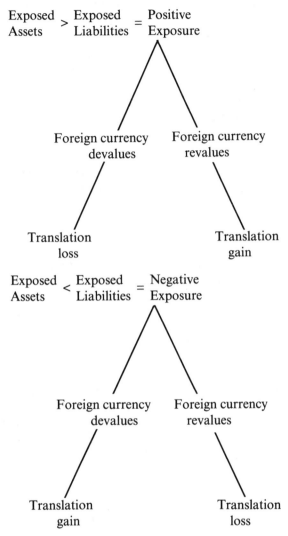

Once the translation process is complete, measuring translation exposure is a straightforward procedure. The problem of measurement is therefore a question of which translation method gives the 'best measurement' of reported exposure. The concept of best measurement cannot be isolated from the question of how the translated figures are to be used; however, the discussion will try to centre on the question of the general applicability of each method as a basis for measuring translation exposure.

The effect of using the alternative methods on the financial statements and the measured exposure of a hypothetical US-based multinational are illustrated below.

An illustration of the translation process The following examples illustrate the translation process and highlight the financial statement effects of the major translation methods described.

Kilim AS, the Turkish affiliate of a UK rug manufacturing company, has a balance sheet as shown below. The current exchange rate is 20 Turkish lira (TL) to the pound Sterling (TL = £0.05).

Cash	TL 6,000	Current liabilities	TL 3,000
Accounts receivable	12,000	Long-term debt	9,000
Inventories	12,000	Shareholders' equity	42,000
Net plant and equipment	24,000		
Total	TL 54,000		TL 54,000

Assume the lira devalues from 20 lira/£ to 25 lira/£ by the end of the accounting period. We will now show how to calculate the translation loss or gain using the monetary–non-monetary method, the current–non-current method and the current rate method.

Example 6.3

	TL accounts	(1) converted at 20 TL/£	(2) Translated at 25TL/£ M/NM	C/NC	CR
Cash	TL6,000	£300	£240	£240	£240
Accounts receivable	TL12,000	£600	£480	£480	£480
Inventories	TL12,000	£600	£600	£480	£480
Net plant and equipment	TL24,000	£1,200	£1,200	£1,200	£960
Total	TL54,000	£2,700	£2,520	£2,400	£2,160
Current liabilities	TL3,000	£150	£120	£120	£120
Long-term debt	TL9,000	£450	£360	£450	£360
Stockholders' equity	TL42,000	£2,100	£2,100	£2,100	£2,100
Exchange (loss) or gain	—	—	£(60)	£(270)	£(420)
Total	TL54,000	£2,700	£2,520	£2,400	£2,160

The balance sheet of a hypothetical Turkish subsidiary of a UK-based multinational appears in the first column of Example 6.3 in Turkish lira (TL). The second column depicts the UK sterling equivalents of the TL balances when the exchange rate was TL = £0.05 or 20 TL = £. Should the TL depreciate to 25 TL = £ a number of different accounting results are possible.

Under the current rate method, exchange rate changes affect the sterling equivalents of the Turkish subsidiary's total assets and liabilities in the current period. Since their sterling values are affected by changes in the current rate, they are said to be exposed, in an accounting sense, to foreign exchange risk. Accordingly, under the current rate method an exposed Turkish lira net asset position (where total assets are greater than total liabilities) would result in a translation loss should the Turkish lira depreciate in value, and an exchange gain should the Turkish lira increase in value. An exposed lira net liability position produces a translation gain in the event of a Turkish lira devaluation and a loss if the lira increases in value. In our example, current rate translation yields a £420 translation loss since the sterling equivalent of the Turkish subsidiary's net asset position after the lira depreciation is £2,100.

Under the current–non-current method, the UK company's accounting exposure is measured by its Turkish lira net current asset or liability position (a positive TL27,000 in net current assets in Kilim AS balance sheet).

Under the monetary–non-monetary method, exposure is measured by its net Turkish lira monetary asset or liability position (net monetary assets 6,000 Turkish lira).

Exposure under the temporal principle depends on whether the Turkish subsidiary's inventories or other assets are valued at historical cost (and are therefore not exposed) or some other valuation basis (net revalued assets 42,000 Turkish lira).

To summarize, the different translation methods illustrated offer a wide array of accounting results, ranging from a £420 loss under the current rate method, through a £270 loss under the current–non-current, to a £60 loss under the monetary–non-monetary method. This is quite a variation in light of the fact that all the results presumably describe the same factual situation! What is more, operations reporting respectable profits before translation at the new rates may very well end up reporting losses or significantly reduced earnings statistics after translation.

Example 6.4

	M/NM	(3) Translated at 14.29 TL/£ C/NC	CR
Cash	£420	£420	£420
Accounts receivable	£840	£840	£840
Inventories	£600	£840	£840
Net plant and equipment	£1,200	£1,200	£1,680
Total	£3,060	£3,300	£3,780
Current liabilities	£210	£210	£210
Long-term debt	£630	£450	£630
Stockholders' equity	£2,100	£2,100	£2,100
Exchange (loss) or gain	£120	£540	£840
Total	£3,060	£3,300	£3,780

Example 6.4 shows the translation gains and losses when Turkish lira appreciate to TL14.29/£. In this case translation gains range from £120 under the monetary–non-monetary method, through a £540 gain under the current–non-current method and to a £840 gain under the current rate method.

The monetary–non-monetary method ('temporal' in the USA) assumes that inventory does not change in value at the time of devaluation, and that long-term debt does change. This method is probably the most meaningful translation method if the inventory assumption is correct, but the approach is controversial even within the USA.

The current–non-current method assumes inventory changes in value at the moment of devaluation. If domestic competition is so strong that sales prices cannot be changed to reflect a change in exchange rates, this is perhaps a more meaningful approach. The current–non-current approach also defers recognition of the change in value of any long-term debt until the debt matures.

The current rate method, used primarily in the UK, assumes that all accounts, including net plant and equipment, change in value when exchange rates change.

None of the methods attempt to show economic (future cash flow) gain or loss resulting from a change in exchange rates.

A critique of the translation methodologies: current–non-current and monetary–non-monetary methods

The idea of using a current–non-current classification to determine whether assets and liabilities should be translated at historical or current rates appears to lack any sort of theoretical or empirical justification. As the National Association of Accountants (1960, p. 17) points out, the method 'reflects the use of an established balance sheet classification for a purpose to which it is not relevant'. The monetary–non-monetary classification departs from the current–non-current method in two main areas: inventory is translated at historical rates since it is not considered to be exposed to exchange rate fluctuations; and long-term debt is translated at the current rate, indicating that it is considered to be exposed to fluctuations in exchange rates.

In practice the second difference is usually the more significant. As Walker (1977) points out, long-term debt is often the largest single component in a company's translation exposure. This can produce very large translation losses if the parent or one of its subsidiary companies holds loans which are denominated in a currency which is appreciating relative to the parent currency. This certainly appears to be an improvement on the current–non-current method, as translation losses relating to long-term debt represent a very real risk to the organization. However, Lorensen (1972, pp. 33–34) points out that the distinction between monetary and non-monetary is, in many areas, open to subjective classification: for example, bonds and negotiable notes have both monetary and non-monetary characteristics. There are other criticisms of both the current–non-current and the monetary–non-monetary distinctions in terms of practical application; however, we will now concentrate on their more general theoretical and empirical shortcomings. Aliber and Stickney (1975) indicate that the use of historical exchange rates for translating non-monetary items assumes that such items are not exposed to fluctuations in exchange rates. Such an assumption rests on the belief that exchange gains and losses, which would have been reported using the current rate, are approximately offset by changes in the local currency price of the translated item. To put it simply, an exchange loss is offset by a holding gain and vice versa. Watt (1970, p. 30) points out that, property and plant accounts are usually considered as not exposed, on the generally accepted assumption that their value will usually rise in proportion to the devaluation of the local currency.

Such a 'generally accepted assumption' rests on the belief that the purchasing power parity (PPP) theory is valid. As discussed in Chapter 5, this theory concerns the relationship between the commodity price levels in two countries and the equilibrium exchange rate between their currencies, and states that changes in the equilibrium exchange rate from one date to another are proportional to changes in the ratio of the prices of similar goods available in the two countries. If the PPP theory holds perfectly for all commodities, exchange losses are offset by changes in local prices of non-monetary assets (which include the majority of non-current items) and are therefore not exposed. Consider now the monetary items. Use of the current rate implies that these items are exposed to the risk of exchange losses. The National Association of Accountants (1960, p. 62) attempts to clarify the rationale of the approach by stating that the dollar equivalent of assets in the form of foreign currency claims to a fixed number of foreign currency units is immediately affected by a change in the rate of exchange because, if the dollar value of a foreign currency rises or falls, assets in that currency will yield a greater or smaller number of dollars on conversion. Such assets are always at risk from unfavourable movements in the exchange rate.

Such reasoning is based on a rejection of the proposition that changes in exchange rates are reflected in the relative differential in interest rates on similar assets denominated in several currencies. This relationship is known as the Fisher Effect. The proposition is that interest rates on assets denominated in currencies expected to depreciate are higher than those on assets denominated in currencies expected to depreciate less or to appreciate in value, and conversely. If the Fisher Effect holds, cumulative interest revenue (expense) over the maturity of the financial asset includes an amount equal to the exchange loss (gain) from changes in the exchange rate. If this offset is exact (as is assumed under the PPP theory for non-monetary items), the net result is that the effective foreign interest rate is equivalent to the domestic interest rate. In this case, monetary items are not exposed to losses from exchange rate changes.

Therefore, the methodology for translating foreign assets and liabilities assumes that the PPP theory holds while the Fisher Effect does not. As Aliber and Stickney point out, such a distinction is not logically consistent. After researching the validity of the PPP theory and the Fisher Effect empirically, they reached the following conclusions: 'the implications of these results on the measurement of exposure to exchange losses should be distinguished from the implications concerning the appropriate translation methodology to be used when periodically determining net income and financial position. The translation methodology considered here was developed primarily for the latter purpose. Our aim has been to examine the appropriateness of this translation methodology when the objective is to measure exchange exposure. Our principal conclusion is that the current translation methodology does not appear to be appropriate when measuring exposure to exchange losses. The empirical data suggests that the classification of the assets and liabilities used by accountants (monetary–non-monetary, current–non-current) is not the critical variable in measuring exposure. Instead, the firm's planning horizon is of critical importance. Over relatively short horizons (two or three years), all assets and liabilities tend to be exposed. Over longer periods, the increased validity of the purchasing power parity and the Fisher theories indicates that most assets and liabilities not exposed to exchange gains are losses.'

Such a suggestion that classification should be based on time horizons rather than the various properties of the assets and liabilities to be translated is a complete departure from any of the methodologies previously outlined. However, one must appreciate that the objective of translation exposure measurement is not the sole consideration when developing a translation methodology. If we accept the reasoning of Aliber and Stickney, many of the arguments for and against the various translation approaches become nonsense. For example, the suggestion that long-term debt provisions are an improvement under the monetary–non-monetary method as opposed to the current–non-current method would be invalidated. If the Fisher Effect is assumed to hold over long time horizons, exchange rate effects would be offset by interest rate changes and long-term debt would not be exposed.

Closing rate (or current rate) method, temporal method and the accounting policies

SSAP 20, 'Foreign Currency Translation', issued in April 1983, required the use of one method in most situations. The favoured method is now called the 'closing rate/net investments method', and this appears to be the method used by the majority of companies in the UK.

The words 'net investments' have been added to the title of the method to indicate the view that the method implicitly takes of the investment in the overseas subsidiary. Most overseas subsidiaries are thought of as independent entities and to operate primarily within their own economic environment. The parent company is considered to have an investment in the net assets of the subsidiary rather than in its individual assets and liabilities. It follows that only the net investment is at risk from exchange rate changes and so the closing rate method is deemed appropriate. In situations where the subsidiary's operations are closely linked with that of the parent company, SSAP 20 requires the use of the temporal method so that the results are included as if they had been undertaken by the parent company itself.

The evaluation of the two approaches cannot be isolated from the question of how the translated data are to be used. If we are studying the accounts with the view to invest or for general interest, the closing rate/net investment method is more appropriate as it maintains the same relationships in the sterling accounts as exist in the foreign currency accounts. However, when considering the translation of the accounts of a subsidiary company prior to consolidation the use of the net investment method would seem irrelevant. Such a translation would result in a loss of the relationship between items of the subsidiary's accounts and those of the parent's. In such situations, maintaining the consistency of the basis of measurement used for the assets and liabilities appears to be more important. The temporal method of translation is consistent with the historical cost basis of accounting. The translation of a historical cost at a historical rate produces the historical cost in sterling; the translation of a historical cost at a closing rate would seem to produce a conceptual nonsense.

However, the temporal method is not without its problems. The application of the method has caused large fluctuations in reported profits which appear to bear little relevance to the underlying operating performance of the subsidiary. This situation arises owing to the requirement of the method to include exchange gains and losses on long-term monetary items in the ordinary profits of the group rather than taking them direct to reserves. For example, consider a UK company which has an overseas subsidiary. In the balance sheet of the overseas subsidiary fixed assets and stocks are shown on the basis of historical cost, while these are usually financed by net monetary liabilities and an equity interest. During a particular year sterling is weakening against the overseas currency, that is, the other currency is becoming more valuable. In such a case the value of the overseas net assets to the UK company would be increasing and any potential dividends from the overseas subsidiary would be more valuable, since a given future dividend stream in the foreign currency would produce a greater amount of sterling. However, using the temporal method of translation we would recognize no gains on the fixed assets but merely losses on the net monetary liabilities. Thus, as a result of the movement in exchange rates the overseas subsidiary is more valuable, but as a result of using the temporal method appears less valuable.

There is evidence that such reported losses have led to 'profitable' overseas projects being rejected because of the misleading figures translated via the temporal method. The closing rate/ net investment method does not produce these misleading figures because it is applied to non-monetary as well as monetary assets and liabilities. Here, exchange losses on foreign currency borrowings are offset against exchange gains on real assets, and so no charge to the profit and loss account needs to be made. The use of such a cover method is felt by many to reflect the reality of the situation where fixed assets and stocks are financed by money raised overseas.

An illustration of the current rate or closing rate method Assume that Polly-Tech plc, a UK company, purchased 75 per cent of the share capital in a Turkish company, Borusan AS, for £75,000 on 31 December 1987. The financial statements (Examples 6.5 and 6.6) show the balance sheets of Polly-Tech plc and Borusan AS immediately after the acquisition and after one year trading from the date of acquisition (Borusan figures are shown in Turkish lira). The profit and loss account statements of both companies for the year ending 31 December 1988 are also shown in Example 6.7.

You are also informed that assets of Borusan have been revalued to their fair value at the date of acquisition and the relevant rates of exchange are as follows:

Rate to £

1 January	1988	30 TL
Average for	1988	25 TL
31 December	1988	20 TL

The exchange rate on 1 January 1988 was £1 = 30 TL. Example 6.8 shows the translation of the balance sheet of Borusan AS as at 1 January 1988.

Example 6.9 shows a consolidated balance sheet for Polly-Tech plc on 1 January 1988 using the closing rate method of translation. Example 6.10 illustrates a balance sheet for Borusan AS on 31 December 1988. A consolidated balance sheet on 31 December 1988 and a consolidated profit and loss account for the year ending on 31 December 1988 for Polly-Tech plc using the closing rate method of translation are shown in Example 6.11. Finally, Example 6.12 shows a statement of consolidated reserves for the year ended 31 December 1988, showing clearly the amount of exchange difference arising from foreign currency translations.

Example 6.5 Polly-Tech plc balance sheet

	1 January 1988 *£*	*31 December 1988* *£*
Fixed assets		
Tangible assets	360,000	300,000
Investment in subsidiary	75,000	75,000
Net current assets	105,000	225,000
	540,000	600,000
Capital and reserves		
Share capital	300,000	300,000
Profit and loss account and revaluation reserve	240,000	300,000
	540,000	600,000

Example 6.6 Borusan balance sheet

	1 January 1988 *TL*	*31 December 1988* *TL*
Fixed assets		
Tangible assets	300,000	240,000
Net current assets	60,000	144,000
	360,000	384,000
Long-term loan	(90,000)	(90,000)
	270,000	294,000
Capital and reserves		
Share capital	180,000	180,000
Profit and loss account and revaluation reserve	90,000	114,000
	270,000	294,000

Example 6.7 Summarized profit and loss accounts for the year ended 31 December 1988

	Polly-Tech plc £	Borusan AS TL
Profit before taxation	105,000	45,000
Taxation	45,000	21,000
Profit after taxation (retained)	60,000	24,000

Example 6.8 Borusan AS Balance sheet on 1 January 1988

	TL	Rate	£
Fixed assets			
Tangible assets	300,000	30	10,000
Net current assets	60,000	30	2,000
	360,000		12,000
Long-term loan	(90,000)	30	(3,000)
Net assets	270,000		9,000
Capital and reserves			
Share capital	180,000	30	6,000
Profit and loss account and revaluation reserve	90,000	30	3,000
	270,000		9,000

Goodwill on 1 January 1988

	£
Cost of investment	75,000
Less net assets acquired	
Share capital and reserves	(9,000)
Group share (75%)	(6,750)
Goodwill on consolidation	68,250

Example 6.9 Polly-Tech plc Consolidated balance sheet on 1 January 1988

	£
Fixed assets	
Intangible assets (goodwill)	68,250
Tangible assets (360,000 + 10,000)	370,000
	438,250
Net current assets (105,000 + 2,000)	107,000
	545,250
Long-term loan	(3,000)
	542,250
Capital and reserves	
Share capital	300,000
Profit and loss account	240,000
	540,000
*Minority interest	2,250
	542,250

*Minority interest = 25 per cent of translated net assets, i.e. 9,000.

Example 6.10   Borusan AS balance sheet on 31 December 1988

	TL	Rate	£
Fixed assets			
Tangible assets	240,000	20	12,000
Net current assets	144,000	20	7,200
	384,000		19,200
Long-term loan	(90,000)	20	(4,500)
	294,000		14,700
Share capital	180,000	30	6,000
Reserves:			
Pre-acquisition	90,000	30	3,000
Post-acquisition	24,000	Balancing figure	5,700
	294,000		14,700

The figure £14,700 represents the increase in net assets since acquisition. This comprises:

(a) The profit for the year since acquisition

Translation of Borusan profit and loss 31 December 1988

	TL	Rate	£
PBT	45,000	20	2,250
Tax	21,000	20	1,050
	24,000		1,200

(b) The exchange difference arising in the retranslation of the opening net assets of the subsidiary

Exchange difference on opening net assets

TL 270,000 at £/20 TL	13,500
TL 270,000 at £/30 TL	(9,000)
	4,500
Profit for the year (24,000 TL at 20TL/£)	1,200
Post-acquisition reserve	£5,700

Example 6.11   Polly-Tech plc Consolidated balance sheet on 31 December 1988

	£
Fixed assets	
Intangible goodwill	68,250
Tangible assets (300,000 + 12,000)	312,000
	380,250
Net current assets (225,000 + 7,200)	232,200
	612,450
Long-term loan	4,500
	607,950
Capital and reserves	
Share capital	300,000
*Profit and loss account	304,275
(see statement of consolidated reserves)	
	604,275
Minority interest (25% of £14,700)	3,675
	607,950

Polly-Tech Consolidated profit and loss account

	£
Profit before tax (105,000 + 2,250)	107,250
Tax (45,000 + 1,050)	46,050
Profit after tax	61,200
Minority interest 25% of 1,200	(300)
Profit attributable to shareholders of Polly-Tech	60,900

Example 6.12   Polly-Tech statement of consolidated reserves for the year ending 31 December 1988

	£
Profit and loss at 1 January 1988	240,000
Exchange difference arising from retranslation of opening net assets of foreign sub. (75% of 4,500)	3,375
Retained profit for the year	60,900
Consolidated reserves	£304,275

TOWARDS A BROADER LOOK AT EXPOSURE AND ITS MEASUREMENT

The Accounting Standards Committee (ASC) balanced the advantages and disadvantages of the two methods in producing SSAP 20. Obviously, neither method was developed with the sole objective of accurate exposure measurement and, although they may well be satisfactory translation methodologies when we consider all the objectives of the translation process, they are not the best methods of exposure measurement.

Choi and Muller (1984) suggest that: a single translation methodology cannot logically serve equally well translations occurring under different conditions and serving different purposes. Thus, more than one translation method seems warranted.

However, it has become clear to many managers and accountants alike that retrospective accounting techniques, no matter how refined, cannot truly account for the economic effects of devaluation or revaluation on the value of a company. As a result of this accounting distortion of economic reality, many multinational firms are now taking a longer-term look at their degree of exchange risk. This involves focusing on a company's economic exposure.

ECONOMIC EXPOSURE

Economic exposure results from the fact that a company's economic value will change as a result of a change in exchange rates. Basically, this means that economic exposure is the present value (see Chapter 12 for an explanation of present value) of assets minus liabilities which change in value with exchange rate changes. This is the change in the net present value of expected future, after-tax, flows. Economic exposure can be split into two types: transaction exposure and real operating exposure. Real operating exposure arises because currency fluctuations, combined with price changes, may alter the amount and riskiness of a company's future revenue and cost streams, i.e. its operating cash flow.

Measurement of economic exposure

Transaction exposure focuses on relatively short-term cash flow effects; economic exposure encompasses these plus the longer term effects of changes in exchange rates on the market value of the company.

The term real operating exposure was used above. Why real? This means the effects on operating exposure after the impact of inflation has been removed. A large change in exchange rates which is accompanied by an equally large change in the price level (inflation) in the foreign country may have no overall effect on the competitiveness or market value of a multinational company; in other words, there will be no change in real cash flows. In order for real operating exposure to exist, exchange rate changes must result in relative price changes, both within and between countries. The most important factor is changes in the purchasing power of one currency relative to another. If a real exchange rate change occurs, the impact on the company will depend upon the price elasticity of demand for its products. The more individual and distinct a company's product, the greater the possibility that the company can alter its prices to maintain the parent currency cash flow. If, however, a company has many foreign competitors, then it may have little flexibility to protect itself from the real exchange rate change, since if it increases its prices demand could fall substantially. Relative price changes can also affect a company's competitors, suppliers and customers. The full effect of economic exposure on an individual company will therefore not only depend on the direct impact of relative price changes on the company itself, but also on the indirect effects that result from the impact of relative price changes on a number of other organizations with which the company deals.

It is not hard to see, therefore, that economic exposure is difficult to quantify, and if this is the case, how should companies react to it? There is no easy answer to this question, but one favoured strategy is to diversify internationally, in terms of sales, location of production facilities, raw materials and financing. Such diversification is likely to significantly reduce the impact of foreign exchange economic exposure relative to a purely domestic company, and provide much greater flexibility to react to real exchange rate changes.

There are two lengths of economic exposure:

1. Short-term: for example when a multinational company lends its parent currency to a subsidiary in the USA
2. Long-term: for example, a subsidiary may have been established in a country with low rates of inflation, readily available funds for borrowing, balance of payments surpluses and low rates of taxation. These factors could have been the main reason for setting up the subsidiary. However, over time the economic situation there could have deteriorated, causing the local currency to devalue and the subsidiary to face operating cost problems.

Therefore, economic exposure, especially in the long term, arises as a result of foreign exchange risk, because of a multinational company's investment, production and other operating decisions. The company will generate both current assets and liabilities and a stream of expected future cash flows. Foreign exchange risk manipulation has to incorporate expectations about exchange rate changes into all the decisions affecting cash flow and financial structure.

Economic exposure management has become more important in recent years as exchange rates have become more volatile, countries are following divergent monetary policies and markets are becoming more global. Exchange rate changes can affect the operational cash flows of companies in globally competitive industries, whether or not they export their products. It is not only multinational companies that need to take note of the implications of economic exposure.

Operating exposure

The real change in exchange rates will affect different aspects of a company's operations. The effect of a real change in exchange rate for a domestic company will depend on its degree of pricing flexibility; that is, can the company maintain its sterling margin both at home and abroad? This will depend on the sterling elasticity of demand. Inelastic demand means that the company will have greater flexibility in responding to exchange rate changes. Elastic demand means that the company will have less flexibility to respond; this could happen if the company has a lot of competition. The more differentiated the company's products, the less competition exists and therefore the more inelastic, and more flexible to exchange rate changes a company will be. Furthermore, if most competitors are based in the same country as the company, then they will all face the same change in costs, so demand is more inelastic.

It has become clear that, no matter how refined, accounting statements do not accurately represent the economic effects of devaluation or revaluation on the value of a company. The impact of exchange rate changes, represented by the company's balance sheet and income statements, become distorted and of little value to investors or managers. In theory there should be no difference between accounting and economic values.

The problem is not that the accounting measures of exposure are distorted, but that information from the historic cost accounting system provides only part of the total information for true exposure. Not all future flows appear there and stocks are not adjusted to reflect the effects of inflation and relative price changes on their associated future cash flows.

True economic exposure

Economic exposure requires detailed knowledge of a company's operations and their sensitivity to exchange rate changes. There are two types of exchange rate: nominal and real. The nominal exchange rate is what we actually see in the market; however, this may only be reflecting the difference between the rate of inflation in two countries. Unless the company's consumption bundle in a particular currency is identical to the bundle in a national inflation index, or all prices in the index change by the same amount, the impact on the company is not described by the change in national index. Purchasing power parity (PPP) theory states that exchange rates are determined by the relative prices of similar goods between countries. Therefore, even when purchasing power parity theory holds there is still some exchange risk. For true exposure we use the real exchange rate which takes into account the rates of inflation when calculating an exchange rate. True economic exposure can occur under four circumstances:

1. *Deviation from purchasing power parity* That is the real exchange rate changes. Changes in exchange rate can benefit some economic sectors while simultaneously having adverse effects on others. It may be noted that a company can face exchange risks even when exchange rates do not change. For example, a Brazilian pen manufacturer exporting to the UK may be placed at a competitive disadvantage if Brazil's rate of inflation is high, but the Brazilian government does not allow the exchange rate to change. This will make Brazilian pen prices relatively high when compared to foreign manufacturers.
2. *Relative price changes* Exchange rate changes have the same effect on all local currency values; however, the rate of price increase is not uniform for all goods and services. For example, if the wholesale price index rose by 9 per cent, agricultural chemicals may only rise by 7 per cent and gas fuels by 30 per cent. Thus, to the extent that changes in the specific prices

faced by a company in its input and output markets differ from changes in the general price level, so a company's gain from devaluation may not offset its losses from inflation even if purchasing power parity holds.

3. *Tax factors* Governments tax nominal rather than real income; therefore, nominal currency changes can lead to real cash flow changes. For example, if a multinational company's foreign affiliate borrows sterling (home currency) and then the foreign currency depreciates relative to sterling, then the affiliate will show a tax-deductible loss even though the sterling cost of repaying the loan has not really changed at all. This increase in the affiliate's real after-tax cash flow is due to the government's confusing the nominal interest rate with the real cost of the loan.

4. *Some cash flows are fixed in nominal terms* Most of a company's costs or revenues are typically non-contractual in nature, i.e. they fluctuate in keeping with changing market conditions. Exchange rate effects on non-contractual cash flows, therefore, are specific to a given business and depend on changes in the markets for these goods and services and for factors of production. As long as prices and exchange rates are free to adjust, the exchange risk and exposure associated with non-contractual flows are likely to be minimal. An example of how real operating exposure might affect a multinational corporation is when a local currency depreciates. A devaluation will reduce import competition, so if a large amount of import competition exists the prices of local currencies will increase, although this increase will not be to the full extent of the devaluation. If import competition is small, local prices will only increase a little, because the prices would have already been raised as much as possible. In either case there will be a decline in local demand and in local currency revenue. Foreign prices that are expressed in the home country's currency should remain the same or decrease slightly, depending on the degree of competition from other exporters. Local currency cost will increase, but not to the extent of the devaluation and the home country's cost of imported inputs should remain the same. The company may show a loss on its net local currency monetary assets and a gain on its liabilities, and the real loss in working capital is equal to the net increase in the home country's currency value of working capital required following a devaluation. This illustrates that the company's sources of imports, domestic traded or non-traded goods, and fluctuations in the real exchange rate, are far more important to the company's economic exposure than accounting definitions.

REFERENCES

Aliber, R. Z. and C. P. Stickney (1975) 'Accounting measures of foreign exchange exposure: the long and short of it', *Accounting Review*, January, pp. 45–52.

Ankrom, R. K. (1974) 'Top level approach to the foreign exchange problem', *Harvard Business Review*, July–August.

Choi, F. D. S. and G. G. Muller (1984) *International Accounting*, Prentice-Hall, p. 379 and pp. 130–33, Englewood Cliffs, New Jersey.

Lorensen, L. (1972) 'Reporting foreign operations of U.S. companies in U.S. dollars', Accounting research study No. 12, p. 2.

National Association of Accountants (1960) 'Management problems in foreign operations', NAA Research Report 36, p.10.

Shank, J. K. (1976) 'F.A.S.B. statement No. 8 – Resolved foreign currency accounting – or did it?', *Financial Analyst Journal*, July–August, pp. 55–61.

Shapiro, A. C. (1986) *Multinational Financial Management*, 2nd edition, Allyn and Bacon, Newton Mass.

The Committee on International Accounting (1975) 'Report of the Committee on International Accounting', *Accounting Review*, p. 92.

Walker, D. P. (1977) 'An economic analysis of foreign exchange risk', The Institute of Chartered Accountants, Occasional paper No. 14, December.

Watt, G. C. (1970) 'Foreign exchange transactions and translations', *Handbook of Modern Accounting*, pp. 1–35.

ADDITIONAL READING

Abdullah, F. A. (1987) *Financial Management for the Multinational Firm*, 1st edition, Prentice-Hall, Englewood Cliffs, New Jersey.
Adler, M. and Dumas, B. (1984) 'Exposure to currency risk: definition and measurement', *Financial Management*, Summer, pp. 41–50.
Demirag, I. (1987) 'A review of the objectives of foreign currency translation', *International Journal of Accounting*, Vol. 2, November, pp. 69–85.
Eaker, M. R. (1981) 'The numeraire problem and foreign exchange risk', *Journal of Finance*, May, pp. 419–26.
Eun, C. S. (1981) 'Global purchasing power view of exchange risk', *Journal of Finance*, December, pp. 639–50.
Heckerman, D. (1972) 'The exchange risk of foreign operations', *Journal of Business*, January, pp. 42–8.
Lessard, D. R. and Lightstone, J. B. (1986) 'Volatile exchange rates can put operations at risk', *Harvard Business Review*, July–August, pp. 109–14.
Shapiro, A. C. (1982) *Multinational Financial Management*, 1st edition and 1986 2nd edition, Allyn and Bacon, Newton, Mass.
Shapiro, A. C. (1975) 'Exchange risk changes, inflation and the value of the multinational corporation', *Journal of Finance*, May, pp. 485–502.
Stern, D. and Chew, D. H. (eds) (1988) *New Development in International Finance*, Blackwell, New York and Oxford.
Thomas, R. D. (1978) 'Foreign currency translation', *CA Magazine*, **111**, October, pp. 76–80.
Walker, D. P. (1978) 'Currency translation: a pragmatic approach', *The Accountant*, **178**, 9 March, pp. 311–313.

CASE STUDY 1

Relay Products Ltd

Relay Products Ltd is the wholly owned South African subsidiary of a UK multinational corporation and is solely engaged in manufacturing gears for bicycles. 60 per cent of all its products are sold in the South African market and the remaining 40 per cent are exported to other African countries. Raw materials and parts of the gears are obtained both locally and imported from various European suppliers. Relay only uses South African labour in its manufacturing process. The effective corporate tax rate is 40 per cent in South Africa and the annual depreciation charge on plant and equipment is 800,000 rand. In addition, the company has 4 million rand of debt, with interest payable at 10 per cent annually.

Based on the current exchange rate of rand 4/£, projected sales, costs, after-tax income and cash flow for the next year are presented in Example A.1. All sales are invoiced in rand. The average collection period for sales is 90 days, and stock is carried at direct cost valued on a last in, first out (LIFO) basis and equals 90 days' worth of sales. Accounts payable average 10 per cent of sales while cash equalling 5 per cent of sales is normally maintained.

The current balance sheet of Relay Products Ltd is shown in Example A.2.

The local management in South Africa expects the rand to be devalued to rand 5/£ by the end of next year.

The parent company treasurer is sent from the parent headquarters to advise the subsidiary's management on its projections. On his arrival he discovers the following:

1. Relay is able to raise the rand price of its products to 25 rand without affecting sales volume.
2. The unit cost of imported materials will increase to 6 rand, yielding no extra contribution to Relay Products Ltd.

3. The company is able to increase locally sourced material from 800,000 units to 1,000,000 units and reduce imported material from 600,000 to 450,000 units.
4. All local input prices will stay at their pre-devaluation level.

He recommends that Relay should increase the price of its products to 25 rand, increase locally sourced material to 1,000,000 units and reduce imported material to 450,000 units.

Required:
(a) Assuming that the rand is devalued by 25 per cent to rand 5/£, calculate translation gains and losses using both current rate and monetary/non-monetary methods of translation, based on the current year's balance sheet presented in Example A.2.
(b) Assuming that the company will maintain the revised level of cash flows for the next three years, pay the loan at the end of year 3 and that all the treasurer's recommendations will be implemented, calculate the economic exposure of Relay Products Ltd for the next year. Use 15 per cent as the cost of capital. Present value factors for 15 per cent are:

Year 1	0.870
Year 2	0.756
Year 3	0.658

Clearly state all the assumptions made.

Example A.1   Summary of projected cash flows for Relay Products Ltd

	Units (*hundred thousand*)	Unit price (*rand*)	Total (*rand*)
Export sales	4	20	8,000,000
Domestic sales	6	20	12,000,000
Total revenue			20,000,000
Local labour (man hours)	1.5	20	3,000,000
Imported material	6	4	2,400,000
Local material	8	3	2,400,000
Total operating expenditure			7,800,000
Net operating income			12,200,000
Less overhead expenses			3,500,000
Less interest on local debt at 10%			400,000
Less depreciation			800,000
Net profit before tax			7,500,000
Income tax at 40%			3,000,000
Profit after tax			4,500,000
Add back depreciation			800,000
Net cash flow in rand			Rand 5,300,000
Net cash flow in sterling (rand 4/£)			£1,325,000

Example A.2   Balance sheet for Relay Products Ltd

	Rand	Rand
Cash		1,000,000
Accounts receivable		5,000,000
Stock		1,950,000
Net fixed assets		10,000,000
Total assets		17,950,000
Accounts payable	2,000,000	
Long-term debt	4,000,000	
Total liabilities		6,000,000
Equity capital		11,950,000
Total liabilities plus equity		17,950,000

Suggested solutions:

(a)

	Before devaluation	
	Rand	Rand 4 = £1
Cash	1,000,000	250,000
Accounts receivable	5,000,000	1,250,000
Stock	1,950,000	487,500
Net fixed assets	10,000,000	2,500,000
Total assets	17,950,000	4,487,500
Accounts payable	2,000,000	500,000
Long-term debt	4,000,000	1,000,000
Equity	11,950,000	2,987,500
Total liabilities and equity	17,950,000	4,487,500

	Rand 5/£	
	Current rate	*M/NM*
Cash	200,000	200,000
Accounts receivable	1,000,000	1,000,000
Stock	390,500	487,500
Fixed assets	2,000,000	2,500,000
Total assets	3,590,000	4,187,500
Accounts payable	400,000	400,000
Long-term debt	800,000	800,000
Equity	2,390,000	2,987,500
Total liabilities and equity	3,590,000	4,187,500

Translation (loss) or gain is the change in equity

For the current rate method this is (2,390,000) − (2,987,500) = (597,500)

For the monetary/non-monetary method the translation (loss) or gain is (2,987,500) − (2,987,500) = 0

(b)

	Units (hundred thousand)	Unit price (rand)	Total (rand)
Domestic sales	6	25	15,000,000
Exports	4	25	10,000,000
Total revenue			25,000,000
Local labour (man hours)	1.5	20	3,000,000
Local material	10.0	3	3,000,000
Imported material	4.5	6	2,700,000
Total operating expenditure			8,700,000
Net operating income			16,300,000
Overhead expenses			3,500,000
Interest			400,000
Depreciation			800,000
Net profit before tax			11,600,000
Income tax at 40%			4,640,000
Net profit after tax			6,960,000
Add back depreciation			800,000
Net cash flow			Rand 7,760,000

Increase in working capital (an incremental outflow in year one)

	Pre-devaluation	Post-devaluation	Net change
Cash (5% sales)	1,000,000	1,250,000	250,000
Accounts receivable (25% of sales)	5,000,000	6,250,000	1,250,000
[a]Stock (25% direct costs)	1,950,000	1,950,000	0
Accounts payable	2,000,000	2,500,000	500,000
			Rand 1,000,000

[a]As sales volume is constant no increase in stock occurs.

Net cash flow after year one working capital increase 6,760,000.

Net cash flow in sterling (Rand 5/£) 1,352,000.

Estimated economic exposure

	Post-devaluation cash flow	*Pre-devaluation cash flow*	*Change in cash flow*	*15% P.V. factors*	*Present value*
	£	£	£	£	£
Year 1	1,352,000	1,325,000	27,000	0.870	23,490
Year 2	1,552,000	1,325,000	227,000	0.756	171,612
Year 3*	1,752,000	1,325,000	427,000	0.658	280,966

Net economic exposure gain £476,068

*Include £200,000 gain on loan repayment, ignoring any tax effects. This example, although much simplified relative to the real world, illustrates some of the problems a company faces in identifying economic exposure.

CASE STUDY 2

Enterprise Plc

Enterprise plc purchased the whole of the share capital of a French company, Tranier et Fils SA, on 1 January 1987. The agreed price of £110,000 was paid in cash. Fixed assets and stocks of Tranier were revalued for the purpose of the acquisition and the current valuations have been included in the balance sheet on 1 January 1987.

Tranier et Fils SA
Balance sheet on 1 January 1987

	French francs
Share capital	200,000
Revaluation reserve	80,000
Retained profits	260,000
	540,000
Fixed assets (at current value)	
Premises	560,000
Machinery	200,000
	760,000
Net current assets (at current value)	80,000
	840,000
Less: Long-term loan	300,000
	540,000

The summarized accounts for 1987 of Enterprise and Tranier et Fils SA are as follows:

Summarized profit and loss accounts for year ending on 31 December 1987

	Enterprise		Tranier	
	£000	£000	FF000	FF000
Operating profit before depreciation		144		100
Less: Depreciation				
Premises	4		8	
Machinery	32		24	
		(36)		(32)
Profit before taxation		108		68
Less: Taxation		(42)		(20)
		66		48
Add: Retained profit brought forward		304		260
Retained profit		370		308

Summarized balance sheets at 31 December 1987

	£000	FF000
Share capital	400	200
Revaluation reserve	—	80
Retained profits	370	308
	770	588
Fixed assets:		
Premises: at cost to group	600	560
Less: Depreciation	(80)	(8)
	520	552
Machinery: at cost to group	360	200
Less: Depreciation	(120)	(24)
	240	176
	760	728
Investment in Tranier:		
at cost	110	—
Net current assets	300	160
	1,170	888
Less: Long-term liabilities	400	300
	770	588

Relevant rates of exchange are: French franc to £:

1987 January 1	9
1987 Average for year	10
1987 December 31	11

Required:

Prepare a set of UK sterling consolidated accounts for Enterprise plc and its subsidiary Tranier et Fils SA using the temporal method of translation. (Stocks included in the net current assets of Tranier on 31 December 1987 may be translated at the closing rate of exchange.)

   Draw up a set of UK sterling consolidated accounts for Enterprise plc and its subsidiary Tranier et Fils SA using the closing rate method of translation. Follow the provisions of SSAP 20; in particular use the average rate of exchange for translation of the profit and loss accounts.

Suggested solution:

Consolidated profit and loss accounts for year ended 31 December 1987
using temporal method

	£
Operating profit (108,000 + 6,446 + 3,718)	118,164
Less: Taxation (42,000 + 2,000)	(44,000)
Retained profit for the year	74,164
Add: Retained profits brought forward (Enterprise)	304,000
Retained profits at 31 December 1987	378,164

Consolidated balance sheet on 31 December 1987
using temporal method

		£
Share capital and reserves		
Share capital		400,000
Retained profits		378,164
		778,164
Fixed assets		
Premises: at cost (600,000 + 62,222)	662,222	
Less: Depreciation (80,000 + 888)	(80,888)	
		581,334
Machinery: at cost (360,000 + 22,222)	382,222	
Less: Depreciation (120,000 + 2,666)	(122,666)	
		259,556
		840,890
Goodwill on consolidation		50,000
Net current assets (300,000 + 14,546)		314,546
		1,205,436
Less: Long-term liabilities (400,000 + 27,272)		(427,272)
		778,164

Consolidated profit and loss accounts for year ended 31 December 1987
using closing rate method

	£
Operating profit (108,000 + 6,800)	114,800
Less: Taxation (42,000 + 2,000)	(44,000)
Retained profit for year	70,800

Consolidated balance sheet on 31 December 1987
using closing rate method

		£
Share capital		400,000
Reserves:		
Retained profits at 1 January 1987 (Enterprise only)	304,000	
Retained profit for 1987	70,800	
Loss on exchange	(11,344)	
		363,456
		763,456
Fixed assets		
Premises: at cost (600,000 + 50,901)	650,901	
Less: Depreciation (80,000 + 728)	(80,728)	
		570,182
Machinery: at cost (360,000 + 18,182)	378,182	
Less: Depreciation (120,000 + 2,182)	(122,182)	
		256,000
		826,182
Goodwill on consolidation		50,000
Net current assets (300,000 + 14,546)		314,546
		1,190,728
Less: Long-term liabilities (400,000 + 27,272)		(427,272)
		763,456

Workings:

(i) *Goodwill*

		£
Equity interest in Tranier		
FF540,000 ÷ 9		60,000
Cost of investment		110,000
Goodwill on consolidation		50,000

(ii) *Temporal method*

Profit and loss account

	FF000	Rate	£
Operating profit before depreciation	100	10	10,000
Less: Depreciation	(32)	9	(3,554)
	68		6,446
Less: Tax	(20)	10	(2,000)
Retained profit for year	48		4,446

Balance sheet

Share capital	200		
Revaluation reserve at 1 January 1987	80		
Retained profit at 1 January 1987	260		
	540	9	60,000
Retained profit for year	48	as above	4,446
Balance: Diff. on exchange treated as ordinary profit		—	3,718
	588		68,164
Premises: at cost	560	9	62,222
Less: Depreciation	(8)	9	(888)
	552		61,334
Machinery: at cost	200	9	22,222
Less: Depreciation	(24)	9	(2,666)
	176		19,556
	728		80,890
Net current assets	160	11	14,546
	888		95,436
Less: Long-term liabilities	(300)	11	(27,272)
	588		68,164

(iii) *Closing rate method*

Profit and loss account

	FF000	Rate	£
Operating profit before depreciation	100	10	10,000
Less: Depreciation	(32)	10	(3,200)
	68		6,800
Less: Tax	(20)	10	(2,000)
	48		4,800

Balance sheet

	FF000	Rate	£
Share capital	200		
Revaluation reserve at 1 January 1987	80		
Retained profit at 1 January 1987	260		
	540	9	60,000
Retained profit current year	48	as above	4,800
Balance: treated as movement on reserve	—		(11,344)
	588		53,456
Fixed assets:			
Premises: at cost	560	11	50,910
Less: Depreciation	(8)	11	(728)
	552		50,182
Machinery: at cost	200	11	18,182
Less: Depreciation	(24)	11	(2,182)
	176		16,000
	728		66,182
Net current assets	160	11	14,546
	888		80,728
Less: Long-term liabilities	(300)	11	(27,272)
	588		53,456

(iv) *Analysis of difference*

Opening net investment	540,000 FF at 9/£	60,000
P&L for year	48,000 FF at 10/£	4,800
Closing net investment	588,000 FF at 11/£	53,456
Loss on exchange		(11,344)

This is due to opening net investment being translated at different opening and closing rates. Also, profit and loss is translated at different rates in the balance sheet and the profit and loss account.

SEVEN

MANAGEMENT OF FOREIGN CURRENCY EXPOSURE

INTRODUCTION

This chapter examines the alternative techniques of currency risk management that may be used to deal with translation, transaction and economic exposure. Managers must identify which type of exposure is likely to have the greatest impact on the operations of the company, and decide to what extent the exposure should be hedged and which exposure reducing techniques should be employed.

The management of foreign currency risk has far-reaching implications for the company as a whole; the financial manager must consider the tax implications of his or her strategy and the effect of this strategy on other parts of the organization. He or she should also be involved in setting foreign currency pricing policy, in conjunction with the marketing department. On a larger scale, there is a need for integration of the currency risk management function into the management structure of the organization, and in particular the decision must be made as to whether this function should be centralized or decentralized. Managers must also decide whether to adopt an aggressive or defensive policy with respect to foreign exchange risk.

WHY HAS EXPOSURE MANAGEMENT INCREASED IN IMPORTANCE?

Over the past 20 years, foreign exchange risk management has significantly increased in importance. Three major reasons for this are:

1. *An increase in international trade and financing* Since the Second World War there has been a large increase in international trade. With an average rate of inflation being taken into account, trade has increased more than sixfold over the period, with much of this rise being attributed to the rapid growth of multinational companies.

Over the past 30 years there has also been a marked increase in international financing. From 1968–90 the Eurocurrency market grew more than twentyfold, and growth in the Eurobond market has also been substantial. Corporate treasurers increasingly look to world financial markets rather than domestic markets to raise funds.

2. *An increase in the volatility of exchange rates* In the early 1970s there was a shift from a relatively fixed to a relatively floating exchange rate regime. Because of this exposure management has become a big problem for international business. Any rumour of an economic problem results in a depreciation of the currency concerned, with significant effects on the performance of the companies trading in that currency. A change in the exchange rate can easily wipe out or double the profit on an international contract.

Hence, in today's primarily flexible exchange rate regime an international company cannot afford to ignore the problem of foreign exchange risk.

3. *The increased visibility of foreign exchange gains/losses*   The first two factors are the source of the foreign exchange risk problem; this third factor helps to explain why the problem is becoming increasingly important for corporate financial managers. The gains/losses from international trade are now more visible because of more stringent accounting reporting rules.

Hedging: when is it necessary?

Hedging may be defined as the partial or total elimination of a risk by some compensating action. In order to assess whether a hedge/no hedge strategy is to be undertaken, it is important to evaluate all of the costs involved before making a decision. Most hedging strategies involve fee or transactions costs, which can be considerable, especially if options are involved (see Chapter 9).

A company must first identify the foreign exchange risks that exist, and then decide whether or not such risks are material and acceptable. If the risk is not considered to be acceptable, the risk should be hedged with the cheapest effective means of protection.

The financial manager must consider whether his foreign currency management policy will adopt an aggressive or defensive style, i.e. should he actively deal with the problem of exposure? Hedging against risk is possible for each of transaction, translation and economic exposure, but costs are involved in implementing such hedges. The arguments put forward in favour of either passive or active exposure management largely reflect opinions as to whether capital markets and foreign exchange markets are efficient or inefficient. A passive approach to this problem would consider that these markets tend to be relatively efficient; many managers, however, believe that markets are imperfect and therefore adopt a more aggressive policy towards hedging.

Hedging transaction and translation exposure
Active management of these exposures is justified by:

1. The degree to which foreign exchange and money markets are not efficient.
2. Management's risk aversion to higher variability in cash flow and reported earnings per share owing to foreign exchange gains and losses.

Foreign exchange and money markets display efficiency at some periods, but are unlikely to be consistently efficient. Managers should take advantage of this inefficiency whenever possible, or at least protect against the exchange risk implied by such inefficiency. Some degree of inefficiency exists in the markets for most of the major currencies. Reasons for such inefficiency include government intervention in the foreign exchange or money markets, political instability, change in tax law and other government restrictions. Even if markets were efficient, managers should be prepared for the eventuality of unexpected changes in future spot rates. In an efficient market the forward rate is an unbiased predictor of future spot rates which implies that it will only correctly predict spot rates on average. Management should therefore prepare itself for some deviations from the predicted rate; volatility of future cash flows of the company should be minimized irrespective of what the future spot rate will be. Protection of future cash flows is the major concern of the financial manager.

It is extremely difficult to eliminate both transaction and translation exposure simultaneously. Translation exposure does not constitute a cash flow whereas transaction exposure does; the latter involves a realized loss or gain. The accounting nature of translation exposure means that it is not taxable; transaction exposure may be. Managers must consider whether it is necessary to implement costly protective techniques for translation exposure management, to avoid the possibility of incurring a loss which does not constitute an actual cash flow.

The management of translation exposure is therefore not advocated (see Chapter 6 for measurement of transaction, translation, and economic exposure).

Hedging economic exposure   As discussed in the previous chapter, actively managing economic exposure is justified by deviations from the purchasing power parity theory. The absolute version of this theory states that the 'price of internationally traded commodities should be the same in every country'. The relative version of PPP states that 'if the spot exchange rate between two currencies starts in equilibrium, any change in the differential rate of inflation between them tends to be offset over the long run by an equal but opposite change in the exchange rate'. There is evidence that PPP holds reasonably well over the long term, but in the short term large fluctuations are possible. Management should therefore manage economic exposure in times when PPP does not hold, which is frequently!

Internal and external hedging   Hedging may be undertaken by using both internal and external hedging strategies. Internal strategies are those that involve the means by which the company organizes its international transactions within the company itself. Such hedges have little direct cost, but may have implications for the operating efficiency of the entity that need to be considered before deciding to use such measures. The main forms of internal hedge are leading and lagging, netting, matching, the selection of the currency of invoice and internal asset and liability management. External hedging involves the use of external contracts whereby the company purchases or sells forward contracts, options, swaps, futures, etc., in order to protect against an exchange rate risk.

It must be stressed that many companies do not protect themselves from foreign currency risk at all, either because they do not consider that it will have a significant effect on their cash flows or because they believe that on average foreign exchange gains will cancel out foreign exchange losses and risk protection is not worth the cost involved. The latter argument is fine if the company can sustain a series of foreign exchange losses and does not go into receivership before the foreign exchange gains arrive to compensate for the losses!

Data needed to hedge the identified exposure

The data that are needed depend on the type of exposure being managed. The hardest information to ascertain concerns the management of transaction exposure and economic exposure. The quality of information has to be good, otherwise any techniques used will be a waste of time.

Information needs might relate to:

1. *Corporate plans*   The information that is most useful here is that of the company's short-term plans. These should contain data on future cash and currency flows, volumes of imports and exports and the extent to which components will have to be imported (which brings with it currency risk). Other data required may include any expansion or acquisition plans.
2. *Settlement procedures*   The data required here concern the settlement dates and terms of business transctions, including currency clauses, that are agreed upon.
3. *Timing problems*   This is the most important factor for exposure management. Transaction

exposure arises from trading flows; timing can be uncertain in this context. If a company does not pay on time then not only will this result in the debtor being exposed to currency risk, it could also lead to a shortage of funds.

Many circumstances can affect the timing of future currency flows. Some examples are:

1. Delays in production
2. Transport delays: the traded product does not reach the market as quickly as envisaged
3. Accounting delays: relevant data do not reach the importer as quickly as expected

In the following sections we will examine the management of transaction, translation and economic exposures and discuss appropriate hedging techniques for each type of exposure.

1. Managing transaction exposure

A company will experience transaction exposure whenever it is committed to a foreign currency denominated transaction. Undertaking this transaction can cause a gain or loss; transaction exposure measures this gain or loss. Examples of such transaction are purchasing goods and services on credit, borrowing or lending funds, being party to an unperformed forward foreign exchange contract and acquiring assets or incurring liabilities in any other manner (all in foreign currencies).

The transaction undertaken incurs an inflow or outflow of cash at a future date. Since exchange rates tend to be volatile, it is almost inevitable that there will be a difference in the exchange rate between the time the original commitment was made for the transaction and the time it is settled in cash. The transaction will therefore cost more or less than originally anticipated. Protection against this type of exposure requires the entering into of foreign currency transactions whose cash flows precisely counteract the cash flows of the transaction exposure. The application of techniques such as forward contracts, price adjustment clauses and currency options and borrowing or lending in the foreign currency will help the manager to guard against such exposure.

The most common form of transaction exposure arises from purchasing or selling on credit. It occurs when a company has a receivable or payable expressed in foreign currency. An example is as follows.

A British company sells goods on credit to a French company for FF900,000. The agreement is that the payment is to be made in 30 days. The current exchange rate is FF10/£ so that the British seller expects to exchange FF900,000 for £90,000 when payment is received.

There is a risk that the seller will not receive the exact amount of £90,000 expected. If the exchange rate were to change such that FF12/£ when payment was received, the British seller would only receive £75,000 (i.e. FF900,000 divided by FF12/£) which is £15,000 less than forecast. If the exchange rate had changed such that FF9/£, the seller would have received £100,000: this is £10,000 more than anticipated. Thus, transaction exposure can take the form of a gain or a loss.

As a means of protection it would be possible for the British seller to fix the terms of sale in pounds, but this might adversely affect the marketability of the product. Sterling invoicing would only transfer the transaction exposure to the buyer and would not achieve a total elimination of the risk.

Hedging techniques for transaction exposure

Leading and lagging Leading and lagging refer to the adjustment of the times of payments that are made in foreign currencies.

Leading is the payment of an obligation in advance of the due date.

Lagging is delaying the payment of an obligation past the due date.

The purpose of these techniques is for the company to take advantage of expected devaluations or revaluations of the appropriate currencies. Lead and lag payments are particularly useful when forward contracts are not possible.

Leading and lagging may be operated in both an aggressive and a defensive manner, as follows:

An English company has a subsidiary in France. The English company regularly provides the French subsidiary with goods, allowing 60 days for payment. An expected fall in the French franc against the pound may encourage the English company to try to make the French subsidiary pay early or even immediately, i.e. without 60 days' credit—the English company is intentionally shortening intra-group credit. In this way the English company will gain if the French franc does fall against the pound. Obviously for this strategy to be successful the franc will need to fall in value in line with the company's expectations. Under defensive currency risk management, leading and lagging will be undertaken to try to bring the English company's net French franc assets nearer to zero, thus reducing the absolute amount of the exposure. This defensive strategy normally involves analysis of the total net exposure positions of all component companies in the group. The treasury of the group is usually involved to ensure that the timing of intercompany settlement is functional from a group standpoint and not simply from a local one.

The performance of some subsidiaries may be affected if they are asked to lead or lag. Involvement in leading incurs a loss of interest on funds used to pay creditors early. The problem can be resolved by evaluating performance on a pre-interest and pre-tax basis.

The tax implications of leading and lagging must also be considered, since when borrowing and interest burdens are transferred internationally the overall consolidated tax burden is altered.

Leading and lagging are often constrained by the exchange control regulations of individual countries; this must be taken into account when deciding on a hedging strategy. Host governments often impose allowable bands on credit terms which must be followed in all international trading.

Both leading and lagging can be fairly easily arranged within a group of companies, subject to government constraints. However, between independent companies lead payments are much more likely than lag payments. To lag a payment to an external creditor will involve contravening the terms of sale. However, this does not mean that it never happens!

The following example illustrates a lead payment. This will later be extended to see how hedging via a lead payment compares with other forms of hedge.

A UK importer has just contracted to buy goods from Germany on 90 days' credit, at a price of DM500,000 (payable in DM). Exchange rates:

Spot DM2.9565–2.9595/£

Three months forward DM2.8826–2.8865/£

The current spot equivalent of DM500,000 is £169,119.

	Borrowing	Lending
Interest rates		
UK	14%	10%
Germany	7%	4%

Hedging through a lead payment would mean paying the DM500,000 early. If it was paid now the cost would be:

$$\frac{DM500,000}{2.9565} = £169,119$$

This would require the cash now in order to make payment. If this was borrowed the total cost after three months is:

$$£169,119 \times 1.035 = £175,038$$

The position at the end of three months is considered in order to put the cost of the lead payment in a form comparable to the time horizon of other hedges, particularly a forward contract where no payment would be made until the end of the three-month period.

Where a lead payment is being made it might be possible for the company to negotiate a cash discount for early payment. This could make the lead payment an attractive form of hedge.

Exposure netting and matching Netting occurs within a group of companies. Companies within the group can settle interfirm debt in different currencies (or in an agreed common currency) for the net amount owed in the currency rather than the gross amount. The effect of this is to reduce the size of currency flows between subsidiaries, and to significantly reduce the size of the net exposure that needs to be hedged, and the transactions costs of currency transfers. The simplest form of netting is bilateral netting, which takes place between two group members. Each company nets its own position with that of the other company such that cash flows are reduced by the lower of each company's purchases from or sales to its netting partner.

Multilateral netting is, in principle, no different from this. Here, more than two associated companies' intergroup debt is involved. Because it is essential to know at all times the exposure positions of all component parts of the group in order to successfully undertake multilateral netting, it nearly always involves the use of a centralized group treasury.

Subsidiaries which are taking part report all intergroup balances to the group treasury at an agreed date. The treasury then advises the subsidiaries of the amounts to be paid or received from the other subsidiaries. This system can give rise to very large savings in foreign exchange commissions and transfer costs.

In some countries bilateral and multilateral netting is restricted, and any limitations on netting or relevant exchange control regulations need to be discovered before a policy is established. The system of netting reduces banking costs and increases the control of intercompany settlements.

Examples 7.1 and 7.2 show how multilateral netting may be undertaken. Payments and receipts are assumed to be due at approximately the same time.

If no form of netting takes place, the total amount of transactions will be £4,620,000, and there will be 19 separate transactions. By calculating the total receipts and payments for each member of the group, netting may be undertaken.

With netting only three payments need to be made, with, for example, Subsidiary 2 paying Subsidiary 3 £380,000 and Subsidiary 1 paying Subsidiary 3 £30,000 and the UK parent company £270,000, with total transactions of £680,000.

Whereas netting applies only to transactions within a group of companies, matching may apply to transactions both within a group and with third parties. Matching involves approximately balancing the expected receipts and payments in different currencies so that only the net unmatched part needs to be purchased on the foreign exchange markets, or hedged against. For matching to work there needs to be a two-way flow in a given currency, with roughly the

Example 7.1 Intergroup transactions

	£000 Receiving company				
Paying company	UK parent	Sub 1	Sub 2	Sub 3	Sub 4
UK parent	—	200	350	110	170
Subsidiary 1	600	—	320	80	80
Subsidiary 2	40	240	—	310	600
Subsidiary 3	—	40	130	—	250
Subsidiary 4	460	300	10	330	—

Example 7.2 Intergroup transactions

	£000 Receiving company					
Paying company	UK parent	Sub 1	Sub 2	Sub 3	Sub 4	Total payment
UK parent	—	200	350	110	170	830
Subsidiary 1	600	—	320	80	80	1,080
Subsidiary 2	40	240	—	310	600	1,190
Subsidiary 3	—	40	130	—	250	420
Subsidiary 4	460	300	10	330	—	1,100
Total receipts	1,100	780	810	830	1,100	
Net receipts/ (payment)	270	(300)	(380)	410	0	

same timing of cash flows. There will commonly be timing differences in the cash flows such that matching will be, to some extent, imperfect.

Matching might be possible even if two-way cash flows do not exist in a currency. As we have seen earlier in the book, many currencies are linked to other currencies, particularly the dollar. If a receivable exists in dollars and a payment is due in a currency linked to the dollar, it is possible to match such cash flows. Even if there is no direct link, in recent years some currencies have tended to move closely together, including currencies within the ERM in Europe. Where close movement is expected matching may be possible. Unfortunately such 'parallel' matching involves the risk that the currencies may not continue to move together, as was seen with the problems in the ERM in 1992 and 1993.

As with netting, efficient matching will only be possible if the treasury function of the organization is centralized.

The decision of whether to centralize or decentralize the treasury management function is important to the efficiency of many forms of hedging, not just netting and matching.

The advantages of centralization are:

1. A centralized treasury knows all the financial dealings in the whole group and so it can control the movements of funds worldwide. Consequently it is in the best position to organize intergroup currency netting and other forms of exposure management.

2. There is greater control over intercompany receivables/payables. This is advantageous to the company as more control means a reduction in currency risk.

3. If the treasury is centralized then larger amounts will be lent and borrowed and used in foreign exchange deals. As bigger quantities are involved, better rates may be obtained.

4. As the movement of funds costs money, centralization can prevent the unnecessary movement of funds around the group.

5. A central treasury could lend money to subsidiaries at favourable rates instead of them incurring high interest rates for overdrafts or loans in foreign markets. The surplus cash of some overseas subsidiaries could be lent to others which are in deficit, at the very least saving the spread which would exist on lending and borrowing via a bank. A cental treasury might also have better access to offshore financial markets, where rates of interest tend to be more favourable than those available in the domestic money markets.

6. A centralized treasury could act as an information centre by sending out any information that may be of use to foreign subsidiaries. This information could be, for example, any changes in exchange controls or it may be about more general economic background. No one foreign subsidiary has all the facts at its disposal, so in instances where the consolidated position of the company is of importance, centralized management is necessary.

7. It is expensive to establish the necessary dealing facilities and expertise to undertake exposure management in each individual subsidiary within a group. Centralized treasury management offers economies of scale.

There are, however, disadvantages of a centralized treasury function, the main one being that it may take away much of the decision-making from the subsidiary companies. The local managers may feel a lack of involvement and motivation if they have to submit all their information to the central treasury, and not be directly responsible for decisions on exposures that directly affect their operations. This may lead to a reluctance to provide the necessary information to the central treasury quickly, and problems may not be alerted to the treasury department as soon as they arise.

If decisions turn out to be wrong, then with a centralized department responsibilities lie fairly and squarely in one place.

The currency of invoice It would be easy for a UK company to avoid transaction exposure risk if all of its exports and imports were to be denominated in pounds. Even if this was feasible, and had the agreement of all trading partners, there are reasons why it might not be desirable. From the perspective of UK exports a foreign customer is protected from foreign exchange risk if invoiced in his or her own currency. In competitive markets it might be easier to obtain export orders if the buyer faced no risk. A further implication is that the foreign customer does not have to obtain sterling, a foreign currency with which to make payment. Access to foreign currencies is restricted by exchange control regulations in many countries.

If sterling is at a discount relative to the foreign currency in which payment is to be made, the UK exporter may sell the foreign currency on the forward market to obtain more pounds than would be available at the current spot rate. This will lead to increased profits, or will allow the UK exporter to quote a lower and more competitive price to the foreign buyer.

Internal asset and liability management Internal asset and liability management refers to the manipulation of foreign currency assets and liabilities in order to reduce foreign exchange exposure. It is most commonly associated with the management of translation exposure, where a company might try to equalize the value of its assets and liabilities in a particular foreign currency to leave a zero currency exposure, but it may also be used as part of transaction exposure management.

Possible manipulation of assets and liabilities might include:

1. Borrowing or investing in foreign currencies in an opposing manner to expected export/ import transaction cash flows (see also below).
2. Moving funds from countries where currencies are expected to depreciate in value into relatively hard currency countries.
3. Collecting in debts as quickly as possible in a depreciation-prone currency, and reducing financial investments in such currencies.
4. Deciding to purchase goods from a country to which export sales are made, the purchase price being met by proceeds from the export sales.

Such manipulations of assets and liabilities will have an impact on the efficient operations of the subsidiaries concerned. As well as the obvious cash flow effects, there are implications for gearing levels, which could affect the ability to raise finance or future trade credit.

Further examples of how assets and liabilities may be manipulated are given later in this chapter when translation exposure hedges are discussed.

Companies should be aware of the opportunities and costs of internal hedging, but many companies concentrate mainly on external contractual hedging, in particular forward market hedges.

Forward market hedges   Forward market cover involves taking a contract to exchange two currencies at an agreed future date at a predetermined rate of exchange. The forward contract is entered into at the time the transaction exposure is created, and requires a future source of funds to fulfil the contract. It is a legally binding contract which must be fulfilled. The use of forward cover is best illustrated by an example.

Forward contracts are a common form of currency hedge which is available to all but the smallest companies. Using the above data from the leading and lagging example, a one-month contract would be arranged to purchase DM500,000 at a cost of:

$$\frac{500,000}{2.8826} = £173,455$$

This is £4,336 higher than the spot rate, but is a fixed rate that the company will pay no matter how exchange rates move. With hindsight it might have been better not to bother with the forward contract if, at the end of three months, the exchange rate was above 2.8826/£. Unfortunately companies do not possess crystal balls that can forecast the future, and cannot know in advance whether they should have undertaken the forward market hedge.

The hedge is thought of as 'covered', 'perfect' or 'square' when funds for the forward contract are on hand or are due because of a future business deal. The reason for this is that no residual foreign exchange risk exists since the funds on hand or to be received are matched by funds to be paid. In this instance forward market hedge provides perfect cover for transaction exposure.

A hedge can also be open or uncovered; this occurs when funds needed for the forward exchange contract are not already available or due later. These funds need to be purchased on the spot market at some future date. A certain amount of risk is involved here, since the financial manager will purchase foreign exchange at an uncertain future spot rate in order to meet the forward contract.

There are, however, limitations to forward market hedges. Forward markets do not exist in many countries, especially smaller developing countries, and even if a forward market does exist it may be restricted in size by the local government trying to preserve foreign currency reserves. Moreover, in a small number of countries foreign currency hedging is illegal. Even where forward markets exist, hedges are rarely available for periods of more than one year.

Money market hedges A money market hedge can be defined as the process of borrowing in the money markets, converting the funds borrowed at the spot rate into the currency in which payment is due, and investing in the second country. The total receipts, principal plus interest from foreign currency investment is then used to make payment for the goods.

For example, a UK company with an obligation to pay French francs in three months' time could protect against the risk of the franc appreciating in value by converting pounds into French francs now at the spot rate, investing the francs acquired for three months, and at the end of the three-month period using the invested francs, plus interest, to make the payment due in francs. As pounds have been switched into francs now, any future foreign exchange risk is avoided. The catch is that, unlike a forward market hedge where pounds need only be found at the end of the three months to fulfil a forward contract, with a money market hedge the pounds will be required now. Whether or not the money market hedge is cheaper than the forward market hedge will depend upon the levels of interest rates in the UK and France. In most cases forward market hedges are cheaper than money market hedges.

This technique is therefore similar to forward market hedge in that it involves a contract and a source of funds to fulfil that contract. The contract in this case is a loan agreement. If the funds to match the contract are generated from business operations, the money market hedge is covered. If, however, funds to repay the loan are bought on the foreign exchange spot market, the hedge is uncovered or open. An example of a money market hedge using the same data as for the forward market hedge is shown below.

Money market hedges involve the use of short-term investment, and often borrowing, in order to protect against exchange risk. In the above example the UK company could protect itself against foreign exchange risk by converting pounds to DM and investing those DM in Germany (or international DM securities) for a period of three months. The proceeds of this investment will be used to make payment to the German supplier. If the UK company wishes to have exactly DM500,000 to make payment, given an interest rate of 4 per cent in Germany on invested funds (this is an annual rate!) it will have to invest

$$\frac{\text{DM500,000}}{1.01} = \text{DM495,050 for the three-month period}$$

(1.04 would be the divisor if the investment was for an entire year. Since the investment is for one quarter of a year the divisor is 1.01.)

The full money market hedge, assuming that the company needed to borrow funds in order to undertake the hedge, is:

Immediately
Borrow £167,444.6 and convert them into DM at the spot rate of DM2.9565/£ to give DM495,050.

Invest DM495,050 at 4 per cent per annum for three months.

In three months
Receive DM500,000 from the investment and use this to make payment to the German supplier.
Repay the pound loan plus interest at 14 per cent per annum (or 3.5 per cent per quarter).
The total cost of the money market hedge is £167,444.6 × 1.035 = £173,305.

This may be compared with the cost of the forward market hedge which was £173,455, and with the lead payment which was £175,038. On this occasion the money market is slightly cheaper, but this ignores transaction costs which are likely to be higher for the money market hedge than for a forward market hedge. A money market hedge will always be cheaper than an immediate lead payment unless a cash discount can be negotiated in association with the lead payment.

Conditions of market efficiency mean that interest rate parity should ensure that costs of forward market hedges and money market hedges are almost the same. Markets are not, however, always efficient. Furthermore, the difference in interest rates encountered by a private firm borrowing on two separate national markets may not be the same as the difference in the risk-free government bill rates.

In most circumstances the forward market will offer a better and cheaper way of hedging than the money market because of differences in the level of transactions costs. The exception might be where opportunities for covered interest arbitrage exist.

Foreign currency borrowing   This is a major foreign currency risk management device. The principle is to borrow in a foreign currency in which the company expects to have cash inflows from exports or other operations; these cash inflows can be used to service the interest and principal payments on the foreign currency loan. The extent of such payments is not subject to foreign exchange risk, although the company must consider the interest rates that are payable on the foreign currency loan. Such loans may be arranged for flexible periods and possibly with variable rather than fixed rates of interest.

Currency risk sharing   This can be achieved through a customized hedge contract which is included in the trade transaction between two or more parties. A currency risk sharing agreement is usually used only by those companies who are involved in long-term trade contracts; these agreements reduce the frequency of contract revisions and the effects of currency fluctuations on profits.

Currency risk sharing can help companies to avoid two pricing extremes:

1. Having to revise prices continuously as the exchange rate changes.
2. Keeping the price constant while other companies experience windfall profits or suffer losses in either profit margin or market share. Effectively, the parties to the agreement are sharing the foreign exchange risk.

Currency and interest rate swaps   Currency and interest rate swaps are new developments in financial techniques which have developed significantly since 1981 when the first large-scale interest rate swap between the World Bank and IBM took place.

Currency swaps are said to be more effective than traditional hedging alternatives in reducing the risks associated with trade finance and asset/liability management in international business. Swaps provide more liquidity, increased certainty and are cheaper than, for example, leading and lagging, offshore funding or short-term hedges in the foreign exchange market. Chapter 8 examines swaps in more depth.

Foreign currency options   In many instances a company is uncertain as to whether the foreign exchange rate will increase or decrease. Rather than being tied to a forward contract with a fixed exchange rate, currency options have been devised which permit the company to protect itself against adverse foreign exchange rate movements, while also offering the opportunity to benefit from favourable exchange rate movements. Naturally there is a price to pay for getting the best of both worlds, and this is an upfront premium or cost of the option itself. Options may be put or call: a put option gives the buyer the right, but not the obligation, to sell the currency at a set price and at any time, right up to the date of maturity; a call option gives the right, but not the obligation, to buy the foreign currency at a set price. This is a valuable commodity as it means that if it is uncertain that a deal will go ahead the company can buy a call option in the foreign currency, so that a maximum price is locked in. Downside risk is limited to the call premium in the event that the deal is rejected. Options are discussed in depth in Chapter 9.

Example 7.3 is a practical illustration of the management of transaction exposure.

The finance director of Ultrapart plc is examining the company's expected foreign trade exposure position for the next six months. The company trades extensively with the USA and France. The following payments and receipts are forecast.

Example 7.3

Payments	$	Francs		Receipts	$	Francs
In 3 months	14m	—		In 3 months	—	22m
In 6 months	8m	18m		In 6 months	4m	11m

Exchange rates	$/£		Franc/£
Spot	1.764–1.770		9.875–9.892
3 months forward	1.5–1.6 c pm		1.6–1.7 centimes discount
6 months forward	3.8–4.0 c pm		2.4–2.5 centimes discount

Money market rates (%)

	Borrowing	Lending
Eurodollars	9.50	7.90
Eurosterling	11.75	9.25
Eurofrancs	13.25	11.00

We will illustrate what actions Ultrapart should take to maximize sterling receipts or to minimize sterling payments for each of its three- and six-month exposures, without engaging in foreign currency speculation or taking any foreign currency risk.

Since the company does not wish to experience foreign currency risk it must engage in hedging. The alternatives available from the data provided are forward market hedging, money market hedging, and lead payments. However, before evaluating any hedging strategy the company should undertake a matching process to find its relevant net exposures. The three-month and six-month exposures will be treated separately, but some companies might also net these off.

Net exposures

	$	Francs
3 months	14 million payment	22 million receipts
6 months	4 million payment	7 million payment

The outright forward exchange rates for three and six months may be found from the premiums and discounts given.

Outright exchange rates

	$/£	Francs/£
Spot	1.764–1.770	9.875–9.892
3 months	1.749–1.754	9.891–9.909
6 months	1.726–1.730	9.899–9.917

$ exposures

Forward market hedge

$$3 \text{ months} \quad \frac{\$14\text{m payment}}{1.749} = £8,004,574$$

$$6 \text{ months} \quad \frac{\$4\text{m payment}}{1.726} = £2,317,497$$

Money market hedge

3 months

Borrow £7,782,798 at 11.75% for 3 months	= £8,011,418
Convert at spot to $ at $1.764/£	= $13,728,855
Invest in the USA for 3 months at 7.9% per year $13,728,855 × 1.01975	= $14,000,000
Use the $14m to make payment for the goods	

6 months

Borrow £2,181,408 at 11.75% for 6 months	= £2,309,566
Convert at spot to $ at $1.764/£	= $3,848,004
Invest in the USA for 6 months at 7.9% per year $3,848,004 × 1.0395	= $4,000,000
Use the $4m to make payment	

For dollar exposures the forward market hedge is cheaper for the three-month exposure and the money market hedge for the six-month exposure. This ignores transaction costs.

Franc exposures

Forward market

3 months

$$\frac{22\text{m francs}}{9.909} \text{ receipts} = £2,220,204$$

6 months

$$\frac{7\text{m francs}}{9.899} \text{ payment} = £707,142$$

Money market hedge

3 months

Borrow FF21, 294,616 at 13.25% for 3 months to repay FF22,000,000
Use the franc receipts to make this payment

Convert FF21,294,616 to £ at spot of FF9.892/£	=	£2,152,711
Invest in the UK for 3 months at 9.25% per year	=	£2,202,492

Total £ receipts after 3 months £2,202,492

6 months

Borrow £671,906 for 6 months at 11.75% per year	=	£711,380
Convert to FF spot at FF9.875/£	=	FF6,635,071
Invest in France for 6 months at 11% per year 6,635,071 × 1.055	=	FF7,000,000

Use the proceeds of the investment to make the payment of FF7m. The forward market is better in both cases for the franc exposures.

Where payments were due, lead payments would also provide a possible hedge, but unless a discount could be negotiated would not be cheaper than the money market hedges at any time.

2.   Managing translation exposure

In preparing consolidated financial statements, foreign subsidiaries' accounts have to be reproduced in terms of the parent company's currency; this may result in a translation exposure gain or loss. By producing a consolidated statement, a single report of the operation of two or more legal entities is presented. There are three major translation practices in use at the present time: the current rate method, the monetary–non-monetary or temporal method, and the current–non-current method (all are discussed in Chapter 6).

The current rate method is the one used by most companies in the UK. It involves translating all assets and liabilities at the current exchange rate; this is the exchange rate operational at the balance sheet date. Items on the profit and loss account, such as depreciation and cost of goods sold under this approach, are translated at their respective exchange rates, i.e. the rate prevailing when the revenue or expense was incurred or at an average rate which is calculated for the year.

Items translated at historical rates include equity accounts, e.g. common stock and paid-in capital. Retained profit for the year comprises retained profit from the start of the year carried forward together with the operating profit or loss for that year. This net income figure does not incorporate the gain or loss which arises on translation; this is treated separately and is accumulated in a separate entity account in the balance sheet.

The main advantage of using this method is that balance sheet ratios remain consistent with respect to the figures before translation; this occurs owing to the fact that the individual balance sheet accounts are translated at the same rate.

Technical aspects of translation

Since different techniques of translation are available, many countries tend to stipulate the required and appropriate method. The accounting regulatory authorities in most countries not only recommend a particular method, they also produce guidelines concerning treatment of the translation gain/loss item in financial statements. For this purpose it is useful to consider the meaning of functional and reporting currency, but first we must remember the important fact that a translation gain or loss is only an accounting item. Given this, we have to decide whether this particular item is to be acknowledged in the present time period or deferred to a later reporting period. We have already seen that transaction gains or losses are recognized immediately; under US accounting regulation FASB 52 recommends accumulating translation gains and losses under consolidated stockholders equity.

Functional or reporting currency?   The functional currency of a foreign affiliate is the 'currency of the primary economic environment in which the affiliate operates and in which it generates cash flows'. The reporting currency is the 'currency in which the parent firm prepares its own financial statements'. A company will base its decision as to which is its functional currency on many criteria, e.g. whether it is integrated into the country in which it operates. If so, it will choose the local currency of that country. If, however, an affiliate exists merely as an extension of its parent company, it may decide that the parent's home currency is the appropriate currency. The implication of employing the parent's currency as the functional currency is that the temporal method of translation will be used.

We have so far defined translation exposure and considered its effects in terms of financial statements; we now proceed to assess the main techniques whereby this exposure is managed.

The balance sheet hedge   A balance sheet hedge involves the management of assets and liabilities and is another name for the process briefly discussed previously. For successful operation of this method, assets and liabilities are required to be equal; only then is it possible to completely eliminate translation exposure.

Manipulating assets and liabilities is the most common means of hedging against translation exposure. However, as was explained earlier, hedging against translation exposure is not a recommended strategy. Exposure management should concentrate on the cash flows of the organization, not the likely effects on the reported financial accounts.

If a balance sheet hedge is desired, a UK multinational company with a foreign subsidiary in a country where the currency is expected to fall in value relative to the pound might:

1. Reduce levels of local currency cash and short-term investments.
2. Try to collect money from local currency debtors as quickly as possible.
3. Borrow locally. Repayment will be less in terms of pounds (but relative levels of interest rates must be considered).
4. Invoice exports from the subsidiary in a foreign currency and imports in sterling.
5. Delay collection of any hard (strong) currency debts which are owed to the subsidiary.
6. If any hard currency payments are due to be made by the subsidiary, make them as quickly as possible.

Asset and liability manipulation can take several days or weeks to implement, and can have spin-off effects on the company's operations which must be considered. There is little point in reducing the level of cash holdings if this means that the subsidiary is unable to continue its normal trading operations because it has too little cash.

3.   Managing economic exposure

This type of exposure is concerned with future cash flows and extends over a longer time horizon than translation and transaction exposure. The economic nature of this type of exposure implies that it is not possible to cope with this risk simply through the use of normal hedging techniques. It is appropriately dealt with by long-term strategic decisions within the many departments of a company including those of finance, purchasing and production.

Economic or operating exposure is concerned only with *unexpected* changes in the exchange rate; any expected changes in the exchange rate should be incorporated into projections of expected operating results and market value (assuming reasonable market efficiency). If we assume equilibrium conditions in the foreign currency markets, the forward rate can be used as an unbiased predictor of the future spot rate. This figure would enable management to make predictions for the purpose of constructing budgeted financial statements, and it is only unexpected changes in the exchange rate which would make them revise their calculations and cause an economic exposure loss or gain, in terms of the market value of the company.

Economic exposure may be split into three separate time horizons:

1.   *Short-term*   The impact of a change in the exchange rates on expected cash flows on the one-year budget. It is difficult to evade this type of exposure since obligations cannot be reversed in the short term, e.g. sales price and factor costs. It is possible to change these elements over a longer time period, but for the time being cash flows will deviate from their expected levels.

2.   *Medium-term*   This relates to a longer time period of two to five years and again concerns the effect of changes in cash flows on budgeted statements. More external factors will determine the extent of the economic exposure such as monetary, fiscal and balance of payments policies of governments both in the UK and elsewhere.

3.   *Long-term*   This extends to a time period beyond five years; the company must consider the possible future strategic actions of its competitors. Any company which competes in the international environment will be exposed to economic exposure in the long run.

Efficient management of economic exposure requires companies to anticipate and influence the effect of unexpected changes in exchange rates on their future cash flows. Economic exposure is very difficult to measure precisely. How then should companies react to something they cannot measure? The key to economic exposure management is flexibility. Companies must be able to respond quickly to significant economic exposure effects. One way to achieve this is to diversify internationally in terms of sales, location of production facilities, raw materials and financing. Such diversification should provide the flexibility to respond to changes in real exchange rates and give a competitive advantage over purely domestic companies.

Marketing management of economic exposure

1.   *Market selection*   The marketing department must decide which international markets the company wishes to operate in, and whether opportunities in the selected markets will achieve the objectives of the company. The department is required to estimate the possible earning capacity of operations in these foreign markets, which will be in part influenced by the economic exposure that exists in the markets. To illustrate this we can take the example of the situation when sterling is strong (it does happen sometimes!). British exporters would find it difficult to market their goods abroad owing to the relatively high price of their products, and their competitors abroad would use this opportunity to increase their own market share.

Market strategy is a factor which is only adjustable in the long term if the change in the exchange rate persists; more practical short-term responses would take the form of adjusting pricing and promotional policies.

2. *Pricing strategy* Price is determined by the enterprise's individual strategy, and should allow for fluctuations in exchange rates. The company should clearly define its intentions as far as price adjustments are concerned; this factor is dependent on corporate objectives, which may be to maximize market share or profit, shareholder wealth or others. The following example shows how a company must choose between these such goals.

Assume that the company in this case is a large German company with significant export operations:

The Deutschmark is rising in value so the company has two options:

(a) Keep the DM price fixed at the expense of losing market share but protecting profit.

(b) DM price is reduced, sustaining the market share currently held, but profit decreases.

The difficulty lies in the reaction of domestic producers. If DM prices are altered, what will be the effect in the domestic market? How will competitors react? The possibility of losing market share may be important to many companies, since it is very difficult to regain market share once it has been lost.

The company is likely to resolve its dilemma by reviewing factors such as its economies of scale, the cost structure of expanding output and consumer price sensitivity; if price elasticity of demand is high it would be advisable for the company to keep its prices at a consistent and low level.

3. *Promotional strategy* This must also take exchange rate changes into consideration, i.e. when allocating a budget for advertising in different countries. Companies will wish to alter their promotional pattern with exchange rate changes; for example, if an exporter finds it difficult to sell his or her goods abroad owing to the stronger position of his or her currency, he or she may wish to reduce advertising expenditure, or change product image through different advertising media and slogans.

4. *Production strategy* This is also affected by exchange rate changes; in times of currency fluctuations new products are unlikely to be launched. The likelihood of introducing a new product onto a foreign market will be a function of the relative exposure that the firm is faced with in that market.

Production management of economic exposure

This can involve varying either the product source or the plant location; for example, a German company may decide to set up its manufacturing base abroad, where production costs are lower, if the Deutschmark is strong.

Important production decisions that are affected by economic exposure include:

1. *Input mix* A change in the exchange rate alters the price of domestically produced goods relative to foreign goods. Consequently the implications of exchange rate fluctuations are such that a multinational company would aim to substitute between domestic and imported inputs to achieve the least cost combination of inputs; this does, however, depend on the degree of substitutability that is possible. Taking measures to increase substitutability of inputs would have the advantage of minimizing economic currency risk, but would also involve increased costs.

2. *Shifting production among plants* The changing costs of production mean that the multinational companies have the option of changing the location of production to countries

whose currencies have been devalued. Hence the MNCs can avoid the majority of exchange risk by shifting production in line with changing relative production costs.

However, all this assumes that the MNC has a portfolio of plants worldwide and also that the shifting of production is actually possible. Companies which have international manufacturing facilities include Ford and General Motors (GM). Ford can theoretically shift production from the USA to Spain, West Germany, the UK, Brazil or Mexico.

3. *Plant Location*   Once a company has decided that it has to 'branch out' and set up a foreign plant, it has to decide on which location will give it its maximum unit profitability. For example, many Japanese companies have found that, in response to a strong yen, it is just as profitable to build plants in the USA as it is in Japan.

Before such a drastic move is made an assessment needs to be undertaken as to how long the particular country will keep its cost advantage. This may depend on local inflationary conditions; if they are expected to persist then a country's apparent cost advantage may soon be reversed.

However, shifting production abroad is not always the best approach. For companies which rely heavily on the coordination of departments and closeness to supplies, cutting costs domestically is preferable to producing abroad.

4. *Raising productivity*   The increasing strength of the dollar encouraged US companies to redouble their efforts to improve their productivity. This was done by cutting back wages, closing inefficient plants, etc. When the dollar weakens, US companies are in a good position to increase their international market share.

Other options when faced with a strengthening currency are to seek government import restrictions on competitors' goods, or for companies to turn to the government for low-cost export financing.

Planning for exchange rate changes

Multinational companies should always have contingency plans that could come into operation when exchange rate changes which were not anticipated take place. Consequently, when a currency change does occur, the company is able to quickly adjust its marketing and production strategies in line with the plan. Its marketing efforts would be redirected towards those markets where it has become more competitive. Its production sourcing and input mix could also be shifted into the direction that would be most cost-effective under the circumstances.

Because the range of possible scenarios is infinite the cost of gathering information is immense. Consequently the company should concentrate on those situations that have a high probability of occurring.

Success in business requires the company to react to changes as quickly as possible. Companies have to be flexible to gain the edge over their competitors; this flexibility can take the form of flexible manufacturing systems which permit faster production response times to the shifting market demand. But the greatest boost to competitiveness comes from reducing the time it takes to introduce new and improved products to the market. If a company is prepared for changes in the exchange rate then such changes may be used as opportunities to get ahead of its less flexible competitors. The ability of companies to adjust to changing markets is an important strategic asset.

SUMMARY

The economic conditions of the past decade have created severe exchange rate fluctuations despite the efforts of monetary authorities to counter these dramatic changes. This has necessitated constant monitoring of exchange rates by companies with international operations, and financial managers must ascertain whether transaction, translation or economic exposure is most relevant to their organizations. We have seen that transaction exposure involves a realized gain or loss, whereas translation exposure consists of potential effects on published statements but does not actually represent a realized cash flow. Economic exposure, like transaction exposure, has important implications for realized cash flow—in this case we are concerned with future cash flows.

The goal of the financial manager or treasury department should be to actively deal with transaction exposure and to do so in a manner which is both effective and efficient, paying particular attention to cost. Economic exposure and transaction exposure have possible realizable negative effects on cash flow, and therefore must be appropriately dealt with. We cannot recommend the same strategy for translation exposure unless it is discovered that the possible negative impact of translation risk is so great that action is imperative.

It has been illustrated in this chapter that forward contracts are by no means the only possible way of hedging against foreign exchange risk. It is the role of the financial manager to choose which technique is most appropriate for each situation.

The ideal strategy for management of risk takes into consideration the explicit and implicit costs of each technique and then makes a comparison between the technique and the exposed risk position of the company, while also making predictions about the possible movements of exchange rates in the future.

It is impossible to simultaneously deal with all types of foreign exchange exposure, and to totally eliminate all exposure. In most circumstances foreign exchange exposure management can be most efficiently undertaken through a centralized treasury function.

REFERENCE

Abdullah, F. A. (1987) *Financial Management for the Multinational Firm*, Prentice-Hall, Englewood Cliffs, New Jersey.

ADDITIONAL READING

Buckley, A. (1976) *Multinational Finance*, 2nd edition, Prentice-Hall, Hemel Hempstead, UK.
Demirag, I. and D. Woodward (1989) 'Playing the market with swaps', *Career Accountant*, December.
Handjinicolau, Wallich, and Siegel (1984) 'Currency and Interest Rate Swaps', World Bank.
Prindl, A. (1976) *Foreign Exchange Risk*, Wiley, Chichester, England.
Rodriguez, R. M. and E. E. Carter (1984) *International Financial Management*, 3rd edition, Prentice-Hall, Englewood Cliffs, New Jersey.
Ross, D. (1988) 'Managing foreign exchange: economic exposure', *Accountancy*, March.
Ross, D. (1988) 'Managing foreign exchange: a balance of variables', *Accountancy*, April.
Shapiro, A. C. (1989) *Multinational Financial Management*, 3rd edition, Allyn and Bacon, Newton, Mass.

CASE STUDY

Intrade plc

On 1 June, Intrade purchased goods from West Germany and the USA. Payment for the German goods, costing DM850,000 is due in six months, while the payment of US$320,000 for the American goods is due in three months' time.

Market information

Exchange rates	$/£	DM/£
Spot	1.4480 – 10	3.8400 – 40
3 months forward	1.4842 – 72	3.7440 – 85
6 months forward	1.5204 – 35	3.6480 – 20

Interest rates	Borrowing	Lending
UK clearing bank	9%	5%
Eurodollar 6 months	14%	9%
Eurodollar 3 months	13.5%	8.5%
Deutschbank DM rate	7%	4%

Futures market	$/£	$/DM
Contract size	£25,000	DM125,000
June	1.4350	0.3768
September	1.4820	0.3964
December	1.5170	0.4155

There are five possible policies that Intrade might consider; these are outlined below. The use of futures contracts is explained fully in Chapter 9.

1. **Do nothing.** Intrade would then be exposed to foreign exchange risk. However, the risk will be partially compensating because the dollar is at a discount and the Deutschmark is at a premium to the pound. Additionally, the transactions are of a similar size. If the forward rates are good predictors of the future spot rate, then the loss due to exchange risk will only be small.
2. **Hedge on forward market.** To consider this alternative, we must first work out the relevant cross rates.

$$\text{For US\$/DM, Spot bank's selling rate } \frac{1.4480}{3.8440} = 0.3767$$

$$\text{Spot bank's buying rate } \frac{1.4510}{3.8400} = 0.3779$$

$$\text{6 month forward bank's selling rate } \frac{1.5204}{3.6520} = 0.4163$$

$$\text{6 month forward bank's buying rate } \frac{1.5235}{3.6480} = 0.4176$$

The spot costs of the payments are DM850,000 = £221,354
and US$320,000 = £220,994

If the German payment is covered forward, the cost becomes:

$$\text{DM850,000}/3.6480 = £233,004$$

Similarly, the cost of the US payment would be:

$$US\$320,000/1.4842 = £215,604$$

(Loss)/Gain from hedging:

German payment	(£11,650)
US payment	£5,390
Overall loss	(£6,260)

The cost of hedging both payments is £6,260.

3. **Money market.** This requires the manipulation of funds to try to minimize the sterling equivalents of the payments due. For the German payment, we would need to invest enough today to have DM850,000 in six months' time. The required amount would be:

$$\frac{850,000}{1.02} = DM833,333$$

The interest rate of 2 per cent is half the annual rate because the money is invested for only six months.

At the spot rate this would require Intrade to borrow £217,014 at 9 per cent for six months. In six months' time Intrade will have to repay £217,014 × 1.045 = £226,780.

The cost of this is therefore:

$$£226,780 - £221,354 = £5,426$$

For the US payment, it is better to invest in Germany for three months because of the currency movements.

The amount to borrow is £208,407. This should be converted to DM at the spot rate, giving DM800,283.

Investing for three months at 4 per cent gives DM808,286.

Next, we require the three-month forward cross-rates of US$/DM. These are:

Bank's selling rate $\dfrac{1.4842}{3.7485} = 0.3959$

Bank's buying rate $\dfrac{1.4872}{3.7440} = 0.3972$

Therefore we could receive from the German bank:

$$DM808,286 × 0.3959 = US\$320,000$$

This, of course, is the amount required for payment.

The cost of this is the charge for borrowing £208,407 in the UK: £208,407 × 1.0225 = £213,096. Compared with the cost at spot, this is a gain of £7,898.

Overall, the money market alternative gives the following figures:

Loss on German payment	(£5,426)
Gain on US payment	£7,898
Overall gain	£2,472

4. **Leading or lagging the payments.** It will be possible to lead the German payment, but to replace the funds would cost a minimum of 9 per cent. The total cost would be £221,354 × 1.045 = £231,315.

The net cost is £231,315 − £221,354 = £9,961.

To lag the US payment would mean a large saving. Over three months the lagged cost would be:

$$\frac{320,000}{1.5204} = £210,471$$

The gain would be £220,994 − £210,471 = £10,523.

Overall, the gain would be £562. However, there is no information on lagging the US payment, and it is very unlikely that this would be agreed to.

5. **Futures** (for further details of futures see Chapter 9)   For the German payment, there is no available £/DM future contract, so both the £/$ and the DM/$ contracts need to be used.

For the payment of DM850,000, seven contracts will be needed at DM125,000 each, totalling DM875,000. In addition, 10 £/$ contracts will be required, totalling £250,000.

Buy 7 December DM contracts at US$0.4155/DM

Sell 10 December £ contracts at US$1.5170/£

This gives DM875,000 × 0.4155 = US$363,563, with DM25,000 left spare. This can be converted back to sterling at the forward rate, yielding £6,846.

Sale of the £ contracts gives £250,000 × 1.5170 = US$379,250. From the above, we need US$363,563, so US$15,687 is surplus and can be converted to £10,297.

The total cost is therefore:

£250,000 − £6,846 − £10,297 = £232,857.

This is marginally better than using the forward market, but worse than the money market.

For the US payment, Intrade will need nine September contracts at US$1.4820/£.

This gives £225,000 × 1.4820 = US$333,450.

The surplus will be US$13,450, which can be converted back to sterling at the three-month forward rate of US$1.4872/£ to give £9,044.

Thus the net cost is £225,000 − £9,044 = £215,956.

In comparison with the forward hedging and the money market, this is slightly more expensive.

The best solution for Intrade would appear to be to use the money markets to prepare for the two payments they will have to make.

QUESTIONS

1. **Runswick Ltd**

(a) Explain what is meant by the terms foreign exchange translation exposure, transactions exposure and economic exposure.

What is the significance of these different types of exposure to the financial manager?

(8 marks)

(b) Runswick Ltd is an importer of clock mechanisms from Switzerland. The company has contracted to purchase 3,000 mechanisms at a unit price of 18 Swiss francs. Three months' credit is allowed before payment is due.

Runswick currently has no surplus cash, but can borrow short term at 2% above bank base rate or invest short term at 2% below bank base rate in either the United Kingdom or Switzerland.

Exchange Rates

	Swiss francs/£
Spot	2.97–2.99
1 month forward	2.5–1.5 premium
3 months forward	4.5–3.5 premium

(The premium relates to the Swiss franc.)

Current Bank Base Rates

Switzerland	6% per year
United Kingdom	10% per year

Required:

 (i) Explain and illustrate three policies that Runswick Ltd might adopt with respect to the foreign exchange exposure of this transaction. Recommend which policy the company should adopt. Calculations should be included wherever relevant. Assume that interest rates will not change during the next three months.

(9 marks)

(ii) If the Swiss supplier were to offer 2.5% discount on the purchase price for payment within one month, evaluate whether you would alter your recommendation in (i) above.

(5 marks)

(c) If annual inflation levels are currently at 2% in Switzerland and 6% in the United Kingdom, and the levels move during the next year to 3% in Switzerland and 9% in the United Kingdom, what effect are these changes in inflation likely to have on the relative value of the Swiss franc and the pound?

(3 marks)
(25 marks)
ACCA, 3.2, June 1986

Answer

(a) **Translation exposure** (often known as accounting exposure)

Translation exposure is the result of the requirement for multinational companies to consolidate the activities of their foreign subsidiaries in a group-wide set of financial statements according to predetermined accounting rules. Assets, liabilities, revenues and expenses must be translated and restated in terms of a company's home currency. Translation exposure reflects the impact of a change in value of a company's foreign currency denominated assets and liabilities caused by a change in exchange rates.

There are four major translation methods, which take a different view on which assets and liabilities are exposed to foreign exchange risk, and when foreign exchange gains and losses should be recognized. The main methods are current–non-current, monetary–non-monetary, temporal, and current rate. The current rate (also known as the closing rate) method is the one recommended for use in the United Kingdom in most circumstances.

Transaction exposure

This exposure is the result of foreign exchange gains or losses when settlement of foreign currency denominated contracts occurs. These contracts include normal trading transactions on credit terms, relating to both exports and imports terms, borrowing or lending funds denominated in a foreign currency, or a company having a foreign exchange contract which has yet to be fulfilled. Transaction exposure is a short-term component of economic exposure.

Economic exposure

Economic exposure is the change in the value of a company, measured by the net present value of the company's expected after-tax cash flows, caused by unexpected changes in exchange rates (expected changes in exchange rates should already be reflected in estimates of the company's future cash flows and therefore the company's value). Unexpected currency fluctuations can affect the size and risk of future cash flows.

If the financial manager believes that foreign exchange exposures will have a significant effect on the company, there are a number of hedging strategies that might be adopted.

Translation exposure may result in large changes in reported earnings, but this is an accounting reporting effect and may not have any impact on the actual cash flows of the company. If efficient capital markets exist in which share prices fully reflect all relevant information, translation gains and losses, which do not involve cash flows, should have no impact on share price. Hedging against translation exposure is therefore not widely advocated.

Any hedging that is undertaken should be designed to protect against the effect of exchange rate changes on expected cash flows, hence transaction and economic exposure management should be of most significance to the financial manager.

(b) (i) There are at least five possible policies that Runswick might adopt.

1. **Take no action**

In this case the company is accepting the foreign exchange risk during the credit period and will have to buy Swiss francs at whatever spot rate exists on the foreign exchange market in three months' time. This rate may be favourable or unfavourable.

2. **Forward foreign exchange market hedge**

This involves contracting now, normally through a bank, to buy Swiss francs at a known price for delivery at an agreed date in the future. Payment for the Swiss francs is made at the future date, not now.

The contract of 54,000 Swiss francs may be hedged by buying Swiss francs three months forward at an exchange rate of 2.925 SF/£ (i.e. 2.970–0.045).

$$\text{The cost will be } \frac{54,000}{2.925} = £18,462$$

If the Swiss franc does not strengthen as much as was expected in forward rate, the company will have made an opportunity loss. If the Swiss franc strengthens more than was expected, the company will make an opportunity gain.

3. **Lead payment**

As the Swiss franc is strengthening relative to the pound, it might be beneficial if Runswick pays early for the goods rather than take the risk of having to pay a greater number of pounds on the due date.

If a lead payment is made now the cost will be:

$$\frac{54,000}{2.97} = £18,182$$

But this will have to be borrowed in order for payment to be made as the company has no spare cash. The overall cost over three months, including interest payments, will be:

$$£18,182 + £18,182 \times 12\% \times \frac{3}{12} = £18,727$$

4. Money market hedge

A money market hedge involves borrowing in one country, converting the funds borrowed at the spot rate into the currency in which payment is due, and investing it in the second country. The total receipts, principal plus interest, from the foreign currency investment will then be used to make payment for the goods.

Hence Runswick might:

Borrow £18,002 for 3 months at 12%

Convert to Swiss francs at 2.97 SF/£ = SF53,466

Invest SF53,466 for 3 months at 4% per year to receive a total of SF54,000 at the end of 3 months. Use this to make payment for the goods.

The total cost is $£18,002 + £18,002 \times 12\% \times \frac{3}{12} = £18,542$

5. Hedge using currency options or futures (see Chapter 9 for more details of options and futures).

On the basis of the above calculations, if the company takes any action to protect itself against the Swiss franc foreign exchange risk, the forward foreign exchange market hedge should be used as it is the lowest cost alternative.

(ii) The cost of the goods if the discount is taken will be SF52,650.

Forward market hedge

$$\frac{52,650}{2.945} = £17,878$$

Borrow £17,878 for 2 months at 12% giving a total cost of £18,235.

Lead payment

$$\frac{52,650}{2.97} = £17,727$$

Borrowing costs for 3 months

$$£17,727 \times 12\% \times \frac{3}{12} = £532$$

Overall cost is £17,727 + £532 = £18,259

Money market hedge

Borrow £17,668.4 for 3 months at 12%

Convert spot to SF at 2.97 = SF52,475

Invest for 1 month at 4% yielding a total of SF52,650. Use this to make payment for the goods.

The total cost is:

$$£17,668.4 + £17,688.4 \times 12\% \times \frac{3}{12} = £18,198$$

It is therefore beneficial for Runswick to take the discount.

The money market hedge is now the least cost alternative, with a total cost of £18,198.

(c) If the Swiss franc/£ exchange rate is currently in equilibrium according to the purchasing power parity theory, the value of the pound will fall by the interest differential between the two countries, i.e. by approximately 6% relative to the Swiss franc.

The depreciation of the pound is expected to be:

$$\frac{.09 - .03}{1.03} = 0.058 \text{ or } 5.8\%$$

As long as existing exchange rates are in equilibrium the current inflation levels should already be fully reflected in the current exchange rate.

2. Oxlake plc

Oxlake plc has export orders from a company in Singapore for 250,000 china cups, and from a company in Indonesia for 100,000 china cups. The unit variable cost to Oxlake of producing china cups is 55 pence, and unit sales price to Singapore is Singapore $2.862, and to Indonesia 2,246 rupiahs. Both orders are subject to credit terms of 60 days, and are payable in the currency of the importers. Past experience suggests that there is a 50% chance of the customer in Singapore paying 30 days late. The Indonesian customer has offered Oxlake the alternative of being paid US$125,000 in three months' time instead of payment in the Indonesian currency. The Indonesian currency is forecast by Oxlake's bank to depreciate in value during the next year by 30% (from an Indonesian viewpoint) relative to the $US.

Whenever appropriate Oxlake uses option forward foreign exchange contracts.

	Foreign exchange rates (mid rates)		
	$Singapore/$US	$US/£	Rupiahs/£
Spot	2.1378	1.4875	2,481
1 month forward	2.1132	1.4963	No forward
2 months forward	2.0964	1.5047	market
3 months forward	2.0915	1.5105	exists

Assume that in the United Kingdom any foreign currency holding must be immediately converted into pounds sterling.

	Money market rates (% per year)	
	Deposit	Borrowing
UK clearing bank	6	11
Singapore bank	4	7
Eurodollars	7.5	12
Indonesian bank	15	Not available
Eurosterling	6.5	10.5
US domestic bank	8	12.5

These interest rates are fixed for either immediate deposits or borrowing over a period of two or three months, but the rates are subject to future movement according to economic pressures.

Required:

(a) Using what you consider to be the most suitable way of protecting against foreign exchange risk, evaluate the sterling receipts that Oxlake can expect from its sales to Singapore and not to Indonesia, without taking any risks.

All contracts, including foreign exchange and money market contracts, may be assumed to be free from the risk of default. Transactions costs may be ignored.

(13 marks)

(b) If the Indonesian customer offered another form of payment to Oxlake, immediate payment in $US of the full amount owed in return for a 5% discount on the rupiah unit sales price, calculate whether Oxlake is likely to benefit from this form of payment.

(7 marks)

(c) Discuss the advantages and disadvantages to a company of invoicing an export sale in a foreign currency.

(5 marks)
(25 marks)
ACCA, 3.2, December 1987

Answer

(a) **Sales to Singapore**

Cross-rates	$Singapore/£
Spot	3.1800
1 month forward	3.1620
2 months forward	3.1544
3 months forward	3.1592

It may be seen that the $Singapore is expected to strengthen relative to the £ for most of the period.

Oxlake plc can hedge against foreign exchange risk on the forward market or the money market.

Forward markets

The suggested contract type is an option forward contract as the date of payment is uncertain and may be anytime between two and three months.

The cost of an option forward contract will be the least favourable rate during the period, in this case $S 3.1592/£.

Sales in Singapore are 250,000 × 2.862 = $S715,500

Oxlake can take an option forward contract to sell $715,500 between two and three months in the future.

$$\frac{\$S715,500}{3.1592} = £226,481$$

£226,481 will be received no matter when the payment is made (although Oxlake would naturally prefer to receive payment in two months as the receipts could be invested to yield extra income by the end of the third month).

Money markets

As the payment date is uncertain, a money market hedge will mean that Oxlake has to take the risk of borrowing and/or lending for an incorrect period, and possibly be subject to future borrowing and/or lending at unknown rates of interest which could change from the current rates. As this scenario involves risk it is rejected, as Oxlake has stated that it does not wish to take risk.

It is possible, however, to look at the worst case scenario, payment in three months' time.

Borrow $S703,194 for three months at seven per cent per year in Singapore. With interest, this will lead to repayment of $S715,500 in three months' time, which may be funded from the proceeds of the export transaction.

Convert $S703,194 to £ at the spot rate of $S3.18/£ = £221,130

Invest £221,130 for 3 months at 6.5% per year in Eurosterling to give a total of £224,724

This is less than the £ receipts for payment in three months using an option forward contract. (If payment is made in two months this will allow investment of $S to yield further income by the end of the third month.) Oxlake should use an option forward contract to protect its receipts, which will yield sterling receipts of £226,481.

Sales to Indonesia

Payment in rupiahs in two months' time will yield an unknown amount of pounds as there is no forward market. In order to eliminate risk, Oxlake must seek some form of currency hedge.

The forecast fall in the value of the rupiah relative to the US dollar is merely an estimate, and does not mean that the rupiah/US$ exchange rate in two months can be accurately forecast. Any form of payment in rupiahs will involve foreign exchange risk, which Oxlake does not wish to take. Payment in US$ must therefore be considered, specifically the payment of US$125,000 in three months' time.

Forward markets

If the forward market is used £ receipts will be:

$$\frac{\$125,000}{1.5105} = £82,754$$

Money markets

Borrow $121,359 for three months at 12% per year in the USA. This will lead to a repayment of US$125,000 in three months' time, which can be financed from the export receipts.

Convert $121,359 to £ at the spot rate of US$1.4875 to £ = £81,586

Invest £81,586 for three months at 6.5% per year in Eurosterling to yield a total of £82,912

As the money market hedge is cheaper than the forward market hedge, the use of the money market is the recommended alternative.

(b) The highest existing return after three months, without Oxlake taking any risk, is £82,912.

If immediate payment is made of the full amount owed less the 5% discount, 100,000 × 2.133.7 rupiahs in US$ this would yield:

$$\frac{213,370,000}{1,667.90} = \$127,927$$

$127,927 could be invested in a US domestic bank for 3 months at 8% per year and then converted to £, with gross proceeds of:

$$\$127,927 + \$127,927 \times \frac{8\%}{4} = \$130,486$$

$$\text{Converted to } \frac{\$130,486}{1.5105} = \pounds86,386$$

Alternatively, the dollars could be immediately converted to pounds and then invested in Eurosterling at 6.5% per year for three months to yield:

$$\frac{\$127,927}{1.4875} = \pounds86,002 + \pounds86,002 \times \frac{6.5\%}{4} = \pounds87,399$$

This is the highest return. This alternative will provide Oxlake with a significantly higher return than the money market hedge which yielded a return of £82,912.

(c) Advantages

1. An overseas buyer is protected from foreign exchange risk if invoiced in his own currency. This might make the overseas buyer more likely to purchase the goods, i.e. the method of invoicing can increase the attractiveness of the export package.
2. A foreign customer does not have to obtain foreign currency, access to which might be limited by government controls. Invoicing in the local currency means that an overseas buyer does not have to worry about such restrictions.
3. If sterling is at a discount relative to the foreign currency on the forward foreign exchange market, the exporter can sell any expected receipts forward and will receive more pounds than he would get at the current spot rate. This will increase expected profit for the exporter or may be passed on to an overseas buyer in the form of more competitive prices.

Disadvantages

1. The exporter must, of course, bear the foreign exchange risk.
2. When sterling is expected to rise in value relative to the foreign currency, the exporter is likely to receive less pounds than he could get at the spot exchange rate. This will reduce the profit margin on the sale.

EIGHT
SWAPS

INTRODUCTION

The volatility of interest rates and exchange rates during the 1970s and 1980s led to the development of many new financial instruments to assist in protecting against adverse rate movements. This chapter examines one of the most significant of these developments, swaps. Although the emphasis will be on hedging against exchange rate risk, interest rate and exchange rate risk management are often undertaken simultaneously; hence the chapter also includes discussion of the main interest rate risk management techniques.

SWAPS

In the past five years the fastest growing area in international capital markets has been that of the swap market. According to the International Swap Dealers Association, between 1982 and 1989 the US dollar swap market grew from an initial base of US$5 billion to an annual rate of US$1,000 billion. Estimates for 1993 suggest that the swap market might now be as large as US$5,000 billion, a phenomenal growth in one decade. Swaps are today one of the most important and flexible tools of corporate treasurers.

Confusion sometimes arises over the usage of the word 'swap' owing to the fact that there are two uses of the word in the financial markets. In the foreign exchange markets the term denotes a spot sale and forward purchase of currency, whereas in the capital markets it denotes the exchange of one stream of future cash flows for another stream of future cash flows with different characteristics. One company, for example, could agree to swap payments of fixed rate interest on an agreed sum for a fixed period for payments on a floating rate basis. Swaps offer many potential benefits to companies including:

- The ability to obtain cheaper finance than would be possible by borrowing directly in the relevant market.
- The opportunity to restructure the company's capital profile without physically redeeming debt or raising new debt. For example, the proportion of debt on which fixed and floating rate interest is paid can be altered without incurring expensive transactions costs associated with redemption or new issues.
- Access to markets in which it is impossible to borrow directly. For example, companies with relatively low credit ratings might not be able to borrow directly in some fixed rate markets, but can arrange fixed rate debt servicing through swaps. In addition, some governments still

impose restrictions on direct international capital movements.

- Long-term hedging. Swaps can be arranged for periods of up to 10 years.
- Hedging against foreign exchange risk. Currency swaps are especially useful in less developed countries with volatile exchange rates and exchange controls.

There are two basic types of swaps:

1. Currency swaps: which include both fixed rate currency swaps and currency coupon swaps or fixed rate to floating rate swaps
2. Interest rate swaps

Many variations on these two types of swap have been developed to meet the needs of individual companies.

Currency swaps

Origins of the currency swap The earliest currency swaps evolved from the back-to-back and parallel loans of the 1960s and early 1970s. Parallel loans were a means of avoiding exchange controls. A UK company, for example, might have wished to invest in Bolivia, but was prevented from doing so by the existence of exchange controls. To avoid this problem the UK company could have lent pounds to the UK-based subsidiary of a Bolivian company, while the Bolivian company lent pesos to the Bolivia-based subsidiary of the UK company. At the end of an agreed period, usually several years, the loans would be paid back in the local currency, therefore locking in the exchange rate that existed at the time of the initial agreement. Interest would be payable according to the prevailing level of interest rates in the two countries. Back-to-back loans could be made directly between companies in different countries, with funds being transferred internationally if no exchange controls existed. However, both types of loan required a counterparty to be found, which could prove difficult and involved considerable risk. If one of the parties failed, the remaining going concern would have to repay the loan, but would only be ranked as an unsecured creditor of the failed company and might receive no repayment. Furthermore, these loans were included as assets and liabilities on the balance sheet, and directly affected financial ratios.

The currency swap was devised to overcome these disadvantages by replacing two loan agreements by one sale and purchase of currency agreement which eliminates any obligation of loan repayment on default and can be an off-balance sheet transaction. Currency swaps are inherently less complicated than the old parallel and back-to-back loans and are favoured by managers involved in off-balance sheet finance (since an exchange of principal is not essential).

What is a currency swap? A currency swap is a contract between two parties to exchange payments denominated in one currency for payments denominated in another. There are two main types of currency swap: fixed/fixed and fixed/floating swaps (currency coupon swaps).

Fixed/fixed currency swaps In a fixed/fixed currency swap one party exchanges fixed interest payments in one currency for a fixed rate interest payment in another currency. This process can be broken down into three stages:

1. Initial exchange of principal (either a notional or a physical exchange, often at the spot rate. This establishes a reference point for calculating interest payments)

2. Exchange of interest (this occurs on agreed dates at a fixed rate based upon the amount of outstanding principal)
3. Re-exchange of principal (the re-exchange rate is mutually agreed upon before the commencement of the swap. This enables the party and counterparties to re-exchange the physical or notional principal on the maturity date of the swap). The principal is therefore fully hedged with the re-exchange at the same rate as the original physical or notional swap

However, foreign currency interest payments forming part of the swap are not hedged, and unless the companies engaged in the swap expect to generate some cash flows in the foreign currency concerned it is wise to consider hedging this foreign currency interest rate exposure through the forward market or other hedging strategy.

Examples of fixed/fixed currency swaps and debt equity swap
Example 1 Multinvest plc
Multinvest plc, a UK company, wishes to hedge a one-year foreign exchange risk on an investment in Chile. The company has been offered a currency swap by a Chilean bank as a possible alternative to conventional hedging. The foreign investment is for 800 million escudos and is expected to yield an after-tax return of 35 per cent for the year.

The bank has offered a currency swap at the rate of 22 escudos/£, with the bank making interest payments of 4 per cent to the UK company in pounds.

The current spot rates are:

$$28.000 \text{ escudos}/£$$
$$1.51600 \text{ US dollars}/£$$
$$18.46965 \text{ escudos}/US\$$$

Interest rates are:

	Borrowing	Lending
UK	15	12
Chile	N/A	25

As another alternative the bank suggests a debt equity swap (discussed earlier in Chapter 3), buying Chilean loans on the secondary market and redeeming these loans through an intermediary for escudos. The loans denominated in US dollars are presented to the Chilean Central Bank. Chilean debt is selling at 70 cents on the dollar face value, and the Chilean Central Bank will pay 92 cents on the dollar. The Chilean bank currently charges an application fee of 0.25 per cent to discourage casual proposals.

Possible scenarios
1. No hedging
If no hedging occurs, the investment will require:

$$800 \text{ million escudos at } 28 \text{ escudos}/£ = £28,571,429$$

If financed by UK borrowing, the interest cost is:

$$£28,571,429 \text{ at } 15\% = £4,285,714$$

2. Currency swap
If the currency swap is used:

$$800 \text{ million escudos at } 22 \text{ escudos}/\text{£} = \text{£}36{,}363{,}636$$

If financed by UK borrowing the interest cost is:

$$\text{£}36{,}363{,}636 \text{ at } 15\% = \text{£}5{,}454{,}545$$

Interest received is:

$$\text{£}36{,}363{,}636 \text{ at } 4\% = \text{£}1{,}454{,}545$$

Total cost £4,000,000

This is a gain over not hedging of £285,714.

3. Debt equity swap
If the debt equity swap is used:

$$800 \text{ million escudos at } 18.46965 \text{ escudos}/\text{US\$} = \text{US\$}43{,}314{,}302$$

Therefore, face value of loans purchased on the secondary market at a redemption value of 92 cents/US\$ = US\$47,080,763
Loan required + 0.25 % charged by Central Bank = US\$47,198,465
Discounted loan face value of US\$47,198,465 at 70 % = US\$33,038,926
Value of investment in £ at 1.516 dollars/£ = £21,793,487
If financed by UK borrowing, the interest cost is:
£21,793,487 at 15% = £3,269,023
   This is a gain over not hedging of £1,016,691.
   In the light of these calculations, on this occasion Multinvest plc is likely to undertake a debt equity swap.
   Currency swaps may be arranged for much longer periods than one year, and may relate to both existing and new debt obligations.

Example 2 Growalot plc
Growalot plc is a UK-based multinational company with an existing 100 million Swiss franc 10 per cent fixed rate bond issue. The bond is due to be repaid in a lump sum maturity in five years' time, and interest is paid annually. The company is worried about a possible appreciation in the value of the Swiss franc relative to the pound, and would like to have sterling interest rate commitments, not Swiss franc.
   Maxicorp plc wishes to undertake capital investment in Switzerland and establish a subsidiary, Minicorp SA. Maxicorp is not a large multinational company, and does not have a good enough credit rating to borrow in the Swiss domestic bond market. It would like to borrow fixed rate in Swiss francs, and would service the interest on such borrowing with cash flows from its Swiss subsidiary.
   How could a swap be arranged?
   The first stage is to establish the present value of the Swiss franc obligations of Growalot. (For those not familiar with present values, they are discussed in Chapter 12.) This may be estimated as:

Five annual interest payments of 10 million Swiss francs.
Using present value of annuity tables and a discount rate of 10% (the Swiss franc interest rate), the present value of the Swiss franc obligation is:

Annual interest	10 million × 3.791 = 37.91
Lump sum repayment of 100 million Swiss francs in five years' time	100 × 0.621 = 62.10
	———
Present value of interest and principal payments	100.01

Assuming a current spot rate of SF2.25 /£ the present value of the Swiss franc obligations is a sterling equivalent of £44.449 million.

In order for the swap to be agreed, a series of sterling cash flows of the same present value must be constructed. In this case the discount rate will be the UK interest rate, which will be assumed to be 14 per cent.

A series of UK sterling cash flows of equivalent present value will be a loan of the same magnitude, £44.449 million, with annual interest payments of £44.449 million × 14% = £6,222,860. The swap will thus involve the following cash flows.

Growalot will pay to Maxicorp each year for five years, interest of £6,222,860, which Maxicorp will use to service the interest payments on a new loan of £44.449 million which it will have to take out. Growalot has swapped from Swiss franc to sterling fixed rate interest payments.

Maxicorp will pay to Growalot interest of 10 million Swiss francs per year for five years, which Growalot will use to service the interest on its Swiss franc loan. The £44.449 million borrowed by Maxicorp is likely to be converted at spot into Swiss francs and used for establishing the subsidiary, Minicorp SA, in Switzerland.

At the end of the five-year period the principal of the swap (which was a notional swap at the outset) will be swapped at the rate of SF2.25/£. The principal is thus protected from any exchange rate movement during the five-year period. Growalot will use the 100 million Swiss francs to repay the bullet maturity of its loan, and Maxicorp will use the £44.449 million to repay its loan. Maxicorp might need to seek further financing at this time.

In this example the swaps have effectively been used to hedge against foreign exchange risk, and to gain access to a form of finance that would not otherwise have been available. Some arbitrage gains on the interest payments might also be possible. Examples of arbitrage gains through swaps are given later in this chapter.

Fixed to floating rate currency swap This is also known as the currency coupon or cross-currency interest rate swap. This is a combination of interest rate and currency swaps. As with a fixed/fixed currency swap, this can be broken down into the same three stages of initial exchange of principal, exchange of interest and re-exchange of principal. However, here one or both of the payments are on a floating basis, e.g. 10 basis points above LIBOR. A basis point is 0.01 per cent. LIBOR is the London Inter-Bank Offer Rate.

Example of a fixed to floating rate currency swap International Business Systems (IBS) has a competitive advantage in the US fixed rate bond market due to its AAA credit rating, but prefers to use LIBOR funds to match its floating assets. The Mexton Group has a competitive advantage in the Deutschmark floating rate banking market.

	US fixed rate bonds	*DM floating*
IBS	10%	LIBOR + 0.3%
Mexton Group	11.75%	LIBOR + 0.75%
	———	———
Difference	1.75%	0.45%
	———	———

The difference shows the total gain (ignoring transactions costs) which is available from the swap transaction, in this case 1.75–0.45 or 1.30 per cent.

Each party enters into a separate swap agreement with Chase Manhattan, an intermediary bank. The Mexton Group's fixed payments and IBS's payments are determined by the intermediary bank, and each includes a 25 basis point handling charge. The Mexton group actually borrows from the German market at LIBOR + 0.75 and pays Chase Manhattan a fixed rate of 10.9 per cent in return for receiving LIBOR + 0.3 basis points. IBS borrows from the US bond market at a fixed rate of 10 per cent and pays Chase Manhattan LIBOR + 0.55 in return for fixed payments of 10.65 per cent.

Swap transaction

	IBS	Chase MH	Mexton
Interest paid (on actual borrowing for IBS and Mexton)	(10.00)		(LIBOR + 0.75)
Swap transactions			
Interest (paid) or received	(LIBOR + 0.55)	LIBOR + 0.55	
	10.65	(10.65)	
		(LIBOR + 0.30)	LIBOR + 0.30
		10.90	(10.90)
Overall cost	LIBOR − 0.10		11.35
Saving from swap (relative to borrowing directly)	0.40		0.40
Benefit to Chase Manhattan		0.50	

The total arbitrage saving from the swap transaction of 1.30 per cent has been split 0.4 per cent each to IBS and Mexton Group and 0.50 per cent to Chase Manhattan.

In practice banks often arrange multi-legged swaps with three or more counterparties, since it is impossible to directly match the requirements of two companies. These are sometimes known as multi-legged cocktail swaps.

The currency swap market enables a company possessing a comparative market advantage to raise funds and swap the loan or repayment schedule with another company in a preferred currency. The most common reason for the existence of a comparative advantage is a difference in the perception of the borrower's credit rating in the different markets. Companies are given credit ratings subject to a number of tangible and intangible criteria.

The best known example of perceived credit differences is on the Swiss franc market. Swiss investors have a preference for household names; this sometimes means that a well known name is more important than the company's formal credit rating. On some occasions A-rated companies have been able to achieve terms on the Swiss market normally only available to AA-rated companies; this has been achieved by issuing bonds on the Swiss franc market and then swapping these liabilities for fixed interest bearing securities on the US market. In general, the counterparties to these transactions were either sovereign states or super-national corporations wishing to maintain in their portfolios a currency spread covering a wide range of different currencies.

Government intervention on the financial markets or changes in fiscal policy (i.e. changes in tax laws) will also have an effect on a borrower's international credit standing in the markets by changing investors' perceptions of risk.

The reasons for a company wishing to raise currency in a market other than the one in which it has a comparative advantage can be split into two main areas:

1. Exploiting market imperfections
2. Hedging income streams

Exploiting market imperfections   Currency swaps provide an important vehicle for circumventing market imperfections. If they are arranged without any initial exchange of principal they constitute an off-balance sheet item which can be used to arbitrage between regulatory regimes, exchange controls or accounting supervisory controls.

Hedging income streams   Currency swaps can be used to hedge existing currency streams or to make it possible for a company to take a speculative position on exchange rates. In practice companies normally use currency swaps to reduce exposure on an existing currency position, e.g. a debt obligation in a foreign currency. Swaps enable a company to do this by effectively extending the existing forward exchange rates beyond what is usually available.

Market saturation   Let us return to the previous example on the Swiss franc swap market. As well as allowing a company to exploit market imperfections, currency swaps allow companies to avoid a potential market saturation. One of the counterparties in the Swiss transactions has been the International Bank for Research and Development (IBRD), which felt that a swap was preferable to raising new finance directly in the Swiss market. While preferring the Swiss franc with its low interest rate, the IBRD feared that its own issues of securities in the Swiss bond market would reach saturation point. When this happens, due to the large borrowing requirements of a single borrower in any one market, there is an increase in the cost of borrowing which may lead to a reduction in the market price and a capital loss for existing investors. This results in a loss of confidence in the borrower's securities.

The currency swap market   It is difficult to estimate the extent of activity in today's currency swap market, since banks have no obligation to report currency swaps to their shareholders or to regulatory bodies. Currency swaps are believed to represent about 25 per cent of the total swap market. At the end of 1990 outstanding currency swaps exceeded US$500 billion.

The interest rate swap market

The interest rate swap market evolved from the currency swap market, and has grown dramatically since 1982. Prior to the development of this market the main instruments available to borrowers for financing debt were :

1. Long-term fixed rate debt
2. Long-term floating rate debt
3. Short-term debt

The introduction of swaps to this market meant that previously unavailable opportunities were made available to companies with appropriate credit ratings.

Interest rate swaps are much more important in terms of trading volume than currency swaps.

Measurement of the interest rate swap market is still very problematic. Conventionally the market adds together the total principal amounts, ignoring the fact that no principal is actually transferred. To add to the difficulties, the problem of double counting occurs all the time within the inter-bank section of the market, since the swap is shown in the books of both banks.

The estimate for new interest rate swaps entered into in 1991 is approximately US$800 billion with outstanding swaps at the end of 1991 totalling US$3,160 billion.

What is an interest rate swap?   An interest rate swap is a contract between two counterparties to exchange one stream of interest rate payments for another. Unlike currency swaps, interest rate swaps involve only an exchange of interest rate streams, not an exchange of principal. Swaps may be fixed/floating or floating/floating, and exist in many different forms; the most common form of swap is the 'plain vanilla' swap between fixed and floating rates. Borrowers who have a high credit rating will have a cost advantage over companies with a lower credit rating in both the fixed rate and the variable rate market, but companies with lower credit ratings, on the other hand, may have a comparative advantage in one of the markets. The company with the comparative advantage in the fixed rate market borrows in that market and swaps the interest rate stream for floating rate interest payments with a counterparty who has physically borrowed in the floating rate market. The gain from the swap is divided between both parties, making both better off.

Example of an interest rate swap   International Oil plc is interested in raising £100 million in order to carry out further oil exploration. International oil is an AA-rated company and, as such, can borrow for six months at a fixed rate of 12 per cent or a floating rate of LIBOR + 30 basis points.

London Property Ltd has a lower credit rating, and wishes to raise a similar sum for investment in the housing market. London Property can only borrow at a fixed interest rate of 14 per cent and a floating rate of LIBOR + 80 basis points.

Security Pacific Bank has been recommended as the best continuous swap managers and the keenest on prices. For arranging a swap, a fee of £50,000 is payable by each party.

	International Oil	*London Property*	*Comparative advantage*
Fixed rate	12%	14%	2%
Floating rate	LIBOR + 0.3%	LIBOR + 0.8%	0.5%

Therefore, it is better for International Oil to borrow at the fixed rate and for London Property to borrow at a floating rate.

If the swap transaction takes place and the benefits from this arbitrage are divided between each partner equally, the swap transaction could be as follows:

1. International Oil borrows at the fixed rate of 12 per cent.
2. London Property borrows at the floating rate of LIBOR + 80 basis points.
3. International Oil pays London Property LIBOR + 80 basis points.
4. London Property pays International Oil fixed rate of 13.25 per cent.

	International Oil	*London Property*
Interest paid	(12%)	LIBOR + (0.8%)
Interest received	13.25%	LIBOR + 0.8%
Net cost or benefit	1.25%	0%
Paid in swap	LIBOR + 0.8%	13.25%
Overall cost (paid in swap—net benefit)	LIBOR − 0.45%	13.25%
Saving from undertaking swap	0.75%	0.75%
	LIBOR − 0.45%	13.25%
	0.75%	0.75%
	(LIBOR + 0.3% − LIBOR − 0.45%)	(14% − 13.25%)

An arbitrage saving of 0.75% on £100,000,000 = £750,000

Minus the arrangement fee of £50,000 = £700,000 for each of International Oil and London Property.

Warehousing Since 1982 the market for swaps has evolved from matching to warehousing, using swap houses and banking intermediaries.

A major problem of early swaps was that a counterparty had to be found before the swap could take place, but finding a suitable counterparty was not always possible. The growth of the swap markets was greatly facilitated by banks undertaking a warehousing function, whereby it is not necessary to immediately match counterparties. With warehousing the bank will arrange a swap with one party and then hedge the swap until a suitable counterparty can be found. For example:

Company A issues a 12 per cent fixed rate bond which is swapped into floating rate debt at a small margin over LIBOR. The bank now has an interest rate exposure which it hedges against by borrowing floating rate funds, the interest payments on which will be covered by payments from company A, and investing in fixed interest securities (e.g. gilts) of an exact amount and maturity to company A's fixed interest debt issue. The fixed interest income from this investment will be used to pay Company A under the swap agreement. Ideally interest costs and receipts from the bank's hedge will offset each other; in practice slight differences are likely to exist.

Some time later the bank might be approached by Company B, which wishes to undertake a floating to fixed rate swap of similar size and maturity to the swap arranged with Company A. A swap can then be arranged with the bank reversing its hedge. Naturally interest rates can change during the period that the bank is engaged in its warehousing operation, and if interest rates were to fall the bank might only be able to arrange a swap with Company B paying 10 per cent fixed to the bank rather than the 12 per cent fixed that the bank is currently paying to Company A. The bank will, however, be compensated for this interest rate differential by the rise in price of its fixed interest investments as the interest rate falls, which will yield a capital gain when the investments are sold.

Interest rate swaps are very flexible and permit the corporate financial manager to alter interest rate payments without redeeming the underlying debt. For example, Company A, which borrowed fixed rate at 12 per cent, and initially swapped to floating rate debt, could take out a further swap to revert to fixed rate debt and lock in the fixed rate financing cost at a lower level than the cost of the debt that was actually borrowed. If fixed rate debt interest rates fell to 10 per cent, Company A could swap its floating rate payments (agreed under the first swap with the bank) for fixed rate payments at 10 per cent. The effect of this is that the company locks in interest payments at 10 per cent rather than the 12 per cent rate at which the fixed rate debt was actually borrowed on the capital market.

Complex swaps and other variations

As the swap market has grown, a large number of new types of swap have been offered or proposed by the leading banks in this field. Owing to the complicated payment schedules associated with them there has also been a move away from the traditional pricing methods used by the market leaders in other fields. These more complicated swaps, some of which are very short-lived, will be discussed only briefly since most are simply variations on the swaps discussed above.

Amortizing swaps   These swaps are structured so that the payments are calculated by reference to an amortizing principal in a similar way to the structure of mortgage repayments. They may be used to hedge a stream of amortizing payments in a foreign currency.

Forward or deferred swaps   The interest payments on this type of swap are agreed today at a prearranged rate and become effective at some future date. This instrument is a means of locking into the implied future interest rates, and can be used as a future hedge. The forward swap's main advantage over the traditional forward market contract and currency futures contracts is that dates further ahead than one year in the future can be agreed, thus providing a means of extending the existing futures and forward markets.

Zero coupon swaps   With this style of swap either the principal or the counterparty's interest payments are compounded over the life of the swap, at an agreed swap interest rate, and all interest is paid at the maturity date. Since the interest payments are only met on the maturity of the swap the associated credit risk (owing to unsecured exposure) for the intermediary bank is potentially at its greatest with this type of swap. Because of this the intermediary party generally demands a greater margin and higher fee for handling such transactions.

Callable, puttable and extendable swaps   These are swaps where one party has the right to terminate the swap before its maturity date (callable or puttable), or to extend the period of the swap (extendable).

Swaptions (options on swaps)   Swaptions integrate swaps and options in one package, and give the purchaser of a swaption the right, but not the obligation, to enter into a forward swap on terms agreed today or to cancel the present agreement on a specific future date. As with options an upfront premium (fee) is payable. An example of a swaption is given in Chapter 9.

Basis swaps   Basis swaps or floating/floating swaps involve the exchange of floating rate interest streams from different sources where credit ratings might differ. For example, a basis swap could be between US floating rate debt and LIBOR, or commercial paper and LIBOR. Once again arbitrage gains are possible.

Asset swaps Asset swaps are concerned with swapping investments (assets) rather than liabilities, and offer the opportunity to convert an existing investment in a security to a different type of income. As the nature of the asset held is changed, a synthetic security is often said to be created. For example, a fixed rate dollar Eurobond issue may be combined with an interest swap to create a synthetic dollar floating rate note.

Risk in using swaps

The amount and type of risk borne by the various parties undertaking swap activity is dependent upon the parties' role in the agreement. Most swaps are arranged by financial intermediaries which have entered into offsetting contracts with two companies. Swap-associated risk can be broken down into four types, as follows:

1. Credit risk
2. Position risk
3. Spread risk
4. Transparency risk

Credit risk The principal party and the intermediary party are both exposed to this risk owing to the possibility that the counterparty to the swap will default. In addition, the intermediary carries extra risk because of the timing and frequency of differences in the payment regime. This unsecured credit exposure occurs due to the possibility of the counterparty defaulting after a payment has been made by the intermediary and before the counterparty's payment date is due. As a means of controlling this risk full investigations of each party's financial situation should be made before trading. The value of open transactions should be limited, and close attention should be paid to the profitability of customers' activities to provide early warning of possible difficulties.

Position risk This risk is borne by the principal party and the counterparty. Position risk can be either positive or negative, and arises from beneficial or adverse movements of the interest rate and associated exchange rate.

Position risk with swaps can be offset to a certain degree by the inclusion of a top-up clause in the swap transaction to maintain the value of the notional debt in proportion to the spot rate.

Spread risk Intermediary banks and trusts which still use the old portfolio matching technique for swap pricing, e.g. warehousing the swap until a matching swap is made and then undertaking a temporary hedge on the futures market, are exposed to this risk. Banks that do this face the risk that the spread between the swap and the hedge may change before a match is made.

Transparency risk This risk affects all three parties: the principal, the counterparty and the intermediary. For example, one party may raise funds in Swiss francs then swap them for US dollars, but the company's accounts still show a Swiss franc liability. As the company's swap activity increases, its true financial position ceases to be reflected in its accounts. This means that beneficial and adverse movements which are of direct relevance to its credit rating are no longer included.

The following example illustrates how currency swaps may be used.

You are advising your client, an international company which has developed a revolutionary watch design and is building a major factory in the USA. The company has no long-term credit rating but has a high short-term credit rating, and is able to issue US dollar commercial paper up to one year at the finest rates, despite a series of bitter legal actions by Swiss companies alleging patent infringement. These actions have delayed the agreed sale of its Swiss operations for SF110 million. Meanwhile, your client urgently needs to raise SF100 million to pay for new machinery available only from Switzerland, and the Swiss supplier refuses to give credit.

You are approached by a rapidly growing, well known but unrated UK travel company specializing in travel to and from Switzerland, which is currently seeking to raise fixed rate US dollars over five years in order to pay for new aircraft. Explain how a swap between this company and your client could be advantageous. What risks could be present in such a swap and how might they be reduced?

Suggested solution

The cheapest source of Swiss franc borrowings is probably the Swiss bond market. However, this is denied to your client because of its poor relations with the Swiss.

Nevertheless, your client needs to raise SF100 million urgently. It could simply borrow Swiss francs from a bank, but it would have no comparative advantage over other borrowers in doing so. Where the client does have a comparative advantage is in its ability to issue US dollar denominated commercial paper at the finest rates.

On the other hand, the UK travel company is well known in Switzerland, no doubt bringing business and tourism to the country and supplying travel facilities to the investment community. It may be reasonable to hope that the UK travel company could make a successful Swiss bond issue at a yield less than your client would have to pay if it borrows Swiss francs from a bank. However, the travel company wants to raise dollars, not Swiss francs.

The travel company thus has a comparative advantage in its ability to borrow fixed rate Swiss francs, while your client has a comparative advantage in its ability to borrow US dollars on a floating basis. There is therefore scope for a swap between the two to their mutual advantage.

Your client would issue US dollar commercial paper at the finest floating rates. The UK travel company would issue fixed rate Swiss franc bonds. The two companies would swap the proceeds and the obligations as shown in Figure 8.1, with the result that the cost of funds to each would be less than if it sought to borrow the currency it requires from a bank.

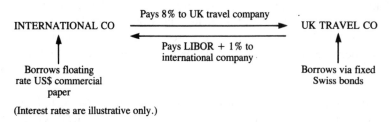

(Interest rates are illustrative only.)

Figure 8.1   Swap transactions

The main risk to the UK travel company is the interest rate risk on its floating rate dollar obligation. This could be eliminated by an interest rate swap with a third party. The third party would pay a floating rate on the nominal amount of the dollars in return for receiving a fixed rate from the UK travel company.

The more significant risk for your client would be the default risk of the UK travel company. The swap is required for five years, and the proceeds are to be used for aircraft which will probably depreciate in value; over such a period it is certainly not unknown for the fortunes of a travel company to be reversed. Default risk can be mitigated to the benefit of the party with the better credit rating by arranging swap terms such that in the event that one party goes into receivership, no amount which is otherwise due to that party by virtue of the swap agreement will be payable.

Exchange rate risk may affect both parties. The UK travel company will have a US dollar obligation, but its income may be denominated in other currencies. Your client will have a Swiss franc obligation, but it is seeking to sell its Swiss operations, and its future revenues are likely to be denominated mainly in other currencies. Foreign exchange risks can be reduced or eliminated by forward purchase of the required currencies, or by the purchase of caps or other options (see Chapter 9).

Further worked examples of swaps are provided in the Questions at the end of this chapter.

ADDITIONAL READING

Bank of England Quarterly Bulletin (1987) February.

Clifford Smith, W., Smithson, C. and Wakeman, L. (1986) 'The evolving market for swaps', *Midland Corporate Finance Journal*, No. 3, pp. 20, 26, 27.

Cooper, R. (1987) 'Swap houses switch to new values', *Euromoney*, January.

Demirag, I. and Woodward, D. (1989) 'Playing the market with swaps', *Career Accountant*, December.

Fierman, J. (1987) 'Fast bucks in latin loans', *Fortune Magazine*, August.

QUESTIONS

Oneup plc

Oneup plc can borrow for six months at a fixed interest rate of 10 per cent and at a floating rate of LIBOR + $\frac{3}{8}$ per cent.

Twodown plc has a lower credit rating and can only borrow at a fixed interest rate of 11.5% and a floating rate of LIBOR + 1 per cent.

Required:

Evaluate, showing relevant swap transactions, whether it is possible for both companies to benefit from a six-month interest rate swap on loans of £10 million.

Solution:

	Oneup	*Twodown*	*Relative advantage*	
Fixed rate	10%	11.5%	1.5%	i.e. 0.875%
Floating rate	LIBOR + $\frac{3}{8}$%	LIBOR + 1%	$\frac{5}{8}$%	Difference or 0.4375% each possible gain

Therefore, it is better for Oneup to borrow fixed rate and Twodown to borrow floating rate.

If a swap occurs and the arbitrage benefits are equally divided:

Oneup borrows fixed rate at 10%
Twodown borrows floating rate at LIBOR + 1%

Swap
Oneup pays Twodown floating rate interest at LIBOR + 1%
Twodown pays Oneup fixed rate interest at 11.0625%

Total costs

Oneup		Twodown	
	10% interest paid		LIBOR + 1% paid
	11.0625% interest received		LIBOR + 1% received
	1.0625% interest gained	Net cost	0%
	LIBOR + 1% paid	Interest paid	11.0625%
Overall cost	LIBOR − 0.0625	Overall cost	11.0625%
Arbitrage saving	0.4375%		0.4375%

(Other ways of achieving this saving are possible.)

An arbitrage saving of 0.4375 per cent on £10 million for six months is £21,875 for each company.

Even with an arrangement fee of £15,000 for each company it is possible for both companies to benefit from an interest rate swap.

Ventus plc

Ventus plc has been offered a currency swap by a bank in Paraguay in order to hedge against the foreign exchange risk of a short-term investment in Paraguay. The investment is for 8,000 million guarani, and it is expected to yield an after-tax return of 40 per cent during the year.

The bank has offered a currency swap at the rate of 1,200 guarani/£, with interest at 4 per cent payable to the UK company in pounds. The current spot rate is 1,598 guarani/£ (mid-rate).

Interest rates

	Borrowing	Lending
UK	12%	10%
Paraguay	Not available	25%

Required:
Estimate by how much the guarani would need to devalue relative to the pound before the currency swap became more attractive than not hedging. Explain whether you consider that the currency swap or not hedging is likely to be more beneficial to Ventus plc.

Solution:
If the swap is used:

8,000m guarani at the swap rate of 1,200/£ = £6,666,667

Interest payable on £6,666,667 at 12% in UK =	800,000	
Interest receivable at 4% =	266,667	
Net cost of swap during the year	533,333	

N.B. The 40 per cent return or 3,200 million guarani will be available at the end of year spot rate whether or not the swap takes place, and has been ignored.

If no hedge occurs, the investment requires 8,000 million guarani at 1,598/£ = £5,006,258
If finance by UK borrowing the interest cost is £5,006,258 at 12% = £600,750

The total cost of not hedging (interest cost + foreign exchange loss) must exceed £533,333 before the currency swap becomes more attractive.

Therefore, foreign exchange loss must be >£533,333 − £600,750 = (£67,417) or a currency gain

The currency swap is thus always more attractive even if the guarani does not devalue.

The appreciation required to produce this exchange gain is:

$$\frac{8,000 \text{ m G}}{X} = £5,006,258 - £67,417$$

$$X = 1,577G/£$$

This is a revaluation of approximately

$$\frac{1,577 - 1,598}{1,598} = 1.31\%$$

If interest rate differentials are reflected in future spot rates the one-year spot rate is estimated at:

$$\frac{.25 - .10}{1.10} = 13.64\% \text{ devaluation}$$

In this case the currency swap would be much more beneficial.

Bank A

Bank A, which wishes to build its reputation in the sterling interest rate swap market, believes a reduction in UK interest rates is imminent and that when this happens there will be a significant increase in demand by its corporate customers for fixed rate positions. Describe how, using the gilt and swap markets, Bank A could enter into a hedged position now which should improve its ability to compete for swap business later.

Bank B also believes that rates will soon fall, but Bank C believes rates will rise sharply before falling in the longer term, and Bank D believes that rates will remain unchanged. Discuss the likely willingness of each bank to be a counterparty in Bank A's hedge. To what extent and how might each bank hedge its own position as Bank A's counterparty?

At 9.00 a.m. Bank A agrees a two-year interest rate swap to commence the following day with a fixed rate of 10 per cent per annum (semi-annual) against six months LIBOR. At 11.00 a.m., following a government announcement, the two-year swap rate rises to 12 per cent per annum (semi-annual). Estimate the value of the swap, assuming the notional principal is £200 million.

Solution:

The rate at which a sterling interest rate swap is quoted is equal to the risk-free fixed rate of interest for a loan or investment of the same term, plus a demand-related spread reflecting the supply and demand of fixed and floating positions.

The risk-free fixed rate for a swap may be taken as the yield on gilts of a similar term. As Bank A believes there will be a fall in UK interest rates it must be unwilling itself to enter into unhedged fixed paying positions. However, it could hedge swaps in which it was the fixed paying counterparty by buying gilts of a value equal to the nominal value of the swaps, and of the same term. Say the risk-free rate is 12 per cent, then the yield on the gilts will be 12 per cent. If risk-free rates fall to, say 10 per cent, the price of the gilts will rise until their yield is 10 per cent.

Since Bank A believes there will be an increase in demand for fixed positions when rates fall, it must expect that there will be an increase in the spread. Thus, the margin over the gilt rate which Bank A, as a fixed rate payer, pays for its initial swap will be lower than the margin over gilts which it will hope to receive as a fixed rate receiver after interest rates fall.

If Bank A's expectations are realized, it will have entered into swaps as the fixed rate payer at, say, 12.5 per cent per annum, hedging by buying gilts yielding 12 per cent per annum (the demand-related margin being 0.5 per cent per annum). When rates fall, its gilts will be sold at a profit worth the equivalent of 2 per cent per annum over the remaining term of the gilts. With this profit, the cost of its fixed rate position is now only 10.5 per cent per annum. However, the spread will increase to, say, 0.75 per cent per annum. Bank A could therefore now enter into offsetting swaps with its corporate clients, receiving fixed rate at 10.75 per cent per annum, while the cost of its original swaps is only 10.5 per cent per annum. Thus, having the original swaps in place at a fixed cost hedged by gilts, it will not sell the gilts until it enters into the offsetting swaps.

Bank B believes that rates will fall, and should therefore be keen to be Bank A's original counterparty. Bank B may well be prepared to keep this position unhedged for the time being.

Bank C believes rates will rise sharply before falling again. It would therefore be reluctant to be Bank A's original counterparty unless it could hedge its own short-term position. This it might do by selling interest rate futures or by entering into forward rate agreements (FRAs) in which it would be the fixed rate payer.

Bank D believes rates will remain unchanged. The costs of hedging through purchase of gilts would not be compensated by prospective profits, and unless it had positions of its own which it could offset Bank D would probably see little benefit in becoming a counterparty in Bank A's hedge.

Analysis of £200 m notional swap
10% p.a. = 5% semi-annually
12% p.a. = 6% s.a. LIBOR is irrelevant

Year	Pay at 5% s.a. £m	Pay at 6% s.a. £m	Difference £m
0			
0.5	10	12	2
1	10	12	2
1.5	10	12	2
2	10	12	2

The NPV of the position may be estimated using present value of annuity tables.
Using a 6 per cent discount rate 3.465 x £2 million = £6.93 million

MBA plc

The treasurer of MBA plc obtains the sterling interest rate swaps quotes as follows:

Years	Semi-annual % p.a.
2	13.06–13.00
3	12.55–12.50
4	12.04–12.00
5	11.56–11.50

(a) Estimate the values to the fixed rate payer of the following interest rate swap positions, all fixed against six months LIBOR on a semi-annual basis:
   (i) A £20 million swap with three years to run fixed at 10 per cent per annum
  (ii) A £50 million swap with four years to run fixed at 14 per cent per annum
 (iii) A £100 million swap with five years to run fixed at 12 per cent per annum
(b) Estimate the payment due for each of the above swaps to or by the floating rate payer at the end of the period commencing today if six months' LIBOR was set at 11.00 a.m. at 14.5 per cent per annum and the period runs for 183 days.

Solution:

(a) (i)

Nominal principal £20,000,000

	Annual	Six months
Initial swap rate %	10	5
Replacement swap rate %	12.5	6.25

Fixed Payer

Years	Receive £	Pay £	Net £
0			
0.5	1,250,000	1,000,000	250,000
1	1,250,000	1,000,000	250,000
1.5	1,250,000	1,000,000	250,000
2	1,250,000	1,000,000	250,000
2.5	1,250,000	1,000,000	250,000
3	1,250,000	1,000,000	250,000

NPV at 6.25% per 6 months   £122,925

(ii)

Nominal principal £50,000,000

		Annual	Six months
Initial swap rate %		14	7
Replacement swap rate %		12	6

	Fixed payer		
Years	*Receive*	*Pay*	*Net*
	£	£	£
0			
0.5	3,000,000	3,500,000	− 500,000
1	3,000,000	3,500,000	− 500,000
1.5	3,000,000	3,500,000	− 500,000
2	3,000,000	3,500,000	− 500,000
2.5	3,000,000	3,500,000	− 500,000
3	3,000,000	3,500,000	− 500,000
3.5	3,000,000	3,500,000	− 500,000
4	3,000,000	3,500,000	− 500,000

NPV at 6% per 6 months   £ − 310,500

(iii)

Nominal principal £100,000,000

		Annual	Six months
Initial swap rate %		12.0	6.0
Replacement swap rate %		11.5	5.75

	Fixed payer		
Years	*Receive*	*Pay*	*Net*
	£	£	£
0			
0.5	5,750,000	6,000,000	− 250,000
1	5,750,000	6,000,000	− 250,000
1.5	5.750,000	6,000,000	− 250,000
2	5,750,000	6,000,000	− 250,000
2.5	5,750,000	6,000,000	− 250,000
3	5,750,000	6,000,000	− 250,000
3.5	5,750,000	6,000,000	− 250,000
4	5,750,000	6,000,000	− 250,000
4.5	5,750,000	6,000,000	− 250,000
5	5,750,000	6,000,000	− 250,000

NPV at 5.75% per 6 months   £ − 1,840,000

(b) Net payment due by floating rate payer:

For example, for swap 1 payment is £20m $\times$ 14.5% $\times$ $\dfrac{183}{365}$ = £1,453,973

Receipts are £20m $\times$ 10% $\times$ $\dfrac{183}{365}$ = £1,000,274

Floating payer

| | Receive | Pay | Net |
	£	£	£
Swap 1	1,002,740	1,453,973	− 451,233
Swap 2	3,509,589	3,634,932	− 125,342
Swap 3	6,016,438	7,269,863	− 1,253,425

The floating rate payer is suffering!

NINE

FUTURES AND OPTIONS

INTRODUCTION

After the collapse of the Bretton Woods fixed exchange rate system in 1971 there was a period of unprecedented volatility in both exchange rates and interest rates. Both companies and financial institutions needed better exchange rate and interest rate exposure management techniques in order to compensate for this increase in risk. The International Monetary Market (IMM), which is part of the Chicago Mercantile Exchange (CME), introduced financial futures in 1972 to allow companies to hedge against these risks. In the UK financial futures have been traded since 1982 when the London International Financial Futures and Options Exchange (LIFFE) opened.

Currency options were first traded in 1982 on the Philadelphia Stock Exchange (PHLX), which has since become the world's largest listed currency options market. This chapter examines how futures and options may be used by the financial manager to protect against both currency and interest rate risk, and illustrates some of the financial engineering techniques that are available to the corporate treasurer.

FINANCIAL FUTURES

A financial futures contract entails the delivery of a specified financial instrument on a specific date (the maturity date) for an agreed price, this price being fixed at the outset. If the futures contract runs to the maturity date the relevant financial instrument will be delivered and the purchase price paid. In practice physical delivery of financial instruments occurs with very few financial futures contracts; the vast majority are reversed prior to maturity by a purchase or sale of contracts which exactly offsets the original purchase or sale. Some contracts, such as stock exchange index futures, cannot be physically delivered. Financial futures may be traded on interest rates, currency rates and stock indexes, although LIFFE (London International Financial Futures and Options Exchange) no longer offers currency futures contracts.

The specifications of future contracts

When buying or selling a futures contract the terms of the contract are always specified in detail. These terms will include the price to be paid for the financial instrument (fixed today but with payment later), the amount and type of asset involved and the maturity date of the contract.

In addition, the contract sets a margin (sometimes called the 'initial' or 'original' margin), which is a sum (either cash or T-bills) that is paid in advance to demonstrate that each party has the funds to honour their side of the contract. The margin is typically between one and five per cent of the value of the underlying financial instrument. The contract may also limit the size of price changes that can occur within a single trading day. In the UK financial futures contracts are traded on LIFFE. The performance of every buyer and seller of futures on LIFFE is guaranteed by a central clearing house to which all of the margins are paid. Although contracts are traded between buyer and seller on the exchange floor, the obligation from the contract is not to each other, but to the central clearing house.

At the end of each trading day any profits or losses on a futures contract are calculated, and the parties involved in the contract must either pay the futures exchange's clearing house for any losses that have occurred or receive any profit. This process is known as 'marked to market' or 'daily resettlement', and is illustrated below.

An oil producer agrees to deliver 1,000,000 barrels of oil to an oil exporter, at US$20 a barrel, at some future date. The next day the price of oil futures falls to US$19.995 a barrel. The oil producer now has a profit on this sale of:

$$US\$(20.000 - 19.995) \times 1,000,000 = US\$5,000$$

The exchange's clearing house pays this US$5,000 to the oil producer. Thus after the first day the oil producer has realized a profit of US$5,000. The oil exporter is not so fortunate: the fall in the price of oil futures leaves him with a loss of US$5,000. (Note that the oil producer's gain is equal to the oil exporter's loss.) The exporter must now pay this loss to the exchange's clearing house in order to maintain the required margin level.

The effect of the daily resettlement process is to reduce risk in the futures market and permit investors with relatively low credit standing to use the market. The margin is aimed at being sufficient to cover any one day price change. This daily resettlement process contrasts with the forward foreign exchange market where the only cash flow is at the delivery date of the contract which can be several months in the future, during which time the exchange rate may move significantly from the current spot rate.

Financial futures are used for two main purposes: hedging and trading (or speculation). From a corporate viewpoint hedging is the primary motive. Futures hedging may be undertaken to reduce the risk of loss through adverse movements in interest rates, exchange rates or share prices. Hedging is most commonly undertaken by taking a position that is equal but opposite to the position that exists in the cash market (e.g. a commitment to pay interest rates or to receive or supply foreign exchange at some future date).

Foreign currency futures contracts

A foreign currency futures contract entails the delivery of one or more foreign currencies at the maturity date for an agreed price (this price being fixed at the outset). On the delivery date the foreign currency (or currencies) is received and the contract price paid. Futures contracts are only available in a limited number of currencies. On the IMM, the largest trader of listed currency futures, contracts are available which relate the US dollar to the pound sterling, Deutschmark, yen, Swiss franc, French franc, Australian dollar, Canadian dollar and ECU. In 1989 more than 25 million foreign currency futures contracts were traded on the IMM with the Deutschmark, yen, Swiss franc and sterling being the most frequently traded currencies.

The main corporate use of currency futures is for hedging, an example of which follows.

It is 1 March. A UK company has arranged to import US$4 million of goods from the USA, which must be paid for on 10 May. The company wishes to protect itself from adverse movements in the spot rate that might occur before the payment is due. Assume that the standard size of a dollar/sterling futures contract is £25,000.

Current market prices:
Spot rate US$1.6149/£
June US$/£ futures US$1.6000

On 1 March the company should sell 100 June sterling futures contracts at a price of US$1.6000/£. The contracts are sold because sterling needs to be sold in order to acquire dollars. June is the nearest contract date. 100 contracts are required as $100 \times £25,000 \times 1.6000 =$ US$4,000,000, the required payment. Obviously the company does not wish to hold the contracts to maturity in June as the payment is due in May. When the payment is due, on 10 May, the company will close out the futures contract by arranging a reverse trade with exactly opposing contracts. In this case it will buy 100 June sterling futures contracts at the market price at that time. If the dollar has strengthened against sterling between 1 March and 10 May then there will be a profit on the futures contracts.

Assume the following rates on 10 May:

Spot US$1.5850
June US$/£ futures 1.5720

The actual payment for the US goods will be made by converting £ for $ on the spot market on 10 May (or thereabouts).

$$\text{This will cost } \frac{\text{US\$4,000,000}}{1.5850} = £2,523,659$$

The spot cost when the deal was agreed in March was:

$$\frac{\text{US\$4,000,000}}{1.6149} = £2,476,933$$

Therefore there is a loss on the spot or cash market of £46,726. By undertaking the futures hedge the company has protected itself against this loss.

The profit on the futures contracts is US$4,000,000 $(1.6000 - 1.5720) = £44,529$.

As the futures market price did not move by exactly the same amount as the spot market price, the futures gain is not the same as the spot market 'loss'. In this case there is an overall 'loss' of £46,726 − £44,529 = £2,197 due to the dollar strengthening, or a hedge efficiency of

$$\frac{£44,529}{£46,726} = 95.3\%$$

This transaction is known as using a short hedge to protect against currency risk. If currency futures had been bought rather than sold, the technique is called a long hedge.

Pricing foreign currency futures   A foreign currency futures contract can be valued using two equivalent instruments. These are riskless domestic debt and riskless foreign debt.

An investor has an amount in dollars and he converts these dollars into pounds. He now invests the money in riskless debt, for example, Treasury Bills. The investor guarantees the rate of exchange back to dollars with a financial futures contract. He writes a futures contract converting pounds to dollars at the maturity date of the treasury bill for an amount equal to the maturity value of the bill. The foreign investment now possesses no exchange risk as the conversion to dollars is at a known rate. Futures are quoted by the number of dollars per currency. Therefore:

Let X be the number of dollars that can be bought with £1 at time 0 (i.e. X is the spot rate). Converting the dollars into pounds and investing these at the foreign riskless rate will yield:

$$[1 + R(£)]$$

The value of the debt at maturity (in dollars) is:

$$[1 + R(£)] \times 1/X \times F$$

where F is the futures price of £1. So the return on the foreign debt is:

$$[1 + R(£)] \times 1/X \times F) - 1$$

Now, since all riskless debt should give the same return:

$$R(\$) = ([1 + R(£)] \times 1/X \times F) - 1$$

Rearranging this gives:

$$F = ([1 + R(\$)]/[1 + R(£)]) \times X$$

i.e. futures sterling rate = $([1 + R(\$)]/[1 + R(£)]) \times$ spot rate.

What is the 30-day sterling futures rate given sterling spot rate US$1.50?

Eurosterling interest rate R(£) = 11%
Eurodollar interest rate R($) = 6%
30-day Eurosterling interest rate = 0.11 × 30/365
30-day Eurodollar interest rate = 0.06 × 30/365
So the 30-day sterling futures rate is:

$$[1 + (0.06 \times 30/365)] / [1 + (0.11 \times 30/365)] \times US\$1.50 = US\$1.494$$

The differences between currency futures and forward contracts

Currency futures used to be available in the UK via LIFFE during the 1980s, but never proved to be a popular form of currency hedging, largely due to the existence of more flexible and convenient forms of currency hedge such as the forward market and currency options. They are still available on several foreign futures markets, including the IMM in Chicago, the Singapore International Monetary Exchange and the Sydney Futures Exchange. Table 9.1 illustrates the major differences between forward contracts and currency futures.

Interest rate futures

Interest rate futures are by far the most important type of financial futures contract. As with all futures contracts, interest rate futures allow the fixing now of prices that will apply to transactions at some specified future time.

In the UK interest rate futures are available on LIFFE. All open positions on the LIFFE market must be taken through a member of the market, and a margin must be deposited with the clearing house. For example, the three-month Eurodollar contract requires a margin of

Table 9.1 Differences between forward contracts and currency futures

Forward contracts	*Currency futures*
Telephone/telex/touch-screen trading, mostly via banks	Trading by open outcry on a futures exchange
Two prices: a buying rate and a selling rate. Price can vary according to size of deal and customer	Single specified price published by the clearing house
Access to individuals and small companies is limited	May be used by banks, companies, financial institutions and individuals
Forward contracts are tailored to the needs of the parties concerned	Contracts are highly standardized both in size and terms of delivery
Forward contracts are usually made with the intention of delivery of currencies	Physical delivery is very rare. Contracts are normally physically liquidated prior to maturity
No payments are made until forward contracts are settled	An initial margin is required, a further variation margin may be necessary

US$1,000 for each US$1,000,000 contract or US$300 if a straddle position is taken. A straddle position is where an equal number of the same currency futures contracts are simultaneously bought and sold. The amount of margin required per contract may be varied periodically. Short-term interest rate futures prices are quoted as 100 minus the rate of interest on the instrument involved. Thus an interest rate of 10 per cent would be priced at 90.00 for one futures contract.

The minimum price fluctuation is known as the tick size, which on most contracts is 1/100 of 1 per cent or 0.01 per cent (also referred to as a basis point). The monetary value of one tick is dependent upon the size and terms of the contract, and is calculated as the minimum price movement multiplied by the contract size.

In the case of the three-month Eurodollar contract this is calculated as:

$$0.01\% \times \$1,000,000 \times \frac{3}{12} = US\$25.00$$

If an investor has a US$1,000,000 floating rate bond yielding 9 per cent and is worried about interest rate fluctuations during the next three months, he or she can use a three-month Eurodollar interest rate futures contract to protect against interest rate changes. The contract can be sold to make a gain or loss if interest rates change. For example, if interest rates fall to 9 per cent the investor could sell the futures contract for 91.00 (100–9) and make a profit of (91–90) = 100 ticks at US$25.00 each = US$2,500. The 9 per cent bond will yield:

$$\frac{9}{100} \times \frac{3}{12} \times US\$1,000,000 = US\$22,500$$

plus profit from futures contract:

$$US\$22,500 + US\$2,500 = \$25,000$$

Effective yield:

$$\$\frac{25,000}{1,000,000} \times \frac{12}{3} \times 100\% = 10\%$$

If interest rates rise to 11 per cent the investor sells futures at a loss:

$$(89\text{--}90) = \text{Loss of 100 ticks at US\$25.00 each} = \text{Loss of US\$2,500}$$

Deducting this loss from interest earned on investment:
   Interest earned on investment:

$$\frac{11}{100} \times \frac{3}{12} \times US\$1,000,000 = US\$27,500$$

minus loss on futures contract:

$$US\$27,500 - US\$2,500 = US\$25,000$$

Effective yield:

$$\$\frac{25,000}{1,000,000} \times \frac{12}{3} \times 100\% = 10\%$$

In both cases, whether actual interest rates rose or fell, the yield for the investor for the three-month period remained at 10 per cent.

LIFFE futures contracts

As at the beginning of 1994 the following futures contracts were available on LIFFE.

	Contract size	Tick size	Tick value	Initial margin
Three month sterling	£500,000	0.01	£12.50	£750
Three month Eurodollar	$1,000,000	0.01	$25.00	$1,000
Three month Euro Deutschmark	DM1,000,000	0.01	DM25.00	DM750
Three month Euro Swiss franc	SF1,000,000	0.01	SF25.00	SF500
Three month ECU	ECU1,000,000	0.01	ECU25.0	ECU750
Three month Eurolira	L1,000,000,000	0.01	L25,000	L1,500,000
ECU 10% bond	ECU200,000	0.01	ECU20.0	ECU600
Long gilt 9%	£50,000	£1/32	£15.625	£1,500
German government bond 6%	DM250,000	0.01	DM25	DM6,250
US Treasury bond 8%	$100,000	$1/32	$31.25	$3,000
Japanese government bond 6%	Y100m	0.01	Y10,000	Y600,000

All of the above are interest rate futures. In addition, LIFFE offers stock index futures based upon the FT-SE 100-share index.

FT-SE 100	—	0.5	£12.50	£4,000

As with currency futures, the main corporate use for interest rate futures is for hedging. An example of an interest rate hedge might be a company that wishes to protect itself from an expected rise in interest rates by undertaking a 'short hedge', i.e. selling futures contracts in the expectation that their price will fall if interest rates rise. The following example illustrates the principle of interest rate futures.

Cango plc has a £2 million floating rate bank loan, currently at an interest rate of 12 per cent, with a rollover date in three months' time when the interest rate is subject to review and is expected to increase by 2 per cent. To hedge against this risk in the quarter year following the rollover date the company could sell now three-month sterling interest rate futures contracts at the current price of 88.10 (an interest rate of 100–88.10 = 11.9%). If interest rates do increase by 2 per cent, the extra cost to Cango during the following quarter will be £2m × 2% × 0.25 years = £10,000. This is the amount that the company would ideally like to gain in the futures market. Sterling three-month futures have a standard contract size of £500,000, hence four contracts will be required. If, by the rollover date, interest rates have altered by the expected 2 per cent then the price of the futures contract will have changed by a similar (but not necessarily the same) amount. Assuming the futures price has moved to 86.10, the gain on the futures market, since identical contracts can be bought more cheaply than the price at which they were sold, will be £10,000. The minimum price movement of three-month sterling futures is one tick, or one-hundredth of 1 per cent. The value of one tick is the contract value of £500,000 × 0.01% × 3/12 months or £12.50. A 2 per cent interest rate movement is a 200-tick movement. The gain to Cango on four contracts will therefore be:

$$200 \times £12.50 \times 4 = £10,000$$

In this situation the loss on the company's interest payments in the cash market is exactly offset by the gain in the futures market (ignoring margin requirements and fees). This situation is known as a perfect hedge with 100 per cent hedge efficiency. Futures rates need not move by exactly the same amount as cash market rates, in which case a perfect hedge will not occur and the futures gain could be smaller or greater than the cash market loss. The risk of this occurring is known as basis risk. Perfect hedges are rare both because of basis risk and because the use of standard contract sizes might prevent hedging against the exact amount of the company's exposure.

In the above example interest rates moved in line with the company's expectations. In reality this will often not occur; indeed sometimes rates might move in the opposite direction to the company's expectations. If, for example, at the rollover date interest rates had fallen to 11 per cent in the cash market what would be the result of the futures hedge?

This will depend upon whether the futures price changes by 1 per cent to reflect the cash market change. If the futures price changes to 89.00, a change of less than 1 per cent reflecting some basis risk, the overall effect is:

Gain on the cash market from lower interest rates:

$$£2m \times 1\% \times 0.25 \text{ years} = £5,000$$

Loss on the futures market:

$$90 \text{ ticks} \times £12.50 \times 4 = £4,500$$

In this case the cash market gain exceeds the futures loss, and the hedge efficiency is

$$\frac{£5,000}{£4,500} = 111\%$$

OPTIONS

While forward contracts and futures contracts may protect the holder against interest rate and exchange rate risks, they also eliminate the possibility of reaping large rewards brought about by favourable rate fluctuations. In contrast, an option allows the holder to benefit from favourable interest rate and exchange rate fluctuations while still gaining protection against adverse movements.

Options have been traded for over 100 years, since privileges, a form of commodity option, appeared on the floor of the US grain exchanges. Options trading was stimulated in 1973 by the creation of the Chicago Board of Options Exchange in the USA, with currency options first offered in 1982 by the International Options Market of the Montreal Exchange and the Philadelphia Stock Exchange (PHLX).

Currency options   A currency option is a contract giving the holder the right, but not the obligation, to buy or sell foreign currency on or before a specified date (the expiration date), at a particular price (the exercise or striking price). The most common types of option are puts and calls.

Puts and calls   A foreign currency call option gives the holder the right, but not the obligation, to buy the contracted currency at a specified exercise price. In some cases the call can only be exercised at the expiration date; these are referred to as European calls. Calls which contain the right to exercise the option at any time up to the expiration date are referred to as American calls. Despite these geographical names most exchange listed options that are traded in the USA, Europe and elsewhere are American options. A foreign currency put option gives the holder the right, but not the obligation, to sell the contracted currency on or before the expiration date. As with calls there are European puts and American puts.

In the money/out of the money   A foreign currency option is said to be 'in the money' if it would be profitable to exercise it at the current exchange rate. Conversely, it is said to be 'out of the money' if it would not be profitable to exercise it at the current exchange rate.

The market structure

Options are traded either on an organized exchange (listed options), such as the PHLX, or 'over-the-counter' (OTC), primarily through major banks. Listed options are standardized contracts, whereas OTC options are generally negotiated to suit the relevant parties of the contract. Branches of foreign banks in major financial centres are generally willing to write options against their home currency; for example, Australian banks in Chicago will write options on the Australian dollar. The OTC option market is much larger than the listed exchange traded options market and has a number of significant differences.

1. OTC options are normally European and can only be exercised at the maturity date.
2. Option sizes are much larger on the OTC market, with most options being in excess of US$1,000,000.
3. A far wider choice of currencies is available on OTC markets.
4. OTC options are designed in size and maturity to meet the specific needs of the multinational company or other client, and have little secondary market trading.

Exchange traded or listed options   Exchange traded options are standardized with the following predetermined elements:

1. Currencies. Only the following options are usually available: pounds, Deutschmarks, Swiss francs, Canadian dollars, French francs, Japanese yen, Australian dollars and ECUs
2. Option size. Each option is for a fixed amount of currency, such as 31,250 pounds or 62,500 Deutschmarks
3. The exercise price: a limited number of alternative exercise prices are available
4. Fixed length maturities: often three, six, nine and 12 months
5. Fixed expiration date, e.g. March, June, September or December
6. Fixed expiration day, for example, the Saturday before the third Wednesday of the month
7. The method and time of delivery

Calls   Concentrating on the conceptually simpler European call, Figure 9.1(a) illustrates the profitability of a call option at its expiration date and shows the gain or loss to the call holder

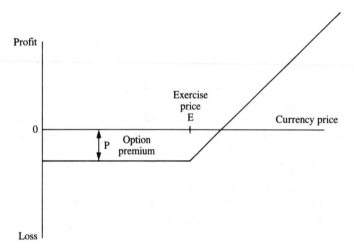

Figure 9.1(a)   Profit/loss of a buyer (long position) of a call option

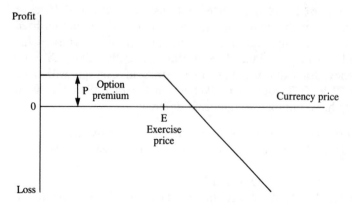

Figure 9.1(b)   Profit/loss of a seller (short position) of a call option

(i.e. the buyer of the call). Figure 9.1(b) depicts the position of the call writer (i.e. the seller of the call option) at the expiration date. Both figures represent a call purchase price P with exercise price E.

It may be seen from Figure 9.1(a) that it would be unprofitable for the call holder to exercise the call when the market currency price is less than E, the option exercise price. This is because the currency could be purchased in the foreign exchange market for less than E.

For market currency prices greater than E it would pay the call holder to exercise the call buying the currency for exchange rate E. The call holder's gain is equal to the difference between the market price and E. It should be noted that the call holder does not make a profit on the transaction unless the market price of the currency is greater than P + E. By examination of Figure 9.1(b), it may be seen that the position of the call writer is the converse of that of the call holder. Note that, for any currency price, the holder's gain is equal to the writer's loss and vice versa.

Puts   Figures 9.2(a) and 9.2(b) illustrate the positions of a put holder and put writer respectively relative to the currency's market price at the expiration date.

Using the same notation as before, if the currency's market price is less than E, the put holder will exercise the put, realizing a pre-put price profit equal to the difference between E and the currency's market price. Again, note that the put holder does not make a profit on the option unless the currency's market price is less than E − P.

If the market price is greater than E, then the put holder will not exercise the option, since he or she could sell the currency on the foreign exchange market for a price greater than E. If either the put or the call option is not exercised, the option holder makes a loss equal to P, and the option writer makes a profit equal to P.

Examples of currency put and call options:

Currency call option   An investor buys a December sterling call option which is selling for a premium of 2.00 cents/£ on an exercise price of US$1.65. The investor has bought the right to purchase one contract of a fixed size, assumed in this example to be £12,500, anytime between now and December.

The effective cost is £12,500 × US$1.65 = US$20,625
The premium cost of the call is £12,500 × US$0.02 = US$250
So, if the call is exercised, the total cost to the investor is:

$$US\$20,625 + US\$250 = US\$20,875$$

The premium of US$250 is payable upfront whether or not the option is exercised.

Currency put option   An investor buys a June sterling put option at a premium of 3.00 cents/£ on an exercise price of US$1.55. The investor has bought the right to purchase £12,500 worth of dollars (i.e. to sell £12,500 for dollars) anytime between now and June.

For £12,500 the investor receives £12,500 × US$1.55 = US$19,375, and the cost of the put premium is £12,500 × US$0.03 = US$375.

A British company has to make a payment of US$16.65 million to a US manufacturer in three months' time. The British company believes that the US$/£ spot rate will decline from the current spot rate of US$1.795 − 1.800/£ to US$1.750 − 1.760/£ in three months' time. The

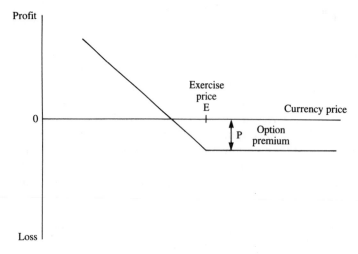

Figure 9.2(a) Profit/loss of a buyer of a put option

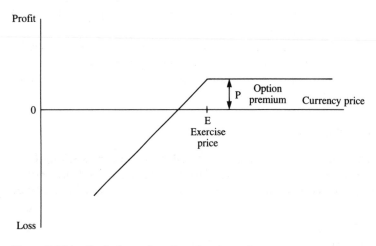

Figure 9.2(b) Profit/loss of a seller of a put option

British company assesses the situation and decides that its best line of action is to minimize its sterling payments by purchasing three-month put options to sell pounds for dollars.

The Philadelphia Stock Exchange is currently selling three-month put options at the following prices:

Exercise price $/£	Price of put options (cents)
1.70	0.9
1.75	1.2
1.80	4.3
1.85	8.0

Of the four put options available, only the US$1.80 and the US$1.85 options would be exercised in three months' time if the expected spot rate prevailed. So the company has a choice between two put options: either US$1.80 or US$1.85.

If the US$1.80 put option is bought:

Number of put options required as a whole number of £12,500 lots

$$= \frac{\$16.65\,M}{\$1.80} \times \frac{1}{12,500} = 740$$

$$\text{Currency cost} = \frac{\$16.65\,M}{\$1.80/£} = £9,250,000$$

$$\text{Cost of option} = 740 \times 0.043 \times 12,500 = \$397,750$$

$$\text{Cost now in pounds} = \frac{\$397,750}{1.795} = £221,588$$

$$\text{Total cost} = £9,250,000 + £221,588 = £9,471,588$$

If the US$1.85 put option is bought:

Number of put options required (as a whole number of £12,500 lots)

$$= \frac{\$16.65\,M}{\$1.85} \times \frac{1}{12,500} = 720$$

$$\text{Currency cost} = \frac{\$16.65\,M}{\$1.85/£} = £9,000,000$$

$$\text{Cost of option} = 720 \times 0.08 \times 12,500 = \$720,000$$

$$\text{Cost in pounds} = \frac{\$720,000}{1.795} = £401,114$$

$$\text{Total cost} = £9,000,000 + £401,114 = £9,401,114$$

Therefore, the company should take out the US$1.85 put option in order to minimize its sterling payments in three months' time.

It must be stressed that this strategy is based upon the company's expectations of future spot exchange rates, and with hindsight might not be the best strategy. If exchange rates move such that it is not worth while exercising the option, the US$1.85 put option, with a high premium cost of £401,114, would prove expensive.

Combinations of options   Puts, calls and the underlying currencies can be combined to give an investor an asset suitably adjusted to his or her view of the currency's future price movements. An example of such a combination is a 'straddle'.

A straddle is a combination of a put option and a call option with the same exercise price and expiration date. Straddle options are bought by investors who believe that there will be a marked difference between a currency's future price and the currency's exercise price, but are not sure which way the currency's price will fluctuate. Conversely, a straddle option would be written by an investor who believes that the currency's price will remain close to the exercise price.

Two combinations similar to a straddle are 'strips' (two puts and a call) and 'straps' (two calls and a put). Calls and puts can also be combined with the contracted currency producing differing results.

Types of option trading strategies

Naked options   A currency option is naked when the buyer or seller does not hold an offsetting position in the contracted currency (or currencies).

Covered options   A currency option is covered when the writer holds an offsetting position in the contracted currency (covered option writing) or when the holder holds an offsetting position in the contracted currency (covered option buying).

Option spreads   An option spread involves the simultaneous purchase and sale of two options of the same type but with differing exercise prices or terms until maturity.

Who uses currency options?   Currency options are primarily used by hedgers and traders, in a similar way to futures.

If an investor's cash position is expected to be subject to lower exchange rates than exist today, he or she might consider selling currency option contracts. Thus, if exchange rates do fall, profits on the options contracts will compensate for the loss on their open cash position owing to the downward fluctuation in exchange rates. If, alternatively, upwardly moving exchange rates are a problem then the investor should consider buying an option currency contract to provide adequate cover for his or her cash position. Unlike a futures hedge which guarantees a single exchange rate, an option hedge will, for a small premium, insure the buyer against any adverse exchange rate movements while still allowing him or her to benefit from some of the favourable exchange rate fluctuations.

An example of hedging with currency options or futures
Chicago Exports Inc., a US company, currently has a £1,000,000 denominated obligation to meet in June. The company wishes to insure against any sudden change in the dollar/pound exchange rate.

The following set of premiums are on offer at the Philadelphia exchange:

Sterling June calls

Exercise price ($/£)	*Premium ($/£)*
1.60	0.028
1.65	0.012
1.70	0.008

As an alternative, IMM in Chicago offers a June futures rate of US$1.645/£.

If the company buys a futures contract to sell dollars forward for sterling it guarantees itself an exchange rate of US$1.645/£.

The company has a choice of three option contracts. If the company buys the:
1.   US$1.70 Call option
     It pays a premium of US$0.008 and so insures itself against the exchange rate being higher than US$1.70 in June. The company will profit by more than if it had bought the futures hedge if the exchange rate falls below :
     (the June futures rate) − (the US$1.70 June call premium) = US$1.645 − US$0.008 = US$1.637
     (In this situation the company will not exercise the option.)

2. US$1.65 call option

The company pays a premium of US$0.012 and so insures itself against the exchange rate being higher than US$1.65 dollars in June. The company will profit by more than if it had bought the futures hedge if the exchange rate falls below:

(the June futures rate) − (the US$1.65 June call premium) = US$1.645 − US$0.012 = US$1.633

(In this situation the company will not exercise the option.)

3. US$1.60 call option

The company pays a premium of US$0.028 and so insures itself against the exchange rate being higher than US$1.60 in June. The company will profit by more than if it had bought the futures hedge if the exchange rate falls below:

(the June futures rate) − (the US$1.60 June call premium) = US$1.645 − US$0.028 = US$1.617

(In this situation the option will be exercised at any price above US$1.60/£.)

The above example is a very simple insight into how options allow the hedger to decide which level of risk to accept and which insurance premium to pay. The best guaranteed rate for an options hedge is always worse than that of a futures hedge because of the premium payable on the option. However, with an options hedge the investor can take advantage of any favourable exchange rate movements. For example, if in the above case the exchange rate in June was US$1.62 an options hedger would not exercise the option at exercise prices of US$1.70 and US$1.65, but would use the market exchange rate of US$1.62/£. The futures hedger is bound by contract to honour the agreed exchange rate contract at US$1.645. This would make a significant difference to any deal.

For example, the futures contracts would cost £1,000,000 × 1.645 = $1,645,000

A foreign currency option hedge would cost:

Exercise price: (i) US$1.70/£

Cost (option is not exercised) £1,000,000 × 1.62 =
US$1,620,000 + US$8,000 (premium) = US$1,628,000

(ii) US$1.65/£

Cost (option is not exercised) £1,000,000 × 1.62 =
US$1,620,000 + US$12,000(premium) = $1,632,000

(iii) US$1.60/£

Cost (option is exercised) £1,000,000 × 1.60 =
US$1,600,000 + US$28,000 (premium) = US$1,628,000

THE ROLE OF FUTURES AND OPTIONS TRADERS

Traders use currency futures and options to pursue profits by exploiting fluctuations in the exchange rates without buying any currency. Traders are necessary for the efficient operation of both the futures and options markets as they assume the risk that hedgers pay to avoid. This thus ensures that the markets' liquidity remains high and hence enables contracts to be bought and sold with ease.

The determinants of currency option prices

The option premium or price depends upon a number of factors:

1. The time to expiry of the option. The longer the time to expiry the more expensive the option will be as there is a greater chance that exchange rates will move in favour of the option buyer.
2. The striking price or exercise price. The more favourable the striking price to the buyer of the option, the higher will be the option price.
3. Current spot and forward market rates for the period of the option.
4. The expected volatility during the life of the option of the currency in which the option is being purchased.
5. Whether an American or European option is to be purchased.
6. Current interest rates that could be earned on the option premium.

Range forward contracts and participating forward contracts

Range forward and participating forward contracts are over-the-counter currency options that have proved popular because of their special characteristics.

Range forwards are an agreement to buy or sell a currency on a specified future date at an exchange rate that lies within an agreed range of values. If the spot rate at the specified date is above the upper agreed limit, the currency will be bought (or sold) for the agreed upper limit. If the spot rate is below the lower agreed limit, the currency will be traded at the lower limit. If the spot rate is between the upper limit and the lower limit, the currency is traded at the spot rate. Range forwards therefore protect against large adverse exchange rate movements (and eliminate gains from large favourable movements), while leaving the company exposed to relatively small gains and losses. The actual exposure depends upon the difference between the upper and lower limits. The hedging company can specify the upper or lower limit, and the option seller (typically a bank) will set the other limit. A risk-averse company would seek a narrow range. The distinguishing feature about range forward options is that no premium is payable by the buyer of the option. Effectively the hedging company is buying a put option and selling (writing) a call option such that a zero net price results from the two contracts. A range forward hedge is illustrated below.

A company wishes to invest in German government bonds to the value of £5,000,000 for a period of six months. The Deutschmark is expected to strengthen against sterling, but the company wishes to ensure, without incurring premium costs, that no significant currency loss occurs if sterling was to strengthen against the Deutschmark. A range forward is the chosen hedge.

Principal amount of the contract: DM14,750,000 (the spot rate now is DM2.95/£)

Upper exchange rate limit DM3.02/£

Lower exchange rate limit DM2.85/£

If the spot rate in 6 months is above 3.02, the sterling value of the investment (ignoring interest) will be:

$$\frac{DM14,750,000}{3.02} = £4,884,106$$

If the spot rate in six months is below 2.85, the sterling value will be:

$$\frac{DM14,750,000}{2.85} = £5,175,439$$

Between the agreed limits a small loss or gain is possible relative to the spot rate when the investment was made. The value of range forwards in reducing the effect of large exchange rate fluctuations may be seen by comparing their results with an unhedged position.

	Change in spot rate by the end of six months		
	− 10%	*no change*	*+ 10%*
	DM2.655/£	*DM2.95/£*	*DM3.245/£*
Investment value			
Unhedged	£5,555,556	£5,000,000	£4,545,454
Hedged	£5,175,439	£5,000,000	£4,884,106

Participating forward contracts for an investor would offer a worst case exchange rate to limit downside risk, but would not have a limit on favourable exchange rate movements. However, if favourable movements occur, the investor could only participate in an agreed percentage from the favourable movement. The investor in this case gets a percentage (the participation rate) of the amount by which the future spot rate is more favourable than the agreed worst case rate. As with range forwards there is no premium cost to participating forwards. Using the data for range forwards, the effect of participating forwards, assuming a 60 per cent participation rate and a worst case rate of DM3.02/£, would be:

	− 10%	*No change*	*+ 10%*
	DM2.655/£	*DM2.95/£*	*DM3.245/£*
Unhedged	£5,555,556	£5,000,000	£4,545,454
Hedged	£5,265,976	£5,000,000	£4,884,106

Effective rate is DM2.801/£
This is calculated as
$3.02 - \{(3.02 - 2.655)0 \cdot 6\}$

Using these assumed data, participating forwards look better than range forwards. This is not always the case; each type of option offers its own risk/return trade-off.

Interest rate options   Although interest rate options are not used exclusively to protect against international risk they have become a common tool of the financial manager. The most common types of interest rate option are the interest rate cap, floor and collar.

An interest rate cap (or ceiling) is an agreement by the seller of the cap to protect the buyer from interest rates moving above a specified level for an agreed period of time. The buyer is usually a company that has borrowed funds and wishes to protect itself from adverse interest rate movements. The cap is agreed with reference to three- or six-month LIBOR rates or some other index, and may be for periods of up to 10 years although most are of much shorter duration. If a six-month LIBOR reference point is agreed, every six months the LIBOR rate that exists at that time is compared to the agreed cap rate. If the LIBOR rate exceeds the agreed cap rate, the seller of the cap will compensate the buyer of the cap for the difference between the LIBOR and the agreed cap rate. If the LIBOR rate is equal to or below the agreed cap rate, then no payment is made to the buyer. The effect of the cap is to ensure that the buyer (who has usually borrowed funds in the money or capital market) never pays more than the cap interest rate. As with any option, the buyer of the cap pays an upfront premium to the seller.

Caps have several advantages for the corporate borrower wishing to manage interest rate risk:

1. They protect against rising interest rates while allowing the corporate borrower to benefit from interest rate reductions.
2. Cash flow planning is facilitated since the company knows its maximum interest commitment over the period of the cap.
3. Caps provide an alternative to fixed interest funding.

Interest rate floors offer the opposite form of protection in that they give the buyer of a floor, usually an investor of funds, compensation if interest rates fall below an agreed level. For example, a company which has invested in a two-year floating rate note currently yielding 10 per cent could buy a floor that would give compensation if LIBOR fell below 8 per cent. In this way the company can fix the minimum yield on its investment at a price, which is the premium cost of the floor.

Collars are a combination of an interest rate cap and an interest rate floor where one party to the agreement will sell the cap, the other the floor. A borrower would buy a cap to protect against interest rate rises and sell a floor to fix the minimum borrowing cost. The advantage of a collar is that the seller of the floor receives payment in the form of a premium which partly (or occasionally entirely) offsets the premium cost of purchasing the cap. One of the major criticisms of options is the 'high' cost of premiums payable when an option is purchased. Use of a collar reduces this cost, but also means that the seller of the floor (the borrower of funds in the money or capital market) gives up possible benefits of low interest rates if LIBOR falls below the agreed floor level, at which point compensation would be payable by the seller to the buyer, eliminating further gains on the actual borrowing costs of the option seller.

Collars, caps and floors are usually arranged for periods in excess of one year, and with a minimum size of approximately US$5 million. For shorter periods of between one month and one year another form of interest option, the interest rate guarantee, is available. Interest rate guarantees offer the same protection as caps and floors in exchange for a premium payment, but cover just one agreed period, e.g. a period of six months commencing in three months' time.

Caps, floors, collars and interest rate guarantees are available in most of the major trading currencies.

Options on futures   As well as straight options contracts and futures contracts it is also possible to buy or sell options on futures. For example, a foreign currency futures option is an option on foreign currency futures at a future date, allowing participants in the currency markets to benefit from exchange rate movements while limiting their exposure. As with foreign currency options, options on futures cannot be valued using the Black-Scholes formula (see Ramaswamy and Sundaresan (1985)).

LIFFE offers options on several financial futures contracts (but not on currency futures), details of which are shown on page 195.

In a similar way to interest rate futures, the best way to describe interest rate options available in the LIFFE market is to use an example.

There are three possible hedging strategies when using options on futures; these are either:

1. To ensure a minimum future return on invested funds
2. To guarantee a maximum cost of funds
3. To maximize portfolio returns

	Contract size	*Options on futures*		
		Tick size	Tick value	Initial margin
Three month sterling	1 futures contract	0.01	£12.50	variable
Three month Eurodollar	1 futures contract	0.01	$25.00	variable
Three month Euro Deutschmark	1 futures contract	0.01	DM25.00	variable
Long gilt 9%	1 futures contract	£1/64	£7.8125	variable
German government bond 6%	1 futures contract	0.01	DM25	variable
US Treasury bond 8%	1 futures contract	$1/64	$15.625	variable

Minimum future return This example uses the three-month sterling instrument, with an option this time to ensure a minimum future return rate and also to enable the investor (with a £500,000 investment) to take advantage of better yields if the interest rate moves higher.

The current cost of a call option with a 90.00 strike price is 15 ticks = 0.15.

Pay 0.15 for one call option with a 90.00 strike price

This guarantees a minimum investment rate of 9.85 per cent

$$(100.00 - 90.00 - 0.15) = 9.85$$

Possible outcome 1

If interest rates fall to 9 per cent:

The investor will sell the call option for 1.00 (91–90) and add profit of (1–0.15) × 100 = 85 ticks at £12.50 = £1,062.50 to the 9 per cent earned on the investment.

Interest on investment:

$$\frac{9}{100} \times \frac{3}{12} \times £500,000 = £11,250$$

Plus profit from option £11,250 + £1,062.50 = £12,312.50

Effective yield:

$$£\frac{12,312.50}{500,000} \times \frac{12}{3} \times 100 = 9.85\%$$

Possible outcome 2

If interest rates rise to 11 per cent:

In this case the investor will allow the call option to expire worthless for a loss of 15 ticks at £12.50 each = £187.50

Deduct this loss from the interest earned on the investment.

Interest earned on investment:

$$\frac{11}{100} \times \frac{3}{12} \times £500,000 = £13,750$$

Minus loss on option:

$$£13,750 - £187.50 = £13,562.50$$

Effective yield:

$$£\frac{13,562.50}{500,000} \times \frac{12}{3} \times 100 = 10.85\%$$

The option has permitted the investor to take advantage of a favourable interest rate movement.

Maximum guaranteed cost of funds A borrower is likely to want to control the cost of funds. An option on an interest rate futures contract allows the maximum cost of borrowing to be fixed while allowing the borrower to take advantage of favourable interest rate movements.

The current cost of a put option with a 90.00 strike price is 0.10 or 10 ticks.
Pay 0.10 for one put option with a 90.00 strike price
This guarantees a maximum borrowing rate of 10.1 per cent.

$$(100.00 - 90.00 + 0.10) = 10.1\%$$

Possible outcome 1
If interest rates fall to 9 per cent:
The put option expires worthless for a loss of 10 ticks at £12.50 each = £125
Add this loss to interest paid:

$$\frac{9}{100} \times \frac{3}{12} \times £500,000 = £11,250$$

Plus loss on option

$$£11,250 + £125 = £11,375$$

Effective cost:

$$£\frac{11,375}{500,000} \times \frac{12}{3} \times 100 = 9.1\%$$

Possible outcome 2
If interest rates rise to 11 per cent:
The put option is sold for 1.00 (90 − 89) giving a profit of (100 − 10) ticks at £12.50 = £1,125

$$\text{Interest paid: } \frac{11}{100} \times \frac{3}{12} \times £500,000 = £13,750$$

$$\text{Minus profit on option: } £13,750 - £1,125 = £12,625$$

$$\text{Effective yield: } £\frac{12,625}{500,000} \times \frac{12}{3} \times 100 = 10.1\%$$

Maximizing portfolio returns   There are three broad categories of option sellers: banks, discount houses and security houses. These institutions already have a broad base of cash deposits from their other operations. In order to augment the return on positions held in these instruments, the institutions can collect option premiums. In a period of stable rising interest rates, banks with low yield deposits sell out-of-money calls and increase their return. In times of declining yield, they sell puts and collect the premiums. Large security houses are constantly adjusting their position in order to remain fully hedged, but this requires good communication with the market.

Could options replace futures?

Hedging a particular currency involves establishing an offsetting currency position such that whatever is lost or gained on the original currency exposure is, in theory, exactly offset by a corresponding gain or loss on the currency hedge. Both currency futures and currency options may be used to hedge a position in the spot currency against exchange rate risks. Chang and Shanker (1986) investigated the substitutability between currency options and currency futures when they are used in portfolios along with the spot currency. Their article endeavours to discover whether the currency option contract could cause a redundancy of the futures contract, by comparing the hedging effectiveness of currency option synthetic futures contracts and currency futures contracts. The study found that when transactions costs and margin requirements were taken into account the currency futures contract performed better as a hedging instrument than the currency option synthetic futures contract.

Swaptions: options on swaps

Swaptions integrate the benefits of swaps (discussed in Chapter 8) and options into one package. The buyer of a swaption has the right, but not the obligation, to execute an interest rate or currency swap during a limited period of time and at a specified rate. Swaptions are available either as:

1. American swaptions which can be exercised on any business day within the exercise period.
2. European swaptions which can be exercised only on the expiry date.
3. Extendable swaptions which allow multinational companies to extend the period of an existing swap at a predetermined rate, usually with an exercise period of several years.

The use of swaptions for debt management purposes is illustrated below.

Bliton plc has borrowed US$50 million floating debt, on which interest payments have increased by 30 per cent during the last year. The company's directors wish to protect future cash flows for at least the next five years from volatile interest rates, but do not wish to swap the floating rate debt for fixed rate as they believe that interest rates will fall. A European swaption is available that requires payment of an annual fixed rate of interest of 10 per cent and receipt of LIBOR for a five-year period. The swaption has an exercise date in six months' time and a premium cost of 1 per cent. By selecting the swaption, the company is keeping its alternatives open. If long-term interest rates in six months' time have fallen below 10 per cent, the swaption will not be exercised, and if the company wants protection from interest rate volatility it can arrange a floating/fixed rate swap. If the long-term rate in six months' time is, for example, 12 per cent the swaption is likely to be exercised to fix interest rates for the next five years at 10 per cent, and, at least initially, to preserve the opportunity gain from lower interest rates. The premium cost of US$500,000 must, of course, be weighed against the potential interest savings from using the swaption.

Risks of using futures and options

Risks affecting futures and options may be subdivided into two types:

1. Credit risk
2. Position risk

The credit risk in futures and options may also be categorized under two headings: the risk that the counterparty is unable to deliver the contract or meet the required call margin, or the credit risk on making margin deposits.

In the first case, if a customer becomes insolvent the contract may then have to be covered at the market spot rate and a loss incurred as the member covers all the customer's open positions. It is also possible for a member to become insolvent and all the customer's open contracts become void.

In addition, there is the risk that marginal deposits held by a member will become insolvent.

As a means of controlling this risk full investigations of each party's financial situation should be carried out before trading. The value of open transactions should be limited and a close eye should be kept on the profitability of customers' activities to provide early warning of possible difficulties.

Position risk, which is not borne by the intermediary, is associated with open positions taken on the market, and is the most significant risk so far as financial futures and options are concerned. As a rule the larger the associated position risk a trade or hedge has, the more opportunity there is for realizing a profit or loss.

The position risk for a futures contract occurs as the price of the future moves and gains and losses on a position occur. With options the purchaser of a position (e.g. the holder of a position) incurs a fixed loss equal to the value paid for the option and possibly unlimited gain. This position is reversed for the writer or seller. These risks due to price volatility can be measured using formulae such as the Black-Scholes model.

REFERENCES

Chang, J. S. K. and L. Shanker (1986) 'Hedging effectiveness of currency options and currency futures', *Journal of Futures Markets*, Vol. 6, No. 2, pp. 289–305.
Ramaswamy, K. and S. Sundaresan (1985) 'The valuation of options on futures contracts', *Journal of Finance*.

ADDITIONAL READING

Bank of England Quarterly Bulletin (1989) 'Currency Options', Vol. 29, No. 2, May.
Bank of England Quarterly Bulletin (1989) 'A Survey of Interest Rate Futures', Vol. 29, No. 3, August.
Brealey R. and S. Myers (1988) *Principles of Corporate Finance*, 3rd edition, McGraw-Hill International, New York, pp. 618–19.
Copeland T. E. and J. F. Weston (1988) *Financial Theory and Corporate Policy*, 3rd edition, Addison-Wesley, Reading, Mass, p. 289.
Cornell, B. and M. C. Reinganum (1981) 'Forward and futures prices', *Journal of Finance*, December, pp. 1036–37.
Elton, E. J. and M. J. Gruber (1987) *Modern Portfolio Theory and Investment Analysis*, Wiley, New York, pp. 548–52.
Fieleks, N. S. (1985) 'The foreign currency futures market', *Journal of Futures Markets*, p. 625.

Kaufman, P. J. (1986) *The Concise Handbook of Futures Markets*, Wiley, Chichester, pp. 13.10–13.12.
Shapiro, A. C. (1989) *Multinational Financial Management*, 3rd edition, Allyn and Bacon, Newton, Mass, pp. 133–136.
Streit, M. E. (1983) *Futures Markets*, Blackwell, Oxford, England, p. 169.
LIFFE publications:
Futures & Options Accounting & Administration
Three Month Sterling
EuroDollar
Currency Futures & Options
UK Gilts
Short Sterling
US Treasury Bonds
CME Publications:
Currency Options Strategy Manual
Inside S&P 500 Options
Options on Deutschmark Futures
Futures and Options: Tools for Currency Trading
Options on Futures

QUESTIONS

This is the last chapter relating to hedging foreign exchange risk. The following questions are good examples of some of the alternative hedging strategies, including options and futures.

1.

(i) Explain briefly what is meant by foreign currency options and give examples of the advantages and disadvantages of exchange traded foreign currency options to the financial manager.

(5 marks)

(ii) Exchange traded foreign currency option prices in London for dollar/sterling contracts are shown below:

Sterling (£12,500) contracts

Exercise price	Calls September	December	Puts September	December
1.90	5.55	7.95	0.42	1.95
1.95	2.75	3.85	4.15	3.80
2.00	0.25	1.00	9.40	—
2.05	—	0.20	—	—

Option prices are in cents per £. The current spot exchange rate is $1.9405 − $1.9425/£.

Required:

Assume that you work for a US company that has exported goods to the UK and is due to receive a payment of £1,625,000 in three months' time. It is now the end of June.

Calculate and explain whether your company should hedge its sterling exposure on the foreign currency option market if the company's treasurer believes the spot rate in 3 months' time will be:

(1) $1.8950 − $1.8970/£
(2) $2.0240 − $2.0260/£

(7.5 marks)
ACCA 3.2, June 1992

Solution:

(i) A foreign currency option allows the purchaser of the option the right, but not the obligation, to buy or sell a currency at a specified rate of exchange at any time up to a specified date. This assumes an American style option that may be exercised at any time.

There are several advantages of currency options including:

1. They offer protection against adverse currency fluctuations, but also permit companies to take advantage of favourable foreign exchange rate movements.
2. They provide a valuable hedge against foreign exchange risk when a company is unsure whether a future foreign exchange risk will occur, or in what direction future exchange rates might move. This is particularly useful when tendering for a contract which the company might not get, or issuing a price list in foreign currencies.
3. They provide an effective currency hedge, especially when foreign exchange markets are volatile.

Disadvantages include:

1. Cost. The option premium is payable when the option is arranged, no matter whether or not the option is exercised.
2. Options that are exchange traded are only available in a limited number of currencies with specific expiration dates (OTC options are much more flexible).

(ii) Any forecasts about the level of future foreign exchange rates that have been made by the company's treasurer are merely a personal viewpoint and, if acted upon, could leave the company exposed to foreign exchange risk as the actual future rates could differ substantially from these forecasts. If the company is worried about foreign exchange risk it must hedge the risk using techniques such as options, swaps, futures or forward contracts, no matter what the treasurer personally believes that future spot rate will be.

If the company were to act upon the treasurer's forecasts it would need to sell sterling for dollars, i.e. buy put options on sterling. £1,625,000 will require 130 contracts.

(1) $1.8950 − $1.8970/£

The relevant future spot rate for selling £ for $ is $1.8950/£. If the future spot rate is $1.8950, the company would receive $3,079,375 using the spot market. The pound is expected to weaken relative to the dollar. September options are available at exercise prices of $1.90, $1.95, $2.0. At all of these prices the option will be exercised.

At $1.90, receipts are 1.625m × $1.90 =	$3,087,500
Less option cost of 1.625m × 0.42 cents =	$6,825
Net	$3,080,675
At $1.95	
Receipts 1.625m × $1.95	$3,168,750
Option cost 1.625m × 4.15 cents	$67,438
Net	$3,101,312
At $2.00	
Receipts 1.625m × $2.00	$3,250,000
Option cost 1.625m × 9.40 cents	$152,750
Net	$3,097,250

All of these three exercise prices result in higher expected dollar receipts than using the spot market in three months (excluding any further transactions costs). Selection of the $1.95 exercise price would give the highest expected receipts.

(2) $2.0240 − $2.0260/£

If the spot rate for buying dollars in three months' time is $2.0240/£ then, if purchased, the options would not be exercised as using the spot rate in three months would give higher dollar receipts than any of the available option exercise prices. Therefore, the company would not purchase currency options.

This strategy would leave the company exposed to foreign exchange risk, as the spot rate in three months' time could be very different to that forecast by the treasurer.

2. **BID (UK) Ltd**

BID (UK) Ltd trades with several countries. During the next six months export and import receipts and payments are due as a result of business with companies in Australia, North Africa, Eastern Europe and Italy. The transactions are in the currencies specified. It is now 31 December.

	Payment date	Exports	Imports
Australia	31 March	$A120,000	£40,000
Italy	31 March	Lire 400 million	Lire 220 million
North Africa	31 March	Francs 565,000	—
Italy	Between 31 March and 30 June	Lire 500 million	—
Eastern Europe	30 June	Tinned meat	—
Australia	30 June	$A180,000	$A260,000
West Africa	30 June	Coffee	Tinned meat
Italy	30 June	—	Lire 700 million

The exports to Eastern Europe will be paid for by a barter exchange of 100,000 tins of meat. BID has arranged for this tinned meat to be exchanged for 70 tons of coffee by its customer in West Africa where tinned meat is in demand. The West African country's currency is tied to the French franc.

Exchange rates

	$A/£	Lire/£	French franc/£
Spot	2.1400–2.1425	2,208–2,210	10.38–10.39
3 months forward	2–2.5 cents dis	3–6 lire dis	5–3 centimes pm
6 months forward	3.5–4.5 cents dis	5–8 lire dis	7–5 centimes pm

Commodities	Futures rate (£/tonne)
Coffee beans	
March	791
June	860

	Interest rates	
	Borrowing	*Lending*
UK bank	15%	10.5%
Australian bank	16%	13%
Italian bank	Not available	16%
French bank	9%	6%

Assume that interest rates will not change during the next six months.

BID proposes to invest net sterling proceeds from foreign trade in a UK bank. The company wishes to hedge against all foreign exchange risk, and currently has no surplus cash.

Taxation, transaction costs and margin requirements on future contracts may be ignored.

Required:

Using the forward market, money market or commodity futures market, as appropriate, estimate the maximum size of cash surplus or the minimum size of cash deficit that will result from BID's foreign trade at the end of six months.

(15 marks)

ACCA, 3.2, December 1990

Solution:

	Exchange rates		
	$A/£	*Lire/£*	*Francs/£*
Spot	2.1400–2.1425	2,208–2,210	10.38–10.39
3 months forward	2.1600–2.1675	2,211–2,216	10.33–10.36
6 months forward	2.1750–2.1875	2,213–2,218	10.31–10.34

3-month transactions
Australian dollars

Forward market

$$\frac{\$120,000}{2.1675} \text{ receipts} = £55,363 \text{ sterling equivalent of receipt in 3 months' time}$$

Money market

Borrow now $\dfrac{\$120,000}{1.04} = \$115,385$ (to repay $120,000 with receipts in 3 months' time)

Convert at spot 2.1425 to £ = £53,855
Invest at 10.5% for 3 months to yield £55,269 at the end of 3 months.
   The forward market is better.

Lire: Net receipts are 180 million lire

Forward market:

$$\frac{180 \text{ million}}{2,216} = £81,227$$

Francs
Forward market receipts

$$\frac{565,000}{10.36} = £54,537$$

Money market:

Borrow $\frac{FF565,000}{1.0225}$ = 552,567 francs (to repay 565,000 francs in 3 months)

Convert at spot 10.39 to £53,183
Invest at 10.5% for 3 months to yield £54,579
  The money market is slightly better.

6-month transactions

The 500 million lire receipt could be hedged using an option forward contract at 2,218/£. Note that there is a 700 million lire payment due in six months. These two transactions may be netted and the remaining 200 million hedged. If the 500 million export is paid before six months, the funds can be invested in Italy and any surplus remitted to the UK after six months.

Forward market:

$$\frac{200\ \text{million}}{2213} = £90,375 \text{ sterling equivalent of payment after 6 months}$$

Money market:
Borrow now £83,870 at 15% for 6 months, repay £90,160 in 6 months
Convert £83,870 to lire at 2208 to £ spot = 185,185 million
Invest in Italy for 6 months at 16% to yield 200 million lire to make the payment.
  The money market is better.

$A Net payments of A$80,000
Forward market:

$$\frac{80,000}{2.175} = £36,782$$

Money market:
Borrow £35,102 for 6 months at 15% to repay £37,734 in 6 months
Convert to $A spot = $75,117
Invest in Australia for 6 months to yield $80,000 to make the payment.
  The forward market is better.
  The export to Eastern Europe will be paid for by tinned meat which will be exchanged for 70 tonnes of coffee. The coffee can be sold for June delivery in the commodity futures market to yield:

$$70 \times £860 = £60,200 \text{ in June}$$

Summary

3 months	£ Receipts	£ Payments	£ Net
$A	55,363	40,000	15,363
Lire	81,227	—	81,227
Francs	54,579	—	54,579
			151,169

£151,169 invested for 3 months (April to June) at 10.5% per year will yield £155,137 at the end of 6 months.

6 months	£ Receipts	£ Payments	£ Net
$A	—	36,782	(36,782)
Lire	—	90,160	(90,160)
Coffee	60,200	—	60,200
			(66,742)

The cash surplus at the end of June is expected to be £155,137 − £66,742 = £88,395.

3. Omniown plc

(a) It is now 31 December 1991 and the corporate treasurer of Omniown plc is concerned about the volatility of interest rates. His company needs, in three months' time, to borrow £5 million for a six month period. Current interest rates are 14% per year for the type of loan Omniown would use, and the treasurer does not wish to pay more than this.

He is considering using either:
  (i) A forward rate agreement (FRA)
 (ii) Interest rate futures
(iii) An interest rate guarantee (short term cap)

Required:
Explain briefly how each of these three alternatives might be useful to Omniown plc.

(10 marks)

(b) The corporate treasurer of Omniown plc expects interest rates to increase by 2 per cent during the next three months and has decided to hedge the interest rate risk using interest rate futures.

March sterling three months' time deposit futures are currently priced at £86.25. The standard contract size is £500,000 and the minimum price movement is one tick (the value of one tick is 0.01% per year of the contract size).

Required:
Show the effect of using the futures market to hedge against interest rate movements:
  (i) If interest rates increase by 2% and the futures market prices also move by 2%.
 (ii) If interest rates increase by 2% and the futures market moves by 1.5%.
(iii) If interest rates fall by 1% and the futures market moves by 0.75%.

In each case estimate the hedge efficiency.

Taxation, margin requirements and the time value of money are to be ignored.

(10 marks)

(c) If, as an alternative to interest rate futures, the corporate treasurer had been able to purchase interest rate guarantees at 14% for a premium of 0.2% of the size of the loan to be guaranteed, calculate whether the total cost of the loan after hedging in each of situations (i) to (iii) in (b) above would have been less with the futures hedge or with the guarantee. The guarantee would be effective for the entire 6 month period of the loan.

Taxation, margin requirements and the time value of money may be ignored.

(5 marks)

ACCA, 3.2, December 1991

Solution:

(i) Forward rate agreements (FRAs)

Forward rate agreements are contracts, normally arranged between companies and banks, that offer companies the scope to fix future interest rates on either borrowing or lending for a specific period. For example, a company may wish to invest £15 million in three months' time at a guaranteed interest rate of 8% per year. The company could arrange a FRA with a bank at the agreed rate of 8% per year whereby if actual interest rates are lower than 8% the bank will pay to the company any difference between 8% and the actual rate. If the interest rate has moved to higher than 8% the company will have to compensate the bank for the difference between the actual rate and 8%. The yield to the company will remain at 8% no matter what happens to market interest rates. FRAs do not involve any actual lending or borrowing of the notional principal sum. They are normally for sums of at least US$1 million (or equivalent) and can be arranged for up to two or three years in the future.

FRAs would be a sensible way for Omniown to fix borrowing costs in 3 months' time, remembering that the actual borrowing of the £5 million would need to be arranged separately from the FRA.

(ii) Interest rate futures

Interest rate futures are legally binding contracts between seller and buyer to make and take (respectively) delivery of a specified interest rate commitment on an agreed date and at an agreed price. They are a means of hedging against expected rises in interest rates using a 'short hedge', and are available for up to two years. To hedge against an expected interest rate rise futures contracts may be sold now in the expectation that, as interest rates rise, the contract value will fall, and they can then be purchased at a lower price to produce a profit on the futures deal. This profit is expected to offset any losses from actual rises in interest rates experienced by companies that have borrowed funds from banks and elsewhere. If interest rates were to move in the opposite direction to that expected a futures loss will occur, but this will be to some extent offset by gains from cheaper interest costs in the cash market. There are only a limited number of types of interest futures contract, the most important on LIFFE (London International Financial Futures and Options Exchange) being 3 month sterling time deposits, 3 month Eurodollar, long gilts and US government Treasury bonds.

Interest rate futures should permit Omniown to hedge against most of the exposure from interest rate movements, although 100% protection (a perfect hedge) is very rare.

(iii) Interest rate guarantee

Interest rate guarantees are a form of short-term interest rate option, for periods of up to one year (longer term interest rate options such as caps, collars and floors also exist). The option guarantees that the interest rate will not rise above an agreed fixed level (or, alternatively, not fall below an agreed fixed level) during a set period commencing sometime in the near future. The interest rate protection is similar to that of a FRA. However, interest rate guarantees involve the payment of a premium to the seller of the guarantee, whereas no premium is payable with a FRA. Additionally interest rate guarantees, while protecting against downside risk (i.e. an interest rate rise for Omniown), offer the option holder the opportunity to take full advantage of favourable interest rate movements by not exercising the option. Neither FRAs nor interest rate futures allow the company to take advantage of favourable interest rate movements.

(b) (i) The value of one tick is $.0001 \times £500,000 \times \dfrac{3}{12} = £12.50$

A tick is one-hundredth of one per cent, a 2% movement is a 200-tick movement.

Omniown needs to borrow £5 million for 6 months. A 2% expected increase in interest rates would result in extra interest costs p.a. of:

$$£5m \times 2\% \times \frac{6}{12} = £50,000$$

Omniown needs to hedge with sufficient contracts to generate an expected £50,000 gain.

A 200-tick (or 2%) movement on one contract would result in an expected gain of $200 \times £12.50 = £2,500$. For £50,000 a 20-contract hedge would be required.

Dec 31 1991:
Sell 20 £500,000 March sterling time deposit contracts at
86.25 (effectively 13.75% per year interest)

March (or whenever interest rates have changed):
Buy 20 £500,000 March sterling time deposit contracts at
    84.25 (effectively 15.75% per year interest)
This closes out the position.

The gain is 20×200 ticks $\times £12.50 = £50,000$
or £10 million (20 contracts) $\times 2\% \times \dfrac{3}{12} = £50,000$

This is a perfect hedge with 100% hedge efficiency.

(ii) In this case the futures gain will be:

$$20 \times 150 \times £12.50 = £37,500$$
$$\text{or } £10m \times 1.5\% \times \frac{3}{12} = £37,500$$

This is a hedge efficiency of $\dfrac{£37,500}{£50,000} = 75\%$

(iii) In this case there is a 'cash market' gain as interest rates fall, but a loss on the futures market hedge.

The cash market gain is:

$$£5 \text{ million} \times 1\% \times \frac{6}{12} = £25,000$$

The futures market loss results from selling at 86.25 and closing out the position at 87.00. The loss is:

$$20 \times 75 \times £12.50 = £18,750$$

$$\text{or } £10m \times .75\% \times \frac{3}{12} = £18,750$$

This is a hedge efficiency of $\dfrac{£25,000}{£18,750} = 133\%$

(c) The total costs with the futures hedge are:

(i) Interest $£5m \times 16\% \times \dfrac{6}{12} = £400,000$ less gain £50,000 = £350,000

(ii) Interest £400,000 less gain £37,500 = £362,500

(iii) Interest $£5m \times 13\% \times \dfrac{6}{12} = £325,000$ plus loss £18,750 = £343,750

The cost (premium) of the guarantee is £5million × 0.2% = £10,000, payable whether or not the guarantee is 'exercised'.

The total cost with (i) and (ii) when the guarantee will be used and will limit interest rates to 14% is:

$$£5m \times 14\% \times \frac{6}{12} = £350,000 \text{ plus } £10,000 \text{ premium} = £360,000$$

This is more expensive than the futures hedge for (i) and cheaper for (ii).
The total cost for (iii) where the guarantee is not used and the interest rate is 13% is:

$$£5m \times 13\% \times \frac{6}{12} = £325,000 + £10,000 = £335,000$$

This is cheaper than the futures hedge as the guarantee has allowed the company to take advantage of lower cash market interest rates.

4. Fidden

(a) Discuss the techniques a company might use to hedge against the foreign exchange risk involved in foreign trade.

(8 marks)

(b) Fidden is a medium-sized UK company with export and import trade with the USA. The following transactions are due within the next 6 months. Transactions are in the currency specified.

Purchase of components, cash payment due in 3 months: £116,000
Sale of finished goods, cash receipt due in 3 months: $197,000
Purchase of finished goods for resale, cash payment due in 6 months: $447,000
Sale of finished goods, cash receipt due in 6 months: $154,000

Exchange rates (*London market*)

	$/£
Spot	1.7106–1.7140
3 months forward	0.82–0.77 cents premium
6 months forward	1.39–1.34 cents premium

Interest rates

3 months or 6 months	Borrowing	Lending
Sterling	12.5%	9.5%
Dollars	9%	6%

Foreign currency option prices (New York market)

Prices are cents per £, contract size £12,500

	Calls			Puts		
Exercise price ($)	March	June	Sept	March	June	Sept
1.60	—	15.20	—	—	—	2.75
1.70	5.65	7.75	—	—	3.45	6.40
1.80	1.70	3.60	7.90	—	9.32	15.35

Assume that it is now December with three months to expiry of the March contract and that the option price is not payable until the end of the option period, or when the option is exercised.

Required:
  (i) Calculate the net sterling receipts/payments that Fidden might expect for both its three- and six-month transactions if the company hedges foreign exchange risk on:
  1. The forward foreign exchange market
  2. The money market

(7 marks)
 (ii) If the actual spot rate in six months' time was, with hindsight, exactly the present six-month forward rate, calculate whether Fidden would have been better to hedge through foreign currency options rather than the forward market or money market.

(7 marks)
(iii) Explain briefly what you consider to be the main advantage of foreign currency options.

(3 marks)

ACCA, 3.2, December 1989

Solution:
(a) Several techniques may be used to hedge against the foreign exchange risk of foreign trade including:
  (i) Forward market hedges. A forward market hedge involves a company making a binding contract with a bank to buy or sell an agreed quantity of foreign currency at a rate of exchange that is fixed when the contract is made. The purchase or sale is fixed to take place either on a specific date, normally corresponding to the date when a company expects foreign currency payments or receipts, or between two specified dates (an option forward contract). Most forward contracts are for periods of up to one year, but contracts of up to five years may be arranged in leading currencies.
  (ii) Money market hedge. In a money market hedge a company borrows funds in one currency and exchanges those funds in the spot market for another currency. The funds are then often invested in the money market of the second currency. For example, a French company due to pay a sterling debt in six months' time might borrow francs now, convert those francs to pounds at the present spot rate (this fixes

the exchange rate) and invest the pounds in the UK for six months at the end of which the total proceeds of the investment may be used to pay the pound debt. The cost of a money market hedge is primarily influenced by the interest rate differential between the two countries concerned, in contrast to a forward market hedge where the cost depends upon the forward market rates quoted by the bank.

(iii) Foreign currency options. Foreign currency options offer the right, but not the obligation, to buy or sell a given amount of foreign exchange at a fixed price (the exercise price) usually at any time during a specified period. Companies using options will normally have a choice of both the exercise price of the option and the maturity date. The price of the option will, of course, vary according to the combination of exercise price and maturity date selected. Influences on the option price are the difference between the exercise price and the spot exchange rate, the time to maturity, relative interest rates in the countries concerned, currency volatility, and the supply and demand for specific options. The option need only be used (or sold) if exchange rates move in favour of the option holder; this limits the 'downside risk' of the holder. Options are available on either major exchanges such as London, New York or Philadelphia, or over-the-counter via major banks.

(iv) Financial futures market hedge. A small number of financial futures markets, e.g. IMM Chicago, offer foreign currency futures. Currency futures offer the purchase or sale of a standard amount of a limited number of foreign currencies at a specified time and price. They are basically an alternative to the forward foreign exchange market, but are much less flexible.

(v) Buy and sell in sterling. If a UK exporter always invoices in sterling or a UK importer insists on paying in sterling there is no foreign exchange risk. However, the risk does not disappear, it is merely shifted to the other party in the foreign trade transaction.

Other possible techniques include matching and netting, currency swaps and leading or lagging.

(b) (i) *3 months' transactions*
The purchase of components is payable in sterling and there is no foreign exchange risk for Fidden.

Outright exchange rates are:

	$/£
Spot	1.7106–1.7140
3 months forward	1.7024–1.7063
6 months forward	1.6967–1.7006

Hedging the sale of finished goods:
Forward market:

$$\text{Sell } \$197,000 \text{ 3 months forward} = \frac{197,000}{1.7063} = £115,454$$

Net sterling payments in three months are:

$$£116,000 - £115,454 = £546$$

Money market:
Borrow $192,665 at 9% per year to repay $197,000 from receipts in 3 months' time
Convert $192,665 spot to £ at 1.7140 = £112,407
Invest £112,407 for 3 months at 9.5% per year to receive £115,076 at the end of 3 months.
   The forward market is the better alternative.

6 months' transactions
Any hedge should be of the net payment, i.e.:

$$\$447,000 - \$154,000 = \$293,000$$

Forward market:
Buy $293,000 6 months forward at $1.6967/£

$$= \frac{\$293,000}{1.6967} = £172,688$$

Money market:
Borrow £166,296 for 6 months at 12.5% per year
Convert to $ spot at 1.7106 = $284,466
Invest $284,466 for 6 months at 6% per year to yield a total of $293,000 which may be used for the payment.
Total cost is £166,296 plus interest £10,394 = £176,690
   The best net sterling payment is £172,688 by using the forward market.

(ii)   The foreign currency option contracts available have an exercise price of $1.70 and $1.80.
   The relevant 6 months forward rate is $1.6967/£ with a total sterling cost of £172,688.
      The $1.70 option at a price of 3.45 cents per £ can be seen by inspection to give a higher sterling cost than the forward market.
Formally: $293,000 at 1.70 = £172,353

This requires $\frac{172,353}{12,500}$ contracts or 14 contracts (to the next whole number)

As sterling is to be sold for dollars a put option on sterling is required.
   The price of the foreign currency option contracts is:

$$14 \times £12,500 \times 3.45 \text{ cents} = \$6,037.5$$

14 contracts selling sterling will provide $297,500 at a cost of £175,000.

The overall cost if the put option is exercised is:

$$£175,000 + \frac{\$293,000 + \$6,037.5 - \$297,500}{1.7006} = £175,904$$

The $1.80 option requires $\frac{293,000}{1.80} = £162,778$

or 13.02 contracts. In practice 13 might be used together with a small amount of forward market cover, but if only options are used 14 contracts will be required to provide the entire $293,000.

The price of the option contracts is:

$$14 \times £12,500 \times 9.32 \text{ cents} = \$ 16,310$$

14 contracts selling sterling will provide $315,000 at a cost of £175,000.
The overall cost if the put option is exercised is:

$$£175,000 + \left(\frac{\$293,000 + \$16,310 - \$315,000}{1.7006} \right) = £171,654$$

This is less than the cost with the forward market hedge.

With hindsight Fidden would have been better to hedge through $1.80 foreign currency options.

(iii) The chief benefit of foreign currency options is that they offer flexibility in that they provide a right, which need not be exercised, to buy or sell foreign currency. If exchange rates move such that exercising the option is favourable, then the option will be sold or exercised. If, however, exchange rates move such that it is better not to use the option, it will mature unexercised and the only cost will be the option price. Options offer a means of limiting 'downside risk' while offering, in theory, unlimited returns.

TEN

THE MANAGEMENT AND FINANCE OF INTERNATIONAL TRADE

INTRODUCTION

The previous chapters have highlighted the problems of foreign exchange rate risk on international operations. The objective of this chapter is to undertake a practical review of some of the other risks that companies face when they engage in international trade, and the influence on such risk of the various alternative ways in which trade may be organized and financed. It also examines an alternative to traditional trade, countertrade, which is becoming increasingly important to exporters from developed countries.

INTERNATIONAL TRADE RISKS

Apart from the foreign exchange dimension, the risks faced by companies in international trade are broadly similar to those of domestic trade, with the added problems caused by increased distance, and dealing within the legal and political framework of the country concerned. These risks may be summarized as follows.

1. *Commercial risk* This relates to the likelihood that the purchaser will not pay for the goods ordered, or will pay at a much later date than was agreed in the terms of sale. This is a major risk for exporters. The business integrity of companies in some parts of the world is much lower than in the UK, and it is quite common for an overseas company to order goods which it has no intention of paying for, or in some cases even taking delivery from a foreign dockyard or other point of entry. The idea in such cases is that the UK exporter will have difficulty in reshipping the goods back to the UK, either for logistic or, more likely, bureaucratic reasons, and the goods will eventually be sold cheaply in the foreign country. If delivery of the goods is taken and the buyer defaults on payment, taking action to recover the debt through foreign courts is expensive and often slow. It is remarkable how many companies cease to trade when they are eventually taken to court, leaving the exporter with nothing but an expensive write-off. The evaluation of the credit risk of potential foreign customers is therefore an important prerequisite to international trade. Even if the customer does not default, significant delays in receiving payment for exports can be very expensive, as the longer the effective credit period taken, the longer the credit has to be financed through overdrafts or by other means. Credit risk may be evaluated in several ways including the use of:

(a) Credit evaluation reports from international credit agencies such as Dun and Bradstreet

(b) Information from government sources such as the Department of Trade which keeps files on several hundred thousand overseas companies

(c) The ECGD (Export Credits Guarantee Department, discussed later), and commercial credit agencies, which also maintain databases on foreign companies

(d) Chambers of Commerce and trade associations

(e) Bank references, although these need to be interpreted carefully as they are rarely derogatory

(f) Trade references. Again, to be used with caution as it is easy for a company to pay a few of its suppliers on time and to use these companies for reference purposes, while paying the bulk of its suppliers late, or not at all

2. *Physical risk* Physical risks comprise normal transit and deterioration risks, but as the time and distances involved in international transportation are normally much greater than for domestic trade, there is a greater chance of damage, theft, fire or loss.

3. *Political risk* The actions of foreign governments may have a significant influence on the success of international trade. The subject of political risk is discussed in depth in Chapter 13, particularly in relation to foreign direct investment, but government influences on foreign trade may take many forms, including exchange controls, export and import licences, quotas and tariffs on imports. It is common for governments to limit the amount of foreign currency that may be used to pay for imports to the country, which may delay or prevent payment being made, and a total block on the movement of funds from the country may be imposed. Bureaucratic delays are common, and may relate to the existence of excessive documentation, unreasonable conditions that have to be fulfilled by the exporter before the trade is allowed to proceed, or merely inefficiency owing to inadequate staffing or poorly trained personnel which holds up the payment process. Advice on political risk may be obtained from the Department of Trade, commercial banks, and UK embassies and consulates abroad. There is little point in accepting an overseas order if the government in the overseas country is likely to prevent payment being made, in an acceptable currency, for that order.

4. *Cultural risk* When dealing with countries of differing culture, religion, attitudes to alcohol and the role of women in society, laws, language and ways of undertaking business it is not surprising that it is sometimes difficult for trading partners to effectively communicate and successfully complete a transaction. Such problems may be overcome by prior research into such cultural factors, and by using the services of local agents or other advisers who can anticipate and smooth over any problems arising from cultural differences. Unfortunately one cultural difference which is still prevalent in some countries is the need for 'sweeteners' (bribery) in order to ensure that the trade is successful; if this is a necessary evil, an allowance for such costs should be built into the exporter's prices if possible.

Methods of payment and settlement

The risk of exporting can be strongly influenced by the terms on which the sale is agreed. Generally speaking, the less risky the terms of sale that are arranged, the more expensive such terms will be for the parties to the trade, especially in fees to banks. Companies should balance the benefits derived from using less risky payment methods against their cost.

Ideally, the exporter would like to receive cash in advance or cash on delivery of goods, but relatively few foreign importers are willing to agree to such terms, although many export transactions do involve the payment of an upfront deposit of between 10 and 20 per cent of the purchase price. Most export sales are on a credit basis, often with longer periods of credit granted than for similar domestic trade. Because of the geographical, legal and language differences between countries it is often more difficult to pursue an overseas overdue debt than one in the UK.

The most risky form of sale is open account, where the documents of title are sent direct to the buyer, and the buyer agrees to pay after a specified credit period, usually not more than 180 days. As the exporter loses control of the goods, open account should only be used where the buyer is known and trusted, possibly as a result of previous transactions. Many exports to European Community countries are on open account terms.

A slightly less risky form of sale is payment upon shipment. Here, the exporter informs the importer when the goods have actually been shipped, and at this time, normally before the goods have arrived, the importer makes payment to the exporter. The exporter retains the legal title to the goods (e.g. through ownership certificates and the bill of lading), which prevents the importer from gaining physical possession of the goods. Once the payment has been received by the exporter the documents of title are sent to the importer.

A further alternative is the use of bills of exchange in an 'export trade collection'. A bill of exchange is a document normally drawn up by the exporter (the drawer) and sent to the buyer or the buyer's bank (the drawee). The drawee shows its willingness to pay the amount specified on the bill at the time stated (or immediately if it is a sight bill) by signing the bill (also known as 'accepting the bill'). Where a bank accepts the bill it is known as a bank bill as opposed to a trade bill and carries less risk. Some bills are clean bills which require no documents, others are documentary bills where the title to the goods, and hence possession of the goods, will only be released after the bill has been paid or accepted. Bills are a legally binding obligation, and offer significantly more security for the exporter than open account. The typical process of a bank bill is as follows:

1. The exporter draws up the bill of exchange on the foreign purchaser.
2. The bill is passed to the exporter's bank (the remitting bank), which then forwards it to a bank in the importer's country (the collecting bank). This may be an overseas branch of the UK bank or a correspondent bank.
3. The collecting bank presents the bill to the overseas customer (the drawee) for immediate payment if it is a sight bill or for acceptance by the customer if it is a term bill. The bank will not release the documents of title to the customer until either payment has been made or the bill has been accepted.
4. Payment is passed to the exporter (sight bill) or the accepted bill is returned to the exporter. The exporter can then either wait for payment to be made at the agreed date specified on the bill (60 days' or 90 days' credit is common), or may discount (sell the bill now at a discount to its face value) in order to raise immediate finance.

Similar risk protection is provided by the promissory note, which is a written promise by the buyer to pay the exporter (or the bearer of the note) an amount of money at a specified time.

Banks may also be used for a 'cash against documents' collection. In this case there is no bill of exchange involved. The bank is instructed only to release the documents of title when payment to the bank has been made by the overseas buyer.

An even more secure form of payment terms is the use of the documentary letter of credit. A letter of credit is arranged by the buyer through its bank and is a guarantee of payment by that bank subject to the exporter fulfilling exactly the terms of the contract, including the error-free provision of specified documents. Documents that are commonly requested include:

1. A bill of exchange
2. The bill of lading. This gives title to the goods and states that the goods were received for transportation in good order
3. Insurance policies
4. Shipping documents
5. Certificate of origin, to prove that the goods did not originate from an unacceptable country (e.g. Iran)
6. The invoice, specifying the quality, quantity and price of the goods

The letter of credit, once drawn up by the importer's bank (the issuing bank) is passed to the exporter's bank or another UK bank (the advising bank) which notifies the exporter of the exact terms that must be fulfilled. Sometimes the exporter's bank will add its own guarantee (confirmation), giving even more security. The full process of documentary credits is illustrated in Figure 10.1.

As may be seen from Figure 10.1, using documentary letters of credit is quite an involved process. It is also relatively expensive. The cost of the letter of credit is normally borne by the importer, but the cost may be shared between the importer and the exporter if this is agreed at the time the sales contract is fixed.

The most secure form of documentary letter of credit is one which is confirmed by a UK bank (which means that this bank is adding its own guarantee that payment will be made to the exporter), and is irrevocable. The terms of an irrevocable letter of credit cannot be altered without the agreement of all parties. It is not recommended that revocable letters of credit are used, as this would mean that the importer could change the terms of credit, and would significantly increase the risk taken by the exporter.

Since documentary letters of credit are relatively expensive to use they are best suited to cases where the creditworthiness of the buyer is not proven or where the export is of high value and the exporter wishes to be sure of payment. For payment to be made under a letter of credit the terms agreed in the credit must be precisely met, including presentation of the documents in exactly the agreed form. It is important that companies using these credits check all details carefully: nearly half of all sets of documents that are presented to UK banks are rejected because they have errors or are incomplete. This causes delays in the payment process, delays which the exporter may have to finance.

Settlement of international trade transactions   The settlement means used can have an important impact on company cash flow. Normally a company wishes to have effective use of the cash as soon as possible, but once again the quicker means of settlement will involve additional costs, which must be weighed against the extra speed achieved. Alternative settlement means include:

1. Cheque. This is normally by post, and is slow and risky. The postal system of some countries is not reliable. If a cheque is received in a foreign currency, the UK bank where it is presented will charge a fee for clearing foreign cheques which must be borne by the exporter.
2. Banker's draft. A cheque is drawn by the buyer's bank, normally on a bank in the exporter's country. The draft is then sent to the exporter who arranges payment via his or her own bank. Drafts are slightly better than cheques, but these too may be lost in transit.
3. Payment orders, either by mail transfer or telegraphic transfer. Payment orders are written

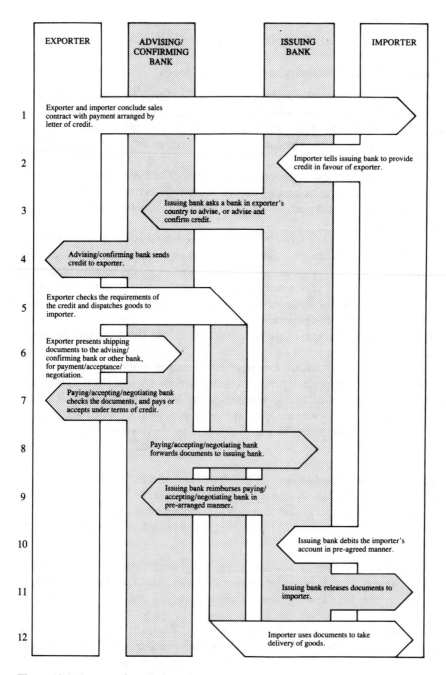

Figure 10.1 Letters of credit flow chart

Source: Midland Bank booklet *Letters of Credit*

instructions from one bank to another. Mail orders are sent by airmail, but may still go astray. Telegraphic orders are sent by telex or cable which considerably speeds up the payment process. Where large sums are involved which need to be paid or received quickly, the use of telegraphic transfer is recommended.

4. SWIFT (Society for Worldwide Inter-Bank Financial Telecommunications). SWIFT is a computer-based payment method, centred in Brussels, that is very rapid, but quite expensive. Transactions only take place between banks and brokers that are members of SWIFT (this includes almost all of the world's leading banks), and are in the form of an international money transfer (IMT) or express international money transfer (EIMT). Settlement by SWIFT is very common for large denomination transactions in Europe and North America.

Foreign trade insurance   Normal transit risks may be insured through Lloyds and other private sector insurance companies, but it is also possible to insure against commercial and political risk.

A condition of obtaining finance for exports is often the existence of adequate insurance against political and commercial risk. In the UK the major provider of such insurance has traditionally been a government department, the export credits guarantee department (ECGD), which offered both short-term and medium- to long-term protection. The ECGD was always intended to be a self-financing department, but during the 1980s it suffered severe deficits. In order to relieve public subsidies to the ECGD the government privatized its short-term activities (up to 180 days) in 1991, when it was purchased by a Dutch company, NCM Holding NV, one of the largest private credit insurers in the world.

NCM offers similar cover to the old short-term ECGD policies, with the most favourable terms for normal export transactions which cover all of a company's exports, although cover is also available, at a higher premium, where a company just wishes to protect against exports to selected countries.

The NCM international guarantee is designed for all companies which sell on credit terms of up to 180 days. Cover is normally available from the date of shipment of the goods, but it is also possible, for a supplementary fee, to insure from the contract date. The risks insured are:

1. Commercial or buyer risk from:
   (a) Insolvency of the buyer (90 per cent cover)
   (b) Failure of the buyer to pay within six months of the due date (90 per cent cover)
   (c) Failure of the buyer to accept dispatched goods (72 per cent cover)
2. Political or country risk including:
   (a) Restrictions imposed by a foreign government on the transfer of money from the buyer's country
   (b) Political events which prevent the performance of the contract or transfer of funds. This would include the effects of war and civil war
   (c) Cancellation of an export licence or the imposition by a government of new restrictions after the contract has been signed

Cover for political risk is normally 95 per cent of the company's loss.

NCM charges an annual premium which varies according to export turnover, and a flat rate fee payable monthly on the amount of export business. For certain high-risk countries an additional premium is payable.

As well as NCM, short-term insurance against commercial and political risk is provided by Trade Indemnity and other insurance companies.

Medium- to long-term protection (two to five years or occasionally longer) is still offered by ECGD through its Project Group. This provides insurance for one-off medium- and long-term export contracts, for example, a contract to construct a power station in a foreign country. Such cover would involve a tailor-made specific guarantee normally giving 90 per cent protection against loss.

Tender to contract insurance against foreign exchange movements between the date of tender and the award of the contract is also possible.

New foreign direct investment in an overseas subsidiary can also be insured by ECGD. Cover includes:

1. Expropriation of assets (this includes the results of severe discrimination by foreign governments against the overseas enterprise)
2. War and revolution
3. Restrictions of remittances from the foreign country to the UK. This includes the remittance of profits, loan repayments and capital
4. Breach of contract by the host government

Insurance is usually for a period of 15 years.

ECGD Project Group is a major provider of both buyer and supplier credits. These are discussed in more detail below.

Export financing

To most companies export financing means obtaining sufficient finance to cover the period of credit that is given to foreign customers. Export customers are frequently given longer periods of credit than domestic customers, 90 days or more being common and the UK exporter requires working capital to continue operating until payment is made by the foreign customer. Although the credit period might be specified as 90 days, customers frequently take longer to pay than the agreed period, and this can make it necessary for the exporter to raise substantial amounts of expensive finance.

There are two types of export credit: the more common supplier credit where the exporter allows credit to the foreign customer and then borrows from a bank or elsewhere to finance that credit; and the buyer credit where a UK bank provides finance direct to the overseas customer who then uses the funds to make payment to the exporter. In all forms of credit it is useful to differentiate between finance which is non-recourse and finance which is with recourse. Non-recourse finance means that the exporter is not responsible to a lender if the buyer defaults on payment.

The finance of exports can be arranged using traditional sources of finance, such as overdrafts and other types of bank loan that are in common use for domestic trade, but some financing methods are particularly suited to exports.

1. *Discounting bills of exchange* Bills of exchange have already been described. If the bill is a bank bill, especially one associated with a documentary letter of credit, it can be sold (discounted) before its maturity date in order to provide the exporter with finance. The exporter, upon receipt of the accepted bill, can either keep it and receive payment on the due date, or can sell it for less than its face value (discount it). For example, if interest rates are 10 per cent and the bill has 90 days until payment is due, a bill with £10,000 face value would be sold for approximately £9,750 (£10,000 less 10 per cent for three months). Bills are often sold to

banks, the bank then collecting the payment from the importer. A fee is normally payable to the bank for the collection operation. If the importer defaults on payment, the bank has recourse to the exporter who must bear the loss.

2. *Negotiating bills of exchange* Banks are also willing, for a fee, to negotiate (purchase) bills before they are accepted by the foreign customer. The exporter receives immediate credit for the full face value of the bill, but must pay interest to the bank until the bank receives payment from the foreign customer. The bank will send the bill to the overseas buyer, and will reimburse itself from the payments of the buyer. Once again, this is a with recourse form of finance.

3. *Clean acceptance credits* An acceptance credit facility provides short-term export finance for a company by a bank agreeing to accept (guarantee) bills of exchange drawn upon itself up to an agreed total sum. Once accepted by the bank the bills can be discounted to provide immediate finance for the exporter. Clean acceptance credits are normally a 'rolling' source of finance; as old bills mature and are paid, new bills are accepted in their place. This form of finance is only available to larger companies. A beneficial feature of acceptance credits is that the exporter can choose when to acquire finance, and can select the times when the discount rates are most favourable in the money market. This may result in acceptance credits providing a cheaper form of finance than overdrafts.

4. *Export factoring* Export factoring involves companies handing over responsibility for the collection of payments from their credit customers to a factoring company. Factoring companies, most of which are subsidiaries of major banks, are able to give advice as to the creditworthiness of overseas customers; one potential problem, however, is that they may refuse to factor the debt of a customer if they do not consider the customer to be creditworthy. The factoring company is usually experienced in the foreign country or has excellent contacts with agents who can act on its behalf to pursue the debts. Some factors offer a non-recourse service, i.e. the factoring company will bear the risk of any bad debts. If this is the case, then the exporter will normally be able to sell on open account terms without bearing any default risk; as was discussed earlier, open account is considerably cheaper than methods such as documentary letters of credit. Naturally, factoring companies charge a fee for non-recourse protection.

Export factoring is normally only available to companies with export credit sales in excess of £250,000.

As well as offering a debt collection service, export factoring companies are willing to provide immediate finance, against the security of the exports to be factored. Finance is normally available for up to 80 per cent of the value of the invoices to be factored, with the remaining 20 per cent being paid either upon collection from the overseas buyer by the factor, or 90 days after the due payment date, whichever comes first. The cost of this finance is usually greater than overdraft or bill finance.

Many factoring companies also provide invoice discounting services, where invoices are sold to the invoice discounting company to provide finance. Up to 75 or 80 per cent of the value of invoices can be immediately advanced in this way. Invoice discounting does not involve any debt collection service, and the responsibility for any bad debts remains with the exporter.

5. *Export merchants or export houses* Export merchants do not directly provide finance to exporters; instead they buy goods outright from companies and then export them. Payment to the UK company is usually within seven days, and the export house takes the risk of any bad debts from the foreign customer.

6. *Confirming houses* Confirming houses act as agents for foreign buyers. They will normally place the order with the exporter and will often arrange for payment to be made to the UK

exporter upon evidence of shipment. There is no overseas credit risk for the exporter; the confirming house usually provides credit to the foreign customer, which eliminates the risk of non-payment for the exporter.

7. *Forfaiting*   Forfaiting is a method of financing medium-term exports of capital goods over a period of between six months and five years. The forfaiting bank agrees to buy, at a discount, a series of bills of exchange or promissory notes, thus providing finance to the exporter. Finance provided by forfaiting is normally at a fixed interest rate and can be provided for up to 100 per cent of the contract value. The forfaiting bank itself normally receives some security in the form of an 'aval' (guaranteeing that payment will be made) from a reputable bank in the foreign customer's country. Forfaiting is unusual in that it is non-recourse; in the event of the foreign customer defaulting, the banks have no claim on the exporter.

8. *Leasing*   Where exports are of large items of capital equipment, the exporter may be able to sell the equipment to a leasing company (the lessor), and receive immediate payment. The leasing company will then receive periodic payments from the overseas buyer over the agreed lease period. This form of leasing is effectively non-recourse factoring to the exporter, and may be arranged with a lessor in either the exporter's or importer's country. Hire purchase finance may also be arranged for the importer, again providing the exporter with immediate finance.

9. *ECGD supplier and buyer credit*   The Project Group of the ECGD facilitates the finance of medium-term capital goods. Exports of expensive capital goods normally involve lengthy credit periods which could prove to be a drain on the exporter's cash flow and could be a deterrent to seeking capital orders if credit had to be financed at normal market rates. ECGD does not itself directly give credit; instead it provides a guarantee to a bank which protects the bank against loss if the overseas customer defaults. Under the supplier credit financing facility (SCF), banks participating in the scheme provide finance to the exporter. Supplier credit is available for sums in excess of £25,000 and for up to 85 per cent of the contract value at fixed rates of interest. Interest may sometimes be at preferential rates, depending on the country of destination of the exports; cheap rate finance is available for many Third World countries. As long as the terms of the loan are complied with, the loan is non-recourse, with no risk to the exporter should the purchaser default. The exporter can thus confidently seek orders without worrying about default risk on 85 per cent of the order value, or how to finance the credit period of the order. Banks are prepared to offer the non-recourse facility because they have the safety of the ECGD guarantee.

The buyer credit financing facility (BCF) is designed to aid large-scale capital exports with a value of at least £1 million and with a credit period of at least two years. Most loans are for in excess of £5 million. With buyer credit the loan is provided by the bank direct to the overseas customer, up to a maximum of 85 per cent of the value of the exports. The buyer must pay an upfront deposit of up to 20 per cent of the total contract price. Since the loan is made direct to the foreign buyer there is no recourse to the exporter should the foreign buyer default. Interest is normally at a fixed rate, and is almost always at a lower rate than prevailing market rates for a loan of the same risk (this is meant to be a marketing attraction to stimulate UK exports). However, most other industrialized nations also have organizations that are prepared to offer relatively low interest rate supplier credit. The loan made to the foreign buyer is used to make payment to the exporter. Payment will be according to the terms of the individual agreement, but will commonly be in agreed stage payments when the exporter has completed various elements of the capital export. The ECGD fees for the guarantee, and any arrangement charges with the bank, are normally paid by the exporter.

A variation on the single project buyer credit is the buyer line of credit. This may relate to either a project line of credit which, in a single agreement, covers a number of relatively small (minimum £35,000) separate contracts with different suppliers in the UK, but all relating to the same capital project, or to general purpose lines of credit. These are made available to foreign banks to offer financial support to overseas companies wishing to place orders in the UK.

Unless export finance facilities are available at a fixed rate of interest, the exporter will face interest rate risk, which can adversely affect the profitability of the exports. Protection against interest rate risk can, of course, be arranged using interest rate options, swaps, or futures (discussed earlier in Chapters 8 and 9), or alternative procedures such as forward rate agreements (FRAs). These offer companies the facility to fix future interest rates on either borrowing or lending for a specific period: for example, a company wishing to invest £5 million in six months' time at a guaranteed interest rate of 8 per cent per annum, might enter into a FRA with a bank at the agreed rate of 8 per cent per annum, whereby if actual interest rates are lower than 8 per cent the bank will pay the company the difference between 8 per cent and the actual rate. If the interest rate is above 8 per cent then the company will have to compensate the bank for the difference between the actual rate and 8 per cent. No matter what level market interests move to, the yield to the company remains at 8 per cent. FRAs do not involve any actual lending or investment of the principal sum, are usually for at least US$1 million (or equivalent in other major currencies), and can be arranged for up to two or three years in the future.

Countertrade

Countertrade is a trade deal in which either no cash changes hands or only a portion of the value of the trade is paid for in cash. Payment is made in goods, services or ideas. Early countertrade was mainly in the form of barter, but more recently many different forms have been devised. The 1980s saw a resurgence of countertrade to the extent that some estimates suggest that up to 35 per cent of all world trade is in the form of countertrade (see, for example, Rowe (1989)). This is probably an exaggeration, but other estimates have suggested a figure of 25 per cent and there is no doubt that both the amount of countertrade and the number of countries using countertrade have substantially increased; more than 100 countries now engage in frequent countertrade deals.

What are the attractions of countertrade? Sometimes the use of countertrade is the only way to arrange an export deal, especially with:

1. Less developed countries with limited supplies of foreign currency with which to make payment for imports
2. Countries with exchange control restrictions
3. Centralized economies whose currencies are not freely convertible or accepted in the 'Western' world. For many years the old Comecon block widely used countertrade in its dealings with the West.

The debt crisis discussed in Chapter 3 has also contributed to the growth of countertrade: many countries, particularly those which are less developed, have found it increasingly difficult to obtain the necessary trade finance to pay for imports, and the commercial banks have been reluctant to further increase their sovereign risk exposure to such countries, even for trade purpose. Countertrade has thus provided the means for countries to maintain a reasonable level of imports.

A further feature of countertrade is that it effectively allows price reductions to be made by raw material or commodity producers in order to gain market share. If agricultural produce is traded at a favourable price to the exporter and brought to a Western market, this may gain market share which would not otherwise exist. Countertrade is also an excellent means to gain entry to a new market, particularly an emerging market with exchange controls and other restrictions, and can provide major growth opportunities for exporters to countries such as China, the former Eastern bloc, and several South American countries.

Many countertrade deals involve quite long-term agreements to purchase raw materials or produce. These agreements may be at fixed prices, or prices with a limited adjustment factor built in according to movements in exchange rates. One effect of such agreements is to provide medium-term price stability and effectively to offer a substitute for the forward foreign exchange market cover that cannot be obtained in the currencies of many countries engaging in countertrade.

Should countertrade be encouraged?   Despite these very sound reasons for the growth of countertrade, there are strong economic grounds for governments to actively discourage the process. Most countertrade is on a bilateral basis and does not necessarily promote economic efficiency. Trade is not based upon free market competition, where efficient economic activity should, in theory, be based upon the principle of comparative advantage. In addition, it is not difficult to see that some countries can produce a particular type of good more efficiently than other countries: for example, the UK is inefficient in the production of bananas owing to the climate, but efficient in the production of grain crops. Therefore it makes sense for the UK to concentrate on grain production, where it has an absolute advantage in productive efficiency, and to trade grain for bananas. However, gains from trade do not only occur when countries have an absolute advantage in production: as long ago as 1817, Ricardo (1948) suggested that trade can benefit two countries even if one country is more efficient at producing all of the traded goods. The theory of comparative advantage suggests that there are gains to be made whenever the relative price ratios of two goods differ under international trade from what they would under conditions of no trade. For example:

	Cost of production (one unit)		
	UK	*Foreign country*	*Ratio*
Textiles	200	100	2:1
Wine	200	50	4:1

The UK in this example is relatively inefficient in the production of both goods. Before trade, one unit of textiles in the UK costs one unit of wine. In the foreign country one unit of wine costs only half a unit of textiles. If the foreign country can import more than half a unit of textiles for one unit of wine it will gain from trade. Similarly, if the UK can import more than one unit of wine for one unit of textiles, it, too, will gain from trade. In this situation the foreign country should specialize in the production of wine, in which it has the greatest relative advantage (4:1), and the UK in textiles, where its relative disadvantage is lowest (2:1). At an exchange ratio of two-thirds (i.e. the price of wine to the price of textiles) the results of trade would be:

UK: one unit of wine now 'costs' $200 \times \frac{2}{3} = 133$ (previously it was 200)

Foreign country: one unit of textiles now 'costs' $50 \times \frac{3}{2} = 75$ (previously it was 100)

Both countries therefore gain from trade rather than producing the traded good themselves.

This is a simplification of reality, however, it assumes that resources can be quickly and freely moved to new uses to take advantage of the gains from trade, whereas adjustments are, in fact, expensive and slow. Retraining the UK wine labour force to produce textiles would take many months, even supposing the workers are willing to move from the vineyard to the factory! It also assumes that world prices are not affected by a single major producer's level of imports and exports, and ignores dynamic effects such as improvements in technology or changes in the factors of production such as population growth.

Although these factors complicate the basic theory of comparative advantage, the conclusion that trade can increase national wealth and welfare still remains valid.

Countertrade does not depend on the principle of comparative advantage and, in economic terms, means that uncompetitive goods may be successfully produced and marketed. It also reduces the economic stimulus to countries to adjust their production to concentrate on products or services where they are relatively efficient. As a result, countertrade may be argued to reduce the quantity, quality and efficiency of world production, and to cause a reduction in world consumption. This argument is to some extent valid, but the reality of today's world is that it contains many restrictions which prevent the principle of comparative advantage becoming fully operational. Every nation to a greater or lesser extent impedes the free flow of international trade, and tariffs, often in the form of customs duties (e.g. 25 per cent of the import price), have been imposed by most countries at some time. The arguments for tariffs centre on the protection of domestic industries. Eventually it is hoped that tariffs can be eliminated through the protracted general agreement on tariffs and trade (GATT) negotiations.

Barriers to trade occur in many forms besides tariffs. These include:

1. Quotas, quantitative limits on imports and exports
2. Technical barriers, including standards imposed by national governments concerning health, welfare, quality, and size of product
3. 'Buy domestic': this particularly relates to the purchasing patterns of governments which favour domestic producers
4. Subsidies by governments, for example, to support industries in less developed regions or areas of high unemployment
5. Taxes, levied on foreign goods and not their domestic competitors
6. Exchange controls, restricting the free flow of funds between countries

The existence of tariffs and other market imperfections stimulates activities such as countertrade. According to Lecraw (1989) there are three valid economic reasons for the existence of countertrade:

1. Where there is some form of market failure, and countertrade is the best means of reducing that failure. The creation of a substitute forward market, the avoidance of tariffs and other barriers are possible examples.
2. Where there is market failure and countertrade is the second-best alternative, the best alternative not being feasible.
3. Where there are principal/agent problems that countertrade can be used to reduce. In competitive market conditions individual companies (the agents) will engage in foreign trade which will maximize the value for their countries (the principals). Where market imperfections exist, the actions of companies may maximize their own benefits, but may not maximize the benefits of the country. The government, in its role as 'principal' for the country, may intervene in the market to directly encourage and stimulate countertrade, and by doing so alter the actions of companies, in order to increase the value of trade deals to the country as a whole.

The attitude of governments and international agencies towards countertrade has been mixed; most governments condone countertrade to some extent, but international agencies such as the International Monetary Fund (IMF), the Organization for Economic Cooperation and Development (OECD) and, understandably, GATT, are opposed to it, largely on the grounds of economic efficiency. The United Nations (UN) takes a more neutral position.

Types of countertrade   Countertrade can take many forms, including:

1. *Barter*   With barter, goods or services are exchanged for other goods or services of equivalent value. Barter may be a direct swap, or a third party may take the goods and make payment to one of the suppliers. For example, a UK exporter could send goods to Eastern Europe; the Eastern European company could supply some raw materials to the Middle East; and a company in the Middle East could make payment to the UK company. Despite its historic origins, barter accounts for only about 5 per cent of countertrade transactions. A good example of barter is Boeing, which traded 10 747 aircraft with Saudi Arabia in exchange for 34.48 million barrels of oil.
2. *Compensation agreements*   Under a compensation agreement the UK exporter will accept payment for the goods partly in goods and partly in money.
3. *Counterpurchase*   Counterpurchase is the most widely used form of countertrade, representing about 50 per cent of all arrangements. The UK exporter agrees to buy goods from the foreign importer, or from a third party nominated by the foreign importer. The value of the counterpurchased goods is an agreed percentage of the price of the goods originally exported.
4. *Buy-back*   The UK exporter agrees to buy goods that have been produced using the equipment that was exported. For example, if a car production plant was exported the exporter would agree to purchase, probably at some later date, cars which had been manufactured abroad in that plant.
5. *Industrial offset*   This represents approximately 25 per cent of deals. The exporter of large capital items, such as ships or aircraft, agrees to purchase components for the production of these exports from the customer for the exports, thereby reducing the effective cost to the customer.
6. *Switch trading*   With switch trading the exporter sells goods to an importer who cannot, or will not, make payment for the goods in a convertible hard currency. The importer maintains a special clearing account in a third country (often a LDC), which can only be used to buy goods in that country, and makes payment to the exporter from this account. The exporter, however, may not want goods from this third country, but instead may use the services of a switch trader who will buy, with a convertible currency, the credit that the exporter has been given by the importer, at a discount to its face value. The exporter thus receives payment, albeit at a discount, and the switch trader will find another company that wishes to purchase goods from the third country and will sell the credit to that company.
7. *Debt swaps*   Debt swaps were discussed in Chapter 3 (in the section on the Third World debt crisis). Lenders of debt to LDCs, faced with the likelihood that large proportions of their loans are unlikely to be repaid, or not repaid for many years, have become increasingly willing to exchange the debt for something else. The main forms of swap are:

(a) Debt for equity swaps, where debt is swapped for shares in a domestic company, and effectively leads to foreign direct investment in that country.
(b) Debt for debt swaps, through which the debt of one country might be swapped for the debt of another country, allowing the lending bank to consolidate its loan portfolio in particular countries.

(c) Debt for product swaps, where debt is directly swapped for products of the country concerned. In most cases the country will require more products to be purchased than debt that is repaid: for example, the repayment of £1 million of debt by a country might be conditional upon £2 million of products being purchased from the country, meaning a further £1 million has to be found by the bank or another company.

(d) Debt for nature swaps. This is an unusual form of swap which involves conservation groups and others buying debt at a large discount from banks and returning the debt to the borrowing LDC in return for guarantees from the LDC that it will undertake agreed conservation measures, for example, that it will preserve an agreed area of tropical rainforest.

The attitude of companies towards countertrade has changed significantly during the last few years. From being a form of trade which was only undertaken as a last resort, countertrade has become an important strategic tool for entering new markets and increasing market share. Countertrade is much more complex than conventional trade, often involving lengthy and expensive negotiations and relying on a large element of trust between the parties to the trade, and the costs of countertrade must be clearly established before a company engages in such a transaction. The larger fixed cost element in countertrade negotiations means that countertrade is more suited to large trade deals than to small ones. There is also a significant learning curve in negotiating and undertaking countertrade deals; the more experience a company has of such deals, the more efficient future deals are likely to be. Many multinational companies have established dedicated teams which specialize in countertrade and actively seek countertrade opportunities. In spite of opposition by international agencies, countertrade has become an important part of world commercial activity.

REFERENCES

Most of the leading commercial banks offer free booklets giving guidance to exporting and importing. These guides often contain useful information on hedging foreign exchange risk.

Lecraw, D. L. (1989) 'The management of countertrade: factors influencing success', *Journal of International Business Studies*, Vol. 20, No. 1, Spring.

Ricardo, D. (1948) *On the principles of political economy and taxation*, Dutton, New York.

Rowe, M. (1989) 'Countertrade', Euromoney Books.

QUESTIONS

1. Briefly discuss five sources of external finance that a medium-sized company might use to finance its export sales.

ACCA, 3.2, December 1990

Solution:
Possible sources of export finance for UK companies include:

(i) Overdrafts, either in sterling or a foreign currency. This is still the most common form of export financing in the UK. With an overdraft a bank allows borrowing up to an agreed credit limit at an interest rate which is dependent upon the credit risk of the borrower. Floating rate interest is payable on the amount borrowed at any time, not on the entire overdraft facility. Overdrafts may sometimes be unsecured, but many are secured by shipping documents or other assets.

(ii) Short-term loans. Loans may also be in a variety of currencies, and are normally fixed rate. Interest is paid upon the entire loan and the cash flow commitment is known at the outset. Foreign currency loans will normally be repaid from the foreign currency proceeds of export transactions.

(iii) Negotiation of bills of exchange. An exporter might arrange with his or her bank to purchase (negotiate) sight or term bills of exchange prior to their acceptance by the foreign customer (often when the bill is remitted abroad to the customer). The exporter in this way can receive immediate finance. Interest at an agreed margin over base rate is payable by the exporter for the period between the date of negotiation and the date the bank receives payment on the bill. If the overseas customer defaults on the bill the bank has recourse to the exporter.

(iv) Discounting of bills under documentary credits. Bills of exchange that are issued in association with a documentary letter of credit may be sold in the discount market to provide immediate finance. If the bills have been accepted by a bank (i.e. the bank undertakes to make payment at maturity of the bill), there is no recourse to the exporter. Bills are commonly of 60, 90 or 180 days' maturity.

(v) Clean acceptance credit. An acceptance credit involves an exporter negotiating a facility with a bank for a fixed amount. Under the facility bills are accepted by the bank (prior to payment of the bill by the overseas customer), and can be discounted at competitive rates. Acceptance credits are often cheaper than overdraft finance.

Clean acceptance credits are normally arranged as a revolving facility, meaning that when existing bills mature and are paid new bills are accepted in their place. In the event of default by the overseas customer the bank has recourse to the exporter.

(vi) Export factoring. Exporters that use the debt collection services of a factoring company may obtain an immediate loan from the factoring company, normally up to 80% of the value of invoiced sales. Interest costs are usually slightly higher than for overdrafts. Many factoring companies offer non-recourse financing.

(vii) Export house finance via:
1. Export merchants
2. Export agents acting on behalf of the exporter
3. Confirming houses acting as agents for foreign buyers.

Export merchants act as principals buying goods outright and exporting them. Export merchants normally pay UK manufacturers within seven days, effectively transforming an export sale into a domestic sale.

Export agents and confirming houses arrange payment to the UK manufacturer on evidence of shipment, and often offer credit to the foreign buyer (reducing credit risk for the exporter).

(viii) Forfaiting. Forfaiting relates to the medium-term export of capital goods. A bank purchases a series of promissory notes on a non-recourse basis after shipment has been made, or some agreed part of a contract has been fulfilled. The bank will usually demand that its own risk is guaranteed (avalized) by the importer's bank.

Hire purchase, leasing, and countertrade are other forms of finance that might be possible.

2. Newlean Ltd

Newlean Ltd has experienced difficulty with the collection of debts from export customers. At present the company makes no special arrangements for export sales.

As a result the company is considering either:

1. Employing the services of a non-recourse export factoring company
2. Insuring its exports against non-payment through a government agency. The two alternatives also provide new possible ways of financing export sales.

An export factor will, if required, provide immediate finance of 80% of export credit sales at an interest rate of 2% above bank base rate. The service fee for the debt collection is 2.5% of credit sales. If the factor is used administrative savings of £12,500 per year should be possible.

The government agency short-term comprehensive insurance policy costs 35 pence per £100 insured and covers 90% of the risk of non-payment for exports. For a further payment of 25 pence per £100 insured the agency will provide its guarantee which enables bank finance for the insured exports to be raised at $\frac{5}{8}$% above bank base rate. This finance is only available in conjunction with the government agency comprehensive insurance policy. Newlean normally has to pay 2.5% above base rate for its overdraft finance.

Newlean's annual exports total £650,000. All export orders are subject to a 15% initial deposit.

Export sales are on open account terms of 45 days' credit, but on average payment has been 30 days late. Approximately 0.5% by value of credit sales results in bad debts which have to be written off.

Clearing bank base rate is 10%.

Required:
Determine which combination of export administration and financing Newlean Ltd should use.

ACCA, 3.2, December 1985

Solution:
As a first step it is useful to establish the alternative combinations of export administration and financing that are possible. These are:

1. Continue with the present system
2. Government agency insurance plus normal overdraft finance
3. Government agency insurance and guarantee with cheaper finance
4. Factoring with normal overdraft finance
5. Factoring with finance from the factor (80%) and overdraft finance (20%).

Alternative 4 is unlikely to be selected as normal overdraft finance is more expensive than finance from the factor.

1. Continue as at present
Annual credit sale £552,500
Average credit period taken 75 days
Overdraft cost 12.5%

	£
Annual cost of granting credit £552,500 $\times \dfrac{75}{365} \times 12.5\% =$	14,191
Cost of bad debts	2,762
Total cost	16,953

2. Agency with normal overdraft

	£
Annual cost of granting credit as above	14,191
Cost of bad debts (10% risk retained)	276
Cost of agency insurance on £552,500 at 35p per £100	1,934
Total cost	16,401

3. Agency insurance and guarantee
   Interest cost $10\frac{50}{8}\%$

	£
Annual cost of granting credit £552,500 $\times \dfrac{75}{365} \times 10\frac{50}{8}\% =$	12,062
Cost of bad debts	276
Cost of agency insurance	1,934
Cost of agency guarantee	1,381
Total cost	15,653

5. Factoring using factor finance
   80% financed by the factor, 20% by overdraft

	£
Annual cost of granting credit £442,000 $\times \dfrac{75}{365} \times 12\% =$	10,899
plus £110,500 $\times \dfrac{75}{365} \times 12.5\%$	2,838
Service fee	13,812
Administrative savings	(12,500)
Total cost	15,049

The use of the factoring company is the cheapest alternative, and unless there are reasons why Newlean does not wish to use a factor, this should be the alternative that is selected.

ELEVEN
INTERNATIONAL INVESTMENT POLICY AND STRATEGY

INTRODUCTION

The decision to invest abroad in a subsidiary or affiliated company normally requires the commitment of millions of pounds for many years. It is arguably the most important decision facing the multinational company, and once taken is not easily reversed. This chapter examines the reasons behind foreign investment decisions and the types of investment that a multinational company can engage in. The latter part of the chapter examines the implications for a company of diversification by means of foreign direct investment, and the benefits to shareholders of investing in multinational companies in comparison with purely domestic companies and in comparison with holding a portfolio of shares of many companies from different countries.

REASONS FOR FOREIGN DIRECT INVESTMENT

Foreign direct investment is essentially a strategic decision which is influenced by political and behavioural factors in addition to financial considerations. Multinational companies take a conscious decision to set up foreign subsidiaries or affiliates rather than rely on exporting or licensing. 'The essence of corporate strategy is creating and then taking advantage of imperfections in the product and factor markets' (Shapiro (1989)). In the multinational sense companies try to create, transfer and preserve their competitive advantages abroad.

Rugman and Verbeke (1990) suggest that four conditions need to be fulfilled before foreign direct investment will take place:

1. The multinational's foreign activities must be competitive when compared with local companies in the foreign country. This is often considered to result from 'monopolistic advantage' available to multinational companies because of market imperfections.
2. The net benefits of foreign direct investment are expected to be greater than for either exporting or licensing. In order for foreign direct investment to be undertaken there must be benefits from 'internalizing'. The theory of internalization suggests that competitive advantage can be maintained by possession of information within the company and control of expertise through skilled employees who can create new information through R&D, marketing and other commercial expertise. The multinational company is motivated to create an internal market for this information to keep possession of and benefit from this unique body of information. According to Rugman (1980): the creation of an internal market by the multinational company allows it to transform an intangible asset into a

valuable property specific to the firm. The multinational enterprise will exploit its advantage in all available markets and will keep the use of information internal to the firm in order to recoup its initial expenditures on research and knowledge generation.

Reasons for internalization are summarized in Table 11.1.

Table 11.1 Reasons for internalization

Natural market imperfections	Unnatural market imperfections
Pricing of public goods, e.g. knowledge	Government imposed, e.g. tariffs
Transactions costs	Foreign exchange control
Buyer uncertainty	Regulations on foreign direct
Quality control	investment
Difficulty in making a contract	

Both natural market imperfections and unnatural market imperfections induce internalization by multinational companies

Source: Rugman, Lecraw and Booth, *International Business: Firm and Environment*, McGraw-Hill, 1986

Rugman and Verbeke (1990) suggest five situations where foreign direct investment will be preferred to exporting or licensing:

(a) Where the reputation or brand name of the company is considered as important by consumers. In order to maintain tight control over quality, multinationals invest directly in foreign operations rather than trust quality control to a third party. This is not always a problem; for example, Whitbread Breweries produce many foreign lagers under licence because the formulae can easily be transmitted and Whitbread itself has the technical skills to produce the lagers to the standards required by the foreign firms.

(b) Where after-sales service is important. Once again, the multinational is unwilling to entrust after-sales service to a third party through a licensing or other agreement.

(c) Where benefits exist from interrelationships in the production of several parts of the multinational's product range. For example, the same equipment may be used for several products, in which case it is much more efficient for the multinational to undertake all manufacturing.

(d) Where new products require the dissemination of significant new information to customers. Internalization through vertical integration may be beneficial in achieving this.

(e) Where international diversification of product lines by foreign direct investment reduces risk.

3. The optimal location for foreign direct investment can be identified. This can be achieved through the analysis of the costs of materials, labour, transportation, etc., in alternative locations, and the attitude of the local government to foreign direct investment.

4. The optimal timing of foreign direct investment can be established.

An early explanation of multinational direct investment is the life-cycle model. Caves (1982) suggests that expansion into international operations is an incremental process, with companies initially gaining information about a foreign market through exporting or licensing, and only when they are familiar with the cultural, political and economic environment of the foreign country will direct investment take place. At an early stage in its life, multinationals will export the new product. As the size of foreign markets for the product increases, it may become economically viable for the multinational to establish production facilities in the foreign markets. The product will eventually become standardized and will be replicated by competitors. At this stage, cost factors such as the availability of cheap labour or a low transportation cost will strongly influence the location of foreign investment. A final stage that has been suggested for some products (e.g. televisions) is a 'dematuring' stage, whereby markets become highly sophisticated and consumers demand an increasing number of varieties of the basic product. In order to respond quickly to the demands of these sophisticated markets, manufacturing facilities need to be located close to them.

Buckley and Casson (1981) extended the life-cycle model to try to identify more directly why multinationals select direct investment as opposed to exporting or licensing. No matter how a foreign market is serviced, three types of cost exist:

1. A non-recoverable set-up cost
2. A recurrent fixed cost which is largely independent of output (e.g. management salaries)
3. Recurrent variable costs of labour, raw materials, etc.

Given these costs the company will service the market by whichever of exporting, licensing or direct investment is the most efficient for the chosen volume of activity.

Exporting will have the lowest fixed costs so long as the exports can be serviced from expanding existing production facilities in the home country. However, transportation costs and possible tariff barriers are high with this method.

Licensing avoids transportation and tariff costs, but will involve costs of monitoring the performance of the licence and ensuring that product quality is satisfactory.

Foreign direct investment obviously requires the highest investment in fixed costs with the establishment of production and distribution facilities, but will avoid the monitoring costs of licensing. At high volumes of activity the market is likely to be serviced by a method that has relatively high fixed costs and relatively low incremental costs, namely direct investment.

Dunning (1980) developed an 'eclectic' model of international production which attempts to explain simultaneously the location of international business activity and the method chosen to carry out that activity. Three groups of factors are significant:

1. Company-specific factors which allow competitive advantage in the chosen activity of the company. The most important of these are:
   (a) Large size, reflecting economies of scale
   (b) Major product differentiating factors, patents and trademarks
   (c) Managerial or marketing skills specific to the company
   (d) Proprietary technology that has been developed by the company
   (e) Large capital requirements in order to operate efficiently.
2. Location-specific factors which mean that it is more efficient to operate in one country rather than another. These might include natural resources, trade barriers and a skilled low-cost labour force.
3. Internalization advantages which make the international transfer through direct investment of capital, technology and sometimes labour more efficient than transfer through open market pricing, exporting or licensing. High costs of making and enforcing contracts, a need to control the use or resale of the product, advantages from price discrimination or

cross-subsidization of products, and uncertainty of the value of any technology that might be sold are all likely to result in internalization.

Direct investment is likely to occur when a multinational company identifies the existence of all three of these factors.

All of these models help to explain the growth of foreign direct investment that has occurred during the last 40 years.

A particularly useful framework of analysis that supplements these theories is that of Eiteman and Stonehill (1989), who recognized three main motives for foreign direct investment: strategic, behavioural, and economic. These three categories are clearly interrelated, since the overall aim of the company is long-term survival and the achievement of a satisfactory level of shareholder wealth.

Strategic motives

Raw materials   Many multinationals, including oil and mining companies, invest abroad in order to extract the raw materials needed for their production, especially if a domestic supply of raw materials is not available or is more costly. Multinationals, rather than local companies, exploit foreign raw material supplies because they have the finance, expertise and technology needed to extract them, which the local companies do not. By having direct control over raw materials, a more certain supply at an acceptable cost can be maintained. The consequences of an uncertain supply are illustrated by Burmah Oil which, after depleting and losing oil deposits, failed to seek further deposits for its distribution and marketing networks. With the OPEC crisis of the 1970s Burmah was left without a satisfactory supply of oil.

Knowledge   The maintenance of technological leadership is an important ingredient of commercial success in the 1990s. One way of keeping ahead is to acquire foreign companies that are heavily involved in research and development, or control key patents and processes. In addition, multinational companies may locate their operations where a high concentration of R&D and expertise exists. Examples of this are Hyundai and Samsung, which set up operations in Silicon Valley. Silicon Valley offers a supply of skilled technicians and possible access to research into the US arms and space programmes which often have commercial spin-offs.

Efficiency   Because of imperfections in the international factor markets, especially labour, companies often locate abroad in regions of cheap labour in order to cut production costs and thereby increase competitiveness. This is especially the case in the electronics industry, which is very labour-intensive. An example of this is Amstrad, which produces most of its components and products in the Far East and has little production capacity in the UK and Europe, which are its major markets.

Political security   In order to avoid interference from governments, companies often locate in regions free from government influence, such as the USA and some European Community countries. The early 1980s saw heavy European investment in the USA, since companies feared that the recession could bring about a swing towards socialism and thus more interference by governments. Two corporate policies result from this motive: safe plants and multiple sourcing.

Safe plants involve locating production facilities in politically stable countries in order to secure supply in case of government intervention in alternative source countries. These safe plants are often in economically suboptimal locations, but the fact that customers can always be sure of supply gives the company extra credibility and thus an edge in a competitive market. Multiple sourcing occurs when companies locate in several locations and produce similar products in each. An example of this is Ford in Europe who, by being in this position, have a stronger hand in dealing with the unions by being able to say that they could increase production elsewhere if the unions take strike action. Again, this is economically suboptimal, since economies of scale are eroded, but the gains outweigh the costs.

Markets   Imperfections and barriers to entry exist in many foreign markets, which might mean that companies have to locate abroad in order to access new markets. An example of this is Ford, which established UK plants during the inter-war period. This was done in order to bypass the tariffs imposed by the government on imported cars to Britain and the old British Empire. The market motive is often defensive, as are the other strategic motives, with companies concentrating on overall survival rather than profitability. Companies often move into developing markets when it is unprofitable to do so in the hope that the market will take off in the future. The 'follow-the-leader' approach is often seen in such situations, with the decision of one company to locate in a foreign country being closely followed by others. This is because of the fear that the first company will benefit from economies of scale and the existence of abnormal profits if the market is successful. It is often important to follow suit quickly because it is possible that the local government will impose tariffs and restrictions on further newcomers, making entry difficult, if not impossible.

These five strategic motives for foreign direct investment have been identified for many years as being of great importance for foreign investment analysis (see, for example, research by The Conference Board (1966) and Stonehill and Nathanson (1968)). Because of the political and foreign exchange risks involved in foreign investment analysis, projections of expected cash flows are subject to large margins of error. The choice of location abroad is usually based upon strategic factors, and only the actual projects undertaken by the subsidiary are evaluated using detailed financial analysis.

Behavioural motives

Aharoni (1966) studied the behavioural motives of foreign investment and identified two categories: external stimuli from the organization's environment, and internal stimuli within the organization.

External factors
1. External proposals that are attractive to the multinational, from clients, distributors and governments
2. Fear of losing a market
3. When competing companies are successful in foreign markets it is important for the company to locate there also
4. Strong competition from abroad in the home market could lead to retaliatory foreign investment abroad

Internal factors
1. Creation of a market for components and other products
2. Utilization of old machinery.
3. Capitalization on know-how, i.e. spreading of research and development and other fixed costs
4. Indirect return to a lost market through investment in a country which has commercial agreements with these lost territories

Aharoni (1966) examined the actual decision-making processes and found that the approach of multinational companies was similar to that of domestic companies, as proposed by Cyert and March (1963). Decisions were observed to be made in response to a motivating force, whether it be internal or external, and involved considering a few alternatives, but not all, because of time and financial constraints.

Thus, multinationals are satisficers in that they do not evaluate all of the options, and consider non-financial as well as financial methods.

Brunnson (1982) recognized the importance of having a motivated workforce in order to put the decision into action. The consideration of too many alternatives is demotivating as it splits loyalties within the organization and thus makes it more difficult to put the final decision into practice.

Economic motives

Economic motives relate primarily to the competitive advantages of the multinational over companies located in foreign markets, and, as discussed earlier, direct foreign investment may result from imperfections in the product and factor markets.

Product and factor market imperfections   Hymer (1976) proposed that market imperfections can be caused both by multinational companies and by governments. Governments produce imperfections through tariffs, tax incentives, preferential purchasing policies and capital controls. In order to profit from such imperfections multinationals must have a large competitive advantage over local firms in order to overcome the communication problems of being based abroad and also to overcome local problems, e.g. adjusting to customs, the local legal system, and nationalistic customers.

Five main areas of competitive advantage exist:

Economies of scale and scope: These can arise in production, marketing, R&D, transport, finance and purchasing. Economies of scale arise as a result of size, in that as the company's size and volume increases, the marginal fixed costs diminish. Examples of this are the marketing policies of Coca-Cola and Shell. Because of their enormous levels of production they are able to finance very expensive commercials with international stars and show them during peak rate viewing like the Superbowl, and to sponsor worldwide events like the Olympics because they have a global distribution network which enables them to fully utilize the exposure. Companies like Honda take advantage of economies of scope. These occur when an investment can support several profitable activities less expensively in combination than separately. Honda produces a wide range of motorized products, for example, cars, motorbikes and outboard engines, and can use the same equipment to produce them and the same distribution and marketing network to sell them. This will increase the economies of scale as it increases volume and thus makes it difficult for rivals who have only one product to compete. Recently Honda's marketing strategy has been based around its success in designing Formula 1 engines, and the company has promoted this success for all its products.

Managerial and marketing expertise Servan-Schreiber (1968) suggested that the US multinationals were successful in the 1950s and 1960s because of better management training through their business schools, and that Europe was far too elitist. (Since that time European and Japanese companies have expanded internationally faster than US companies, even though business schools are still more developed in the USA.)

An alternative explanation is that multinationals have more experience than the local producers, through expertise gained in their home markets and in other foreign ventures, and have acquired prior knowledge of the local market from exporting to it.

Technology Gruber *et al.* (1987) indicate a strong relationship between R&D and foreign investment. This is due to the fact that the multinational has monopolistic rights over the innovations it has developed in the form of patents when it produces abroad, thus giving it a competitive advantage over local companies.

Financial strength By diversification of operations, multinationals are able to reduce overall riskiness, because different markets have different economic cycles. So a downturn in one market can be compensated by an upturn in another, which reduces the overall cost of debt because there is less risk. Compounded with this is the fact that entry to new product markets might give access to new financial markets.

Differentiated products Caves (1971) noted that, by heavy R&D and marketing, companies are able to differentiate their products from those of their competitors and thus turn them into 'brand names' like Persil and Walkman. By continually modifying their products and by regular advertising, they create a difficult time-lag for competitors to overcome, and use levels of advertising and R&D which competitors cannot afford.

Foreign investment in the form of joint ventures

Recently there have been many foreign investments made by multinationals in the form of joint ventures, for example, General Motors and Toyota. By merging their divergent skills and resources, multinational companies can break into new markets and gain access to technology that would otherwise be either more difficult or impossible to acquire. The basis of joint ventures is that all the companies involved will benefit from the venture. There are three main motives for joint ventures.

1. Market access
2. Technology
3. Economies of scale

The first two factors are usually closely related and will be considered together.

Market access and technology Even large multinationals face barriers to entry of new markets, especially those of Japan and some EC countries. To counter these barriers the multinational can form a joint venture with a local company which has the facilities to get around these obstacles and gain market access. In return the multinational is able to offer the local company access to the technology behind the product (it is usually technologically ahead of the local competition). An example of this is the joint venture between Armco and Mitsubishi to sell and manufacture Armco's lightweight plastic composites in Japan.

As well as the technology of the product itself, the technology of production methods, quality control and inventory systems are often of interest to the local company. An example of this was the joint venture between Rover and Honda which existed until Rover was taken over by BMW in 1994. In return for increased access to the British and EC markets and a way to bypass the quota system in operation there, the Japanese were able to give the UK car industry an insight into the low cost and high quality methods of car production about which the UK was ignorant at the time.

Economies of scale   In high-technology industries, the R&D costs necessary to develop new products are enormous, and this has led to the creation of joint ventures in order to spread the fixed costs and lower the burden of risk on the individual companies. An example of this is AT + T and Philips, where a joint venture was arranged to develop, manufacture and market sophisticated telecommunications equipment. By combining their similar facilities they were able to increase the probability of success. As well as economies in R&D, joint ventures often offer economies in production, for example, the agreement between Alfa and Nissan to produce car engines in Italy.

Although in theory joint ventures are attractive, in reality there have been problems as conflicts often occur between parties over transfer pricing, the allocation of products and markets to each plant, and the maintenance of quality control. These problems have led to some companies, such as IBM, preferring to 'go it alone' in the global market and to maintain full control over their subsidiaries. Zenoff (1978) recognized these problems, and likened them to a marriage in that although in theory it works, careful advanced planning is necessary for it to work in practice. To achieve this all parties must agree to a 'pre-nuptial agreement', spelling out what each company is expecting from and willing to contribute to the venture, and the future plans each company has for it. If there is a proper match reached from the discussions, then the joint venture should be seriously considered.

One problem which cannot be avoided is the rapidly changing environment of the 1990s. As the environment changes, different companies' views and objectives are also subject to change, potentially putting pressure on the venture in the future.

INTERNATIONAL PORTFOLIO DIVERSIFICATION

Financial theory normally assumes that investors are risk-averse. By this it is meant that for a unit of expected return they prefer as little risk as possible. In order to minimize risks many investors hold diversified portfolios, as the returns on different investments are not perfectly correlated. Even if the individual security returns within the portfolio fluctuate and thus are risky, the fact that they are not perfectly correlated means they fluctuate differently to one another and thus the overall portfolio risk is reduced, since the differing fluctuations to some extent cancel one another out.

Eun and Resnick (1984) estimated the average correlation coefficient within a country's domestic portfolio. Their research showed that the average correlation between the securities of eight markets ranged between 0.698 in the UK and 0.439 in the USA. They also estimated the correlations between the markets and found that these were far less than within markets; for example, the UK's correlation rates with other countries ranged from 0.209 with Japan to 0.431 with Switzerland (the internal correlation was 0.698). These results reveal a great potential for risk reduction by international diversification. These lower correlations can be explained by the fact that different countries have different business cycles, which means that when one country is experiencing a boom another will be facing a downturn. Furthermore, different countries have different industrial bases and economic policies. Germany, with a major base in car production and exporting, could be affected to a greater extent than the UK by a change in oil prices.

Solnik (1974) carried out research into the extent to which risk can further be reduced by investing in an international portfolio, and by using the US market as a comparison concluded that the systematic (non-diversifiable) risk could be reduced from 27 per cent (which it was in the domestic US portfolio) to 12 per cent by diversifying internationally. This means that holding the US portfolio can reduce risk to 27 per cent of that of holding one averagely risky stock, and going international can reduce it further to 12 per cent. This leads to the conclusion that international diversification offers significant opportunities for the reduction of portfolio risk.

Investors are concerned with return as well as risk. Eun and Resnik in a later study examined both the risk and return characteristics of stock markets. The results of the study confirmed that an investor in any market could improve his or her overall risk/return position by investing in an international portfolio. For example, a Canadian investor, in their analysis, could increase average monthly returns from 0.93 per cent to 1.21 per cent and at the same time reduce the standard deviation (risk) from 5.94 to 4.40.

A major problem with investing in foreign portfolios is the added risk of fluctuations in the foreign exchange markets. Although the above study took into account such fluctuations, as it was conducted while the foreign exchange market was floating freely, it is obvious that free floating exchange rates might lead to a reduction in potential gains from international portfolio diversification because of the increased risks it imposes.

Although Eun and Resnik (1984, 1987) showed there to be an advantage in holding an international portfolio they made a number of subjective assumptions in the creation of the different optimal international portfolios for each foreign investor, including one that all investors can borrow and lend at the risk-free rate of 5 per cent. This is unrealistic as different domestic markets have different interest rates, and few investors can invest and borrow at the same rate. Proffit and Seitz (1983) looked at the returns of international funds (portfolios containing 50 per cent or more of foreign securities) against a purely domestic index (Standard and Poors 500 Index). Their research was able to conclude that the international funds by far outperformed domestic ones, which gives added credence to the work of Eun and Resnik.

Atkinson and Madura (1984) analysed the potential gains that could be achieved by British investors when diversifying internationally. Using national stock market indices they estimated the risk and return of 11 major countries between 1970 and 1983. Both risk and return were adjusted to take into account exchange rate fluctuations relative to the pound during the period. In order to estimate the potential gains from international diversification, efficient portfolios were identified (an efficient portfolio produces the highest return for a given level of risk or minimizes risk for a given level of return). Their results are summarized in Table 11.2 and show that there has been a wide divergence in risk and return between countries (from the perspective of a UK investor), and that all efficient portfolios except Portfolio 8 generated both higher returns and lower risks than the UK stock market. The choice of efficient portfolio ranged from the maximum return Portfolio 1, which comprised 100 per cent investment in

Table 11.2 The performance of country stock markets and efficient international portfolios between 1970 and 1983

	Mean quarterly return (%) (adjusted for exchange rate fluctuations)	Standard deviation of adjusted returns
United Kingdom	1.89	0.1722
Australia	0.91	0.1283
Canada	1.77	0.0976
France	1.36	0.1529
Japan	3.83	0.1082
Netherlands	1.13	0.1024
Sweden	2.57	0.1104
Switzerland	1.72	0.0956
USA	1.43	0.0984
West Germany	1.67	0.0924
Portfolio 1	3.83	0.1082
Portfolio 2	3.54	0.0990
Portfolio 3	3.25	0.0917
Portfolio 4	2.95	0.0854
Portfolio 5	2.66	0.0800
Portfolio 6	2.37	0.0768
Portfolio 7	2.08	0.0748
Portfolio 8	1.79	0.0742

Source: From Atkinson, S. and Madura, J., 'International stock diversification for British investors', *The Investment Analyst*, July 1984

Japan to the minimum risk Portfolio 8, which involved investment in all countries except Japan and Australia. The potential benefits of international diversification for UK investors are substantial.

Diversification through multinational companies

The opportunity for international portfolio diversification and management may be limited by high information and trading costs, exchange controls and the poorly developed state of some overseas stock markets. Where these conditions exist it has been suggested that investment in multinational companies might be an acceptable substitute for international portfolio investment (see, for example, Rugman (1977)). Jacquillat and Solnik (1978) examined the benefits of international diversification by means of investment in both multinational companies and portfolios of shares from different stock markets, and their conclusion was that investing in US multinational companies could not be regarded as a valid substitute for international portfolio diversification. The share prices of the multinationals behaved in a similar manner to domestic companies and were not extensively affected by foreign factors.

Research by Fatemi (1984) concluded that benefits could be obtained by investing in the shares of multinationals. He found that there was no significant difference in returns between multinational companies and purely domestic companies, but there was less fluctuation in the returns of multinationals which led to lower betas (the beta coefficient is a measure of relevant risk, see Chapter 12) and thus lower risk, which shareholders prefer. He also found that as companies internationally diversified further, the beta fell further.

Thompson (1986) examined the international diversification benefits from purchasing shares in a sample of 46 UK-based multinational companies. Portfolios with a high multinational content (measured by the foreign to total sales ratio) were found to reduce domestic systematic risk by approximately 20 per cent (systematic risk is measured using the beta coefficient, see above). However, if the analysis is disaggregated to the individual company level then the risk reductions are very small, casting doubt on diversification as a motive for multinational growth. Investors may not value highly multinational companies that have diversification as their main motive for international expansion, as the investors could themselves obtain the benefits from diversification more easily and more cheaply than the multinational, by purchasing an international portfolio of shares, for example, through a well diversified international unit trust. Whether or not diversification by multinationals brings benefits to investors depends largely upon market segmentation. If the multinational can obtain access through direct investment to market sectors which are not available through portfolio investment, investors might pay a premium for shares in such multinationals. In addition, if investors in international portfolios face significant additional costs to those incurred when investing in the domestic market, such as extra information costs, additional taxation in some markets, and legal restrictions on the ownership of shares by foreigners, then investment in the shares of well diversified multinational companies might be preferred to international portfolio investment. However, the increasing globalization of markets is gradually resulting in the erosion of such restrictions, and as they disappear it is becoming more advantageous to invest in the form of international portfolios rather than in the shares of multinational companies.

SUMMARY

This chapter examined the main motives behind foreign investment and highlighted the wide range of possible influences on international investment, including many non-financial factors. A detailed discussion of the financial implications of foreign direct investment is the subject of the next chapter.

REFERENCES

Aharoni, Y. (1966) 'The foreign investment decision process', Harvard Graduate School of Business Administration, Division of Research.

Atkinson, S. and Madura, J. (1984) 'International stock diversification for British investors', *The Investment Analyst*, July, pp. 30–32.

Brunsson, N. (1982) 'The irrationality of action and action rationality: decisions, ideologies and organisational actions', *Journal of Management Studies*, **19**, 1.

Buckley, P. and Casson, M. (1981) 'The optimal timing of a foreign direct investment', *Economic Journal 91*, March, pp. 75–87.

Caves, R. E. (1971) 'International corporations: the industrial economics of foreign investment', *Economica*, February, pp. 1–27.

Caves, R. E. (1982) *Multinational Enterprise and Economic Analysis*, Cambridge University Press, Cambridge.

Conference Board, The (1966) *US Production Abroad and the Balance of Payments*, NY, p. 63.

Cyert, R. and March, J. (1963) *A Behavioral Theory of the Firm*, Prentice-Hall, Englewood Cliffs, NJ.

Dunning, J. (1980) 'Towards an eclectic theory of international production: some empirical tests', *Journal of International Business Studies*, Spring/Summer, pp. 9–31

Eiteman, D. K. and Stonehill, A. I. (1989) *Multinational Business Finance*, Addison-Wesley, Reading, Mass.

Eun, C. and Resnik, B. (1984) 'Estimating the correlation structure of international share prices', *Journal of Finance*, December.

Eun, C. and Resnik, B. (1987) 'International diversification under estimation risk: actual vs. potential gains', S. Khoury and A. Gosh (eds) *Recent Developments in International Banking and finance*, Vol. 1, D. C. Heath, Lexington.

Fatemi, A. F. (1984) 'Shareholder benefits from corporate international diversification', *Journal of Finance*, December.

Gruber, W., Mehta, D. and Vernon, R. (1987) 'The R&D factor in international trade and international investment of US industries', *Journal of Political Economy*, February, pp. 20–37.

Hymer, S. (1976) *The International Operations of National Firms: A Study of Direct Foreign Investment*, MIT Press, Cambridge, Mass.

Jacquillat, B. and Solnik, B. (1978) 'Multinationals are poor tools for diversification', *The Journal of Portfolio Management*, Winter, pp. 8–12.

Proffit, D. and Seitz, N. (1983) 'The performance of internationally diversified mutual funds', *Journal of the Midwest Finance Association*, December.

Rugman, A. M. (1977) 'International diversification by financial and direct investment', *Journal of Economics and Business*, Vol. 30.

Rugman, A. M. (1980) 'Internalisation as a general theory of foreign direct investment: a reappraisal of the literature', *Weltwirschaftliches Arch*, Vol. 116, pp. 365–79.

Rugman, A. M. and Verbeke, E. (1990) 'Strategic capital budgeting decisions and the theory of internalisation', *Managerial Finance*, Vol. 16, No. 2, pp. 17–24.

Servan-Schreiber J.J. (1968) *The American Challenge*, Hamish Hamilton, London.

Shapiro, A. (1989) *Multinational Financial Management*, 3rd edition, Allyn and Bacon, Newton, Mass.

Solnik, B. (1974) 'An equilibrium model of the international capital market', *Journal of Economic Theory*, August, pp. 500–25.

Stonehill, A. and Nathanson, L. (1968) 'Capital budgeting and the multinational corporation', *California Management Review*, Summer, p. 40.

Thompson, R. S. (1986) 'Multinational companies and portfolio diversification', *The Investment Analyst*, January, pp. 9–12.

Zenoff, D. B. (1978) Presentation at the University of Hawaii Advanced Management Program, August.

TWELVE

INTERNATIONAL CAPITAL BUDGETING

INTRODUCTION

The decision to invest abroad is often based on strategic, economic or behavioural motives, either as defensive or aggressive actions to strengthen the company's position. Even though many decisions are taken for other than financial reasons it is essential that most foreign direct investment is financially viable, otherwise the multinational company will not survive in the long run. Financial managers have numerous tools available to them to assist in the financial evaluation of foreign investments and to provide a basis for choosing between competing projects. Most of these evaluation methods are applicable to both domestic and international projects, but the international dimension introduces complexities and risks that are not faced in a domestic context. This chapter examines the evaluation techniques that are available to the multinational company, and the theoretical and practical problems that multinationals face in appraising foreign capital investments.

INVESTMENT APPRAISAL METHODS USED BY MULTINATIONAL COMPANIES

Investment appraisal decisions, in practice, range from those that are largely subjective to those based upon sophisticated mathematical models. The majority of the decisions that use quantitative analysis are based upon one or more of four techniques:

1. Accounting rate of return
2. The payback period
3. The internal rate of return
4. Net present value

Accounting rate of return assesses the percentage return on capital invested in the project, usually the average annual percentage profit before taxation relative to the average amount of capital invested in the project. This technique may be criticized, since it is based upon expected accounting profits rather than the expected incremental cash flows that are associated with the investment. The main purpose of investment appraisal is to make the best possible use of the resources that are available to the company. This will involve assessing the size and timing of cash inflows and outflows of the investment. Profit is a reporting concept developed by accountants, and is not a suitable basis for making future economic or resource allocation decisions. Capital investment is a resource allocation decision which should be judged on the cash flows that it generates.

Further problems of the accounting rate of return are that investment is judged as a percentage return, which takes no account of the size of projects when alternatives are being considered, and that the time value of money is ignored. Ignoring the time value of money means that a cash inflow of £1 million now is treated as being of exactly the same value to a multinational company as a cash inflow of £1 million in 10 years' time. If the £1 million inflow now could be reinvested to earn 10 per cent per annum for the 10-year period, the amount available to the multinational company at the end of 10 years would be £2,593,743. This example clearly illustrates the weakness of any evaluation method which does not take into account the time value of money.

The payback method assesses how quickly the initial outlay in an investment is paid back from after-tax cash flows that are generated from the investment. Only projects which are paid back within a period of time that is considered acceptable to the investing company would be undertaken. Payback has an advantage over accounting rate of return in that it is based upon cash flows rather than profits, but it has two major disadvantages: it ignores both the time value of money, and any cash flows that occur after the initial investment has been paid back. It is possible to modify the basic payback technique to incorporate the time value of money (discounted payback), but ignoring some of the cash flows generated by the project could lead to incorrect investment decisions when two or more competing (mutually exclusive) projects are being evaluated. Payback might favour a project that has good initial cash flows but small cash flows after payback is complete, rather than an alternative project which has a longer payback period but much larger cash flows over the entire life of the project.

Internal rate of return and net present value are both discounted cash flow techniques that take into account the time value of money. Net present value (NPV) is based on cash flows and takes account of the time value of money by restating or discounting all future cash flows in today's value. The discount rate used is the minimum rate of return required by the company's investors, and is normally found by estimating a weighted average cost of capital (WACC), taking into account the risk of the investment. The cost of capital will be discussed in more detail later in the chapter.

Net present value can be estimated using the following formula:

$$NPV = \sum_{t=0}^{n} \frac{CF}{(1 + r)} \quad \text{where } CF = \text{cash flow in period } t$$
$$\text{(either inflow or outflow)}$$
$$r = \text{annual discount rate}$$

A zero or positive NPV means that, on financial grounds, the company should invest in the project. A negative NPV project should be rejected on financial grounds as it would not produce sufficient cash flows to repay the financial cost of undertaking it. However, as previously discussed, investment decisions are often based upon other than purely financial factors.

The internal rate of return (IRR) (sometimes referred to as the yield) is the discount rate which, when applied to the cash flows of a project, results in a NPV of zero. It is estimated using the formula:

$$\sum_{t=0}^{n} \frac{CF}{(1 + r)} = 0 \quad \text{where } CF = \text{cash flow in period } t$$
$$r = \text{internal rate of return}$$

The IRR is a percentage measure, unlike NPV which measures the absolute financial benefit of a project. A project is considered to be acceptable if the IRR exceeds some predetermined hurdle rate, usually the cost of capital that would be used to estimate the NPV of the project. Although NPV and IRR both allow for the time value of money, NPV is the recommended appraisal method as IRR and NPV may result in different investment decisions where mutually exclusive alternative projects are being considered. IRR incorrectly assumes that cash flows generated during a project can be reinvested at the IRR rate, and may conflict with NPV when competing projects are of differing size or time horizons. NPV is the only one of the four techniques that will result in decisions which consistently lead to shareholder wealth maximization, given the existence of efficient capital markets that accurately reflect the decisions of management. Shareholder wealth maximization through capital gains and dividend payments is normally considered to be the primary objective of financial decision-making.

Despite the theoretical superiority of the NPV method (and even this has its limitations) evidence from both the UK and the USA suggests that multinational companies use a variety of investment appraisal techniques. Table 12.1 summarizes the results of surveys of the capital budgeting practices of multinational companies.

Table 12.1 Investment appraisal techniques of multinational companies

	UK		USA	
	Primary method	*Secondary method*	*Primary method*	*Secondary method*
Accounting rate of return	28.6	8.8	10.7	14.6
Payback	24.3	35.3	5.0	37.6
Internal rate of return	24.3	11.8	65.3	14.6
Net present value	7.1	17.6	16.5	30.0
Other	15.7	26.5	2.5	3.2
	100%	100%	100%	100%

Source: USA: Stanley, R. and S. Block, 'An empirical study of management and financial variables influencing capital budgeting decisions for multinational companies in the 1980s', *Management International Review*, Vol. 23, 1983
UK: Questionnaire to 59 UK multinational companies, Goddard, S., unpublished research

UK-based multinationals rely more heavily on traditional appraisal techniques, such as accounting rate of return and payback, despite their theoretical limitations. Discounted cash flow techniques were a primary method of appraisal for only 31 per cent of UK companies in comparison with 82 per cent in the USA. The main 'other' evaluation technique used in the UK was contribution to earnings per share.

Estimation of relevant cash flows

The accuracy of any investment appraisal is dependent upon the identification of the after-tax incremental cash flows that will result from that investment. The rationale behind the focus on incremental cash flows is that a new foreign project might affect current operations, for example, by reducing sales of existing products or by creating new sales. It is the overall effect on the company's cash flows that is of importance, not just the cash flows that are directly attributable to the project. For example, any loss of cash flows from export sales falling as a direct result of a foreign investment project must be included as an incremental cash outflow when evaluating the foreign project. It is not always easy to identify relevant cash flows: those which might be difficult to identify include the effects of intra-company transactions. Multinationals often manipulate transfer prices between subsidiaries and use unrealistic (judged by 'arms length' market prices) levels of royalty fees or management fees, primarily to reduce their global tax liability. Through manipulation of the transfer prices of inputs and outputs, a company can 'adjust' the profitability of a project to divert tax liability from a high tax country to a subsidiary in a lower tax country.(Transfer pricing is discussed further in Chapter 13.) In order to determine and measure the incremental cash flows to the multinational company, the decision-maker should charge the project with the market values of inputs and outputs and only look at additional expenditure caused by the project. In this way a more meaningful basis for decision-making will be established.

The multinational company faces many new risks and opportunities arising from international factors, most of which have an influence on cash flows.

Taxation policies   Taxation policies differ substantially between countries, and may therefore complicate estimates of the magnitude and timing of cash flows. Many tax systems recognize the injustice of taxation in two or more countries upon the same income, and subsequently provide relief to avoid this extra burden. The effects of taxation do, however, depend upon how cash flows are remitted and transferred between countries. Taxation is discussed further in Chapter 17.

Political risks   Multinational companies may face varying degrees of intervention from the governments of countries in which their subsidiaries are located. Such intervention might reduce the cash flows available to a project, in the extreme case through the expropriation of assets without compensation. Blocked funds are particularly common, where the remittance of cash to the parent country or another desired location is restricted or prohibited by the local government through the imposition of exchange controls or other regulations. This can lead to cash flows generated by the project in the foreign country deviating significantly from cash flows that are available for repatriation to the parent company, and raises the question as to whether project cash flows or remittable cash flows should be considered in the appraisal of foreign investments. The multinational company can, however, partially avoid this problem by remitting funds through supervisory fees and royalties, or by adjusting transfer prices. The measurement and management of political risks are examined in Chapter 13.

Inflation and exchange rate differentials   These factors are closely related to political risk, since they are influenced by government policies. As foreign direct investment involves the use of different currencies, which even in a formal exchange rate system such as the European exchange rate mechanism (ERM) experience changes in relative values, the estimation of cash flows that could be remitted to the parent company requires an estimate of exchange rate relationships over the period of the investment. Potential gains or losses arising from movements in exchange rates can substantially affect project cash flows. Some protection against long-term exchange rate movements is, of course, available through the use of swaps and other hedging strategies discussed earlier.

It is difficult to estimate future prices and costs owing to uncertainties relating to the level of inflation in the foreign country and its effect on exchange rates. Decision-makers must also consider possible changes in future demand as a result of a devaluation of one currency against another.

Parent cash flows versus project cash flows

The appropriate evaluation measure is normally considered to be the funds flowing back to the parent company. Cash flows remitted to the parent company usually form the basis for dividend, reinvestment and other decisions, and are likely to have a direct impact on shareholder wealth as the multinational's share price responds to expected cash flows that are usable by the parent company. Funds that are blocked in a foreign country will not be available to the parent company to use for dividend payments or repayment of loans, and may not be regarded by investors or creditors as part of the value of the company.

In practice, multinational companies normally consider both project and parent cash flows (Wicks Kelly and Philippatos (1982), Stanley and Block (1983)). The project may effectively be considered as a separate company which would be judged against local competitors. In theory, the project should only be undertaken if it can earn a higher risk-adjusted discounted return than local competitors. If it cannot, the investors in the project will be better off if they buy shares in the local company and let it undertake the project. However, as well as ignoring the question of whether cash flows can be remitted to the parent company, focusing upon project cash flows in this way also ignores the potential benefits that exist from being a multinational company. Such benefits might include lower financing costs than are available to a local company, and the ability to reduce tax liability through transfer pricing or other means. Evaluation based upon project cash flows would not incorporate any indirect costs and benefits of the project on other group activities.

The suggested evaluation process is:

1. Estimate incremental cash flows in the foreign country, taking account of any foreign tax effects.
2. Estimate remittable cash flows to the parent company and translate those cash flows into the parent country's currency at the expected exchange rates for the relevant periods.
3. Incorporate into parent company remitted cash flows any indirect costs and benefits which arise directly as a result of undertaking the project. All parent company tax effects must be considered at this stage.
4. Discount parent company incremental cash flows at a rate which reflects the risk of the project to produce the expected NPV of the project.

The following case study illustrates some of the problems of international capital budgeting.

Broomhill plc

Broomhill plc is considering whether to start manufacturing in Spain. A suitable local factory has been located which would cost 1,400 million pesetas, including all machinery and fittings. Working capital of 400 million pesetas is also required. The project is expected to last for five years, and Broomhill would then sell the machinery to a local company for an estimated 600 million pesetas. The historic cost of the machinery is 750 million pesetas.

Market values of the other assets are likely to increase in line with inflation in Spain. Broomhill may deduct tax allowable depreciation on machinery to the value of 750 million pesetas on a straightline basis at the rate of 10 per cent per annum. No tax allowable depreciation is available on any other fixed assets.

Production schedule:

Annual production 140,000 units

Each unit needs a component from the UK parent company plant, which is sold at the fixed price of £2 per unit. This is contributing £0.50 to the parent cash flows.

Spanish costs and prices:

Variable costs: 2,400 pesetas per unit in year 1

Fixed costs: 70 million pesetas in year 1

Price: 6,000 pesetas per unit in year 1

Costs and prices (except for the UK component) are expected to increase in line with inflation in Spain.

Corporation tax: Spain 40 per cent, UK 35 per cent, payable one year in arrears. A bilateral tax treaty exists between the UK and Spain which allows tax paid in Spain to be set against any UK tax liability.

Inflation in Spain is expected to be 13 per cent per annum for the next five years. The peseta is expected to fall in value by 8 per cent per annum against the pound. (This could be estimated using the purchasing power parity (PPP) theory.)

Peseta/£ spot rate: 201.57–201.94

Broomhill believes that the appropriate risk-adjusted discount rate for the project is 17 per cent.

The first step is to estimate the exchange rates for the five years ahead.

Exchange rates	*Pesatas/£*
Spot	201.57–201.94
Year 1	217.70–218.10
Year 2	235.11–235.54
Year 3	253.92–254.39
Year 4	274.23–274.74
Year 5	296.17–296.72
Year 6	319.87–320.45

Peseta cash flows are then estimated, to establish Spanish taxation. It is assumed that all the units produced are sold in the year of production and that all associated cash receipts and expenditures also occur during the same year. Tax allowable depreciation on machinery is 10 per cent of 750 million, i.e. 75 million pesetas each year.

Cash flows estimates in pesetas (millions)

Year	1	2	3	4	5
Sales	840	949	1,073	1,212	1,370
Variable costs	(336)	(380)	(429)	(485)	(548)
UK part	(61)	(66)	(71)	(77)	(83)
Fixed costs	(70)	(79)	(89)	(101)	(114)
Depreciation	(75)	(75)	(75)	(75)	(75)
Taxable	298	349	409	474	550
Tax 40%	(119)	(140)	(164)	(190)	(220)

Depreciation is not a cash flow, but needs to be deducted to find the tax liability in Spain.

Actual cash flows

Year	0	1	2	3	4	5	6
Sales		840	949	1,073	1,212	1,370	
Costs		(467)	(525)	(589)	(663)	(745)	
Tax			(119)	(140)	(164)	(190)	(220)
Investment	(1,400)						
Working capital	(400)						400*
Sale of assets						600**	(90)
Realizable value						1,198	(219)
Net	(1,800)	373	305	344	385	2,233	(129)

* It is assumed that the money tied up in working capital will be released when the project has ended. In practice investment in working capital will vary during the life of the project.
** The assets are sold for 600 million pesetas. Written-down value is $750 - (5 \times 75) = 375$. The gain on disposal of 225 is subject to tax at 40%, i.e. 90. The gain has been calculated by taking the proceeds less the written down value of the assets.

Realizable value is estimated by the historic cost of fixed assets, 1,400 million, less disposals, 750 million, adjusted for Spanish inflation at 13 per cent per annum or $650 \times (1.13)^5 = 1,198$. Tax would be payable on any gain on disposal. The tax is estimated by 1,198 less the original cost of 650, or a gain of 548 taxed at 40 per cent, giving a liability of 219.

This enables the estimation of the cash flows in UK£ (millions), assuming that all cash flows are remittable at the year end.

Year	0	1	2	3	4	5	6
Remitted	(8.93)	1.710	1.295	1.352	1.401	7.526	(0.403)
Contribution from UK part		0.07	0.07	0.07	0.07	0.07	
Tax on this			(0.025)	(0.025)	(0.025)	(0.025)	(0.025)
Net flows	(8.93)	1.780	1.340	1.397	1.446	7.571	(0.428)
Discount factors	17%	0.8547	0.7305	0.6243	0.5337	0.4561	0.3898
Present value	(8.93)	1.521	0.979	0.872	0.772	3.453	(0.167)

The discount factors have been calculated based on the rate of 17 per cent.

Since Spanish tax is at a higher rate than UK tax, no further tax liability will arise on remitted cash flows. (Nor can the extra 5 per cent paid in Spain be recovered from the UK tax authorities.)

This results in a negative NPV of £1.5 million. On the basis of the financial analysis the project should not be undertaken as it does not result in a positive NPV. However, these calculations are based on estimates and will be subject to a margin of error, so unless the estimated NPV is significantly positive or negative it is unwise for a company to rely upon one single NPV estimate, even if this is based upon the most likely scenario of future cash flows. Financial modelling packages usually offer 'what if' simulations, which permit the main variables affecting the investment decision to be altered to examine the implications if variations from the most likely scenario occur. The final investment decision is often based upon several alternative financial forecasts and non-financial influences.

Other examples are provided in the Appendix, which illustrates other aspects and problems of the investment appraisal of overseas operations.

THE INTERNATIONAL COST OF CAPITAL

The cost of capital is an important concept to the financial manager as it is used as the discount rate for future cash flows. As previously indicated, it is a central component in the investment appraisal process. Multinational companies operate in a highly complex environment and are faced with many risks and opportunities; some of the factors which influence the cost of capital in multinational corporations are examined here.

The cost of capital is normally defined as the minimum risk-adjusted rate of return required in order for the investment to be accepted. The overall cost will depend on the type of capital employed and the degree of risk associated with the investment project. It is important, however, to distinguish between the company's overall cost of capital and the cost related to a specific project; this is because unless the capital structure and the degree of risk of the new project are both similar to those of the company's existing portfolio of investments, it is incorrect to use the company's cost of capital as the discount rate. The discount rate for new projects should reflect the risk of the project itself, and each project might require an individual estimate of its own risk-adjusted discount rate.

Since most corporations use multiple sources of funds, it is generally accepted that the weighted average cost of capital (WACC) is the most appropriate cost of capital for multinational companies. The WACC is defined as the costs of the various types of funds weighted according to their relative proportions of the company's overall capital structure. This is illustrated by the following formula:

$$WACC = Kd \times (1 - T) \frac{D}{D + E} + Ke \times \frac{E}{D + E}$$

where Kd = cost of debt
T = tax rate $0 < T < 1$
Ke = cost of equity
D = market value of debt
E = market value of equity

The introduction of debt to a company's capital structure will initially lower the overall cost of capital, since debt is normally cheaper than equity (as it is less risky the return required by investors is lower), and interest paid on debt is a tax-deductible expense, i.e. there is a tax shield associated with borrowed funds. The WACC can be used as the discount rate in the evaluation of foreign projects. The most common sources of capital used to finance a foreign investment are parent company funds, earnings retained by the foreign subsidiary, and foreign debt (especially debt borrowed in the local currency).

Cost of equity

The cost of equity is normally considered to be the minimum rate of return necessary to induce investors to buy or maintain their holding of a share. There are two main models covering the cost of equity capital.

1. *The dividend valuation model* The underlying assumption of this model is that the rate

of return required is determined by the expected level of dividends that the company will pay and the risk (more specifically the systematic risk, see below) of the expected future stream of dividend payments.

Under this model:

$$\text{Share price (P)} = \frac{D}{k_e - g}$$

where g is the annual growth rate of dividends, k_e is the cost of equity and D is the expected dividend in 12 months' time.

Rearranging the equation:

$$k_e = \frac{D}{P} + g$$

A weakness of the model is that the growth rate, g, is assumed to be constant.

2. *The capital asset pricing model (CAPM)* This model is based on the assumption that for each asset there is an equilibrium relationship between its required rate of return and its associated risk level. It reflects the fact that shareholders require higher rates of return for investing in risky assets, and defines the cost of equity by adjusting the risk-free rate of return by a risk premium related to the systematic risk of the investment. The systematic risk is the risk that cannot be diversified away by owning a broad portfolio of investments and, according to the model, is the only relevant risk in determining the return required by an investor and hence the cost of equity to a company. Systematic risk is estimated by relating the covariance of returns on the investment and returns on the market as a whole to the variance of returns on the market. Thus, the risk of any investment is related to the risk of the overall market. An investment with the same systematic risk as the market will have a beta coefficient of 1, a project that is riskier than the market has a beta coefficient of greater than 1, and a project less risky than the market has a beta of less than 1.

There are, however, some weaknesses inherent in the model itself, and in an international context further problems occur because some of the underlying assumptions no longer hold. The main problem is the identification of the risk and returns of the market. This point was first raised by Richard Roll (1977), who claimed that it is virtually impossible to define the market portfolio, since all durable goods, as well as intangible assets, e.g. human capital, should be included. There are also differing views as to whether investors do differentiate between systematic and unsystematic risk when they evaluate potential investments.

Another problem is the lack of data to estimate beta. Estimates of the beta of a company's equity are usually based upon relating company and market returns using monthly observations over a five-year period. However, as individual projects often differ in risk to the company, the use of a company beta to estimate the cost of equity for the project would be incorrect as it would not reflect the systematic risk of the project. The returns on new projects cannot be compared on an ex-post basis with historic market returns. (In theory, this model requires the use of ex-ante returns, but accurate forecasts of future returns are not possible.) The systematic risk of individual projects which differ in risk from the company may only be estimated indirectly. One estimation method is the 'pure play' technique (see, for example, Fuller and Kerr (1981)), which requires the identification of a company or companies with similar risk characteristics to the proposed project. The equity beta of the comparable risk company is then used as the estimate for the beta to be used to calculate the project discount rate, after adjusting for any difference in capital structure (financial gearing) between the comparison company and the company undertaking the project. This technique involves some subjectivity, and can only produce an approximate estimate of the project cost of equity.

In the international context the assumptions within the model that all investors have the same opportunity set, tastes and patterns of consumption, are no longer valid. Despite these theoretical and practical problems, the model is commonly used in finance theory and is the best operational tool that theory can offer to financial managers.

The capital asset pricing states that:

$$Ke = Rf + [E(Rm) - Rf] \times B \quad \text{where}$$

$$
\begin{aligned}
Ke &= \text{cost of equity} \\
Rf &= \text{risk-free rate of return} \\
E(Rm) &= \text{expected return on the market} \\
B &= \text{beta for the company or project}
\end{aligned}
$$

$$
\begin{aligned}
\text{Risk premium} &= \text{price of the risk} \times \text{quantity of risk} \\
&= [E(Rm) - Rf] \times \text{Beta}
\end{aligned}
$$

The use of the model to estimate the cost of equity can be illustrated by the following case study.

Glasnost plc

Glasnost plc is considering a possible major foreign investment in the western non-communist market, which is considered to be an integrated market where there are no barriers to the free movement of money and capital. Returns on this investment are expected to have a covariance with the market of 200.12 (this, in practice, is difficult to estimate).

The project will be financed with a £30 million floating rate loan, initially at an interest rate of 12 per cent, on the Eurobond market. Glasnost has relatively low financial gearing, and the proposed investment is not thought to have any significant effect on its financial risk.

First, the return of the market portfolio is estimated. This is assumed to be represented by a weighted average of the equity returns on the London, Tokyo and New York stock markets, although even this broad measure will not fully represent the entire market portfolio. The equity return is the sum of the dividend yield and the capital gain (or loss) on the market. (The data below are illustrative and do not show the actual returns for these markets.)

Year	Capitalization equity £ billion	Price change %	Dividend yield %	Treasury bill yield %
London:				
1987	102	23	3.8	8
1988	145	25	4.2	11
1989	206	15	4.0	11
1990	290	23	3.9	9
1991	310	5	4.7	8
New York:				
1987	742	15	3.2	7
1988	946	20	3.5	10
1989	1,148	20	3.8	9
1990	1,624	35	3.6	8
1991	1,650	2	3.8	7

Year	Capitalization equity £ billion	Price change %	Dividend yield %	Treasury bill yield %
Tokyo:				
1987	214	10	5.2	6
1988	254	15	5.8	5
1989	384	40	5.4	5
1990	580	45	5.6	4
1991	560	−8	4.9	4

The weighted average return on the Western market can be calculated as follows:

1987		1988		1989	
102 × 26.8 =	2,734	145 × 29.2 =	4,234	206 × 19.0 =	3,914
742 × 18.2 =	13,504	946 × 23.5 =	22,231	1,148 × 23.8 =	27,322
214 × 15.2 =	3,253	254 × 20.8 =	5,283	384 × 45.4 =	17,434
1,058	19,491	1,345	31,748	1,738	48,670
WA = 18.42%		WA = 23.60%		WA = 28.0%	

1990		1991	
290 × 26.9 =	7,801	310 × 9.7 =	3,007
1,624 × 38.6 =	62,686	1,650 × 5.8 =	9,570
580 × 50.6 =	29,348	560 × (3.1) =	(1,736)
2,494	99,835	2,520	10,841
WA = 40.03%		WA = 4.3%	

The overall estimated return on the market $\overline{Rm}$, is found by

$$\overline{Rm} = (18.42 + 23.60 + 28.0 + 40.03 + 4.3)/5 = 22.87, \text{ i.e. } 22.87\%$$

Secondly, the risk-free rate of return is estimated by taking the weighted average of treasury bill yields over the five years.

1987		1988		1989	
102 × 8 =	816	145 × 11 =	1,595	206 × 11 =	2,266
742 × 7 =	5,194	946 × 10 =	9,460	1,148 × 9 =	10,332
214 × 6 =	1,284	254 × 5 =	1,270	384 × 5 =	1,920
1,058	7,294	1,345	12,325	1,738	14,518
Rf = 6.89%		Rf = 9.16%		Rf = 8.35%	

1990		1991	
290 × 9 =	2,610	310 × 8 =	2,480
1,624 × 8 =	12,992	1,650 × 7 =	11,550
580 × 4 =	2,320	560 × 4 =	2,320
2,494	17,992	2,520	16,270
Rf = 7.19%		Rf = 6.46%	

The average over the five years:

$$Rf = (6.89 + 9.16 + 8.35 + 7.19 + 6.46)/5 = 7.61, \text{i.e. } 7.61\%$$

To find the B equity, B = Covariance Rm, Ri/σ^2_m the variance of the market returns is required.

Rm	(Rm − $\overline{Rm}$)	(Rm − $\overline{Rm}$)^2
18.42	(4.45)	19.80
23.60	0.73	0.53
28.00	5.13	26.32
40.03	17.16	294.47
4.3	(18.84)	344.84
Rm = 22.87%		685.96	$\sigma^2_m = 685.96/4* = 171.49$

* The variance has been divided by n − 1 instead of n due to the number of observations (loss of one degree of freedom). The data can now be inserted into the formula for the cost of equity.

$$K_e = Rf + (\overline{Rm} - Rf) \times B \quad \text{Our Beta: } B = CovRm,Ri/\sigma^2_m$$
$$= 200.12/171.49$$
$$= 1.16.$$

Thus $K_e = 7.61 = (22.87 - 7.61) \times 1.16 = 25.31\%$

This estimate would then be input into the weighted average cost of capital equation, along with the cost of debt, to estimate the appropriate discount rate to use in the project evaluation.

Cost of debt

This cost is more easily identifiable as it is based upon the current market interest rate payable on the debt. For debt that is quoted on a stock market this will be the yield to redemption of the debt which incorporates all interest payments (net of any tax relief which is available, as interest is a tax-allowable expense) plus any capital gain or loss on the debt, i.e. change in price between the current market price and the redemption price of the debt. For unquoted debt it is the current after-tax interest rate payable on new debt. The tax shield associated with the use of debt may result in the overall cost of capital being lowered by introducing borrowed funds.

FACTORS AFFECTING THE COST OF CAPITAL

The multinational company operates in an environment which is much more complex than that of the domestic company. Thus, its cost of capital is influenced by variables related to many foreign markets and their imperfections. It is often assumed that the multinational faces more risks than a domestic company and that its cost of capital will increase because of these extra risks. There are differing views on this matter, but the multinational company's ability to diversify internationally, and perhaps reduce its level of systematic risk, must also be taken into consideration.

Factors which might influence the multinational's cost of capital include:

Access to capital

The increased availability of capital from foreign markets may lead to a lower marginal cost of capital. This may be due to the fact that domestic markets are illiquid, both in terms of equity and debt. The market may not be able to absorb another issue of shares, or there might be limited access to borrowing. Therefore, providing that tax, exchange and interest rates are favourable to the multinational, availability of capital from foreign markets may mean that they can reduce their overall cost of funds. Greater availability of capital may also allow the multinational to maintain its desired capital structure more easily.

Market segmentation

Segmentation is closely linked with the availability factor discussed above, and means that returns on the same type of security vary from market to market and that some investment opportunities may only be available to companies or investors within individual market segments. This situation is generally caused by governments imposing restrictions on the movement of capital. Segmentation leads to restricted availability of capital within a particular country or market segment.

The multinational company, by undertaking capital investment in many different countries (which may be separate market segments), may gain access to new risk and return combinations that are not available within its domestic economy and may reduce the systematic risk of its portfolio of capital investments. If this is the case, international investment might result in a lower cost of capital for the multinational. Another problem of market segmentation is that a multinational company will mostly be operating in a market which is neither completely segmented nor completely integrated. When attempting to calculate the cost of equity to be used in the discount rate estimate (i.e. using $Ke = Rf + [E(Rm) - Rf] \times B$) how should Rf and $E(Rm)$ be estimated? For a segmented market Rf and $E(Rm)$ would be based upon the parent country risk-free rate and market return; for an integrated market the rates for the whole world (or the market, if smaller) would be used. It is not possible to directly identify the appropriate rates for a market which is not completely segmented or completely integrated, which is the normal situation given the restrictions imposed by many governments on currency and capital flows. How then should the discount rate be estimated? A pragmatic, although somewhat subjective, solution is to estimate the cost of equity for both a segmented and an integrated market (in many cases there will be little difference), and to use a cost of equity which lies somewhere between the segmented and integrated rates. The actual selection of rate will depend upon how integrated or segmented the market in which the multinational company operates is perceived to be.

Foreign currency risk

The introduction of exchange rate risk may lead to an increase in the cost of debt raised abroad and hence the cost of finance and discount rate, although it is arguable that much of this risk can be hedged away (at a price) using swaps and options.

Taxation policies

The tax factor is normally associated with the tax shield created by the use of debt. However, the tax treatment of debt can differ between countries as can the tax treatment of remitted funds and funds which are reinvested in a foreign country. Such factors can influence the cost of capital: for example, if remitted funds are subject to parent country tax and reinvested funds are not, then the cost of equity for funds retained in the foreign subsidiary will be lower (effectively due to tax deferral until remittance to the parent company is made). This reduction in the cost of equity will result in a fall in the company's overall cost of equity.

Disclosure of financial information

The signalling role of disclosure of financial data is of importance to banks, creditors and other investors. The last decade has seen a trend towards more comprehensive and standardized disclosure requirements internationally, leading to investors being able to place greater reliance on the information given (the process is, however, by no means complete!). This means that investors experience less risk when they invest in multinational companies, owing to the fact that they have access to more detailed and more reliable information about the companies they are investing in. The result is that the cost of capital might be reduced, since investors experiencing lower risk are happy to accept a lower return, and a lower return to investors means a lower cost of funds to companies.

Capital structure

Financial theorists have long debated the importance of the choice of capital structure to the market value of the company. The consensus view is that a company can maximize shareholder wealth by moving to an optimal capital structure which minimizes the weighted average cost of capital. This view may still be valid in a multinational company, but the international environment introduces many new variables which complicate the estimation of a company's optimal capital structure and the weighted average cost of capital. Again, the question of project or parent company viewpoint arises; should the subsidiary's capital structure conform with:

1. The capital structure of the parent company
2. Norms within the country where the subsidiary operates, or
3. Should it vary to take advantage of opportunities to minimize the cost, i.e. assuming that the markets are at least in part segmented?

Point 2 is supported by Stonehill and Stitzel (1969), who state that the cost of capital and the structure should conform with those of appropriate local competitors within the same industry. The benefit, they argue, is that adopting the capital structure of similar local companies can reduce the exposure to political risk and criticism that the multinational is not providing enough investment within the foreign country in the form of equity capital. However, both points 1 and 2 ignore the possible benefits that the multinational can derive through its ability to access many financial markets.

Shapiro (1989) suggests that the capital structure of foreign subsidiaries is only relevant in so far as it affects the overall group capital structure. The implication is that multinational companies should attempt to raise funds wherever in the world will minimize the group's weighted average cost of capital, taking account of foreign exchange risk and local taxation. If this results in extremely high or extremely low levels of financial gearing in different subsidiaries, this is not a problem. Subsidiaries can have high gearing levels without paying a very high cost for funds, because the ultimate risk of the subsidiaries' financing is associated with the group as a whole and its capital structure. It is common for subsidiary financing to be guaranteed by the group or parent company.

Lee and Kwok (1988) explored the differences in capital structures between multinational companies and domestic companies based in the USA. They found a tendency for multinational companies to have lower debt to equity ratios than the domestic companies. These results are consistent with those of Michel and Shaked (1986), but contradict what theory would suggest. Lee and Kwok also found significant differences in capital structure between industries, with companies in highly volatile environments, e.g. high-technology firms, having a lower debt ratio. This reflects the higher general level of risk these companies face, and hence the need to have a more flexible capital structure.

RISK ADJUSTMENTS

Given the above complexities in estimating the cost of capital for a multinational company, any estimate will be subject to error, possibly as much as + or − 2 per cent from the calculated discount rate. In many cases this will not be significant to the investment decision because the discount rate is rarely the most significant variable affecting project cash flows. Much of the problem of estimating the discount rate arises from trying to allow for the degree of risk involved in the project. Even in domestic investment appraisal it is not easy to incorporate the effects of a change in risk (through, for example, a change in financial gearing of the company), into the discount rate. Alternatives to attempting to adjust the discount rate for risk are adjusting cash flows, or using a different appraisal technique to net present value (the adjusted present value technique).

Adjustment of cash flows

This approach is regarded by many as the most appropriate one, as it allows the multinational company to more specifically reflect the impact of the risk during the investment. Shapiro (1989) also argues that better information is usually available regarding the impact of risk on cash flows than on discount rates. Adjustment of cash flows can be achieved using the certainty equivalent approach. The certainty equivalent technique requires the uncertain future cash flows of an investment to be reduced to a smaller risk-free cash flow which the market would accept as a direct alternative. This adjustment should be made separately for each period of the project. The adjusted risk-free cash flows are then discounted at the risk-free rate to estimate the net present value of the project. Time and risk are separately considered by the certainty equivalent, but are treated jointly if a risk adjusted discount rate is used. Although theoretically superior, the certainty equivalent method is not widely used because there are significant practical problems in identifying the equivalent risk-free cash flows.

Adjusted present value

The adjusted present value (APV) technique avoids many of the problems of estimating a unique correct discount rate, as is required to calculate a NPV. The method first evaluates the project as if it were all equity financed (the base case NPV), and then makes adjustments to directly take into account the 'side-effects' caused by the specific method of financing that has been used. Each financing side-effect is discounted at a separate rate which reflects its level of systematic risk. Typical financing side-effects include tax relief on the interest paid on debt capital, tax savings from depreciation or capital allowances, and the effect of subsidized loans or other incentives that might be available in the foreign country. The APV for a foreign investment might be estimated by the present value (PV) of:

Capital outflows (net of any residual value)
+ PV of remittable operating cash flows
+ PV of tax savings from depreciation or capital allowances
+ PV of subsidies to the project
+ PV of any other tax savings
+ PV of the project's effect on corporate debt capacity
+ PV of other cash inflows or outflows which occur directly from undertaking the project

All of these present values are estimated using a discount rate which reflects their own level of systematic risk. Operating cash flows, for example, are likely to be discounted at a higher rate than tax savings from depreciation since they involve a higher level of systematic risk.

The difficulty with the APV technique is that it requires considerable expertise to correctly identify all relevant financing side-effects and to establish the correct individual discount rates to apply to the financing side-effects.

SUMMARY

The appraisal of foreign investments exposes multinational companies to two main problems: first, they have to decide how to measure and reflect the more complex international situation; and secondly, they have to decide on which basis they should make their decisions—project cash flows or parent cash flows.

All evaluation methods have their weaknesses as they are based on simplistic assumptions. There are, therefore, doubts about the usefulness to decision-makers of models like the NPV model owing to the very wide range of possible outcomes.

Surveys have shown that companies are rather reluctant to adopt more sophisticated, and theoretically better, methods of appraisal, because of a general lack of understanding of the models themselves, and the possible inaccuracy of the NPV estimates. However, as long as appraisal methods are applied with care, including the appraisal of alternative scenarios, and the manager has an understanding of the complexities involved, the models should provide a good basis for decision-making.

REFERENCES

Fuller, R. J. and Kerr, H. S. (1981) 'Estimating the divisional cost of capital: an analysis of the pure play technique', *Journal of Finance*, December, pp. 997–1009.

Lee, C. K. and Kwok, C. (1988) 'Multinational corporations vs domestic corporations—international environmental factors and determinants of capital structure', *Journal of International Business Studies*, Summer.

Michel, A. and Shaked, T. (1986) 'MNC vs DCs: financial peformance and characteristics', *Journal of International Business Studies*, Summer.

Roll, R. (1977) 'A critique of the asset pricing theory's tests', *Journal of Financial Economics*, March, pp. 129–76.

Shapiro, A. (1989) *Multinational Financial Management*, 3rd edition, Allyn and Bacon, Massachusetts.

Stanley, R. and Block, S. (1983) 'An empirical study of management and financial variables influencing capital budgeting decisions for multinational companies in the 1980s', *Management International Review*, Vol. 23, March.

Stonehill, A. and Stitzel, T. S. (1969) 'Financial structure and multinational corporations', *California Management Review*, Fall.

Wicks Kelly, M. E. and Philippatos, G. C. (1982) 'Comparative evaluation of foreign investment evaluation practices used by US based manufacturing multinational companies', *Journal of International Business Studies*, Winter, pp. 19–42.

CASE STUDIES

These case studies supplement those shown earlier in the chapter.

Case study 1 – Baumain plc

Baumain plc, a leading construction company, is negotiating with two foreign governments regarding large capital investment projects. The Gwumban government wishes to construct a 300 megawatt hydroelectric scheme on the Gwumba river. The Sunnovian government is proposing to build a new 80,000 seat stadium. Both projects have been offered to Baumain, but the company only has the capacity to undertake one project. The expected cash flows relating to each project are detailed below. Both projects are expected to take four years.

	Year				
	0	1	2	3	4
Gwumba					
Outlay (in million Gwumban francs)	50	150	150	100	50
Sunnovia					
Outlay (in million Sunnovian sols)	100	200	300	75	75

The contracts will be paid for in US dollars. The terms of the proposed Gwumban contract are such that payments, each of 20 per cent of the purchase price of US$225 million, will be made at the start of year 1 and year 3, with the balance payable at the end of year 4. The Sunnovian government will agree to an advance payment of 25 per cent of the purchase price of US$180 million, with the balance payable on completion.

Baumain has produced estimates of possible exchange rate changes each year for four years for the Gwumban franc and Sunnovian sol relative to sterling.

Current spot exchange rates

Gwumba (francs)	5/£
Sunnovia (sols)	10/£
US dollars	2.3/£

Expected exchange rates

	Year			
	1	2	3	4
Gwumba (francs)				
Expected % devaluation	20	20	23	23
New rate	6/£	7.2/£	8.9/£	10.9/£
Sunnovia (sols)				
Expected % devaluation	35	35	31	31
New rate	13.5/£	18.23/£	23.86/£	31.3/£

The pound is expected to appreciate by 5 per cent per annum relative to the US dollar.

New rates $/£	2.42/£	2.54/£	2.66/£	2.80/£

UK corporation tax of 35 per cent is payable on net cash inflows the year after they arise. Net cash outflows in one year are allowable against future tax charges. Baumain estimates the Gwumban project's beta coefficient to be 2.0 and the Sunnovian project's beta to be 2.5. Market return is 12 per cent and the average yield on treasury bills is 8 per cent.

Should Baumain accept one of the projects, and what other factors should be taken into account in making the decision?

Evaluation of Gwumban project

		Year				
	0	1	2	3	4	5
Outflows (Fr m)	50	150	150	100	50	
(£ m)	10	25	20.83	11.29	4.59	
Inflows (\$ m)	45	0	45	0	135	
(£ m)	19.57	0	17.74	0	48.28	
Net flows (£ m)	9.57	(25)	(3.09)	(11.29)	43.69	
Tax 35%	0	(3.35)	0	0	0	(1.51)
	9.57	(28.35)	(3.09)	(11.29)	43.69	(1.51)

The appropriate discount rate for Gwumba using CAPM is:

Rf = Return on treasury bills = 8%

Beta = 2.0

Rm = Return on market = 12%

Discount rate = Rf + beta (Rm − Rf) = 8 + 2.0 (12% − 8%) = 16%

	Year				
	0	1	2	3	4	5

	0	1	2	3	4	5
Discounted cash flows	9.57	(24.44)	(2.30)	(7.24)	24.12	(0.72)

The expected NPV is −£1.01m

On financial grounds the project should be rejected.

Evaluation of Sunnovian project

		Year				
	0	1	2	3	4	5
Outflows (sol m)	100	200	300	75	75	
(£ m)	10	14.82	16.46	3.14	2.40	
Inflows ($ m)	45	0	0	0	135	
(£ m)	19.57	0	0	0	48.28	
Net flows (£ m)	9.57	(14.82)	(16.46)	(3.14)	45.88	
Tax (35%)	0	(3.35)	0	0	0	(4.01)
	9.57	(18.17)	(16.46)	(3.14)	45.88	(4.01)

The appropriate discount rate for Sunnovia using CAPM can be calculated by using the formula Rf + beta (Rm − Rf). This time beta is 2.5, but the other variables are the same as for the Gwumban project.

Rf + beta (Rm − Rf) = 8 + 2.5 (12 − 8) = 18%

		Year				
	0	1	2	3	4	5
Discounted cash flows	9.57	(15.39)	(11.82)	(1.91)	23.67	(1.75)

The expected NPV is £2.37m

From a financial perspective this looks a viable project and should be accepted. However, there may be non-financial factors that need to be considered before a final decision is made.

Case study 2 – Bekosan Inc.
Bekosan Inc., a New York-based manufacturer of domestic waste disposal units, is re-evaluating its UK sales strategy. Since the entry of the UK into the EC, Bekosan has had to face a 30 per cent common external EC tariff on its exports to the UK, compared with a 10 per cent UK tariff in force prior to the UK joining. This, together with the downward floating of the pound against the dollar, has led Bekosan to increase the UK price of its product, the Omnigrind. Although the company has reduced its profit margin, its share of the UK market has fallen considerably in the face of competition from companies that do not have to pay the 30 per cent tariff. Bekosan is now considering whether to set up a manufacturing subsidiary in the UK, or to pull out of the market completely.

In 1991 Bekosan's UK sales totalled US$15 million and produced an after-tax net cash flow of US$1 million. It is expected that this net cash flow will fall steadily to $0 over the next five years. If the company immediately pulls out of the UK market it is thought that some production could be diverted to the Canadian market, yielding an after-tax net cash flow of US$500,000 for the foreseeable future.

A UK manufacturing subsidiary, based in a development area, would cost £10 million to establish, 20 per cent of which would be met from a grant by the British government. The UK investment would be depreciated on a historic cost straightline basis over five years. After five years it is expected to have an after-tax realizable value of £5 million. Production would commence in six months, and full production is anticipated by the end of the first year. All components would be produced locally in the UK except the control device which would be exported from the parent company and would be subject to the external tariff. The parent would charge the subsidiary US$10 per unit for this component, yielding a contribution of US$3 per unit to overhead.

Bekosan has a five-year planning horizon. Sales by the proposed UK subsidiary are expected to be 50,000 units in the first year (1992), and 150,000 units in each of the next four years. The UK price is to be fixed initially at £60 per unit, and will be varied at the beginning of each year in direct relation to the rate of inflation experienced during the previous year. UK fixed and variable costs are also expected to vary directly with inflation in the same manner. Estimates of these costs for the first year are: fixed costs £500,000, variable costs £30 per unit. Bekosan has proposed a royalty payment to the parent of US$10 per unit sold by the UK subsidiary, payable at the end of each year. There are no restrictions on remittances from the UK to the USA, and corporation tax is levied at a rate of 35 per cent in both countries, with a full double taxation agreement in force. Tax is payable in the year the profit is earned.

Bekosan's estimates of future US$/£ spot rates and UK inflation rates are as follows:

| | Spot rate $/£ | | Expected UK |
Year	Average for year	31 December	Inflation
1991	1.55	1.50	12% (historic data)
1992	1.60	1.55	8%
1993	1.65	1.70	5%
1994	1.75	1.75	5%
1995	1.70	1.60	6%
1996	1.50	1.50	10%

Bekosan's managers believe that the appropriate discount rate for this project is 20 per cent. The present value of £1 at 20 per cent is:

Years hence	£
1	0.833
2	0.694
3	0.579
4	0.482
5	0.402

Assume that it is now 31 December 1991. Should Bekosan accept the proposal to invest in the UK or not?

Cash flows to the UK subsidiary

	£000				
	1992	1993	1994	1995	1996
Inflows sales	3,000	9,720	10,206	10,716	11,360
Outflows UK variable costs	1,500	4,860	5,103	5,358	5,680
Imported materials	406	1,182	1,114	1,147	1,300
Fixed costs	500	540	567	595	631
Royalty	323	882	857	937	1,000
Depreciation	1,000	1,000	1,000	1,000	1,000
Net inflows	(729)	1,256	1,565	1,679	1,749
Tax	0	184	548	588	612
	(729)	1,072	1,017	1,091	1,137
Add back depreciation	1,000	1,000	1,000	1,000	1,000
Realizable value					5,000
Cash flow repatriable	271	2,072	2,017	2,091	7,137

Notes:

	Sales price per unit £	VC PU£	FC £000	Imported materials PU£
1992	60	30	500	(10/1.6) + 30% = 8.125
1993	64.8	32.4	540	(10/1.65) + 30% = 7.878
1994	68.04	34.02	567	(10/1.75) + 30% = 7.428
1995	71.44	35.72	595.35	(10/1.7) + 30% = 7.647
1996	75.73	37.86	631.07	(10/1.5) + 30% = 8.667

Cash flows to parent company

	$000				
	1992	1993	1994	1995	1996
Inflows					
Repatriated cash flow	420	3,522	3,530	3,346	10,706
Royalties	500	1,500	1,500	1,500	1,500
Contribution to OH	150	450	450	450	450
	1,070	5,472	5,480	5,296	12,656
Outflows					
Tax on royalties and contributions	228	683	683	683	683
Incremental cash flow	842	4,789	4,797	4,613	11,973
PV with 20% discount rate	701	3,324	2,777	2,223	4,813

Total present value	= $13,838,000
Initial investment	= $12,000,000
NPV of incremental cash flows	= $1,838,000

This is the estimated NPV from the UK investment. However, there are other relevant cash flows. If the investment is undertaken, Bekosan is free to sell to the Canadian market, yielding an after-tax incremental cash flow of US$500,000 per year. The present value of a perpetuity of US$500,000 per year is:

$$\frac{500,000}{.20} = US\$2,500,0000$$

The total expected NPV is therefore US$4,338,000. (The Canadian cash flow is only relevant if Bekosan has no spare capacity and is to supply the Canadian market without investing in the UK subsidiary.)

If the investment is not undertaken, the after-tax net cash flow from exporting to the UK is expected to fall steadily to zero. If cash flows in years 1–5 respectively are: US$800,000, US$600,000, US$400,000, US$200,000 and US$0, these cash flows will have a NPV of US$1,410,000 (assuming a discount rate of 20 per cent which might not be appropriate since exporting will involve a different level of risk to foreign direct investment). This NPV is much less than the that produced by investing in the UK and exporting to Canada.

Therefore, based on the financial information Bekosan should invest in the UK.

Case study 3 – Axmine plc

Axmine plc has been contacted by Traces SA, a mining company based in a South American country. Traces has proposed a four-year joint venture to mine copper, using a new technique developed by Axmine. Axmine would supply machinery, at an immediate cost of 800 million pesos, and 10 supervisors, at an annual salary of £40,000 each at current prices. In addition, Axmine would pay half of the 1,000 million pesos per year (at current prices) local labour costs and other expenses in the South American country. The supervisors' salaries and local labour and other expenses will be increased in line with inflation in the United Kingdom and the South American country respectively.

Inflation in the South American country is currently 100% per year, and in the UK 8% per year. The government of the South American country is attempting to control inflation, and hopes to reduce it each year by 20% of the previous year's rate.

The joint venture would give Axmine a 50% share of Trace's copper production, with current market prices at £1,500 per 1000 kilogrammes. Trace's production is expected to be 10 million kilogrammes per year, and copper prices are expected to rise by 10% per year (in pounds sterling) for the foreseeable future. At the end of four years Axmine would be given the choice to pull out of the venture or to negotiate another four-year joint venture, on different terms.

The current exchange rate is 140 pesos/£. Future exchange rates may be estimated using purchasing power parity theory.

Axmine has no foreign operations. The cost of capital of the company's UK mining operations is 16% per year. As this joint venture involves diversifying into foreign operations, the company considers that a 2% reduction in the cost of capital would be appropriate for this project.

Corporate tax is at the rate of 20% per year in the South American country and 35% per year in the UK. A tax treaty exists between the two countries, and all foreign tax paid is allowable against any UK tax liability. Taxation is payable one year in arrears, and a 25% straightline writing-down allowance is available on the machinery in both countries.

Cash flows may be assumed to occur at the year end, except for the immediate cost of machinery. The machinery is expected to have negligible terminal value at the end of four years.

Required:
(a) Prepare a report discussing whether Axmine plc should agree to the proposed joint venture. Relevant calculations must form part of your report or an appendix to it.
State clearly any assumptions that you make.

(16 marks)
(b) If the South American government were to fail to control inflation, and inflation were to increase rapidly during the period of the joint venture, discuss the likely effect of very high inflation on the joint venture.

(4 marks)
(c) Explain whether you consider Axmine's proposed discount rate for the project to be appropriate.

(5 marks)
(**25 marks**)
ACCA, 3.2, December 1991

Solution:
(a) *Report on the proposed joint venture*
The proposed joint venture must be appraised using both financial and non-financial considerations. Based upon the expected cash flows the proposed joint venture is financially viable. The expected net present value is £4,724,000. Full details are provided in the appendix to this report.

Please note that cash flow estimates such as these are subject to a large margin of error, and sensitivity analysis is advisable on the key variables, especially copper prices, labour costs, the discount rate, and the exchange rate. Exchange rate estimates have been based on the purchasing power parity theory, but future exchange rates are likely to deviate from these estimates. One reassuring fact is the size of the expected NPV; there would need to be very large errors in the estimates to produce a negative NPV and make the project not financially viable.

Important factors to consider in addition to the expected NPV are:

(i) How trustworthy is the proposed partner in the joint venture? Will Traces SA fulfil its obligations?
(ii) Political risk. What political risk is Axmine likely to experience? Many South American countries are known for their political volatility. What is the possibility that the company's assets will be expropriated?
(iii) Is there a danger of technology transfer, as Traces will have knowledge of the new mining technique?

(iv) What is the value of the option to negotiate a new joint venture after four years? This option might have a positive expected NPV which would make the joint venture even more attractive.

(v) Is the proposed project significant in terms of Axmine's overall future success?

It is recommended that, on the basis of available information, the joint venture should be undertaken.

Appendix

Year	South American inflation (%)	UK inflation (%)	Forecast rates (pesos/£)
1	80	8	233.3
2	64	8	354.3
3	51.2	8	496.0
4	41	8	647.6
5	32.8	8	796.3

$$\text{For example, year 1 is } \frac{1 + 0.80}{1 + 0.08} \times 140 = 233.3$$

Year	Forecast copper prices for 5 million kg (£000)	Supervisory labour costs (£000)
1	8,250	432
2	9,075	467
3	9,983	504
4	10,981	544

Axmine's share of copper production
Cash flows (pesos million)

	0	1	2	3	4	5
Sales (copper)		1,925	3,215	4,952	7,111	
Outlays						
Initial outlay	800					
Local labour		900	1,476	2,232	3,147	
Supervisors		101	165	250	352	
WDA		200	200	200	200	
Taxable		724	1,374	2,270	3,412	
Taxation (20%)			(145)	(275)	(454)	(682)
Add back WDA		200	200	200	200	
	(800)	924	1,429	2,195	3,158	(682)

Cash flows (£000)
Year

	0	1	2	3	4	5
Net cash flow	(5,714)	3,961	4,033	4,425	4,876	(856)
UK tax[1]			(465)	(582)	(686)	(790)
	(5,714)	3,961	3,568	3,843	4,190	(1,646)
Discount factors (14%)		.877	.769	.675	.592	.519
Present values	(5,714)	3,474	2,744	2,594	2,480	(854)

Expected NPV is £4,724,000

[1] As UK tax is 35%, tax equivalent to 15% of foreign taxable income will be payable in the UK (20% has been paid in South America). Tax liability in year 1, for example, is:

$$\frac{724}{233.3} \text{ million pesos} \times 15\% = \text{£}0.465 \text{ million payable in year 2}$$

(b) Although it is not intuitively obvious, on this occasion the very high inflation is likely to increase the expected NPV of the joint venture.

   If exchange rates alter in line with the purchasing power parity theory, the pound sterling cost of labour and other expenses in South America will increase by the level of inflation in the UK, 8% per year, no matter what the inflation level is in South America. Supervisory salaries also increase by 8% per year. However, copper prices are expected to increase by 10% per year, leading overall to increased net cash flows and an increase in the NPV of the joint venture.

   Although most of the benefit of the writing-down allowance is lost with very high inflation, there will be a significant present value gain from paying tax one year in arrears. This is a further reason for the higher expected NPV if very high inflation occurs.

(c) The discount rate in any investment should reflect the systematic risk of that investment. Axmine's approach of a reduction in the UK rate for UK mining operations (which might have a different systematic risk, higher or lower) is not satisfactory.

   Any diversification into overseas operations is likely to reduce the total risk of the company (by reducing unsystematic risk), but might have little or no effect on the company's systematic risk. The project discount rate should be based upon the systematic risk of the project itself, not on company-wide factors.

   Foreign diversification is only likely to reduce systematic risk if the domestic and foreign markets are significantly segmented and the joint venture offers investment opportunities to Axmine's shareholders that they could not have previously undertaken themselves. This could be possible for a South American country, where exchange controls and other market imperfections often exist.

THIRTEEN
POLITICAL RISK

INTRODUCTION

Governments, in theory, exist to serve the needs of the country's citizens through the application of monetary, fiscal, social and other policies. Companies are responsible to their shareholders and to broader interest groups, including employees, customers, suppliers and the 'community' (at local and national levels). Given that the objectives of a host country and of a multinational are likely to differ, some degree of political risk is inevitable. Abdullah (1987) points out that all international trade and finance transactions involve political risk, and the longer the term of investment the greater the exposure. Companies, whether small or multinational, may consciously decide to accept these risks in order to make profits. When companies are evaluating a project they may analyse the risk by attempting to quantify it (for example, by the use of beta coefficients), decide to what extent risk may be controlled, and whether the expected returns are sufficient to make the venture worth while. To this extent political risk should be treated no differently from any other sort of risk, with the intelligent business person compromising between risk and return.

Multinational corporations are not merely economic entities; they are also social entities whose actions and reactions have significant effects on the political and social environment (Shubik (1983)). The multinational company will inevitably cause some social change within the host country.

The response of host governments to multinational companies can take many forms, ranging from minor currency controls to complete expropriation of assets. This chapter examines the reasons for political risk, how it might be predicted and measured, and what responses a multinational company might make when faced with political risk.

THE IMPORTANCE OF POLITICAL RISK

Despite the possible extreme consequences of political risk, multinationals typically undertake little formal political risk analysis. Studies in both the UK and the USA (see, for example, Rummel and Heenan (1978), Wicks Kelly and Philippatos (1982), Goddard (1990)) suggest that *ad hoc* methods are still relied upon for political risk analysis by the majority of UK and US companies. This is not because managers do not recognize that there is such a risk, as Kobrin (1979) points out; managers perceive political risk to be one of the dominant factors in foreign investment decisions, but analysis of the political scene is for the most part superficial, subjective and is not formally incorporated into any decision-making apparatus. Kobrin also found that the most common action taken against political risk was that of avoidance, with companies simply not investing in countries that were seen as being too risky, no matter how high the level of expected return. Political risk decisions are commonly made using information found within the company, or from banks or the general media.

As international trade and investment increase with the globalization of money and capital markets, so does the importance of managing international risk. The relevance of political risk has grown recently in the eyes of corporate decision-makers. In the pre-OPEC era, political risk assessment took low priority, but after the oil crises of the 1970s the effects of political events on economic conditions became more apparent. However, political risk assessment was still not given high priority. The events in Iran and Nicaragua at the end of the 1970s changed that perspective, and the political environment of the last two decades has become an important factor in the strategic decisions of the multinational firm.

Definition of political risk

Before political risk can be quantified it is necessary to examine what is meant by political risk; Shubik (1983), for example, differentiates between political risk and political uncertainty. Rummel and Heenan (1978) claim that political uncertainty is a subjective doubt, an unquantified aspect of the political arena, and that political risk is a relatively objective quantification of that doubt, often leading to probability estimates. However, Shubik (1983) and Friedmann and Kim (1988) disagree. They say that uncertainty is the situation where a lack of information means that future alternatives are unpredictable. Such alternatives have no objective probabilities. Uncertainty is an environmental characteristic, whereas risk is a value assessment of the importance of the uncertainty to a particular entity. Therefore, risk does not exist without the entity and its goal structure.

Political risk definitions fall into two main categories. The first describes political risk in terms of government interference, the second in terms of events. Typical definitions are:

that uncertainty stemming from unanticipated and unexpected acts of governments or other organisations which may cause loss to the firm (Greene (1974))

and

possible occurrence of political events of any kind (such as war, revolution, coup d'etat, expropriation, taxation, devaluation, exchange control and import restriction) at home or abroad that cause a loss of profit potential and/or assets in international business operations (Root (1968)).

The two definitions stem from two different, although interdependent, perspectives. What is relevant? Is it the actual events, with the potential to cause loss to the firm, that are relevant? Or is it the political factors behind the events that are relevant? These two perspectives will have different implications for how political risk is measured or assessed.

Simon (1982) noted that a study on available literature revealed no general consensus as to the meaning of political risk. Friedmann and Kim (1988) agree with the proviso that it represents unwanted consequences of political activity. However, Eiteman and Stonehill (1986) and Goddard (1990) argue that political risk can imply either positive or negative effects for a company. Nevertheless, it is the possible adverse effects of political changes which concern most companies.

Identification of political risk

It is often difficult to separate political risk from other types of risk such as economic, social and cultural and country risks. Friedmann and Kim (1988) illustrate the problem by examining the views of three authors. Kobrin (1982) argues that the difference between economic and political contingencies are fairly obscure; when splitting the environment into areas for study (e.g. political, economic, legal) reality is merely being broken down into analytical abstractions. These abstractions are interrelated in the world as a whole, so that precise definitions are difficult to derive. Overholt (1982) dismisses attempts to differentiate political from economic risk by stressing the importance of their interaction. He claims that the dichotomy of politics and economics for academic study creates the false impression that the differentiation can actually be done. In Herring (1983) political, economic and social and cultural risks are all treated as aspects of country risk. However, as noted in Friedmann and Kim (1988) country risk is seen in some works as synonymous with political risk and in other works as distinct from it.

A further area for disagreement is that of geography: can political risk occur in the home country? Shubik (1983) states that companies must contend with political risk in their home countries, merely because each country has its own political environment. However, others, such as Eiteman and Stonehill (1986), talk only of host countries, so implying that the company is investing abroad. Reid (1983) states that investments and trans-actions abroad are different from the same operations in the home market. For most industries, this is not a difference in kind, but one of degree. Clearly, political risks do occur in the home market. The purely overseas definitions can then be looked upon as putting the emphasis on the differences in degree of each type of political risk in the particular country.

The lack of a standard accepted definition of political risk has affected its assessment and study. One consequence of this is the lack of agreement on what constitutes a political risk event. For instance, Rodriguez and Carter (1976) limit political risk to those types related to foreign exchange and expropriation, usually in countries with unstable governments. As Brewer (1982) notes, these may be important types, but they do not constitute an exhaustive list, nor are they necessarily the most important. The lack of agreement is also responsible, at least partly, for the haphazard conceptual development of political risk. Friedmann and Kim (1988) identify six types of theoretical frameworks for political risk, and give examples of authors who have adopted that framework:

1. The actor/source approach: this suggests that groups (or actors) generate political risk events and that these groups are brought about by sources more fundamental and abstract (e.g. Robock (1971)).
2. The relative deprivation approach: developed from the theory of relative deprivation. This suggests that the important component in the decision to expropriate is the level of national frustration.
3. The product/venture type approach: claims that different products or industries suffer from various levels of sensitivity and exposure to potential risk, purely because they are different (e.g. Overholt (1982)).
4. The structural approach: the variables in the structural characteristics of the industry or organization mostly determine the vulnerability of that industry to political risk (e.g. Kobrin (1980)).

5. The bargaining power approach: this suggests that political risk is determined by the relative bargaining powers of the host government and the foreign company.
6. The government type approach: the risk of high political instability depends on the national structure of government (e.g. Brewer (1983)).

There have been many attempts to formalize political risk analysis, but there is still no general theory. The area of study is not bounded rigorously enough by most analysts to allow theory building. Quite often, the dependent variable is not clearly specified: it may be industry-, company- or project-specific, making a generalization to a broader theoretical framework difficult. No single approach can establish why or how political risk (in its variety of forms) can affect the interests and goals of a multinational company.

A consequence of this lack of consensus is that it is very difficult to develop a reliable system for measuring and analysing political risk. When decisions involving political judgements need to be made, it is not surprising that quite often corporate managers resort to subjective procedures.

Political risk assessment

Brewer (1981) details three aspects in which present assessment methods are deficient. First, they focus too narrowly on expropriation, exchange controls and government instability. Secondly, the information collection techniques are either too intuitive and subjective or too mechanistic and objective. Finally, the adjustments with respect to capital budgeting techniques are too simple. There are barriers to improving political risk assessment techniques, the most important of which are conceptual rather than operational (Kobrin (1981)).

First, a general framework needs to be developed. It is important to distinguish between macro and micro political risks: macro risks are those which affect all foreign companies in a country, while micro risks are those which are industry-, company- or project-specific. Simon (1982) makes distinctions between governmental and societal related events and policies, and internally and externally based events, as these help to distinguish the sources of types of political risks.

Brewer (1982) suggests that what is needed is a comprehensive list of political risk events, with a similar list of the potential political sources of these risks. These could then be combined in a matrix form: type of risk against source of risk. This would assist in two ways: it provides a checklist of each risk and source, so encouraging a more systematic approach; and also helps to focus attention on the analytic dimensions that require close scrutiny. Not all cells of the matrix would be relevant in any given decision.

Simon (1982) provides a similar table using a list of possible risks in cells generated by the distinctions given above (Table 12.1).

Eiteman and Stonehill (1986) consider that the traditional view of political risk, i.e. political interference by the host government, is dated and counterproductive, in the sense that it implies that a company has the right to do abroad what it does at home. They claim a better framework is that of problems arising owing to conflicts of interest/objectives between the host government and the multinational enterprise. Although this does not provide a comprehensive list of risks and their political sources, it may highlight the more probable and directly relevant risks (in the sense that the company can do something about them) which can be the subject of more in-depth analysis.

Once political risk events have been identified, there are various methods of assessing the

Table 12.1   Simon's general framework for political risk (1982)

	Macro		Micro	
	Societal	*Governmental*	*Societal*	*Governmental*
I N T E R N A L	revolution coup civil war	nationalization bureaucratic policies	selective strike	expropriation price controls
E X T E R N A L	world public opinion	alliance shifts	foreign MNE competition	import/export restrictions

likelihood of their occurrence and their possible effect on the multinational company. Reid (1983) suggests that assessment methods should:

1. Allow predictions concerning the future
2. Allow decision makers the chance to take action to avoid the risks
3. Suggest feasible actions which are cost effective

Political risk assessment is a two-stage process: first, a forecast of the general political environment over the relevant time period is required: and secondly, it is necessary to assess how the general political environment will affect a specific project of the multinational company. In other words, political risk must be examined from both a macro and micro perspective. A macro analysis alone is not adequate; within the same country a government might expropriate the assets of companies within extractive industries or the financial sector while leaving untouched or even offering subsidies to companies in other industries, typically those with a high advanced technology content.

Kobrin (1981) split political risk assessment methodologies into two main types, those using observational data and those using expert generated data. Friedmann and Kim (1988) produce five categories: purely qualitative unstructured methods, aggregation of expert opinion, scenario approaches, decision tree approaches, and rating indices approaches.

Macro techniques   Macro techniques are typically country or political indices. They assess political risk by giving each country a score and produce a relative ranking of political risk within the country as a whole. Most of them rely on opinions from experts on the country under assessment; the experts, for example, would be asked to rate each country in the survey on a scale from 1 to 10 with respect to important variables that are considered to influence political risk. Such variables might include political stability, currency convertibility, cultural compatibility, social conditions, internal conflict and the state of the legal, financial and accounting infrastructure.

In a recent political risk ranking by *Euromoney* in 1992, countries were judged on economic performance, political risk, debt indicators, access to bank lending, access to short-term finance, access to capital markets, discount on forfaiting, credit ratings, and debt in default or rescheduled.

The total possible score was 100, which reflected virtually no risk. The top 10 countries according to this rating were:

Japan	99.55
The Netherlands	99.08
Switzerland	98.49
Germany	98.20
France	98.18
United States	98.08
Austria	97.46
Canada	97.14
United Kingdom	96.89
Belgium	95.99

The bottom 10 rankings were:

Rank		
169	Cambodia	2.56
168	Iraq	6.07
167	N. Korea	6.30
166	Somalia	7.67
165	Cuba	8.08
164	Mozambique	10.46
163	Sudan	11.66
162	Liberia	12.19
161	Nicaragua	12.45
160	Guyana	12.53

Source: Euromoney, September 1992

Macro techniques often concentrate on the possibility of expropriation or nationalization. Although the effect of expropriation might be the most extreme for the multinational, expropriations are rare. Political actions that result in remittance and operational restrictions are likely to have a much greater impact on the cash flow of multinationals than expropriations.

Haendel, West and Meadow (1975) developed a well-known macro model, the political systems stability index. This model comprises three equally weighted subindices concerned with socioeconomic characteristics, social conflict characteristics and governmental processes characteristics, all of which are derived from objective measures. Socioeconomic characteristics are measured by growth in per capita gross national product, per capita energy consumption and ethnolinguistic fractionalization within a country. Governmental processes examine legislative effectiveness, constitutional changes per year, number of irregular changes in chief executive and a political competition index. Societal conflict is further subdivided into three sections:

1. Public unrest, comprising riots, demonstrations and government crises
2. Internal violence, measured by armed attacks, assassinations, *coups d'états* and guerilla warfare
3. Coercion potential, the number of internal security forces per 1,000 population

All of these measures are defined and observable. The three subindices are combined to produce an overall country score, with a confidence estimate to allow for missing data or questions about the reliability of data (consider, for example, different versions of events in Tiananmen Square, Beijing in 1989). The index is more suited to less developed countries, and in 1975 ranked the Dominican Republic the worst country surveyed; by the early 1990s the Dominican Republic was a popular destination for UK package holidays. Frequent revisions of the political stability index are necessary to reflect the rapidly changing environments of many countries, in particular the effects of debt servicing payments. A country with debt servicing problems is more likely to impose restrictions on remittances to the parent company and to introduce exchange controls.

The main advantage of macro techniques is that they sum up numerous complex variables into a meaningful quantitative index. There are, however, many drawbacks to political indices. A political event will convey a different political risk to each company and project. A general index of a country's political risk will be of minimal value to a randomly selected company with its individual projects, since such indices cannot account for variations in risk exposure for different investments. Further criticism is levelled at their subjective nature; assigning ratings to the findings gives a pretence of objectivity to subjective data (Simon 1982). The margin of error may be large, but its exact magnitude is difficult to estimate.

Not all indices give the same results: Eiteman and Stonehill (1986) compare two indices produced by Frost and Sullivan (World Political Risk Forecasts) and by Business International (Country Assessment Service):

	Frost and Sullivan	*Business International*
Seven best		
	USA	Singapore
	Denmark	Holland
	Singapore	Norway
	Finland	Kuwait
	West Germany	Saudi Arabia
	Austria	Switzerland
	Canada	West Germany
Seven worst		
	El Salvador	Iran
	Iran	Yugoslavia
	Nicaragua	South Korea
	Zaïre	Algeria
	Zambia	Brazil
	Libya	Nicaragua
	Bolivia	India

Source: *Business Week*, 1 December 1980

Friedmann and Kim (1988) blame this difference in the results of indices on the lack of consensus regarding the definition of political risk and the lack of a conceptual framework. Despite these problems, macro techniques do offer a cost-effective overview of potential investment climates.

Micro techniques Micro analyses are undertaken by a multinational company with a particular investment in mind. Rummel and Heenan (1978) claim the four most popular forms of analysis are: the grand tour, old hands, delphi techniques and quantitative methods (such techniques may be used for both macro and micro analyses).

The grand tour The grand tour involves a manager or team of executives from the company visiting the potential host country to meet with government officials, businesspeople and local leaders and to view at first hand conditions within the country. First-hand impressions may be of value, but such tours can easily be stage-managed by government or other officials eager to attract foreign investment.

Old hands This approach seeks the opinions and advice of experts who have many years of experience of the country. Such experts might include academics, diplomats, journalists and businesspeople. The use of such experts is well established, and there is undoubted value in their knowledge of local customs, protocol and history. However, the value of such knowledge depends upon how it can be directly applied to the investment under consideration.

Delphi techniques Delphi techniques provide a more systematic approach to political risk analysis. A delphi study comprises of a controlled feedback questionnaire. A group of experts are chosen and each individual asked, independently, to answer a comprehensive questionnaire about his or her assessment of and predictions for a set of possible developments. These answers are then collected, aggregated and returned to the experts, who then have the chance to change their minds having seen the answers of their peers. In order to produce meaningful results delphi studies require:

1. A comprehensive and accurate list of the main determinants of political risk
2. Well-thought-out and up-to-date opinions from the experts
3. A means of weighting and aggregating the opinions

Shubik (1983) notes four main problems with using a delphi study for political risk assessment. These are: difficulty in design of the questionnaire and choice of variables; the selection and availability of experts; the control and motivation of experts; and the interpretation and utilization of the results.

Quantitative methods Quantitative methods usually involve some form of country risk analysis, often incorporating sensitivity or simulation analysis to examine the effect on the multinational of different possible scenarios.

An early warning system Simon (1982) suggests a more flexible approach is required for anticipating political risk. By moving from rigid models to an adaptable early warning system (EWS), reductions in uncertainty can be achieved. To be effective, such a EWS must meet certain criteria. First, it must be able to monitor both country- and industry-specific conditions, due to the wide variety of risks faced. Secondly, it needs a mechanism for coordinating and analysing information from many diverse sources, since multinational companies involve vast information networks. Thirdly, it has to be able to account for any recent development, since situations can change rapidly. Finally, the EWS must have a feedback procedure available to it, to allow revision and updating of information when needed and to prevent false alarms.

Simon suggests the separation of political risk assessment into its macro and micro components, with the responsibility for each component resting mainly with the corporate headquarters and the overseas subsidiary respectively. Macro developments will generally be reported in public sources, and so will be available for the corporate headquarters to use in analysis. Since they are company-specific, micro developments are rarer and will rely upon the expertise of overseas managers who will be in a better position to monitor the nuances in government policies and social attitudes, as they will have developed contacts in the government, the business community and with local leaders.

In order to obtain regular reports from the overseas subsidiary, they should be sent a questionnaire every month. This will also have a 'Further Information' section to allow an expansion on an answer or to cover points not set out in the questionnaire. These reports should be circulated among subsidiaries in the same and different countries. The first analysis of these reports is carried out at regional headquarters and the probability estimates passed on to corporate headquarters. At the same time macro risk analysis is conducted at corporate headquarters. This consists of two files; a country profile system covering basic country attributes, for example, the type of political system; and, the current macro risk file directed at the changes in inter- and intra-national developments. This will cover the political, social and economic sectors. The macro reports are contrasted with the micro reports and initial probability estimates, and are then referred back to the subsidiaries for further consideration. Hence, the feedback procedure is set in motion. These adjusted assessments from the subsidiaries are then transferred back to corporate headquarters for integration with the macro file. There are also many independent sources of information available to the multinational, which can be incorporated into the EWS if more information is deemed necessary, such as an expert opinion for further consultation on the micro file. Finally, a unit at corporate headquarters coordinates the input from both files, which is then dispatched to relevant departments. Feedback is encouraged, and forecasts are adjusted as new information becomes available.

The EWS stresses the ongoing monitoring of the political environment so that it becomes an integral part of the decision-making process.

When an assessment has been made of the degree to which political risk will affect a particular project, the multinational is faced with further decisions about what courses of action to take to combat political risk in all stages of the project.

Management of political risk

The first decision to be made once the company has undertaken a political risk assessment is whether or not to invest in the foreign country. A multinational will often reject a project which it views to be too risky, no matter what the expected return. However, in theory, the multinational should undertake a risk/return analysis to establish how much risk the company is willing to take and how much return is needed to compensate for this risk.

If the multinational takes the decision to invest overseas, it is in its interests to minimize the political risks which it faces. Political risk cannot be completely eliminated.

Management techniques   Political risk may be incorporated into the capital budgeting process (see Chapter 11), but the difficulty lies in integrating the various aspects of this risk into the quantitative evaluation. Predicting all aspects of risk affecting the real world is clearly impossible; including only a small number of these risks makes capital budgeting techniques incomplete.

Concession agreements   A more practical way of managing political risk is to undertake negotiations with the host government prior to investment. This usually takes the form of a concession agreement, and involves negotiating investment arrangements with the host government, as well as attempting to solve anticipated problems before investment proceeds. The biggest problem with this policy is that host governments in developing countries are very volatile, which sometimes results in radical political change. Consequently, agreements made with previous administrations can be repudiated by the new government. Wells (1977) argues that the terms of a concession agreement will not normally remain unchanged, even with the same host government. He cites several reasons for this:

1. The terms and conditions required to entice a company to invest in a particular country are different to the terms and conditions required to make a company remain, once it has committed and developed its investment. Thus, the host government has an incentive to alter an agreement immediately after the investment has been fully developed.
2. The standard terms and conditions which a government agrees upon will change with the passage of time, owing to the structure of industry changing and also new multinationals investing and giving the host government a better deal. Therefore, the host government has another incentive to renegotiate an agreement to reflect its new-found expectations.
3. If the multinational's subsidiary is more successful than both parties anticipated at the beginning of the investment, the government might wish to renegotiate to take account of the windfall.

As advanced nations have renegotiated concession agreements, less developed countries feel that they can be justified in following suit. Consider, for example, Britain's renegotiation of North Sea oil exploration licences, as the potential of the oilfield developed.

Although concession agreements have their limitations they are not all subject to renegotiation, and they offer one way of preventing any misunderstandings which could otherwise have appeared, at some future date, between the multinational and the host government. Rational governments are unlikely to renegotiate agreements to the point where multinationals feel they have to leave that particular country, if that country has a need for the company.

Items which should form part of a concession agreement include:

Transfer risks   These are restrictions placed by host governments on the overseas transfer (in or out) of capital, dividends, patent and management fees, loan repayments, equipment, technology, personnel and even the export of some products. Governments sometimes consider that the transfer of some or all of the above items may result in 'illegal' profits, and may be detrimental to the country's balance of payments. It is wise to agree the basis for all remittances and transfers in a concession agreement before investment takes place.

Access to local capital markets   This is important for a multinational company as it can reduce the risk of government intervention. The larger the proportion of the investment that is financed from local sources, the less the potential benefit to the host government from expropriation.

Ownership and control risks This is intervention by, or on behalf of, the host government which prevents the efficient management and performance of local operations, often where the foreign subsidiary is in the form of a joint venture. This is common throughout the developing world, and the company should seek to establish terms in the concession agreement.

Transfer pricing According to Abdullah (1987), transfer pricing is probably the most controversial aspect of a multinational's worldwide operations. Transfer pricing is the pricing of goods sold to (or by) the subsidiary by (or to) the parent multinational or other foreign subsidiaries. Transfer pricing at substantially different prices from arm's length market prices enables subsidiaries to send profits back to the parent. It is therefore important that the basis of such pricing should be agreed upon to minimize the possibility of future dispute.

Social and economic obligations Host governments sometimes require multinational companies to contribute to the economic or social infrastructure of the area in which they are investing. Wells (1977) believes that any commitment by the multinational to social and economic infrastructure such as hospital, road or school building should be minimized, since past research suggests it has rarely prevented government intervention. This is probably sound reasoning, except in the case where a government requires a company to contribute to the social economy, as a condition of investing, or where it is expected to result in tangible benefits to the multinational and possible extra profits from the provision of better education, health and similar facilities.

Price controls Agreement should be reached before investment on any price controls on the multinational's sales in the host economy or export markets.

Taxation The level of taxation to be levied on the company and the methods of calculating taxation should be agreed.

Employment of expatriate personnel Developing countries which wish to increase the skills, education and training of their workforce, or other countries with high levels of unemployment may impose strict limits on the employment of foreign personnel. Most countries have some kind of restriction in place. Agreement should be reached on the number of foreign workers that can be admitted into the country.

Political risk insurance Political risk insurance is available to multinationals in most countries, and is a popular means of risk management. It is normally arranged prior to undertaking the investment, often through government agencies in the parent country. A few private companies, such as Lloyd's of London, do offer cover, but between 75 and 85 per cent of political risk insurance is provided by government agencies.

In the UK, political risk insurance for new foreign direct investment is provided by the Export Credits Guarantee Department (ECGD). ECGD cover protects against most forms of foreign hostility including:

Expropriation and nationalization The seizure of investments of the multinational company, with no, or only partial, compensation. Cover is also provided for indirect forms of expropriation where the host government discriminates against the multinational company.

Currency inconvertibility This is the company's inability to convert the local earnings back into sterling, or to repatriate capital, or in the case of loans, to convert repayments of principal and interest.

War, revolution, insurrection and civil strife Cover is normally for up to 15 years and for 90 per cent of any loss arising from the above three risks. No insurance is given in respect of the commercial risks of foreign subsidiaries. Although negotiation and planning before the investment reduce the political risk facing the multinational, they cannot be expected to totally eliminate risk when the investment is undertaken.

Strategies to reduce risk after investment has taken place After investment has taken place, the multinational can use a number of effective risk management techniques and strategies. The objective behind them is to make intervention unprofitable or politically unacceptable to the host government. The multinational will be expected to continually adapt to new host government demands, as its priorities and aspirations change. According to Eiteman and Stonehill (1986), 'anticipation of host country priorities is the key to a successful operating strategy'.

Production and logistics Production and logistics strategies can help to reduce the chance of government intervention through:

Local sourcing The decision to be made here by the multinational is how much of a particular product should be produced in a foreign country. The more local sourcing the company undertakes, the more valuable it is to the local economy; therefore, the firm should tend to face less risk of government intervention. However, the more local sourcing, the bigger the investment and the greater the potential loss. With local sourcing, the company will gain benefits through lower risk by contracting parts of the production process out to local companies. However, handing out local contracts will cause the multinational to lose full control over its investment, might adversely affect the quality of components, and could result in supply shortages through industrial disputes. It also offers more possibilities for intervention by the host government.

An example of how Chrysler managed to avoid expropriation of its automotive plant, while other expropriation was occurring in Peru, is shown by Bradley (1977). Chrysler prevented intervention because it only sourced 50 per cent of the components it needed for its automotive assembly plant in Peru, importing the rest from a number of other countries. Chrysler was still valuable to the host country because the plant was useless without the remaining foreign sourced Chrysler parts.

Location of facilities This is a very important factor in the management of political risk for companies in extractive and natural resources industries and those with a high level of vertical integration in the production process. An excellent example of the significance of locating productive facilities is provided by the oil industry. The majority of the world's oil is located in politically sensitive and high-risk countries, such as those in the Middle East. However, although it would be cheaper to have the refineries near the oil wells, the major oil companies have located their refineries in low-risk countries to prevent their expropriation.

Control of transportation   This is another way of reducing the probability of expropriation. Both Eiteman and Stonehill (1986) quote the United Fruit Company having power over the banana exporting countries, since it possessed the large refrigerator ships and 'controlled the market outlets'.

Control of patents and processes   Abdullah (1987) and Eiteman and Stonehill (1986) quote Coca Cola as a prime example of how the control of patents and processes reduces political risk. The secret ingredient in Coca Cola has never been divulged, although bottling takes place worldwide. Without this ingredient, host government intervention would be of little use, being unable to re-create the 'feeling' of Coca Cola! Patents are internationally recognized and, if abused by an expropriating authority, companies can often bring the offenders to justice in an international court of law.

Marketing   A second strategy for reducing the risk of government intervention is marketing. Intervention into a multinational's operations is of little use if the host government cannot reach the multinational's intended customers. This strategy still gives the oil companies some leverage over the oil producing nations. The final market for products made from crude oil still lies, to a large extent, in the hands and expertise of the oil companies.

Financial policies and strategies   This is probably the most complicated way of combating political risk, once foreign operations have commenced. The strategies are limited only by the imagination of the multinational's financial managers. There are several basic policies for reducing political risk. One popular technique is for the multinational to borrow a considerable proportion of the funds needed to finance its foreign subsidiary from local financial institutions. In such circumstances any damaging intervention from the host government also damages local institutions. However, Abdullah (1987) suggests caution in this policy, since it is risky to depend upon local borrowing because credit may be stopped at any moment, by host government influence, and the cost of such funds may be relatively expensive. Many governments place restrictions on the multinational companies' borrowing facilities from the local money and capital markets.

Given that the multinational is unable to finance all its operations from within the host country, it has the option instead of financing worldwide, using institutions from several countries. This discourages expropriation, since if the government intervenes in the company's operations, default on the loans may cause a diplomatic backlash from a number of countries, not just the multinational's own parent country.

Another important strategy that has become very popular among multinationals over recent years is obtaining unconditional guarantees from the host government. Shapiro (1981) states that this is especially important for multinationals in the natural resources industry. The guarantee is made by the government for the amount of the investment; this means that if the terms of the project agreement are not met by successive host governments, then the multinational involved is able to take legal action against any transactions involving the host government and any third party. This, says Moran (1973), gives multinationals 'a potential weapon against a nationalistic government', without having to rely on the 'uncertain diplomatic support of their home government'. An example of this, given by Moran, is the threatened confiscation of Chilean aircraft by Kennecott on landing in the USA, due to the Chilean government expropriating Kennecott's copper mine in Chile.

Multinationals in the high-risk natural resources industries, such as copper and oil, have also come up with another innovative strategy to try to reduce their political risk. This involves selling forward the future proceeds of contracts made with buyers to financial institutions worldwide, who, for the interest plus a fee, act as a collection agency. If the government prevents the multinational from fulfilling the contracts, it will incur pressure from countries involving the buyers and the financial intermediaries, as well as the multinational's parent country.

Organizational policies   There are several ways of organizing an investment so as to reduce the risk of expropriation.

Location of subsidiary headquarters   The location should have good facilities: health, education, communications, safety and recreation, and a degree of political and economic stability which will satisfy key personnel.

Management contracts   These are often a way of keeping an interest in a foreign investment after the company has lost the controlling interest, often through political actions. For example, Kennecott demanded a 10-year management contract to run its Chilean copper mine, when it voluntarily divested a controlling 51 per cent interest to the host government. This was due to Kennecott's perception of a more uncertain investing climate in that particular country (which turned out to be good prophecy).

Joint ventures   Joint ventures may be used to discourage political intervention. International joint ventures have two or more partners, usually from different countries, possibly with one of the partners being a company from the host country. The advantage behind the joint venture is that it lowers the political (and commercial) risk, because expropriation would damage relations between the host country and at least two other countries, as well as possibly damaging a local company. The disadvantages of joint ventures include the loss of control and adverse publicity when problems occur. Eiteman and Stonehill (1986) cite the example of Union Carbide's Indian plant and the Bhopal chemical disaster. From news reports, the multinational appeared to own 100 per cent of the operation, when it actually owned only 50.9 per cent. Government restrictions on the amount of expatriate personnel Union Carbide could employ meant that the multinational was forced to use a high proportion of underqualified domestic managers. Therefore, some of the blame of the disaster lay in the hands of the Indian government. Joint ventures also face management problems: shared management being the biggest cause of project failure.

Ventures with partners in the host country are also riskier than they might intuitively appear. Bradley (1977) reports that historically the rate of expropriation of a joint venture with the host government is ten times greater than that of a 100 per cent owned US subsidiary. He goes on to say that there is considerable evidence of a reduction of risk in ventures with local private companies, owing to the elimination of 'the stigma of 100% foreign ownership', which particularly befalls the 'imperialistic' USA.

Countering intervention and expropriation

If the host government either threatens to interfere with the operations of the multinational or actually does interfere in some way, how should the multinational react?

Intervention may take many forms. Eiteman and Stonehill (1986) suggest a useful classification of the forms of government action into non-discriminatory regulations, discriminatory regulations and wealth deprivation.

Non-discriminatory regulations do not specifically discriminate against foreign direct investments, but have more impact on a multinational company than on a local company. Examples include requiring that all production must have a specified proportion of local components; local nationals must form a significant part of senior management; transfer prices must be set to benefit local taxation; and contributions must be made to the local economic or social infrastructure.

Discriminatory regulations involve more severe government action, which is aimed at putting the multinational at a disadvantage relative to local companies. Special taxes, fees, wage levels or regulations (for example, strict pollution controls) which are only imposed on foreign companies are examples of such regulations.

Wealth deprivation causes significant cash flow loss to the multinational company. It might involve severe price controls or production constraints which will gradually force the company out of business, or to sell the business to local interests at a bargain price. The extreme form of wealth deprivation is expropriation of assets, which includes the nationalization of assets. Approximately 90 per cent of all expropriations involve some compensation payments to multinational companies, but few payments are made promptly owing to protracted legal negotiations, and often the compensation that is received is less than the multinational's valuation of the expropriated assets.

Doz and Prahalad (1980) define intervention as a limitation to strategic freedom: where the government restricts the multinational's operations through laws and regulations; or a threat to managerial autonomy: where the government affects and attempts to alter the multinational's internal decision-making. Together they are an infringement on the strategic autonomy of the company.

Coping with intervention

Encarnation and Vachani (1985) state that nationalistic pressure placed on multinationals is on the increase and few companies remain unaffected. Governments, especially in the developing countries, want greater control and local ownership.

Both Encarnation and Vachani and Doz and Prahalad are clear on the two basic strategies open to the multinational: adaptation and withdrawal. Adaptation can take one of two forms: strict compliance, and negotiation with the use of bargaining strength.

Strict compliance   This involves agreeing to the wishes of the host country. The Indian government, for example, introduced a policy of 'Indianization', under which all multinationals were required to reduce their equity ownership to 40 per cent and float 60 per cent off to Indian investors, although there were exceptions. This regulation on foreign corporate ownership caused many companies to divest their interests in India. IBM was one such company, although it managed to fend off the regulations for more than 10 years before actually leaving. However, as Doz and Prahalad (1980) report, IBM quit its Indian operations because it was not prepared to accept Indianization, since it wanted to have full control over product development in order to maintain compatibility, and also full control of leased products.

Negotiation with the use of bargaining strength   This involves the careful use by the multinational of its bargaining strength to negotiate with the host government, in order to gain a competitive advantage over others and also a position more acceptable to the multinational. One important bargaining strength is the ability of the multinational to provide products which are unavailable from elsewhere (these tend to be high-technology products and/or products requiring high marketing and R&D expenditures). Such companies in India are allowed to retain majority ownership (74 per cent). Another bargaining strength is the proportion of exports the multinational produces. A high proportion may significantly improve the balance of payments of the host country, and will import valuable foreign exchange reserves. This seems to be of the highest priority in India, since multinationals exporting 100 per cent of its output are permitted to retain full ownership of their Indian subsidiaries. Encarnation and Vachani (1985) provide the example of Hindustan Lever, an Indian subsidiary of Unilever, which, because of the above bargaining strengths, was able to avoid serious dilution of its equity. The core of this strategy was sustained efforts to increase high technology production and export sales.

Local R&D expenditure also enabled its detergents to be considered as high-technology products. Coupled with this, Hindustan Lever set up an export agency, through which small local companies in similar industries were allowed to sell. Since it operated successfully in the priority sectors laid down by the government of India, Hindustan Lever was allowed to maintain majority ownership. The management adapted extremely well in preventing 'Indianization' from removing full control from Unilever. Encarnation and Vachani (1985) observe that:

local management hiked the company's bargaining power by transforming a low technology, domestic producer of limited consumer goods into an exporting, R&D intensive, high technology diversified company.

Encarnation and Vachani also illustrate how Indianization could actually increase profits for flexible multinationals after equity dilution has taken place. Through satisfaction of the new regulations, subsidiaries became Indian companies and thus became open to government concessions: licences to expand and diversify, subsidized loans, and tariff protection from foreign competition. These raised entry barriers to companies exporting to India, and gave the multinationals with Indian interests a significant competitive advantage. The Indian subsidiary of Ciba-Geigy, a high-technology Swiss pharmaceutical company, qualified for 51 per cent ownership owing to the nature of its industry. However, it volunteered to reduce this to 40 per cent, in order to be considered as an Indian company. Hence it was able to expand and double its pharmaceutical sales.

Expropriation

Expropriation seldom occurs without some advance warning. When faced with the prospect of expropriation, the multinational must make a fast and thorough review of the situation to ascertain whether any policies could be effected to reverse government action. In most cases, continuing the operations of a foreign subsidiary will be more beneficial than receiving an uncertain level of compensation from the host government, if compensation is paid at all. If expropriation occurs, Hoskins (1970) suggests four stages of action, with each stage worsening relations between the company and the host government and having less chance of restoring operations and relations to anything approaching those seen in the pre-expropriation period.

1. *Rational negotiation* The first stage is negotiating in a rational way with the government. This can take the form of offering concessions such as the use of local components, or favourable transfer prices, in order to keep the subsidiary as a going concern. Negotiations

may be of value if the multinational can either make sufficient concessions to satisfy the local government or persuade the government that it has miscalculated the pros and cons of expropriation.

2. *Bargaining with power tactics* If the situation is reached where the multinational calculates that further negotiations are pointless, it can try to apply different forms of power. Political power can be applied positively and negatively. Hoskins (1970) believes that emphasis should be placed on the positive approach, trying to satisfy the needs of the host government. If this does not work, the multinational has little to lose by applying negative tactics: gathering home or neighbouring country support or supporting a local opposition party. However, unless the government is weak and unstable, dependent on aid, for example, these tactics are rarely going to be successful, and are likely, as Shapiro (1986) observes, to 'strengthen the government's resolve'.

The multinational is also likely to possess economic power which it can apply. This is the most powerful tactic a multinational has at its disposal if it is well vertically integrated and operating as a monopolist or oligopolist. This would allow the company to cut off supplies of other components, technology and expert management. Consider Chrysler in Peru, as mentioned above, which escaped expropriation because it controlled the supply of components and operated in an oligopolistic market.

3. *Legal remedies* Once negotiations and power tactics have failed, the multinational might consider legal action. However, legal action against host governments in many less developed countries is often futile, as the courts may be controlled by the expropriating government. Occasionally it might be possible to gain legal judgment in the multinational's parent country to sequestrate assets of the offending country which are located in the parent country.

Multinationals are also able to seek redress through an international body, the International Centre for the Settlement of International Disputes (ICSID). The Centre provides a service of binding arbitration for disputes between a member country and a multinational from some other member country. Abdullah (1987) states that, by the beginning of 1985, 91 countries had signed ICSID's convention and become member nations. If a case is taken to the Centre, then 'neither party can unilaterally withdraw' (Shapiro (1986)). He goes on to say, however, that the practical decisions made by ICSID unfortunately have little influence (and no legal enforcement) when decisions go against member countries.

4. *Management surrender* The final stage is for management to surrender their investments and attempt to maximize compensation or salvage value. If insurance has been taken out against political actions this will reduce some of the loss. Hoskins (1970) states that the biggest obstacle when seeking compensation or attempting salvage appears to be how strained relations between the host country and the multinational become during the process of expropriation.

If the multinational was an integral part of the host country's economic system, then legal ownership, in an economic sense, may not be important. The multinational may be able to operate and profit in other ways, such as:

1. Acting as an export agency (marketing and selling abroad), under a commission arrangement
2. A management contract
3. Sales of components, licensing technology, etc., to the host country

However, this is usually less profitable for the multinational than its former operations were.

SUMMARY

Because of the wide range of risks posed by changes in the political environment it is difficult to produce a generally accepted definition and conceptual framework for political risk. Any framework must be strategic and anticipatory, active and not just reactive. The goals of the multinational company must be compared with the goals of the host government.

Kobrin (1981) claims improvements in forecasting are more likely to come from understanding the nature of contingencies faced by companies and their relationship to organizational characteristics and political events, rather than from increasing the sophistication of methodologies.

Inter- and intra-national affairs change constantly, as do the political risks faced by the multinational. Multinationals must try and anticipate these developments, but political changes are even harder to predict than economic ones.

Managing political risk should be one of the multinational's highest priorities. One adverse host government reaction to the investment could lead to an investment salvage value of zero. The multinational has to decide whether to invest, given the political environment and risk levels. If it does decide to invest, then it has to structure the investment so that its exposure to political risk is minimized. Keeping ahead of the host government, through maintaining a good bargaining position, is essential.

The benefits to the host country from foreign direct investment often diminish with the passage of time. The multinational should try to continually maintain these benefits, in order to remain valuable to the host country.

REFERENCES

Abdullah, F. A. (1987) *Financial Management for the Multinational Firm*, Prentice-Hall, Englewood Cliffs, NJ.

Bradley, D. G. (1977) 'Managing against expropriation', *Harvard Business Review*, July–August, pp. 75–83.

Brewer, T. L. (1982) 'Political risk assessment for foreign direct investment', *Columbia Journal of World Business*, Spring, pp. 5–12.

Brewer, T. L. (1983) 'The instability of governments and the instability of controls on fund transfers by multinational enterprises; implications for political risk analysis', *Journal of International Business Studies*, Winter, pp. 147–157.

Doz, Y. L. and Prahalad, C. K. (1980) 'Host Government Intervention', *Harvard Business Review*, March–April.

Eiteman, D. K. and Stonehill, A. I. (1986) *Multinational Business Finance*, Addison-Wesley, Reading, MA.

Encarnation, D. J. and Vachani, S. (1985) 'Foreign ownership: when the hosts change the rules', *Harvard Business Review*, September–October, pp. 153–60.

Friedmann, R. and Kim, J. (1988) 'Political risk and international marketing', *Columbia Journal of World Business*, Winter, pp. 63–73.

Greene, M. K. (1974) 'The management of political risks', *Best's Review*, July, pp. 71–74.

Goddard, S. (1990) 'Political risk in international capital budgeting', *Managerial Finance*, Vol. 16, No. 2, pp. 7–12.

Haendel, D., West, G. T. and Meadow, R. G. (1975) 'Overseas investment and political risk', Foreign Policy Research Institute, Philadelphia Monograph 21.

Herring, R. J. (1983) *Managing International Risk*, Cambridge University Press, Cambridge, England.

Hoskins, W. (1970) 'How to counter expropriation', *Harvard Business Review*, September–October, pp. 102–12.

Killing, P. J. (1982) 'How to make a global joint venture work', *Havard Business Review*, May–June.

Kobrin, S. J. (1979) 'Political risk: a review and reconsideration', *Journal of International Business Studies*, Spring–Summer, pp. 67–80.

Kobrin, S. J. (1980) 'Foreign enterprise and forced divestment in LDCs', *International Organisation*, Winter.

Kobrin, S. J. (1981) 'Political assessment by international firms: models or methodologies', *Journal of Policy Modelling*, May, pp. 251–70.

Kobrin, S. J. (1982) 'Managing political risk assessment. Strategic response to environmental change', University of California Press, Berkeley.

Moran, T. H. (1973) 'Transnational strategies of protection and defence by multinational corporations: spreading the risk and raising the cost for nationalisation in natural resources', *International Organisation*, Spring.

Overholt, W. H. (1982) *Political Risk*, Euromoney Publications, London.

Reid, J. T. (1983) 'Perspective: managing country risk for a manufacturing corporation', in Herring, R. J., *Managing International Risk*, pp. 184–90, Cambridge University Press, Cambridge, England.

Robock, S. H. (1971) 'Political risk: identification and assessment', *Columbia Journal of World Business*, July–August, pp. 6–20.

Rodriguez, R. M. and Carter, E. F. (1976) *International Financial Management*, Prentice-Hall, Englewood Cliffs, NJ.

Root, F. R. (1968) US business abroad and political risks, *MSU Business Topics*, Winter.

Rummel, R. J. and Heenan, D. A. (1978) 'How multinationals manage political risk', *Harvard Business Review*, January–February, pp. 67–76.

Shapiro, A. C. (1981) 'Managing political risk: a policy approach', *Columbia Journal of World Business*, Autumn, pp. 63–70.

Shapiro, A. C. (1986) *Multinational Financial Management*, Allyn and Bacon, Newton, Mass.

Shubik, M. (1983) 'Political risk: analysis, process and purpose', in Herring, R. J., *Managing International Risk*, pp. 109–32.

Simon, J. D. (1982) 'Political risk assessment: past trends and future prospects', *Columbia Journal of World Business*, Autumn, pp. 62–70.

Wells Jnr., L. T. (1977) 'Negotiating with Third World governments', *Harvard Business Review*, January–February, pp. 72–80.

Wicks Kelly, M. E. and Philippatos, G. C. (1982) 'Comparative analysis of foreign investment evaluation practices used by US based manufacturing multinational companies', *Journal of International Business Studies*, Winter, pp. 19–42.

CASE STUDIES

A series of examples follows, showing some theoretical instances of political risk analysis.

Case study 1 – Worrylot plc

Worrylot plc is a multinational corporation. It is examining the political and commercial risk associated with its proposed investments in Peru, Indonesia and Afghanistan.

Worrylot is particularly concerned with three factors:

1. Political stability (including the probability of expropriation)
2. Currency convertibility
3. The level of inflation and the exchange rate

Political stability is considered to be twice as important as either currency convertibility or the level of inflation.

An independent panel of experts has assessed each country on a scale − 5 (very poor) to + 5 (excellent) for each factor. The results are presented in the form of a probability distribution.

Political stability

Peru		Indonesia		Afghanistan	
Probability	*Score*	*Probability*	*Score*	*Probability*	*Score*
.1	− 2	.2	3	.1	2
.2	− 3	.3	2	.1	1
.6	− 4	.1	1	.2	0
.1	− 5	.2	0	.4	− 1
		.1	− 1	.2	− 2
		.1	− 2		

Currency convertibility

Peru		Indonesia		Afghanistan	
Probability	*Score*	*Probability*	*Score*	*Probability*	*Score*
.1	5	.2	2	.2	1
.4	4	.6	1	.4	0
.3	3	.1	0	.2	−1
.1	2	.1	−1	.1	−2
.1	1			.1	−3

Level of inflation

Peru		Indonesia		Afghanistan	
Probability	*Score*	*Probability*	*Score*	*Probability*	*Score*
.2	2	.2	0	.3	4
.3	1	.3	−1	.5	3
.2	0	.4	−2	.1	2
.1	−1	.1	−3	.1	1
.1	−2				
.1	−3				

Required:

An evaluation of the relative political and commercial risk associated with investments in Peru, Indonesia and Afghanistan.

The formula $\sigma_p = \sqrt{x^2\sigma_a^2 + y^2\sigma_b^2 + z^2\sigma_c^2}$ may be used in the analysis. Assume that the covariance between political instability, currency convertibility and the level of inflation is zero.

Solution:

	Expected values ($P_i.S_i$)		
	Peru	*Indonesia*	*Afghanistan*
Political stability	−3.7	1.0	−0.5
Currency convertibility	3.3	0.9	−0.5
Level of inflation	0.1	−1.4	3.0

Political stability holds twice the weighting of the other two measures.

Thus, total weighted expected value (EV) is:

0.5EV (political stability) + 0.25EV (currency convertibility) + 0.25EV (level of inflation)

$$\text{Peru EV} = 0.5 \times (-3.7) + 0.25 \times 3.3 + 0.25 \times 0.1$$
$$= (-1.85) + 0.825 + 0.025$$
$$= -1$$

$$\text{Indonesia EV} = 0.5 \times 1.0 + 0.25 \times 0.9 + 0.25 \times (-1.4)$$
$$= 0.5 + 0.225 + (-0.35)$$
$$= 0.375$$

$$\text{Afghanistan EV} = 0.5 \times (-0.5) + 0.25 \times (-0.5) + 0.25 \times 3.0$$
$$= (-0.25) + (-0.125) + 0.75$$
$$= 0.375$$

The expected values for Indonesia and Afghanistan are the same, and better than for Peru. To distinguish between them, their standard deviation may be estimated.

Indonesia

Political stability EV = 1

V–EV	(V–EV) (V–EV)	Pi	Pi(V–EV) (V–EV)
2	4	.2	0.8
1	1	.3	0.3
0	0	.1	0.0
− 1	1	.2	0.2
− 2	4	.1	0.4
− 3	9	.1	0.9

$$\sigma^2 = 2.6$$

Currency convertibility EV = 0.9

V–EV	(V–EV) (V–EV)	Pi	Pi(V–EV) (V–EV)
1.1	1.21	.2	0.242
0.1	0.01	.6	0.006
− 0.9	0.81	.1	0.081
− 1.9	3.61	.1	0.361

$$\sigma^2 = 0.690$$

Inflation EV = − 1.4

V–EV	(V–EV) (V–EV)	Pi	Pi(V–EV) (V–EV)
1.4	1.96	.2	0.392
0.4	0.16	.3	0.048
− 0.6	0.36	.4	0.144
− 1.6	2.56	.1	0.256

$$\sigma^2 = 0.840$$

SD (Indonesia) = $\sqrt{(.5)(.5)2.6 + (.25)(.25).69 + (.25)(.25).84}$
= 0.86

Afghanistan

Political stability EV = − 0.5

V–EV	(V–EV) (V–EV)	Pi	Pi(V–EV) (V–EV)
2.5	6.25	.1	0.625
1.5	2.25	.1	0.225
0.5	0.25	.2	0.050
− 0.5	0.25	.4	0.100
− 1.5	2.25	.2	0.450

$$\sigma^2 = 1.450$$

Currency convertibility EV $= -0.5$

$V-EV$	$(V-EV)(V-EV)$	Pi	$Pi(V-EV)(V-EV)$
1.5	2.25	.2	0.450
0.5	0.25	.4	0.100
-0.5	0.25	.2	0.050
-1.5	2.25	.1	0.225
-2.5	6.25	.1	0.625
			$\sigma^2 = 1.450$

Inflation EV $= 3$

$V-EV$	$(V-EV)(V-EV)$	Pi	$Pi(V-EV)(V-EV)$
1	1	.3	0.3
0	0	.5	0.0
-1	1	.1	0.1
-2	4	.1	0.4
			$\sigma^2 = 0.8$

SD (Afghanistan) $= \sqrt{(.5)(.5)1.45 + (.25)(.25)1.45 + (.25)(.25).8}$
$= 0.709$

Thus, Indonesia has a higher standard deviation than Afghanistan. Hence, in this respect Afghanistan is the least risky.

Case study 2 – Groit plc

Groit plc is evaluating two mutually exclusive foreign investments.

The first investment is in Worriland. The investment will cost 28 million centavos, half of which would be payable immediately and half after one year. Forecast pre-tax net operating cash flows of the project are shown below:

			WC (million)			
Year	1	2	3	4	5	6
Cash flow	6	15	28	20	12	7

Groit would additionally charge the project an annual management fee of £400,000, payable at the end of the year.

Corporate taxation in Worriland is at a rate of 20 per cent and no tax treaty exists between the UK and Worriland. The Inland Revenue has indicated that it will not allow any credit for tax paid in Worriland against UK corporation tax, and will tax remittances from Worriland at the full corporation tax rate of 35 per cent. It is thought, however, that a double tax treaty between the UK and Worriland will exist by the end of the third year of the project. At the end of year 6 the investment is expected to have a residual value of 10 million WC (after all taxes).

The second investment is in Explodia, at a cost of 43 million pesos (payable immediately). In order to attract foreign investment the Explodian government has offered a tax holiday for the first three years of the investment. Corporation tax in Explodia stands at 35 per cent and there is a full double tax treaty between Explodia and the UK.

At the end of six years the investment will be sold to the Explodian government as a going concern for a tax-free sum equal to the original outlay adjusted for half the subsequent level of inflation in Explodia.

The forecast pre-tax operating cash flows are:

Explodia pesos (million)

Year	1	2	3	4	5	6
Cash flow	−6	29	41	64	83	102

An election will be held in Explodia during the next year. There is believed to be a 50 per cent chance of a change in government to the Banga Nationalistic Party, in which case the investment would be nationalized by the new government. Compensation equivalent to the value of the initial investment would be payable two years after nationalization.

The systematic risk of the Worriland investment is estimated to be 1.5, and of the Explodian investment, 2.0. The risk-free rate is 8 per cent, and market return 15 per cent.

All taxes are payable one year in arrears. Corporate taxes are payable on net cash flows. It is the company's policy to remit the maximum funds possible to the parent company.

Exchange rates

WC/£	Explodian pesos/£
spot 3.262–3.296	5.269–5.312

Forecast inflation rates

Year	UK	Worriland	Explodia
1	5%	10%	15%
2	5%	12%	20%
3	5%	14%	25%
4	5%	14%	30%
5	5%	14%	35%
6	5%	14%	40%
7	5%	14%	45%

An evaluation is required of which project, if any, Groit should invest in. The relative form of the purchasing power parity (PPP) should be used to estimate future exchange rates.

Solution:

Forecast exchange rates

Worriland (WC/£)   Explodia (P/£)

	Worriland (WC/£)		Explodia (P/£)	
Spot		3.296		5.312
Year 1	$\dfrac{.10 - .05}{1.05} = 0.0476$:	3.453	$\dfrac{.15 - .05}{1.05} = 0.0952$:	5.818
Year 2	$\dfrac{.12 - .05}{1.05} = 0.0667$:	3.683	$\dfrac{.20 - .05}{1.05} = 0.1429$:	6.649
Year 3	$\dfrac{.12 - .05}{1.05} = 0.0667$:	3.929	$\dfrac{.25 - .05}{1.05} = 0.1905$:	7.916

Year 5 $\dfrac{.14 - .05}{1.05} = 0.0857 : 4.266$ $\dfrac{.30 - .05}{1.05} = 0.2381 : 9.800$

Year 4 $\dfrac{.14 - .05}{1.05} = 0.0857 : 4.631$ $\dfrac{.35 - .05}{1.05} = 0.2857 : 12.600$

Year 6 $\dfrac{.14 - .05}{1.05} = 0.0857 : 5.028$ $\dfrac{.40 - .05}{1.05} = 0.3333 : 16.800$

Year 7 $\dfrac{.14 - .05}{1.05} = 0.0857 : 5.459$ $\dfrac{.45 - .05}{1.05} = 0.3810 : 23.201$

Discount rates (using the capital asset pricing model):

Worriland 8% + (15%–8%) × 1.5 = 18.5%
Explodia 8% + (15%–8%) × 2.0 = 22%

Worriland				*WC (million)*			
Year	1	2	3	4	5	6	7
Operating cash flows	6	15	28	20	12	7	—
Management fee	1.38	1.47	1.57	1.71	1.85	2.01	—
Taxable	4.62	13.53	26.43	18.29	10.15	4.99	—
Taxation (20%)	—	0.92	2.71	5.29	3.66	2.03	1.00
Residual value						10.00	
	4.62	12.61	23.72	13.00	6.49	12.96	(1.00)
				£(000)			
Remitted	1,338	3,424	6,037	3,047	1,401	2,578	(183)
Tax on remitted funds		(468)	(1,198)	(1,009)	(643)	(329)	(149)
Management fee	400	400	400	400	400	400	
Tax on management fee		(140)	(140)	(140)	(140)	(140)	(140)
	1,738	3,216	5,099	2,298	1,018	2,509	(472)
Discount factor (18.5%)	.844	.712	.601	.507	.428	.361	.305
Present value	1,467	2,290	3,064	1,165	436	906	(144)

Years 2–3: tax at 35% on remitted funds; years 4–7: tax at an effective rate of 15% on the amount taxable in Worriland due to tax treaty.

Total present value = £9,184,000
Initial outlay   = £4,292,000 + £4,097,000 × .844 = £7,750,000
(based on buying rates)
Net present value = £1,434,000

Explodia

With no change of government:

			Pesos (million)				
Year	1	2	3	4	5	6	7
Operating cash flows	(6)	29	41	64	83	102	—
Taxation	0	0	0	0	(22.4)	(29.1)	(35.7)
Sale value						92.8	
	(6)	29	41	64	60.6	165.7	(35.7)

			£(000)				
Remitted	(1,031)	4,361	5,179	6,531	4,809	9,863	(1,539)
Discount factor (22%)	.820	.672	.551	.451	.370	.303	.248
Present values	(845)	2,931	2,854	2,945	1,779	2,988	(382)

Present value = £12,270,000
Initial outlay = £8,161,000
Net present value = £4,109,000

If there is a change of government:

	Pesos (million)		
Year	1	2	3
Operating cash flows	(6)	—	—
Compensation	—	—	43
	(6)	—	43

	£(000)		
Remitted	(1,031)	—	5,432
Discount factor	.820		.551
Present value	(845)		2,993

This assumes no tax effects on the negative outflow.

Total present value = £2,148,000
Initial outlay = £8,161,000
Net present value = £(6,013,000)

Expected net present value = (0.5 × £4,109,000) +
(0.5 × (6,031,000)) = £(961,000)

On the basis of these calculations, with this information we would invest in Worriland.

Case study 3 – Saycheese Plc

Saycheese plc is evaluating a possible direct investment in Iceland. The investment would be the purchase of an existing cheese factory outside Reykjavik for the sum of 40 million Icelandic krona. In addition, IKr 10 million would be needed for working capital and IKr 12 million for rationalization and modernization of existing production facilities.

Sales of cheese in Iceland are expected to be 1.5 million kilograms per year, at an initial price of IKr 25 per kilogram, and export sales to the UK are expected to be 500,000 kilograms at the same price. After the first year, prices are expected to increase in line with the previous year's rate of inflation in Iceland.

Variable costs of cheese production are IKr 11 per kilogram, and fixed costs are IKr 6 million per annum. Both of these costs are expected to increase, after the first year, in line with the previous year's rate of inflation. A fixed management fee of £500,000 would be charged by Saycheese plc to its Icelandic subsidiary.

The cheese exports to the UK from Iceland are expected to reduce sales in the UK from Saycheese's Barnsley cheese factory, and to result in a fall in UK pre-tax profits of £180,000 per year.

Assumptions

Corporation tax is at a rate of 35 per cent in the UK and Iceland, and a comprehensive bilateral tax treaty exists between the two countries. Tax is payable one year in arrears. Assume that no taxes other than corporation tax exist, and that funds can be freely remitted from Iceland to the UK.

Fixed assets in Iceland may be depreciated for tax purposes at 25 per cent per annum on a straightline basis, and the Icelandic factory is expected to have a realizable value of IKr 50 million at the end of four years. Saycheese evaluates all its investments over a four-year period.

The proposed investment would be financed by a bank loan at an interest rate of 12 per cent per annum. The company's cost of capital is 14 per cent.

Exchange rate (mid-market)
Spot: 9.790 krona/£

| Year | Forecast inflation levels | | Discount factors | |
	UK	Iceland	12%	14%
1	4%	6%	0.893	0.877
2	5%	8%	0.797	0.769
3	6%	10%	0.712	0.675
4	6%	10%	0.636	0.592
5	5%	10%	0.567	0.519

Required:
Evaluate whether Saycheese plc should buy the factory in Iceland.

Suggested solution:

Future exchange rates may be estimated using the relative form of the PPP theorem.

			Krona/£
Spot			9.790
Year 1	$\dfrac{0.06 - 0.04}{1.04}$	$= 0.0192$	9.978
Year 2	$\dfrac{0.08 - 0.05}{1.05}$	$= 0.0286$	10.263
Year 3	$\dfrac{0.10 - 0.06}{1.06}$	$= 0.0377$	10.650
Year 4	$\dfrac{0.10 - 0.06}{1.06}$	$= 0.0377$	11.052
Year 5	$\dfrac{0.10 - 0.05}{1.05}$	$= 0.0476$	11.578

Estimated taxation in Iceland

	Icelandic krona (millions)			
Year	1	2	3	4
Sales	50	53	57.24	62.96
Less:				
Variable costs	22	23.32	25.19	27.70
Fixed costs	6	6.36	6.87	7.56
Management fee (£0.5m)	4.99	5.13	5.33	5.53
Depreciation[1]	13	13	13	13
Taxable flows	4.01	5.19	6.85	9.17
Tax payable at 35%	1.4	1.82	2.4	3.21

[1] Depreciable fixed assets are assumed to total IKr 52 million

Subsidiary's cash flows
Icelandic krona (millions)

Year	0	1	2	3	4	5
Fixed asset investment	(52)					
Working capital[2]	(10)					10
Sales		50	53	57.24	62.96	–
Less:						
Variable costs		22	23.32	25.19	27.70	–
Fixed costs		6	6.36	6.87	7.56	–
Management fee		4.99	5.13	5.33	5.53	–
Tax on operations		–	1.4	1.82	2.4	3.21
Realizable value		–	–	–	(50)	–
Imputed tax on realizable value		–	–	–	–	17.5
Net cash flows	(62)	17.01	16.79	18.03	69.77	(10.71)

[2] Assumed working capital is released in year 6.
All cash flows are assumed to take place at the year end. This underestimates net present value.

Cash flow remitted from Iceland
£(000)

Year	0	1	2	3	4	5
Remitted from Iceland[3]	(6.333)	1.705	1.636	1.693	6.313	(.925)
Management fee		.5	.5	.5	.5	
Less:						
Tax on management fee			.175	.175	.175	.175
Lost profits (LP)		.18	.18	.18	.18	
Tax saving on LP			(.063)	(.063)	(.063)	(.063)
Net cash flows	(6.333)	2.025	1.844	1.901	6.521	(1.037)
Discount factors (14%)	1	0.877	0.769	0.675	0.592	0.519
Present values	(6.333)	1.776	1.418	1.283	3.860	(0.538)

[3] The remitted cash flows from Iceland, for each year, are converted into sterling, using the corresponding future exchange rates (calculated above).

$$\text{Net present value} = \sum (\text{present values})$$
$$= £1,466,000$$

On the basis of the projected figures, Saycheese's proposed investment in Iceland should be undertaken.

Practical reflections on the questions

The examples given above are very much simplified when compared to the real world.

Example 3 (Saycheese) assumes certain cash flows, and does not even consider any kind of political, commercial or economic risk. The opportunity cost of investing in Iceland is lost sales in the UK. Surely there must be some kind of alternative market for the excess capacity—an alternative dairy product, for example.

Example 2 does consider elements of political risk (i.e. outright expropriation), but does not mention what the company has done to try to offset this risk (e.g. with insurance). There is no discussion of non-financial factors, such as the company's bargaining strength and the structure of its investment. Because of this there is no consideration of how the multinational would act if the project did not progress as predicted.

In the real world, decision-makers would want to know how data such as probabilities and cash flows were calculated. What techniques were used? In example 1, how did the independent panel of experts arrive at the assessment factors for each country? Was it a joint effort or was each contributor sent a questionnaire to enter his or her views? The latter avoids group and social pressures, but the former has the advantage of group thinking.

As with all forecasts, the predictions are never likely to be correct; the margin of error could be large. Confidence interval estimates for the predictions, e.g. on inflation figures, would give a more reliable insight into the potential fortunes of the company.

FOURTEEN
GLOBAL TRANSFER PRICING

INTRODUCTION

This chapter examines the various economic, tax and legal factors which may influence the choice of transfer pricing used in multinational corporations. Methods of determining transfer prices are analysed, along with their practical implications, and limitations for the management of transfer prices. The chapter concludes with an analysis of the empirical studies carried out to determine the types and objectives of transfer prices used among multinational corporations.

The expression 'transfer pricing' often carries a derogatory meaning in today's business world, especially in the context of multinational operations. It gives the idea of systematic manipulation or control of transfer pricing policies for tax avoidance (or evasion) in intra-firm trade by manufacturing companies operating in different countries. Intrafirm trade is defined here as transactions involving international shipments of products between branches or subsidiaries operating under the control of one company. In practice, there are more reasons for companies to use transfer pricing than merely for tax purposes. Transfer prices are also used for risk reduction, control and evaluation purposes between the subsidiaries of a company operating in one country. However, as purely domestic companies' transfer pricing policies are guided by a strict and separated legal status, manipulation of transfer pricing for tax avoidance purposes is less likely to be achieved in these companies than in those operating in international markets, where large differences in taxation rates exist. In this chapter the focus is upon the determinants of transfer prices from the perspective of a multinational firm.

Subsidiaries operating in different countries are subjected to different sets of laws, different degrees of competition in markets, different social and economic conditions, different political climate, and different rules and regulations set by various government policies, particularly in tax matters. It should not therefore be surprising that determination of transfer prices for international sales is difficult and unpredictable. Despite these issues, successful transfer pricing methods can bring a substantial amount of profit to a parent or subsidiary company. Transfer pricing policy has become an essential and critical element of the multinational corporation, and virtually all companies treat their transfer pricing policy and operating procedure as highly secretive.

Many factors complicate the determination of corporate behaviour for transfer pricing in practice. The lack of theoretical base and of operational evidence, owing to the reluctance of managers of multinational corporations to provide information on their practices, prevents precise conclusions and recommendations. Transfer pricing impacts on an extremely wide range of corporate activities and is a function which requires much expertise and judgement.

Organizations which are very similar in nature may employ entirely different techniques to determine transfer prices. This diversity occurs because the methods selected by a company are influenced by the internal management control process (Benke and Edwards (1980)).

The internal management control process (IMCP) has two objectives in controlling the diversity of activities within an organization: first, it guides the members of the company towards the aims of the company; and secondly, it helps to evaluate the performance of each division against the company objectives. One of the main tasks within the IMCP is to determine transfer pricing policies for the company. Therefore, the objective of transfer pricing must be consistent with the objectives of the IMCP.

Intra-firm sales in multinational corporations perform an essential and legitimate function across national boundaries. They require an actual transfer of materials, ownership and a compensating transfer of funds. Costs which may be included in a subsidiary's account are royalty or dividend payments, payments for know-how and trademarks, payment of R&D expenses, and allocations of overhead and administrative and selling costs. All of these can be added to the cost of intra-firm sales to justify high transfer prices. At first, one might think that this would be an extra burden on the buying unit; however, it would not necessarily be disconcerting to either buying and selling unit. This is because a higher than market price for intra-firm sales would probably be desirable to achieve some company objectives. These objectives in setting transfer prices will be discussed later in the chapter.

It should now be clear to the reader that transfer pricing considerations in multinational businesses are numerous, complicated and risky. Knowles and Mathur (1985), for example, group basic objectives of transfer pricing as goal congruence, performance evaluation, and motivation. Within each of these broad categories of objectives there are, however, further factors which may determine a MNC's transfer pricing policies, and each of these determinants is briefly examined below.

DETERMINANTS OF TRANSFER PRICING

In setting transfer pricing policies, many factors should be taken into consideration. These may include:

1. Tax considerations
2. Management incentives and performance evaluation
3. Fund positioning
4. Marketing considerations and competition
5. Risk and uncertainty
6. Government policies
7. The interest of joint venture partners

All of these factors may complicate transfer pricing decisions, along with non-economic considerations.

Tax considerations

Multinational corporations use transfer pricing to manoeuvre profits out of high tax rate countries into lower ones. A parent company may sell goods at lower than normal prices to its subsidiaries in lower tax rate countries and buy from them at higher than normal prices. The resultant loss in the parent's high tax country adds significantly to the profits of the subsidiaries in low tax countries, and in the process the multinational corporation may achieve a considerable reduction in global taxes, as Examples 14.1 and 14.2 illustrate.

A Hong Kong manufacturing subsidiary exports to a US company 500,000 pairs of trousers for US$6 a pair. Assume jeans sell at US$12 per pair in the USA. Both companies are part of Global Enterprises and income tax is 16.5% in Hong Kong and 46% in the USA.

Example 14.1

	Hong Kong	*US*	*Global*
		$000	
Sales	3,000	6,000	6,000
Cost of sales	2,100	3,000	2,100
Gross margin	900	3,000	3,900
Operating expenses	500	1,500	2,000
Before tax income	400	1,500	1,900
Income tax (16.5% in HK, 46% USA)	66	690	756
Net income	334	810	1,144

Now assume that the Hong Kong subsidiary sells jeans at $8.50 per pair.

Example 14.2

	Hong Kong	*US*	*Global*
		$000	
Sales	4,250	6,000	6,000
Cost of sales	2,100	4,250	2,100
Gross margin	2,150	1,750	3,900
Operating expenses	500	1,500	2,000
Before tax income	1,650	250	1,900
Income tax (16.5% in HK, 46% USA)	272.5	115	387.5
Net income	1,377.5	135	1,512.5

Therefore, take advantage of lower tax in Hong Kong.
Increased profits in Hong Kong:

When TP = $6.00	Global tax	40% (756/1,900)
When TP = $8.50	Global tax	20% (387/1,900)

Approximately 40 per cent of all international trade is thought to be between subsidiaries.
The amount of import duties paid should also be considered if the duties were levied on the invoice price, as the total duties will be increased under the high mark-up policy. If the import duties are levied against internationally posted prices rather than the stated invoice price,

transfer pricing policy will not be useful. In the absence of any government interference, multinational corporations would use transfer policies to reduce their tax burden. However, tax authorities are becoming increasingly concerned about the potential income distortion from transfer pricing manipulations by multinational corporations. Several government regulations have been developed to determine the reasonableness of transfer prices—for instance, until 1962 many US-based multinational corporations had subsidiaries in 'tax haven' countries, but the Internal Revenue Act of 1962 (section 482) helped to close the loopholes of massive tax avoidance. Many other countries have also modified their tax laws to eliminate the use of transfer pricing to avoid tax payments. These laws require the use of arm's length market prices (discussed later) whenever they are available.

The regulations governing transfer prices provide general guidance only, and are questionable on many issues. It is therefore important that sound business judgement is exercised in their application, and that flexibility still exists for multinational companies to benefit to some extent through their transfer pricing policies.

Global regulation Saunders (1989) points out that Article 9.2 of the OECD Model Double Taxation Treaty provides that where one of the states includes in the profits of an enterprise of that state, profits on which an enterprise of another state has been charged tax, that other state shall make an appropriate adjustment.

However, he indicates that unfortunately negotiated double tax treaties do not generally oblige the contracting states to make such automatic reductions.

Burns and Ross (1983) state that no one group has the authority to establish international transfer pricing standards of taxation; each country generally establishes rules for companies operating within its boundaries. However, many factors are now causing greater interest in the establishment of international standards for taxation of inter-company transactions; for example, in the USA, Canada, Germany and the UK, transfer prices are required to be 'arm's length', i.e. the price that would obtain if the two companies were unrelated. Nevertheless, each country may differ as to what it terms an arm's length price. Transfer prices develop from tax legislation, tax authorities and the courts. Tax legislation concerning transfer pricing tends to be brief; therefore, the tax authorities have assumed much of the responsibility for a practical definition of an arm's length standard.

Growth in international transactions between related parties has led to a need for international standards. Groups involved in this process include the Organisation for Economic Co-operation and Development (OECD), the United Nations (UN), and International Chamber of Commerce (ICC). The main aim of these groups is to establish a transfer price which is acceptable to all nations, as far as is practical, given differing legal, social, political and environmental constraints in each country. Burns and Ross (1981) argue that, along with the increase in international transactions, has come an increase in the conflict between taxing authorities of different countries, and tax treaties are aimed at reducing these conflicts. Because of the vast difference in the laws of the taxing jurisdiction, a multitude of treaties are required, for example the OECD's model tax treaty issued in 1963. Although no one group has the authority to establish transfer pricing standards for tax audits of MNCs, the arm's length standard is widely accepted. There is, however, still no acceptance of what constitutes an arm's length price, and because of this ambiguity the role of the bilateral treaties in resolving international pricing conflicts is very important.

US requirements In the USA evidence from three separate studies has revealed that adjustments to transfer prices are most commonly based on methods other than those described by the legislation. While the arm's length standard is generally accepted for transfer pricing, this standard remains undefined. The definition evolves slowly from negotiations between the tax authorities and company officials. In the USA, Internal Revenue Code (IRC) Section 482 provides comprehensive and clear statutory rules concerning transactions between related companies. It defines an arm's length price as the price an unrelated party would have paid under the same circumstances for the property. Since unrelated parties normally sell products at a profit, an arm's length price also incorporates a profit to the seller. Criteria for adjusting prices have been predominantly developed by the IRS in the USA: Section 482 of the IRC lays down the criteria for determining an arm's length price. Careful use of transfer pricing should be made: the IRS may scrutinize inter-corporate transactions for section 482 reallocation and the tax manager should be aware of these matters before submitting accounts.

Substantial reporting regulations are also laid down in the USA. Citizens who are US taxpayers must file form 5471 each quarter in relation to transfer pricing. The form states the relationship of the taxpayer in the equity of the foreign affiliate. It is possible to avoid tax liability by abnormal legal arrangements; however, most countries have adopted a 'substance over form' principle to develop anti-avoidance legislation.

Europe in general In the UK, the Taxes Act 1970, section 485 (which subsequently came under the Income and Consolidation Act 1975) allows the Inland Revenue to adjust taxable profits of a UK company if such profits have tended to be diminished by transfer pricing with other group companies. The criterion used by the Inland Revenue is the market-based price for transfer of goods between companies within the group. Although most cases are settled out of court, up to 1982 the Inland Revenue won the majority of cases brought to court, indicating that that is where the balance of power seems to lie. Under UK law, law lords treat each transaction separately to decide whether it is in accordance with the law or not.

In France, under Article 238A of the CGI the taxpayer is burdened with the onus of proof. The authorities also stipulate what will and what will not be acceptable as losses. Any loss which does not arise as a result of those deemed acceptable will be investigated, and any artificial pricing found to be the cause of the loss will be adjusted.

In the Netherlands, Article 31, Algemone wet inzake rijksbelastingen introduces the principle of correct exposition tax. The tax authorities must obtain authorization from the Ministry of Finance before invoking Article 31. However, this only applies where tax avoidance is a primary motive.

The MNC needs to understand such legislation in order that its transfer pricing policy can be as effective as intended, and tax managers need to keep up-to-date with all the legislation in the countries in which they operate since even where the transfer pricing is within the law, differences in legislation between countries can distort its effectiveness.

Management incentives and performance evaluation

In purely domestic companies with decentralized profit centres and organization structures, transfer pricing can be a vital consideration in evaluating subsidiary management and their operations. In multinational organizations, performance evaluation issues are further complicated by the less efficient channels of communication and the need to consider unique variables which influence international transfer pricing. If the transfer price set by the parent company management is not agreed by the subsidiary management, managerial disincentives may arise.

Transfer pricing policies purposely designed to minimize global taxes often produce aberrations in the multinational performance evaluation and control systems. When each subsidiary is evaluated as a single profit centre, transfer pricing policies that are designed to minimize global tax payments will result in inequitable reported performance for the subsidiary managers. A subsidiary manager would then be in a position to accept an operating policy in order to maximize corporate goals at the expense of poor performance results. Unless performance evaluation measures used by the parent company management somehow eliminate the adverse effects of the transfer pricing policy on the operating performance of the subsidiary, the results could lead to suboptimal behaviour by the managers evaluated against the overall corporate objectives.

Halpern and Srinidhi (1991) found that the headquarters' degree of negotiation power with the manufacturing units has an influence on the final outcome of transfer pricing policy used by the MNC. Looking at the resale price method first, Halpern and Srinidhi found that when the negotiation power of manufacturing units is low, after-tax profits are maximized. As the manufacturing units' negotiation power increases beyond a certain point, company-wide optimal profits are not attained, and the final product is produced beyond the company-wide optimum after-tax profit. Under the cost plus method of transfer pricing, the production of the final product is decreased with low negotiating power. As the negotiation power of the distribution division increases, the production of the final product will increase, and there will be no guarantee of profit to the manufacturing unit. Furthermore, it is unlikely that company-wide after-tax profits will be maximized.

Fund positioning

Transfer price setting is one of the techniques by which funds can be transferred within a multinational corporation. If a parent company wishes to remove funds from one of its foreign subsidiaries it can charge a higher transfer price for its intra-firm sales. A higher transfer price would allow funds to be accumulated within the selling country. If the subsidiary is short of funds, it can be financed by the reverse technique of lowering the transfer price.

Transfer pricing can also be used to channel profit into a subsidiary to raise its credit rating. This option is important when low reported earnings can damage the foreign subsidiary's chances of obtaining the required capital. In addition, access to the local capital markets may be obtained for the foreign subsidiary in this way.

Marketing considerations and competition

Multinational corporations may become dependent on their foreign subsidiaries for the sales of finished goods for the following reasons:

1. The desire to control distribution facilities where there is a lucrative market
2. The desire to have a specialized after-sales service (pure sales outlets)
3. The need to communicate information to and from customers on their requirements, designs and plans
4. The need to retain direct representation in order to maintain government contacts and influence policy

All these marketing considerations should be built into the transfer pricing policies of multinational companies.

To strengthen the establishment of a foreign subsidiary abroad, a parent company may grant a fairly low price for products/services to its subsidiary. The competitive foothold in the foreign market can therefore be strengthened through price subsidies. Likewise, lowered transfer prices may be used to shield an existing operation from the effects of increased foreign competition. Transfer prices can also be used to weaken the subsidiary's competitors; the companies which employ this strategy would most probably be those who have control over raw material supplies. The gaining of the market share is thus viewed as being more important than high profit margins per unit of sales since it emphasizes the importance of gaining a competitive foothold. The competitive position is therefore a vital element to be considered in the transfer pricing policy of a multinational company.

Risk and uncertainty

Multinational companies operate in different countries around the world, and possess substantial amounts of assets and liabilities in foreign currencies. Therefore, all their assets and liabilities are exposed to exchange risk. The exchange rate change is beneficial to the holder of the foreign currency asset if the foreign currency revalues; however, losses may occur if it devalues. Inflation is also an important consideration, because it erodes the purchasing power of the company's monetary assets. Balance of payments problems often prompt foreign governments to devalue their currencies and impose a number of restrictions on the repatriation of profit from foreign subsidiaries. In addition, multinational companies' assets are exposed to the risk of expropriation by foreign governments. The use of high transfer prices can help to reduce all of these risks.

Government policies

The policies of home country governments generally require the parent company to use domestic facilities to supply other affiliates. This may be in conflict with host government policies, especially where the investment is established in less developed countries. The policies of host governments will be likely to encourage multinational companies to reduce the import content of production and to increase local inputs over the longer term. Thus, the location of subsidiaries of multinationals in countries which are at different levels of industrial development and have different government policies will affect their abilities to undertake intra-firm trade.

Anti-cartel legislation in the EC may affect transfer pricing, although its main purpose was to prevent independent unrelated companies from colluding on prices. Thus, low transfer prices to a foreign subsidiary which are planned to discourage competition from accessing the local market may be hindered by the existence of anti-trust legislation. When there is a low transfer pricing, a multinational company can provide a comparative advantage for its local production; however, if the price is set too low relative to the market level the multinational may be accused of dumping.

The interest of joint venture partners

Joint venture operations with a local partner may enable multinational companies to reduce economic and political risks, as the local partners would contribute capital and increase the political acceptability of the multinational. Transfer pricing policies can then be used to preserve the multinational shares of profit in the joint venture. However, joint ventures could raise a special problem in transfer pricing policies of the multinational corporation in that fulfilling the interest of the local partners by maximizing local profit may be less than optimal for the overall corporate objectives of the multinational. Therefore, it is important that the determination of fair transfer prices should be resolved before the establishment of joint venture arrangements.

Negotiating power with financial institutions

Enhanced negotiating power with financial institutions is sometimes suggested as an important determinant of transfer pricing policies. If a subsidiary has an increased local currency profit as a result of low transfer prices on its input and high transfer prices on its output, it might be considered to be a better lending risk by local financial institutions. On the other hand, lower reported profit may improve the subsidiary's bargaining power in wage negotiations with trade unions. However, there may be conflicts between the advantages of the enhancement of the negotiating position and the tax and control advantages for the subsidiary. Other considerations also need to be taken into account when quantifying numerous trade-offs, including high income tax rates, high import tariffs, government price controls, a thin capital market, a chronic rate of inflation, foreign exchange rate, and unstable economic and political conditions.

METHODOLOGY OF TRANSFER PRICING

The influences from external and internal environments directly affect the type of transfer pricing techniques employed by a company. In general, transfer pricing techniques can be classified into two broad categories: profit centre techniques and cost centre techniques.

Profit centre techniques

Transfer pricing techniques are generally used when evaluating subsidiary performance with profit related measures. The profit centre technique can be subdivided into market-based pricing and non-market-based pricing.

Market-based pricing Market-based pricing policies include the use of prevailing market price, adjusted market price, contribution margin, and negotiated price.

Prevailing market price With this technique the transfer price of the product is set at the same level as the external market price. In the USA the provisions controlling the transfer pricing policy of companies in the Internal Revenue Code, Section 482, have also adopted the 'arm's length' principle, which equals the market price in open, wide markets. However, this method has its limitations when determining the prices of those commodities unobtainable in certain markets.

Adjusted market price Usually, relatively higher administrative and operational costs are involved in external, rather than in internal, sales; for instance, the sales and marketing expenses, and the costs of documentation are much lower in the latter cases. Any costs which are saved in internal sales will be deducted from the prevailing market price. In some companies, the buying unit receives a large discount for its intra-firm purchases which would normally be given to external buyers with a large quantity of purchases.

Contribution margin Here, the selling and the buying units negotiate either a share of the profit margin earned from sales or a share of the profit margin based on the standard full cost incurred. In some companies, these decisions are determined by top management, who may also transfer a portion of the selling unit's assets to the books of the buying unit in order to maintain an equitable and fair return on investment measure for both buying and selling units.

Negotiated price   Under this approach the selling and buying units determine the transfer price of the internal sales by negotiations. Usually, the buying unit is freed from making the choice of purchasing from the external suppliers and the selling unit is allowed to reject any internal selling if the terms of sale are not as good as the external opportunities. Negotiated transfer prices will, however, influence sub-unit managers' performance, and may lead to excuses for inferior performance.

Non-market-based pricing   Non-market-based pricing includes the use of opportunity cost, marginal or variable cost, and cost plus approaches.

Opportunity cost   The transfer price is determined by an amount equal to the sacrifice suffered by the supplier for not selling to external customers. With this approach there is a need to estimate the optimizing output of the manufacturing resources of the company and the market demand of the product. Furthermore, if the price of the product is not obtainable in the market, then it will be difficult to determine such a transfer price.

Marginal or variable cost   Here, transfer prices equal the direct production costs incurred by the selling unit or the manufacturing unit. Under the variable costing procedure, the variable overhead costs are also added to the direct labour and material costs.

Cost plus   In this approach, an arbitrary mark-up is added either upon the standard full cost or the actual cost of the product being transferred. This method is used to determine the transfer prices of the good without any reference to the external market. The determination of the mark-up margin must be very carefully selected because it will be the focus of conflict between the two units involved.

Cost centre techniques

Cost centre techniques are generally used where the subsidiaries do not operate as a profit centre. These can be divided into actual and standard cost-based pricing.

Actual cost   Using actual cost transfer pricing, the transfer price is set either at the actual full cost or at the actual variable cost. Actual full cost is obtained by dividing all fixed (including any depreciations and adjustments) and variable expenses for a period by the number of units produced. For the variable cost calculation, only the direct labour and materials and other variable expenses involved in the process are included. Since these calculations involve valuing inventory, allocating joint product costs, costing of the by-products, management judgement, and consensus of opinions of the parties involved are required.

Standard cost   Transfer prices under this approach are set to equal either the standard full cost or the standard variable cost. Standard costs are the expected unit costs of producing a product for a period under conditions of given volume, raw materials and other expenses, and are obtained by assuming that manufacturing plants are running at their full capacity. A good standard cost system should monitor the changes in volume or raw material costs that cause the deviation between the actual costs and standard costs.

Dual pricing technique

The buying unit receives the goods at cost and the selling unit charges the goods at the market price. The difference between the buying and selling costs is treated by the company as a compensation for the restriction of purchasing its own goods internally; the buying unit receives the goods at lower than the market price, which enables it to show a higher profit.

In a recent study, Al-Eryani, Alam and Akhter (1990) surveyed 164 MNCs in order to determine factors which may influence the choice of transfer pricing techniques. They found that larger MNCs operating in restrictive legislative environments were more likely to use market-based transfer pricing. It is suggested that this was probably because they are highly exposed to public scrutiny, and therefore it would be difficult to use their own transfer pricing policies given the problems associated with their complex sales networks. The stability of political and social environment, and the number of subsidiaries operating in less developed countries, did not seem to influence the choice of transfer pricing policies used by the US MNCs.

Another interesting finding of the study was that economic restrictions, such as exchange controls, price controls and restrictions on imports, were not found to be significant determinants of a market-based transfer pricing policy. Performance evaluation considerations for foreign subsidiary operations and their managers were also not found to be statistically significant determinants of transfer pricing policies.

These results contradict some of the earlier studies, and have implications for the theoretical framework of transfer pricing. For example, if we accept the findings of these studies without further examination we may be led to believe that transfer pricing policies are not very sensitive to the global positioning of funds, as discussed earlier in this chapter.

In an earlier study, O'Burns (1980) carried out a survey to determine the most important factor in setting transfer prices among 62 US-based multinational companies. The results of her survey indicated the following ranking of the transfer pricing considerations:

1. Market condition in the foreign country
2. Competition in the foreign country
3. Reasonable profit for foreign affiliates
4. US federal income tax
5. Economic conditions in the foreign country
6. Import restrictions
7. Customs duties
8. Price control
9. Taxation in the foreign country
10. Exchange control
11. US export incentive
12. Floating exchange rates
13. Management of cash flow
14. Other US federal taxes

Hoshower and Mandel (1986), examining transfer pricing policies of 25 large, divisionalized

US MNCs, found that the majority of these companies located their transfer pricing decisions at the divisional, rather than the central, corporate level. They also found that the majority (15 companies) used market-based transfer pricing.

As with any survey, there may be some biases in these transfer pricing survey results. It is a very sensitive issue to ask questions about manipulation of taxes through transfer prices, and it is perhaps not surprising that tax considerations were not mentioned as one of the important determinants of transfer pricing policies for the US companies in the survey. The results of this kind of survey must therefore be interpreted very carefully, as it would be unacceptable for companies to admit in a study that they use techniques which break tax laws and violate ethical behaviour.

RELATIVE ADVANTAGES AND DISADVANTAGES OF TRANSFER PRICING TECHNIQUES

The use of market-based systems is suitable for measuring the profitability of intercompany divisions or subsidiaries. It helps management to evaluate subsidiary performance more effectively because resource allocation decisions, which involve return on investment and capacity, are based on the existing market supply and demand functions. Furthermore, as market prices are established on the basis of outside forces, performance indicators which are based on these prices cannot be manipulated by individuals whose interest may be in conflict with that of corporate objectives. This puts managers under pressure to improve their performance in line with corporate objectives.

However, there are some limitations of market-based systems. As previously discussed, the product being transferred may be incomparable with any other product in the market, and therefore market prices cannot be obtained. Moreover, under certain internal management control systems and economic conditions, the use of market pricing policy would distort the investment decision. For example, if a company is operating below its optimal capacity of production, it would be unrealistic for the buying manager to purchase the goods from outside suppliers and hence suboptimize the overall company profit. Conversely, if the company is producing in excess of its normal plant capacity it would be better for the buying unit to source their requirement outside the company, because each extra unit of production by the company would cost more than obtaining it from the open market under perfect competitive conditions.

For the non-market-based pricing systems, the opportunity cost approach could distort the investment decisions because it would make the buying division more profitable and the selling division less profitable.

Under the marginal cost approach, marginal revenue is equated with marginal cost of the product in order to maximize the overall company profit. However, since the marginal cost schedule varies from division to division, managers may be tempted to falsify their report on the marginal cost curve of their own division or subsidiary in order to improve their own profitability. Such attempts will reduce the overall profit of the company as a whole.

The use of cost plus pricing methods could show an unprofitable division to be profitable. This in turn will distort the information used for performance evaluation and decision-making.

The cost-based systems are simple, easily understood and based on readily available data. The use of standard cost can avoid passing on cost inefficiencies to other companies or divisions. A good standard cost system can eliminate the effects of unanticipated change in purchasing volume from the buying unit (some companies adopt a 'take or pay' policy for internal transfer). A company employing the standard full cost transfer can reduce the variation in price received by the buying unit, which in turn will enable the parent company to measure more precisely each unit's contribution. It also helps to clearly distinguish the profit-centre (external sales) and cost-centre (internal sales) roles of the selling unit, and hence reduce the interdependence effect on performance measures.

Some difficulties arise with actual full cost transfers. Since the price is charged at the level of cost actually involved, a change in internal or external demand will cause a fluctuation in the transfer price. Therefore, the buying unit cannot know their payment until the period has already passed and the selling unit has calculated the overall expenses incurred in production.

Halpern and Srinidhi (1987) examine the effects of resale price and cost plus method of transfer pricing on resource allocation decisions of MNCs when the tax rate abroad is lower than in the USA. They found that under the resale price method when transfer pricing is high, sales of the final product will be higher than in a 'no-tax' world and will decrease as the transfer price decreases, to a point below sales of the final product in a 'no-tax' world. The company will use more domestic resources than it would in the absence of taxation, regardless of the amount of foreign resources used. Under the cost plus method, the company will increase its imports over the optimal level in the no-tax world. As transfer pricing increases, both imports and sales of final product also increase.

Both transfer pricing rules cause distortions of resource allocation, although the distortion will vary with the transfer pricing method employed. The distortions arise under both methods as a result of the tax differential and the transfer pricing regulation. If either of these factors were absent, there would be no necessary distortion in the resource allocation pattern. Halpern and Srinidhi (1987) also state that where transfer pricing regulations differ between the two countries, the input/output level distortions in this case are not sensitive to the tax rate differentials. The company's overall pre-tax profit would be lower than in the unconstrained situation; the resource allocation level would be used to reduce taxes. They found that no general assertion could be made on the total after-tax profits of the company or on the amount of taxes paid to the foreign country.

Having discussed the various methodologies used in practice, it is important to consider a criterion to determine the fairness of the transfer pricing policies.

In the USA, Section 482 of the Internal Revenue Code indicates that 'all prices charged by US parents to foreign subsidiaries and/or affiliates must be arm's length, or competitive'. The meaning of arm's length price is defined in the Treasury Regulation $1.482 - 2(e)(2)(ii)$ as 'comparable uncontrolled price'. The uncontrolled price is further clarified as follows:

> ... Uncontrolled sales are considered comparable to controlled sales if the physical property and circumstances involved in the uncontrolled sales are identical to the physical property and circum-stances involved in the controlled sales, or if such properties and circumstances are so nearly identical that any differences either have no effect on price, or such differences can be reflected by a reasonable number of adjustments to the price of uncontrolled sales. ... Some of the differences which may affect the prices of property are differences in the quality of the product, terms of sale, intangible property associated with the sale, time of sale, and the level of the market and the geographic market in which the sale takes place.

This regulation suggests some of the following criteria which management should consider when setting out fair market-based transfer prices:

1. The price of the product must be comparable to those of the same or similar products in the industry in terms of size, quality, etc.

2. Circumstances which may make different prices necessary include location, tradition, trade regulations, local government policies, etc.
3. The price set must reflect the current market price, i.e. there would be no time lag between obtaining the information and publishing the price.
4. The amount of intra-company transactions should not be big enough to affect the open market price if the product were bought or sold on the open market, otherwise the market price could not be used as a benchmark for price setting.

The integrity of the cost-based system of pricing depends on the design of the system and how the company operates it. It is important that the managers believe the costs adopted are what the costs really would be for an efficiently run operation. Furthermore, the buying unit must have confidence that the selling unit is doing its best to forecast raw material costs accurately. It is a common controversy that these forecasts are purposely conservative so that the selling unit can show positive variances in its budget revision.

Standard costs are acceptable for tax purposes if they are revised periodically to reflect the actual cost conditions. However, the adoption of this system would involve the arbitrary nature of the profit mark-ups which would in turn distort the managerial performance evaluation. In certain circumstances, it would be fair to use the marginal or variable costing methods. Such transfer pricing deviations from full costing are acceptable for income tax purposes as long as the economic circumstances warrant their use.

There appear to be many potential conflicts between the alternative methods of transfer pricing. Given these difficulties, what is the current practice among MNEs? In a recent empirical study of 164 US MNEs by Al-Eryani, Alam and Akhter (1990) only 35 per cent of the companies in their survey indicated that they used 'market-based' methods to determine 'arm's length' transfer prices. The remaining majority of the companies used either a 'cost-based' price or a 'negotiated' price.

Transfer pricing techniques and their conflicting objectives are illustrated in the following example.

Rag Enterprises
Rag Enterprises is a multinational company with operations in many parts of the world. The head office is located in Turkey. This example focuses on two of the subsidiaries which produce and distribute Turkish Delight.

One subsidiary in the UK has a production facility where the average unit cost of manufacturing Turkish Delight (Cm) is given as:

$$Cm = 16 + 0.4Q \text{ per batch of one ton of Turkish Delight}$$

The subsidiary in Italy also produces and distributes Turkish Delight, and the following average unit cost and revenue data are relevant for batches of one ton of Turkish Delight:

Cm	$= 20 + Q$	Manufacture
Cd	$= 13 + 0.4Q$	Distribution
R	$= 473 + 0.4Q$	Demand

Rag's policy is to treat each subsidiary as a profit centre with managerial performance being evaluated by return on investment (ROI) and a comparison of actual and budgeted absolute profits, both in terms of the local currency and pounds sterling. Subsidiaries are expected to interact on an arm's length basis, although they are required to purchase within the group any products which they need rather than use external suppliers, but are charged at around the same prices of independent suppliers of similar items.

For the budget year commencing 1 June 1989, the Italian subsidiary estimates that total demand for Turkish Delight in Italy will be 270,000 tons. The manager there believes that his plant cannot operate at its most effective level of production and meet this demand. Hence, he has contacted the manager of the British subsidiary, who quotes the unit cost of $16 + Q$ per ton, plus freight charge of $0.4Q$ per ton.

The following general information is available. The cost of raising finance in Italy is greater than in the UK. Corporation tax is levied at a higher rate in Italy than in the UK, and the *ad valorem* tax on imports is also relatively higher. Political changes in Italy cast doubts on the ease of future repatriation of dividends from Italy to Turkey. Associated with these changes is a likelihood that the Italian lira will shortly be devalued, resulting in the Turkish lira becoming relatively stronger.

We now wish to determine, from the company's point of view, whether the internal trade between the UK and Italy should take place. Furthermore, at what transfer price may it take place?

As the workings suggest, the internal trade should take place from the company's point of view. In Italy, the total costs are obtained by multiplying the given average costs by the production quantity, Q (where Q is in '000s). Therefore:

Total cost:	$TCm = 20Q + Q^2$	Manufacture
	$TCd = 13Q + 0.4Q^2$	Distribution
Total revenue:	$TR = 473Q + 0.4Q^2$	Demand

Marginal costs and marginal revenue are obtained by differentiating the above equations, which are:

Marginal cost:	$MCm = 20 + 2Q$	Manufacture
	$MCd = 13 + 0.8Q$	Distribution
Marginal revenue:	$MR = 473 + 0.8Q$	Demand

For profit maximization $MR = MC$; therefore profit maximization quantity (Q) is found where:

$$473 + 0.8Q = 20 + 2Q + 13 + 0.8Q$$
$$2Q = 440$$
$$Q = 220$$

However, estimated demand for Turkish Delight equals 270,000 tons, so, Italy cannot meet total demand and should contact the UK for the shortfall quantity. Will the UK supply Turkish Delight and at what price?

If the total demand is sourced from the UK subsidiary, the costs would be:

Costs:	$TCm = 16Q + 0.4Q^2$	Manufacture
	$FC = 0.4Q^2$	Freight Charge
Total cost of UK:	$TC = 16Q + 0.8Q^2$	therefore by differentiating
Marginal cost:	$MC = 16 + 1.6Q$	

Substitute the MR of Italy. Apply to the MC of the UK, plus the distribution costs of Italy, i.e. substitute the Italian marginal manufacturing costs for the UK's:

$$473 + 0.8Q = 16 + 1.6Q + 13 + 0.8Q$$
$$1.6Q = 444$$
$$Q = 277.5$$

It therefore seems reasonable to supply up to the 270,000 tons of Italian demand. But what price should be charged?

The UK might argue for MR = MC where the UK's MC was $16 + 1.6Q$ and the UK would apply its profit maximization quantity of 277.5 tons.

$$16 + (2 \times 277.5)$$
$$= 571$$

found by substituting 277.5 tons, i.e. optimal output level into manufacturing marginal cost.

If Italy applies its optimal output to the marginal manufacturing cost, the transfer price should be:

$$20 + (2 \times 220)$$
$$= 460$$

Arguments arise between different transfer prices for each subsidiary. However, estimated demand for Turkish Delight is equal to 270,000 tons, and even if full capacity utilization is budgeted for, Italy still cannot meet the full demand. Total demand can be met by 220,000 tons being produced locally and a further 50,000 tons being transferred from the UK subsidiary. Total profit of the company is much higher with international trade than without it.

Let us now support our findings:

Total company profit without international trade:

$$473(220) + 0.4(220)^2 - [13(220) + 0.4(220)^2 + 20(220) + 220^2]$$
$$= 48,400 \text{ Total company profit}$$

Total company profit with international trade:

$$473(270) + 0.4(270)^2 + [16(50) + 0.8(50) + 20(220) + 220^2 + 13(270) + 0.4(270)^2]$$
$$= 68,600 \text{ Total company profit}$$

which is shared by the UK subsidiary:

$$571(50) - [16(50) + 0.8(50)^2]$$
$$= 25,750$$

and by the Italian subsidiary:

$$473(270) + 0.4(270)^2 - [571(50) + 20(220) + 220^2 + 13(270) + 0.4(270)^2]$$
$$= 42,850$$

While the total company profit is increased with the international trade, the profit of the Italian subsidiary will suffer; its profit is now reduced from 48,400 to 42,850. This will have implications in the performance evaluation of the Italian subsidiary manager.

Other problems may arise for intra-firm trading, for instance:

In order to maximize total company profit we need to charge high transfer prices for goods exported from the UK into Italy as Italy has high corporation taxes. The effect of higher transfer prices from the UK will reduce Italy's tax liability where taxes are higher than in the UK. However, this might be against the transfer price determined on the basis of optimal output. Similarly, if import taxes into Italy are high, then we need to charge low transfer prices from the UK into Italy. If the cost of finance in Italy is high, we need to accumulate profit (and cash flows) into Italy so that these can be used for financing future projects. This, however, requires a low transfer price from the UK. If there is political instability in Italy, then we need to accumulate cash flows in the UK by charging higher transfer prices. If Italian currency is likely to be devalued against Turkish lira, a low transfer price would help to keep the profit in a relatively stronger British currency. Similarly, if the Italian subsidiary has vast growth potential, a lower transfer price would keep higher profits in Italy.

These might be more important than the internal economic problems.

MANIPULATION OF TRANSFER PRICING

There are some specific reasons that may tempt the multinational corporation to manipulate transfer pricing to their advantage. (We have already briefly mentioned some of them in the section on determinants of transfer pricing.) In this section we consider them in more detail. If the multinational corporation manipulates transfer prices substantially, real harm will be done to the home and host governments involved. They will both suffer from loss of tax revenue and, in addition, there will often be some other undesirable effects on the third parties, such as the joint venture partner, consumers and trade unions.

The main reasons for transfer pricing manipulations fall into four categories:

1. Minimizing global tax on profits
2. Customs duties
3. Exchange risk exposure
4. Profit and capital repositioning

Minimizing global tax on profits

The problems of transfer pricing for corporate taxation is one of the most controversial issues in multinational finance. If, in Country A, Company 1 has a heavier burden of corporation tax, in Country B, where Company 2 operates, the multinational corporation will be rewarded when it underprices the sales made by Company 1 to Company 2, or conversely, when it overprices the sales from Company 2 to Company 1. As a result of this manipulation of the transfer price, the profit will be accumulated in the country with lower tax rates, thus saving the multinational company from tax payments at the higher rate of taxation.

Any assessment of transfer pricing potential in the corporate tax field must enter into the complicated tax law, principles and overall practices. Plasschaert (1979) found that the home country only considered a claim when income was effectively remitted by the foreign subsidiary to the parent company; that the double taxation resulting from the concurrent claim of both the home and host countries is alleviated by unilateral concessions by the home country and by bilateral tax treaty arrangement between the countries. In the framework of prevailing international tax arrangement, transfer pricing manipulation would allow tax savings to the multinationals. Table 14.1 illustrates this point.

It is assumed here that unilateral tax relief consists first, of a foreign tax credit system, and secondly, of a foreign tax exemption system. Taxable profit is transferred from a high to a low tax country.

Transfer prices shift 25 per cent of a given real taxable profit base from a high to a low tax jurisdiction. Outgoing dividends are subject to 8 per cent withholding tax in the host country.

Table 14.1   Foreign tax credit system: full remittance of profit

	Without transfer pricing			With transfer pricing		
	Sub A	Sub B		Sub A	Sub B	
Taxable profits	500	500	1,000	375	625	1,000
Taxes in host country:						
Corporate profit tax	125	100	225	93.75	125	218.75
Withholding tax on dividend	30	32	62	22.5	40	62.5
Total	155	132	287	116.25	165	281.25
Taxes in home country:						
Domestic tax before credit	300	300	600	225	375	600
Foreign tax credit	155	132	287	116.25	165	281.25
Matching domestic tax	145	168	313	108.75	210	318.75
Total taxes	300	300	600	225	375	600

General assumptions: Home country tax rate 60%
Host country tax rate (A) 25% (B) 20%
Withholding tax on dividends 8%
(Treaty provisions); Home country applies credit against tax system

Assume that the parent company is subject to a 60 per cent tax rate on total profit for the year whereas subsidiaries of Country A, Company 1 and Country B, Company 2 are subject to 25 per cent and 20 per cent of tax rates respectively. Each subsidiary has £500 million of operating profit which is liable to tax.

In the analysis, the profits are remitted fully as dividend. Transfer pricing manipulations on transactions between Company 1 and Company 2 divert £125 million of profit from Country A to Country B. The result shows that under the foreign tax credit mechanism, transfer pricing manipulation is useless. Any gain from horizontally reshuffling profits between Country A and Country B is offset and recouped vertically by a higher or balancing tax in the home country (see Table 14.2).

In this case the home country only taxes when income is actually remitted by the foreign subsidiary. Transfer pricing becomes profitable, and the overall tax liabilities are reduced from 225 to 218.75. However, in the longer run, the hypothesis of full retention of profits within the subsidiaries is unrealistic, as eventually the multinational must remit dividends for the remuneration of its shareholders and the financing of investment in the home country.

Foreign tax exemption   The result shown in Table 14.3 is slightly different from the two previous analyses. The home country does not exert its claim on foreign income, the remittance notwithstanding. In this case withholding tax is levied on the outgoing dividend from the host country which explains the difference. Therefore, overall tax liability was reduced, thereby transfer pricing yields some benefits.

Table 14.2   Foreign tax credit system: no remittance of profit

| | Without transfer pricing | | | With transfer pricing | | |
	Sub A	Sub B		Sub A	Sub B	
Taxable profits	500	500	1,000	375	625	1,000
Taxes in host country:						
Corporate profit tax	125	100	225	93.75	125	218.75
Withholding tax on dividend	0	0	0	0	0	0
Total	125	100	225	93.75	125	218.75
Taxes in home country:	0	0	0	0	0	0
Total taxes	125	100	225	93.75	125	218.75

General assumptions as in Table 14.1
Home country applies credit against tax system
Host country applies foreign tax credit, no dividends are remitted
Home country exempts foreign source profits, no dividends are remitted

In the analysis of the tax manipulation, one important feature for the group (parent and subsidiaries) is tax havens. The virtues of tax havens are such that they act as a function of company profit 'repository'. Multinationals that enjoy substantial advantages from tax haven facilities can benefit substantially from transfer pricing for the purpose of corporate tax minimization. However, for UK companies the opportunities for lucrative transfer pricing in the corporate tax field are rather limited.

Double taxation agreements typically exclude tax haven subsidiaries from their tax reducing provisions. Furthermore, it would be wrong to view the tax haven subsidiary as merely for tax avoidance. Those subsidiaries may perform specific roles which cannot readily be accommodated within the legal framework of the home country.

Table 14.3   Exemption system: full remittance of profits

| | Without TP | | | With TP | | |
	Sub A	Sub B		Sub A	Sub B	
Taxable profits	500	500	1,000	375	625	1,000
Taxes in host country:						
Corporate profit tax	125	100	225	93.75	125	218.75
Withholding tax on dividend	30	32	62	22.5	40	62.5
Total	155	132	287	116.25	165	281.25
Taxes in home country:	0	0	0	0	0	0
Total taxes	155	132	287	116.25	165	281.25

General assumptions as in Table 14.1
Home country exempts foreign source income, dividends are fully remitted

The tax treatment of non-trade items   Non-trade flows of funds consist of some expenses which are indivisible for the parent and subsidiaries, for example, overhead costs, intangible capital, loan capital. The apportionment of R&D expenses between the parent and the subsidiaries is still a debatable issue. The present treatment in national tax laws of non-trade items varies greatly between countries; no specific set of international rules exists.

Double taxation agreements between developed nations normally state that royalty payments should be deductible; this means that the income will only be taxed in the country of the licenser. However, there are still many countries who do not allow deductibility.

Customs duties

Customs duties (mainly import duties) constitute one of the areas in which multinational companies can manipulate the transfer price of goods.

This type of manipulation is easier because it does not involve corporate figures. If an imported commodity was priced at £180 and it was subject to import duties of 50 per cent in Country A, the exporter could save tax payment by declaring the value of the commodity at £100, thus reducing the import duties by £40 for each commodity.

However, there may be some conflicts between corporate taxation and customs duties. First, the value-lowering method may be profitable to the exporting company, but if the tax rate in the importing country is much higher than that in the exporting country, profits will accumulate in the higher tax country and the company as a whole will suffer higher tax payment. Secondly, there may be a conflict of interests between the customs and tax authorities. The customs officials will wish to increase the value declared, but the tax authorities of the import country will wish to reduce the value, since high import values depress taxable profits.

Exchange risk exposure

Exchange risk arises in international trade if a company owns assets denominated in foreign currencies. Plasschaert (1979) found that the change in the price tag of internationally traded commodities and services does not in itself affect exchange risks. Changes in exchange risk were only achieved when manipulations were complemented by a change in the timing of payments, i.e. by leading (anticipatory move) or lagging (delaying payment).

Two propositions were used to illustrate this situation.

Assume: on 1 January 1988, the British subsidiary of a French multinational incurred a debt of £4 million to the parent company, payable in six months' time. The pound was expected to devalue slightly on 25 February 1988.

1 January FF10.478/£
25 February FF10.128/£

However, the financial manager of the French parent company was pessimistic about the sterling, and changed the normal price of £4 million to a transfer price of £4.5 million. If the date of the effective payment is left unchanged at due date, which is 1 July 1988, the French parent company will receive £4.5 million which can then be converted into FF45,576 million. Through the transfer pricing device, an extra FF5.064 million was siphoned into French francs. But this positive outcome is offset by the outflow of an extra £0.5 million from the subsidiary, which at the new exchange rate is worth FF5.064 million. Transfer pricing helps to improve the overall profit figures.

Judicious leading (or lagging) effectively eliminates the exchange risk. Let us suppose that the payment was brought forward to 10 February 1988, just before the pound is devalued. The £4 million claim would then yield FF41,912 million to the parent company, and exchange loss risk would have been averted.

The use of leading and lagging is limited by several factors, however. It is virtually impossible to accurately anticipate the exchange rate shift. In addition, governments often impose restrictions on lead and lag periods.

Profit and capital repositioning

In relation to the foreign exchange problem, another area which causes much concern is profit and capital repositioning. Many countries impose strict constraints on the remittance of profit to the parent company, and such restrictions may give incentives for reinvesting profits within the subsidiary. Transfer pricing manipulations, in both trade and non-trade channels, can circumvent the explicit restriction on the remittance of profits. The motivation of profit remittance often clashes with other inducements to practise transfer pricing. High transfer prices on the exporting country extract profits from the host to the home country, but the more profits being extracted the heavier the overall tax burden. In this case, the multinational is also liable to higher import duties. Likewise, when the multinational uses transfer pricing to repatriate capital invested in a subsidiary, it may run the risk of its assets being nationalized.

Limitations of transfer price manipulations

Managerial restriction   It is often difficult to determine the subsidiary management's responsibilities in relation to transfer pricing issues. The communication of information on taxes, tariff controls and government policies from subsidiaries located in many countries with different regulations may result in information overload for the parent company, since the capacity of the parent company for processing this vast quantity of information is often limited. Furthermore, when the cost of processing a large quantity of information is also taken into account, manipulation of transfer pricing could become an expensive operation. Moreover, it is often not an easy task to persuade the subsidiary manager to show a loss or low profits when, in reality, he or she is running a profitable operation. As discussed earlier, this could result in performance evaluation problems for the subsidiary management.

In order to have an optimal transfer pricing system, the manipulation techniques need to be updated in line with the many modifications being imposed in tax rates, tax law, import duties and the like, which are subject to amendment from time to time.

How can we avoid transfer price manipulations?

Need for more adequate disclosure   There is a need to disclose more about the business practices of internal price setting. Attention should be paid not only to a particular subsidiary, but also to overall operational aspects of multinationals. An adequate degree of disclosure can extend the knowledge to the multiple users, but this disclosure must not exceed the extent that it could breach the company's confidentiality.

The merits of international harmonization of taxes and regulations   When the regulation on tax matters can be agreed in specific guidelines and principles among all countries, the internal pricing practice will become more acceptable to the governments involved. It would be unrealistic to expect a global harmonization; however, some steps can be effectively taken within regional groupings (for example, there have been rigorous attempts to harmonize taxes within the EC states).

International cooperation and adjustment Cooperation between governments can maintain their sovereign rights to protect their own regulations, and also improve the exchange of relevant information.

Conceptual clarification and the need for more research There are some 'misty' concepts in transfer pricing which need to be clarified. The arm's length principle needs more attention and modifications; the difference between the fair price (which relates to internal control) and the arm's length price (which is concerned with anti-monopoly measures) needs to be explained. The treatment of the non-trade expenses and complicated tax matters also need more clarification. More research is needed on conceptual and technical issues in order to enhance our understanding of the transfer pricing practices.

Establishing transfer prices is embedded in a complex mechanism of price setting at various stages of production. The determinants of prices vary greatly, according to the circumstances discussed at the beginning of this chapter. The principles that lie behind the setting of transfer prices must be made consistent with business principles. If fraud is detected, the government should be empowered to intervene and regulate.

NATIONAL DIFFERENCES IN TRANSFER PRICING SYSTEMS

Arpan (1972) found that among the 60 non-US multinational companies and their US subsidiaries studied, transfer prices were always set by the top-level parent company executives, regardless of nationality or degree of decentralization for the company. The study also found that American, French, British and Japanese management seemed to favour cost-oriented prices, while Canadian, Italian and Scandinavian management preferred market prices. German companies appeared to be least concerned about transfer pricing policies.

Although foreign-based companies generally considered the same environmental variables when formulating guidelines for transfer prices, especially the larger companies, there were distinguishable national differences in the relative importance attached to the considerations. Canadian, French, Italian and US companies indicated that the tax effect was the most important consideration, while British companies emphasized the financial appearance of the host countries, and Scandinavian companies considered the acceptability of the host government to be paramount.

Apart from British-based firms, most other companies in the study viewed transfer pricing more as a means of controlling subsidiaries' operations than as a technique for motivating and evaluating subsidiaries' performance. Choudhury (1979) suggested that transfer pricing could have important effects on autonomy, efficiency and motivation, and suggested that if subsidiary managers responsible for profit centres were granted substantive autonomy they would perform better. He also argued that transfer prices are likely to come under the close scrutiny of relatively highly taxed host nations who would wish to curtail any large-scale evacuation of capital and earning. In his arguments he referred to the example of the Swiss pharmaceutical company, Hoffman-La Roche, reducing the transfer prices of Librium and Valium to its UK subsidiary, which was being charged over 40 times the price in the open market (Chlordiazepoxide and Diazepam Monopolies and Mergers Commission, HC 197, HMSO 1973).

SUMMARY

The development of overseas subsidiaries has become one of the most important topics in the management planning of MNCs. It has been assumed that one of the most significant objectives of companies is to maximize the welfare of its shareholders, and this assumption can easily be extended to multinational companies. This objective may be in conflict, however, with the objectives of the parent and the host country's economies. The management of MNEs have an incentive to manipulate the intra-firm prices so as to reduce their overall tax liabilities and/or to increase their competitive position in the foreign markets, and in certain cases, a MNE could even act against the interests of the host country shareholders. Therefore, the control of transfer pricing for the intra-firm transaction is a significant issue for governments and other stakeholders of multinational companies.

The effects of losing control over transfer pricing policies of multinational companies would be significant for the governments involved. It would reduce their revenues and could distort their planning, which in turn could result in misallocation of scarce resources in the long term. In the USA, the Inland Revenue has applied the 'arm's length' pricing principle and has tried to control the transfer pricing policies adopted by US companies. However, this principle has given rise to controversies in its practical applications.

The manipulation of profits in order to reduce the tax liability of MNEs has encouraged the tax authorities to look at the legislation governing the use of transfer prices to avoid tax liability. As a result, they have developed the legislation to such an extent that the scope for tax avoidance has been dramatically reduced. Tax legislation differs from country to country, and may cause double taxation to occur where tax treaties do not exist. It has also been shown that transfer pricing regulations may cause distortions in the resource allocation of the multinational corporation: not only are resources distorted from their optimal level of allocation, but also the pre-tax profits of the company will be lower than in the unconstrained situation.

Many studies have been undertaken to determine the best way of setting out transfer prices, in order to make policy recommendations to governments on controlling transfer pricing manipulations. The consensus of opinion seem to suggest that there is no one 'best' way of determining transfer pricing, and that each method should be evaluated on its own merits. Governments, therefore, should seek the most appropriate method to meet their particular requirements.

REFERENCES

Al-Eryani, F. Mohammad, Alan, P. and Akhter (1990) 'Transfer pricing determinants of US multinationals', *Journal of International Business Studies*, Vol. 21, No. 3, (third quarter), pp. 409–25.

Arpan J. S. (1972) 'Multinational firm pricing in international markets', *Sloan Management Review*, Winter.

Benke Jr., R. I. and Edwards, J. D. (1980) 'Transfer pricing: techniques and uses', *Management Accounting*, June.

Burns, J. and Ross, R. (1981) 'Establishing international transfer pricing standards for tax audits of multinational enterprises', *International Journal of Accounting, Education and Research*, Vol. 17, pp. 161–79.

Choudhury, N. (1979) 'Transfer pricing practices: room for debate', *Accountancy*, **90**, August.

Halpern, R. and Srinidhi, B. (1987) 'The effects of the US income tax regulations' transfer pricing rules on allocating efficiency', *Accounting Review*, Vol. 62, pp. 686–706.

Halpern, R. and Srinidhi, B. (1991) 'US income tax transfer pricing rules and resource allocation: the case of decentralised multinational enterprises', *Accounting Review*, Vol. 66, pp. 141–57.

Hoshower, L. B. and Mandel, L. A. (1986) 'Transfer pricing policies of diversified US based multinationals', *International Journal of Accounting, Education and Research*, Vol. 22, No. 1, Fall, pp. 51–59.

Knowles, L. L. and Mathur, I. (1985) 'International transfer pricing objectives', *Managerial Finance*, Vol. 11, No. 2, pp. 12–16.

O'Burns, J. (1980) 'Transfer pricing decision in US multinational corporations', *Journal of International Business Studies*, Fall, p. 25.

Plasschaert, S. R. F. (1979) *Transfer Pricing and Multinational Corporation: An overview of concepts, mechanisms and regulations*, Saxon House.

Saunders, R. (1989) 'The price is right', *Taxation International*, November, pp. 163–67.

ADDITIONAL READING

Arpan J. S. (1972) *International Intracorporate Pricing, Non-American Systems and Views*, Praeger, New York.

Arpan, J. S. and Radebaugh, L. H. (1981) *International Accounting and Multinational Enterprises*, Warren, Gorham and Lamont Inc.

Casey, M. P. (1986) 'International Transfer Pricing', Chapter 7, Appendix 7A, *Handbook of Management Control System*, Quorum, New York.

Choi, F. D. S. and Mueller, G. G. (1978) *An Introduction to Multinational Accounting*, Prentice-Hall, Englewood Cliffs, NJ.

Cowen, S. S., Phillips, L. C. and Stillbower, L. (1979) 'Multinational transfer pricing', *Management Accounting*, January.

Davies, J. R. (1978) 'How to determine transfer prices', *Management Accounting*, October.

Eccles, R. G. (1983) 'Control with fairness in transfer pricing', *Harvard Business Review*, November–December.

Eiteman, D. K. and Stonehill, A. I. (1982) *Multinational Business Finance*, Addison-Wesley, Reading, MA.

Evans, T. G., Taylor, M. E. and Holzmann, O. (1985) *International Accounting and Reporting*, Macmillan Publishing Co., New York, p. 378–381.

Finnie, J. (1978) 'Transfer pricing practice', *Management Accounting*, December.

Kugan W. J. (1969) 'Multinational pricing: how far is arm's length?', *Columbia Journal of World Business*, May–June.

Lall, S. (1980) *The Multinational Corporation*, The Macmillan Press Ltd, Basingstoke.

Parry, T. G. (1980) *The Multinational Enterprise: International Investment and Host-Country Impact*, Tai Press Inc.

Rahman, M. Z. and Scapens, R. W. (1986) 'Transfer Pricing by Multinationals: Some Evidence from Bangladesh', *Journal of Business Finance and Accounting*, Vol. 13, No. 3, Autumn.

Shapiro, A. C. (1986) *Multinational Financial Management*, 2nd edition, Allyn and Bacon, Newton, MA.

Tugendhat, C. (1971) *The Multinationals*, Penguin Books, London.

United Nations (1978) *Transnational Corporations in World Development: A Reexamination*, United Nations, New York.

Willard, S. (1960) 'Tax considerations in intracompany pricing', *Accounting Review*, **35**, January.

Yunker, P. J. (1982) *Transfer Pricing and Performance Evaluation in Multinational Corporations, A Survey Study*, Praeger, New York.

FIFTEEN

EVALUATION AND CONTROL OF GLOBAL OPERATIONS

INTRODUCTION

This chapter examines the nature of the control function within the multinational company (MNC), with particular emphasis on the effects of various forms of control upon performance evaluation. This is followed by a brief discussion of the role and design of performance evaluation and control systems, and the main factors which may affect evaluation of foreign subsidiaries. The final section discusses the advantages and disadvantages of various measures of performance, with particular emphasis on developing budgets for global operations.

EVALUATION AND CONTROL IN MULTINATIONAL COMPANIES

Control, according to Daniels *et al.* (1979), is 'the planning, implementation, evaluation and correction of performance in order to achieve organisational objectives.' In Shapiro's view (1989), control contains three basic elements: 'setting objectives, measuring results and comparing results with objectives', with the broad aim of 'communication, evaluation and motivation'.

In this section, following the identification of factors peculiar to the international environment which can affect the control systems of MNCs, various forms of control, decentralization, divisionalization, centralization and coordination will be outlined, and their relative advantages and disadvantages highlighted. The main issues concerning performance evaluation, i.e. the distinction between managerial and operations performance and the use of performance evaluation as a motivator, will be introduced. Finally, the question of whether or not any attempt is made by MNCs to modify domestic control and evaluation systems when applied to foreign operations is examined.

The control function in multinational companies

When considering the control function within MNCs as opposed to domestic-based companies, it is important to recognize several factors which make the control process more difficult in an international context. According to Daniels *et al.* (1979), there are four principal factors.

1. The geographic and cultural distance separating both the parent company from its subsidiaries and those subsidiaries from each other tends to increase the time and expense involved in the control process, and make errors in communication more likely.
2. The diversity of subsidiary operations means that differences in areas such as market size,

product, labour cost and currency make the setting of standards, performance evaluation and correction, and inter-subsidiary comparisons extremely complicated.
3. Factors beyond the corporation's control, such as host government regulations and the objectives of foreign shareholders, impede the control system.
4. The uncertainty attached to the economic and political conditions of the host country makes long-term planning difficult, in that final results may differ from those expected at the time of implementation if conditions alter in the meantime.

Difficulties arising from economic and political uncertainty are discussed further later in the chapter, when the impact of fluctuating exchange rates and inflation on performance evaluation in particular is considered.

The identification of the above four factors as those responsible for difficulties encountered by control systems in MNCs seems to suggest that any such difficulty is, directly and solely, a result of the exposure to the international business environment. However, additional problems may arise from the administration of the control system.

Problems of administration

Bursk *et al.* (1971) agree that there are very definite difficulties stemming from the peculiar nature of the international environment which must be recognized in the design of control systems. However, they also argue that the added problems of controlling foreign operations are a matter of the administration of the control system. They found that those responsible for designing financial control systems within MNCs encounter problems because they do not fully appreciate the relevance of the peculiar characteristics of the diverse international environment to their task, nor do they have a clear concept of what a control system is intended to accomplish.

One particular part of the administration of overseas control, and evaluation in particular, is the translation of financial data from local currency into parent currency and vice versa. Difficulties arising from different methods of translation are discussed in detail in the next section.

One of the most important aspects in the design of a control system is the responsibility for, and location of, decision-making. Who makes the decisions and where in the organization they are located determines the form of control, and since performance evaluation is an integral part of the control function, it is also affected by the location of decision-making.

Centralization versus decentralization

In MNCs, decisions made at the subsidiary level can be considered to be decentralized, whereas those made above the subsidiary level are said to be centralized. Generally speaking, organizations tend to decentralize responsibility for decision-making as much as possible. Decentralization works better the fewer the connections between activity areas (i.e. subsidiaries in the case of MNCs). The main device used by organizations to implement decentralization is, according to Solomons (1965) the 'profit centre'.

Divisionalization and the profit centre concept

Divisionalization adds to decentralization the concept of delegated profit responsibility. A profit centre is an operating subdivision which encompasses a sufficient scope of operations to permit the measurement of a profit, clearly presupposing that the manager of the subdivision, or subsidiary, has either complete autonomy of decision-making, or complete control over operating revenues and expenses. An operation should only be treated as a profit centre if its basic goal is profit, so that its performance might be fairly judged. The theory behind divisionalization and the profit centre concept is that if each profit centre maximizes its profits, then the organization's total profits will be maximized. But since one division may not take into account the benefits conferred or the cost imposed by its activities on other divisions of the company, the substantial independence of divisions from one another is essential.

Problems of decentralization and divisionalization

The interaction between a MNC's subsidiaries is often great. Complete decentralization or divisionalization, both of which demand subsidiary independence, may therefore prove to be suboptimal, since subsidiaries, if forced to act as virtually independent companies, would be unable to take advantage of the opportunities existing in the international environment. It is also likely that individual managers have experience and expertise limited to one or two countries only; this means that they are unlikely to appreciate the effect upon the MNC as a whole resulting from decisions taken in the best interests of their own subsidiary. In this way complete decentralization, allowing subsidiary managers to take decisions of company-wide importance, may prove suboptimal. In addition, not all subsidiaries of MNCs have their individual profit optimization as their basic aim: for instance, it is possible that certain subsidiaries were created to ensure a source of supply or to improve relations between the MNC and a particular government. In these cases the application of the profit centre concept may be inappropriate.

Just as complete decentralization appears to have certain drawbacks, full centralization is not without its disadvantages.

Problems of centralization

Complete centralization involves all decisions being referred to the top management level. If employed in a MNC, the result would be that top management would be faced with too great a volume of everyday decisions to be able to devote the necessary time and attention to major corporate-level decisions. The removal of virtually all decision-making responsibility from the subsidiary can also reduce motivation and inhibit the use of initiative by subsidiary managers.

According to Scott (1972), the location of decision making is one of the main distinguishing features between the operations of MNCs and domestic companies. Domestic operations tend to be decentralized as profit centres are oriented towards short-term planning by the profit centre for the profit centre, whereas MNCs use local plans in an attempt to coordinate on a worldwide basis, allowing the company to achieve both its comparative advantage and many of its objectives. MNCs are clearly centralized compared with the decentralization of domestic companies.

One probable explanation for the apparent preference of MNCs for a more centralized form of control is, as Bodinat (1974) suggests, that only a centralized and integrated organization with a global outlook is in a position to take advantage of the opportunities created by the differences between countries. Such opportunities include a greater variety of sources, the possibility of operations in several currencies, the manipulation of differing legal structures, and heterogeneous taxation and interest rates.

Yet, according to Scott (1972), there are strong indications that MNCs may be heading towards a new form of management, which he refers to as 'co-ordinative management'. Coordination is a mixture of cooperative, centralized and independent management, in which corporate headquarters and subsidiary managers work together. Despite the fact that headquarters retain the right to final approval of major decisions, a great deal of cooperation takes place between headquarters and local operations. Coordination differs from centralization in that local managers participate actively in operating decisions by providing information, representing the local needs to headquarters and working closely with headquarters to decide what is in the best interests of the corporation as a whole. It would seem that a coordinative approach is particularly appropriate to MNCs, since it allows managers to acknowledge the interactions between subsidiaries to permit greater economies of scale and the exploitation of differential advantages between countries. Coordination also avoids part of the suboptimization inherent in more independent approaches, such as use of the profit centre concept.

Goold and Campbell (1987) broadly classify companies under financial control, strategic planning and strategic control.

With **financial control** the company's headquarters is slim, supported only by a strong finance function. Underneath, there are layers of general management, but prime profit responsibility is pushed right down to the lowest level. These companies focus on annual profit targets. There are no long-term planning systems and no strategy documents. The centre limits its role to approving investment and budgets, and monitoring performance. Targets are expected to be demanding, and once they are agreed they become part of a contract between the business unit and the centre. Failure to deliver the promised figures can lead to management changes. The businesses which make up the financially controlled company are likely to have few linkages with each other, operate in relatively stable competitive environments, and do not involve large or long-term investment decisions.

In **strategic planning** companies, while divisionalization is consistent up to a point, the centre participates in and influences the development of divisional strategies. Their influence takes two forms: establishing demanding planning processes; and making contributions of substance to strategic thinking. In general, in comparison with financially controlled companies, they place less emphasis on corporate control. Performance targets are flexible, and are reviewed within the context of long-term strategic progress. The pay-off to strategic decisions is sought in the long term, and it is accepted that there may be hiccoughs along the route to building up the core businesses.

Strategic control companies are also concerned with divisional planning, but they are more diverse than strategic planning companies, and are accordingly 'chunked' into strong and largely independent divisions. The centre focuses more on establishing demanding planning processes, and on reviewing and criticizing divisional proposals, than on advocating particular ways forward. The role of the centre is seen to be a sympathetic and knowledgeable 100 per cent shareholder.

Companies may use a combination of strategies, and it may be difficult to seek a 'correct formula' for success. This is because all styles must cope with basic conflicts or tensions which exist in the role of central management. Clear responsibilities are highly desirable, since they enable tight control to be retained over the business unit, which in turn leads to greater motivation to perform well. Broad responsibility and autonomy at the business unit level leads to a greater sense of responsibility and support efforts to meet long-term objectives, but at the same time strong leadership produces purpose and direction. However, a dilemma exists because the benefits of each style are polar opposites.

Both strategic control and planning may be consistent with divisionalization in organizations. However, if the profit centre is adapted with clear responsibilities in an organization, then it is difficult to have a matrix form of organizational structure designed to bring people together over major decisions. Development of an organizational strategy may be carried out by managers closest to the business, but at the same time imposing strong leadership from the centre is not consistent with the profit centre approach in an organization. Similarly, tight controls cannot be combined with a softer response to performance evaluation. A strict financial control regime may therefore be inappropriate with strategic planning. It is likely that, in practice, most organizations will strike a balance between an extreme profit centre approach and strategic planning. A detailed analysis of control styles and financial pressures exerted upon companies is examined in Chapter 16.

Empirical studies on the control function of multinational companies The following section examines the findings of two surveys, one carried out by Irene Meister (1970) for the Conference Board, the other by Sidney Robbins and Robert Stobaugh (1973).

The Conference Board study This study, carried out in 1970, surveyed 252 US multinational companies. The findings indicate that MNCs can be grouped into three organizational archetypes:

1. Centralized at corporate headquarters
2. Centralized at the headquarters of an international management unit
3. Split between corporate headquarters and some subordinate headquarters (e.g. regional headquarters or central international unit)

1. *Centralization at corporate headquarters* More than 50 per cent of MNCs in the study centralized virtually all aspects of the international finance function at corporate headquarters. Several reasons were given for this: centralization was intended to provide more sophisticated and specialized international financial services to the management of international operations, as well as helping to coordinate financial activities on a company-wide basis; to integrate international and domestic subsidiaries; and also, in many cases, to play the role of watchdog in controlling international activities.

2. *Centralization at international headquarters* According to the Conference Board study, companies which centralize their international finance function at international headquarters can be divided into three groups. In the first group, the foreign operations of several MNCs were organized under a legally and operationally independent international subsidiary. In the second group, the international division had historically operated independently with its own financial department. In the third group, international divisions had their own financial staff but financial variables were relatively unimportant in the determination of corporate strategy.

3. *Split between corporate and subordinate headquarters* A large proportion of MNCs in this study split the responsibility for the international finance function between the corporate level and a subordinate headquarters, such as regional headquarters. Policy was determined at the corporate level, while day-to-day decision-making was handled at the subordinate level.

The Robbins and Stobaugh survey This study, carried out in 1973, surveyed 187 US multinational companies. It indicates that the financial system of a multinational company develops in a predictable pattern as the company's business grows, and that three phases can be discerned in the development of such systems:

1. Ignoring the system's potential
2. Exploiting the system's potential
3. Compromising with complexity

1. *Ignoring the system's potential*   This phase was found to occur in 'small' MNCs, i.e. those just beginning their overseas expansion. At this stage, little is known at the corporate level of the unique problems of multinational business, and so little attention is paid to the international finance function. This stage is usually characterized by a small financial staff with neither the experience nor the time to deal with decisions concerning foreign operations; it merely monitors the foreign subsidiaries which are generally allowed to operate without much supervision. As the relative importance of their international business increased, MNCs were seen to pass into the second phase.

2. *Exploiting the system's potential*   Progress into the second phase occurs when corporate management becomes aware that international financial decisions demand different skills than domestic ones. At this stage, they tend to centralize the most important financial decisions with an expert central staff. Such awareness increases in line with the profit importance of foreign operations, and management is forced to consolidate foreign subsidiaries into parent financial statements. As foreign operations continue to increase, the MNC passes into the third stage.

3. *Compromising with complexity*   By this stage, the MNC finds itself facing a dilemma. On the one hand, experience, the scale of foreign operations and the relative importance of foreign operations encourage tight controls. On the other hand, the greater number of financial options resulting from an increase in the number of subsidiaries makes it impossible for headquarters to make a separate decision on each financial transaction between subsidiaries in the enterprise. The solution chosen by MNCs appears to be a large central international financial staff which delegates responsibility to subsidiaries in the form of guidelines or a 'rule book'. Actual decisions are made at the subsidiary level.

Both studies point out that no single form of organization predominates and that each MNC has an individually designed control system. The location of decision-making determines the form of control, and is also of relevance when considering the way in which performance is to be evaluated.

PERFORMANCE EVALUATION IN MULTINATIONAL COMPANIES

It is generally accepted that performance evaluation is an essential part of the control system. Just as domestic-based companies must be able to compare actual results with pre-set goals, so must MNCs. Evaluating the performance of foreign operations and managers is essential, not only to judge how existing subsidiaries are performing, but also to indicate in which direction they seem to be moving, how corporate strategies and policies should be modified to improve future performance, and the likelihood of corporate objectives being realized. The data produced are also useful for decisions concerning the allocation of limited resources to new projects, and give an indication of which products are the most profitable and which strategies, subsidiaries and managers are performing best.

During performance evaluation, performance is measured relative to pre-set standards, and modifications to operations are introduced, based upon any apparent disparities. However, since the achievement of a particular subsidiary is a function of the manager's ability and the operating environment, it is important to distinguish between operational and managerial performance.

The main measures used to evaluate performance, and their advantages and limitations, are discussed later. The initial focus is on the importance of separating the evaluation of subsidiary managers' performance from the evaluation of the subsidiary.

Operating versus managerial performance

Demirag (1987) states that the evaluation of managers' performance separately from that of the subsidiary helps to indicate the extent to which managers are accomplishing the objectives of the MNC as a whole. The distinction made between managerial and operating performance is especially important in globally integrated MNCs since, as we noted with the use of centralized decision-making, many factors which affect subsidiary performance are outside the local manager's control, and actions taken by one subsidiary manager may be reflected in the performance of other operating subsidiaries. For this reason, according to Hopwood (1972), the financial data available for performance evaluation may be an inadequate reflection of managerial performance. Financial reports are concerned with representing the outcome of the subsidiaries' operations, whereas managerial performance is concerned with the efficiency of the process which results in this outcome. This suggests that those factors which are uncontrollable by the manager should in some way be eliminated during the evaluation of managerial performance. Financial data may also prove inappropriate for managerial performance evaluation, since their emphasis is on short-term performance, whereas managerial performance evaluation may be more concerned with long-term considerations.

For these reasons, many MNCs choose to use non-financial criteria for the separate evaluation of managers' performance.

Non-financial criteria for performance evaluation

Demirag (1987), in a survey of 105 UK multinationals, found that non-financial criteria commonly used include market share as measured by sales, personnel development measured in terms of numbers of people promoted relative to numbers of promotable employees, employee morale ascertained through in-house surveys, productivity, and the relationship between local management and the host government. Demirag also noted that in addition to formal financial reporting and non-financial measures, some MNCs use more subjective judgements in the evaluation of subsidiary managers by allowing them, for example, to explain why certain financial objectives were not met.

Use of performance evaluation for motivation

Eiteman and Stonehill (1989) suggest that managerial performance evaluation can also be used to motivate managers, by relating compensation to the results of evaluation. For example, evaluation can serve as an input for promotion and salary decisions. Managers who feel that they are neither rewarded nor punished as a result of performance evaluation may be tempted to put less effort into their work. Similarly, some managers may work hard, yet tend to shy away from new ventures offering greater potential gains but involving a lot of risk. Incentives to take such risks can be increased by the use of significant rewards for success; otherwise, the manager's use of initiative may be minimal. However, care must be taken when dealing with managers from different cultural backgrounds that they do not consider such a relationship between evaluation and compensation as inappropriate, thus ruling out the possible use of compensation based on evaluation as a method of motivation.

Ideally, performance evaluation should be unique for each manager and separate from the performance evaluation of the operations of the subsidiary.

Overseas performance evaluation is made more complex than that of domestic operations by additional factors such as fluctuations in exchange rates, and foreign inflation, all of which affect the financial data used in performance evaluation. The existence of such factors might suggest that, since the operating environment of MNCs differs so greatly from that to which domestic companies are exposed, MNCs would be encouraged to adapt and develop their domestic control and evaluation systems to cater specifically for overseas operations. Yet this does not appear to be the case in practice.

Applying domestic systems overseas

According to Miller (1979), when MNCs first began to evolve, foreign operations were virtually controlled and managed from the corporate headquarters, and domestic methods of performance evaluation that had proved to be of value were used.

Indications are that the strong similarities between those control systems used at home and abroad result from a conscious choice, based on the desire to use a system overseas which has been used effectively at home and with which managers are familiar. Such 'transplantation' of systems would clearly be of most value to those companies whose objectives for foreign and domestic operations are similar. There are also clear initial cost advantages of simply exporting the domestic system.

Demirag (1987) found that a significant majority of UK MNCs employed the same perform-ance evaluation measures to overseas operations as they did to domestic ones. In the few cases where differences did arise, they were mainly in the amounts of information required and the emphasis placed upon each measure. Control systems may have to be adjusted for various factors peculiar to the overseas environment: as Hawkins (1965) points out, those responsible for foreign operations need to create management control systems tailored to the specific objectives, organization and environment of their international operations.

COMPLICATIONS OF MULTINATIONAL PERFORMANCE EVALUATION

There are five features in general which affect the evaluation of foreign subsidiaries and their managers: exchange rate fluctuations; inflation rate changes (both of which are unforeseeable and largely out of corporate control); transfer pricing; cost allocation; and translation (the latter three are all within corporate control). Transfer pricing and cost allocation affect the actual financial information which is going to be evaluated whether translation is involved or not, whereas translation alters the information by bringing in the effects of exchange rates directly, when evaluating the performance of a foreign subsidiary and its manager.

Exchange rate and inflation rate fluctuations

According to Bennett Stewart (1983) exchange rate fluctuations can be linked to three causes: inflation rates, relative economic competitiveness, and government policies. In the short term government policies and economic competitiveness are the dominant factors determining exchange rates, but in the long term the main cause is inflation.

The effect of inflation on exchange rates can clearly be seen in countries which have consistently high or low inflation rates. In Brazil, for example, where inflation is very high, the Brazilian currency suffers against other currencies, whereas in Switzerland, the Swiss franc appreciates against other currencies owing to its low level of inflation.

However, there is a tendency for exchange rates to offset inflation differentials between two countries, through PPP adjustments. The PPP theory relies on the notion that products of similar qualities will, at roughly the same point in time, cost approximately the same price. This happens because when traders buy where products are cheap and sell where expensive, they ensure that similar products all over the world do not differ in price when translated at current exchange rates. If the prices of products are the same at current exchange rates then, in order to stay the same when translated at future exchange rates, any price level change must have an equal and opposite change in exchange rates to offset it.

Unfortunately, exchange rates deviate from PPP. This is because of factors such as taxes, financing, import costs, transportation costs, and restrictions that affect the risks and profits of international trade.

International competitiveness is another reason why exchange rates fluctuate, and causes problems for the evaluation of foreign subsidiaries and their managers. Changes in supply and demand within a market result in price level changes which may have effects on exchange rates. For example, after 1976 the pound appreciated against the US dollar for several years, yet the UK had a higher rate of inflation (this was partly due to the increase in value of North Sea oil). In this instance the pound could have been compared to a share of stock in the British economy, so as the wealth of Britain rose, so did the pound.

Government policy also has a profound effect on exchange rates. Governments have many reasons for manipulating exchange rates including, for example, as a means of encouraging economic growth and cushioning economic shocks. Having a stable currency is usually a major objective of a government; for example, in 1989 the UK tried to hold the pound constant against the Deutschmark, as a depreciating pound would have led to a rise in UK inflation. As a result, the UK had an overvalued currency, thus enabling organizations to trade products abroad at more profitable prices than would have been possible had the pound depreciated. The implication of government manipulation of exchange rates for the evaluation of foreign subsidiaries and their managers is that top management should not be fooled: they must realize that when the local currency is overvalued, the results of the subsidiary will be improved when translated into the parent currency. The opposite effect will result if the local currency is undervalued.

Interest rates controlled by banks and governments also play a significant role in the determination of exchange rates. The link between exchange rates and interest rates is known as interest rate parity (IRP). IRP operates under the notion that identical risky investments throughout the world must offer the same real rate of return, thus not allowing investors to make profits. As governments have a say, to a certain degree, in the level of interest rates that are set, interest rates, like government policy and economic competition, affect exchange rates in the short term. In order for evaluation to be carried out adequately, the effects of fluctuating exchange rates on financial information must be taken into account. It should follow that by understanding what causes fluctuating exchange rates, i.e. inflation, economic competition and government policies, top management should be able to evaluate the performance of the subsidiaries and their managers more effectively, by not holding them responsible for the effects of these uncontrollable and unforeseeable exchange rate fluctuations.

Transfer pricing

Transfer pricing is a controllable factor which can often lead to gross distortions when evaluating foreign subsidiaries and their managers. The accuracy of evaluating a foreign subsidiary and its managers also depends upon the degree of responsibility that a subsidiary manager has, as to the effects of transfer prices on the overall performance of the subsidiary. It is important that this degree of responsibility is taken into account because, as is generally the case, most multinational corporations decisions on transfer pricing are made from headquarters. Transfer pricing is often centralized because of the lack of knowledge of local subsidiary managers concerning the broader legal, tax and liquidity calculations involved in forming a transfer policy for the multinational as a whole.

When setting the budgeted profits for foreign subsidiaries, the transfer pricing policy should be taken into consideration and the budgets adjusted for the effect of the transfer prices. This can be achieved by a decoupling process being formed between managerial evaluation and the transfer price used. Decoupling can be used by charging the marginal cost of production and transport to the buyers and crediting the sellers with a fair profit for their sales. Often, foreign subsidiaries selling to other subsidiaries of a multinational corporation may be instructed to sell products at a cost lower than if they were to sell on the market. This will lower the revenue and thus cause a reduction in profits. Therefore, they should only be evaluated on their production costs, as they have no control over their revenues.

In using transfer price mechanisms, it is likely that problems will arise with the use of profit related measures such as return on investment in evaluating the performance of foreign subsidiaries and their managers. Top management should ensure that no subsidiaries receive undue profits or losses due to transfer pricing; however, if they do, then these should be recognized.

Allocation of costs

The allocation of company costs or headquarters costs is a controllable factor which affects evaluation in a similar way to that of transfer pricing, i.e. it affects the profits of a subsidiary. Allocation costs are the costs allocated for the company as a whole rather than the division in particular. In computing the divisional profits when evaluating the performance of a subsidiary and its manager in a divisionalized company, the best thing to do may be to forget the allocation costs and evaluate those costs which are directly controllable by the subsidiary manager (see Kollaritsch (1984)).

Translation of foreign currency financial statements

Another factor which can be controlled by multinational companies and which affects the evaluation of foreign subsidiaries and their managers is translation. First, multinationals should decide whether they are going to evaluate their subsidiaries from financial information that has been translated or from financial information remaining in local currency. Secondly, if they are going to translate the financial information, they should then decide upon the method of translation to be used.

If multinational corporations decide to evaluate without translation, but with financial information in the local currency of the subsidiary, then all effects of fluctuating exchange rates will be ignored. As pointed out by McInnes (1971), the effectiveness of the subsidiary and its manager is more meaningful if measured in the local currency. If the reporting currency strengthens, the financial statements of the multinational appear worse (the opposite happens when the reporting currency weakens). Translation also often causes the financial statements to show different trends owing to the fluctuating exchange rates.

If multinational companies use translated financial statements in evaluating their foreign subsidiaries and managers, the effect of exchange rate fluctuations will be included in the translated statements. Therefore, top management should be aware of the effects of translation on the financial information being evaluated. Financial information is often translated because it enables top management to understand it more easily than if it were shown in the foreign currency. It is argued (Ijiri (1983)) that if multinational corporations see their subsidiaries as an investment, then they will wish to see the recovery of that investment in the parent currency.

Another aspect of whether translation should or should not be used for evaluation purposes is the degree to which managers are held responsible for fluctuating exchange rates. If a manager is not held responsible, the evaluation of his or her performance from translated data may be blurred by fluctuating exchange rates; therefore, it seems sensible to evaluate a manager's performance from local currency financial information. If, however, a manager is held responsible for the effects of exchange rate fluctuations, evaluation from translated financial information would show how he or she operated under fluctuating exchange rates, thus enabling the subsidiary and its manager to be evaluated on more appropriate criteria. In fact, it was found in a survey carried out by Robbins and Stobaugh (1973) that organizations which evaluate under local currency on the whole do not hold their subsidiary managers responsible for the effects of fluctuating exchange rates. Therefore, they protect them against fluctuating exchange rates when evaluating their performance. However, although organizations which evaluate under translated statements do not protect their subsidiary managers from fluctuating exchange rates, they do in general hold them responsible for the effects of exchange rate changes.

A number of surveys have been conducted on the use of translation when (mostly US) multinational corporations evaluate their foreign subsidiaries and managers (for example, see McInnes (1971), Robbins and Stobaugh (1973), Mauriel (1969), Morsicato (1978), Persen and Lessig (1979)). For a detailed review of these empirical studies see Demirag (1992).

A summary of the surveys indicate that throughout the 1960s the parent currency was used in evaluation; in the early 1970s there was a split between parent and local currencies: and later in the 1970s the majority of companies used both currencies. A more recent survey on the use of translation by UK multinational corporations (Demirag (1988)) concluded that most companies used both parent and local currencies. Further evidence showed that there was no significant difference in the use of parent or local currencies when evaluating the performance of foreign subsidiaries and their managers.

The findings of the surveys are not consistent with literature presenting the advantages that can be gained from evaluating operations and managers from translated or untranslated financial information. This may be put down to the ignorance of MNCs concerning the advantages of using one or other of the methods; by using both, they avoid making the wrong choice.

Translation methods   If an organization chooses to evaluate from translated financial information, it then has the problem of deciding how it is going to translate these statements. There are several methods of translation available, the four most common being current–non-current, monetary–non-monetary, temporal, and closing rate methods (these were discussed in detail in Chapter 6).

The major issues of translation are which rate should be used to translate the financial statements and how should any gains or losses or differences arising out of translation be treated?

The rate to be used is a basic choice between historic, current and average rates. The treatment of gains and losses can either be included in the earnings/profit, or treated as adjustments to shareholders equity. There have been several opinions as to how gains and losses should be treated with respect to the evaluation of foreign subsidiaries and their managers (for example, see Morsicato (1978)). The four most common methods of translation use different exchange rates and treat gains and losses arising from the different rates used in various ways.

The current–non-current method translates all current assets and liabilities at the current (closing) rate. Non-current balance sheet items are translated at the rates existing at the transaction dates (historic). Income statement items (revenues and expenses), except depreciation which is translated at historical rates, are translated at average rates for the period. Realized gains and losses are charged directly to the income statement.

Under the monetary–non-monetary method, all monetary accounts are translated at current rates and all non-monetary accounts at historic rates.

The basis of the temporal method is that the translation rate adopted must preserve the accounting principles used to value assets and liabilities in the original financial statements. Accordingly, historic rates are used to translate items stated at historic cost and the closing rate for items stated at replacement cost, market value, or expected future value. Under this method, all exchange gains and losses are immediately taken to the income statement and not deferred.

Under the closing rate method, all foreign currency denominated items are translated at the closing rate of exchange. Therefore, since all foreign assets and liabilities are assumed to be equally at risk the accounting exposure in each foreign subsidiary is simply its net equity. All translation gains and losses are taken directly to and shown separately in reserves.

The ways in which gains and losses occur and are treated have significant impacts on the evaluation of foreign subsidiaries and their managers, and it is important that top management fully understand that translation, if used, will affect the financial information. Furthermore, if local managers have been given responsibility for the effect of exchange rates, top management should not simply assume that they can evaluate accurately from translated statements, since each particular translation method used produces considerable differences in the profits due to the way in which gains and losses occur and are then treated.

Demirag (1988) found that a significant majority of UK multinational companies (61.19 per cent) used the closing rate method in translating their foreign subsidiary results for internal performance evaluation purposes (see Table 15.1).

Currency orientation in performance evaluations

In order to determine whether multinational companies use local currency, parent currency or both, Demirag (1988) estimated the number of MNCs consistently using foreign currency only,

Table 15.1 Summary of foreign currency translation methods

Translation methods	%*
All-current method (closing rate)	61.19
Current–non-current method	1.9
Monetary–non-monetary method	—
Temporal method	4.8
Do not translate	30.5
Other	1.0

*These figures represent the percentage of the total 105 MNCs that report using each particular translation procedure.

Source: Istemi Demirag, 'Assessing foreign subsidiary performance: the currency choice of UK MNCs', *Journal of International Business Studies*, Summer 1988, p. 269

consistently using sterling only, or using both foreign currency and sterling performance measures. In addition, he used the mean value of performance measures used in local currency, sterling or both currencies as a measure of companies' currency orientation in internal performance measures. The mean values were calculated as the average number of performance measures used for local currency, sterling or both (see Table 15.2).

The results of Demirag's (1988) study showed that the majority of MNCs (57 per cent) use both foreign currency and sterling financial measures in the evaluation of their foreign subsidiary operations (see Table 15.5). It is argued that MNCs use both types of currencies because they are unable to determine the usefulness of each type of performance measure. The results of the appropriate statistical analysis indicate that UK MNCs use more local currency only, or both sterling and local currency, than sterling only financial measures (the results were statistically significant at the 5 per cent level).

Comparative measures by definition include comparisons between domestic and foreign operations, and the use of parent currency information provides common numeraire for these comparisons. It is therefore suggested that the reason for using both currencies in comparative measures may be for the sake of convenience. The same tests were carried out for comparative measures, but no statistically significant difference between the mean values of comparative measures used in each type of currency was found.

Performance evaluation measures

Owing to the increasing volatility of exchange rates and the increase in size and number of foreign subsidiaries of multinational corporations, current performance measures on the whole provide an inadequate and inaccurate indication of performance when assisting in the evaluation of foreign subsidiaries and their managers. Furthermore, the use of domestic-based measures for evaluation of overseas subsidiaries is not necessarily suitable.

More than one measure of performance is used by most multinational corporations when evaluating a foreign subsidiary and its managers. Demirag (1988), in a survey of 105 UK MNCs, found the results to be similar to those of the US surveys.

It can be seen from Table 15.3 that the most popular financial measures are: budget compared

Table 15.2   Performance evaluation of operations

Financial measures used	No. of firms	% of firms	Mean value of measures used in foreign currency, sterling or both
Foreign currency only	36.0	34.0	2.76
Sterling only	9.0	9.0	0.89
Both foreign currency and sterling	60.0	57.0	2.55
	105.0	100%	

Friedman's $X^2 = 20.748$ df 2 p $= 0.000*$

*p < 0.05

Comparative measures used	No. of firms	% of firms	Mean value of measures used in foreign currency, sterling or both
Foreign currency only	0.0	0.0	0.77
Sterling only	0.0	0.0	0.61
Both foreign currency and sterling	105.0	100.0	0.63
	105.0	100%	

Friedman's $X^2 = 1.471$ df 2 p $= 0.479$

Source: Istemi Demirag, 'Assessing foreign subsidiary performance: the currency choice of UK MNCs', *Journal of International Business Studies*, Summer 1988, p. 265

with actual profits; return on investments; budget compared with actual sales; and absolute amount of profit in monetary units.

The survey results showed that the most popular comparison was that of historical data (i.e. prior period(s) balance sheets and income statements); a further two comparisons of approximately the same popularity were with other similar manufacturing units of the same company in different countries; and with other similar manufacturing units of the company in the UK (see Table 15.4).

Financial measures used as indicators of internal performance evaluation of management were also studied by Demirag. The results of these findings were very similar to those for the evaluation of operations, and the results of comparative measures used for the evaluation of managers were even more alike to those of comparative measures used by MNCs when evaluating operations.

Other surveys and studies have also been carried out over the years to discover which performance measures are most popular with multinational corporations. For example, see McInnes (1971), Robbins and Stobaugh (1973), Morsicato (1978), Persen and Lessig (1979), Choi and Czechowicz (1983). The overall outcome of these and other surveys conducted on US

Table 15.3 Financial measures used as indicators of internal performance evaluation of operations

After translation in UK sterling (%)	Before translation in local currency (%)	Both in UK sterling and local currency (%)*	Financial measures
11.4	41.0	36.2	Return on investment (assets)
5.7	16.2	17.1	Return on equity
1.0	5.7	4.8	Residual income
8.6	27.6	32.4	Absolute amount of profit in monetary units
3.8	12.4	4.8	Value added
17.1	19.0	25.7	Cash flow potential from foreign subsidiary to UK operations
12.4	34.3	30.5	Budget compared with actual return on investments
10.5	42.9	41.9	Budget compared with actual profits
9.5	41.9	36.2	Budget compared with actual sales
6.7	24.8	17.1	Ratios
1.9	10.5	8.6	Others

*These figures represent the percentage of the total 105 companies that report using each particular measure.

Source: Istemi Demirag, 'Assessing foreign subsidiary performance: the currency choice of UK MNCs', *Journal of International Business Studies*, Summer 1988, p. 262

MNCs is that budgets compared to actual performance, and return on investment, are the performance measures most preferred for evaluation purposes. It was also found that non-financial measures used in evaluation purposes are becoming increasingly important, especially when evaluating a manager's performance.

Foreign currency orientation Various empirical studies attempted to determine whether MNCs use local currency or parent company currency in evaluating performance of their foreign subsidiaries. The following section briefly refers to these studies and draws conclusions regarding MNCs' currency orientations in their internal performance evaluation measures.

The National Association of Accountants (1960) carried out research to explore the problems of providing management with the financial information needed for control and decision-making purposes. Interviews were initially held with 51 companies engaged in foreign operations. The report stated that in addition to the responsibility for earning an adequate profit in local currency, the majority of the foreign subsidiary managements were held responsible for protecting the investment of the US parent company and its equity in retained earnings against erosion from devaluation of the local currency. It also indicated that only a few companies centralized their financial management responsibility at parent company level, and in these companies foreign subsidiary managements were evaluated by performance measures in their own currencies.

Table 15.4 Measures used as a basis of comparison for internal performance evaluation of operations

After translation in UK sterling (%)*	Before translation in local currency (%)*	Both in UK sterling and local currency (%)*	Does not apply	Comparative measures
12.4	43.8	32.4	2.9	Historical data of the subsidiary (i.e. prior period(s) balance sheet and income statements)
5.7	6.7	5.7	39.0	Other similar manufacturing units of your firm in the same country
20.0	14.3	10.5	19.0	Other similar manufacturing units of your firm in different countries
20.0	10.5	10.5	18.1	Other similar manufacturing units of your firm in the UK
2.9	1.9	3.8	2.9	Others

*These figures represent the percentage of the total 105 firms that report using each particular comparison.

Source: Istemi Demirag, 'Assessing foreign subsidiary performance: the currency choice of UK MNCs', *Journal of International Business Studies*, Summer 1988, p. 263

Mauriel (1969) conducted a study to examine the evaluation and control of the overseas operations of 15 MNCs, each with foreign sales exceeding US$5 billion. He found that, in the main, the companies exhibited a lack of concern for and understanding of the impact of currency fluctuations on performance evaluation. MNCs were US dollar-oriented at the time.

In 1971, McInnes undertook a survey in which 30 US manufacturers of industrial products with sales of $100–300 million took part. Five companies (17.0 per cent) reported using only local currency information for performance evaluation; 15 companies (50.0 per cent) used both local currency and US dollars; nine (30.0 per cent) used only US dollar information; and one (3.0 per cent) reported that the company's requirement varied with the operating environment of the subsidiary.

Bursk *et al.* (1971) studied 34 US MNCs. Their study indicated some awareness of the impact of environmental factors, including foreign exchange fluctuations, upon the performance of foreign subsidiaries. There was an equal use of local currency and parent currency in the reporting of performance. No distinction was made between the performance of the subsidiary and that of the manager.

The evaluation practices used by MNCs in evaluating foreign operations were again studied by Robbins and Stobaugh (1973). Thirty-nine MNCs were interviewed, and the published records of a further 150 were studied. The results indicated that untranslated information was required by 44.0 per cent of the firms, translated data by 44.0 per cent, and that both types were required by 12.0 per cent. Robbins and Stobaugh reported that companies which evaluate subsidiary performance in terms of local currency financial information see the responsibility for protecting against foreign currency exchange gains and losses as belonging to corporate

headquarters. These companies believe that an evaluation of a subsidiary manager's performance should be based upon his operating efficiency and that this is best accomplished by
reviewing local currency results. Companies also pointed out that the use of untranslated data
also avoided the fluctuation of profit figures which resulted from a period of rapid inflation
during the reporting period followed by a devaluation of the local currency during the next
reporting period.

In 1978, Morsicato carried out research to establish whether US MNCs used translated and/
or untranslated accounting data in performance evaluation of foreign subsidiaries. Seventy
firms in chemical-related industries participated in the study. The results indicated that for each
financial measure used, except budget compared to actual sales, the rate of use of the after-
translation measures was higher than that for the before-translation measures. There was also a
statistically significant difference between the number of financial measures a company used
for internal performance evaluation translation in US dollars and the number before translation
in local currency (more financial measures were used after translation in US dollars than before
translation in local currency). However, the companies did not show a statistically significant
difference between information used before and after translation for comparative performance
evaluation purposes. When the participating companies were asked whether financial statements
presented in terms of US dollars or local currency provided better information for internal
performance evaluation of foreign subsidiaries and managers, 46 companies (65.7 per cent)
stated a preference for local currency information; 15 (21.0 per cent) for dollar information;
and nine (12.9 per cent) commented that it was impossible to choose one or the other as better
and reported that they consider both when internally evaluating the performance of foreign
operations.

In 1979, Business International Money Report (BIMR) carried out a survey in order to
determine the methodology used by US MNCs to incorporate exchange rate considerations in
their evaluation of foreign subsidiary operations. The study was conducted among 12 US-
based MNCs, but the characteristics of these companies were not mentioned in the report. The
result of the survey indicated that seven (58.0 per cent) measured the performance of their
overseas operations in both local and parent currencies, while the remaining five (42.0 per cent)
evaluated in parent company currency terms.

In 1979, Persen and Lessig found that of the 125 companies they studied, 57 per cent
reported that Financial Accounting Standards Board (FASB) No. 8 was leading their companies
to highlight local currency results in addition to US dollar results, as a result of the distortion
on profit margins. The results of their study showed that five companies (4 per cent) used only
local currency measures; 48 (38 per cent) only parent company currency; and 72 (58 per
cent) used both local and parent company currency measures in their internal performance
evaluations.

Czechowicz, Choi and Bavishi (1982) evaluated how US and European manufacturing
MNCs assessed overseas operations and their managers' performance. A questionnaire was
sent to 300 MNCs: 64 US and 24 (mainly UK, Swedish and Swiss) responded. Interviews took
place with 10 US and 10 European MNCs' financial executives. The results of the study
indicate that while on average 28.0 per cent of the US MNCs employed both parent and local
currency performance measures, 44.0 per cent on average used strictly parent company
measures. Only 9.0 per cent of the US MNCs used only local currency measures. The results
also indicated that while US MNCs preferred a dollar perspective, non-US MNCs preferred a
local perspective. The US preference was found to be influenced by financial reporting
regulations which at the time emphasized translation gains and losses.

Table 15.5 Comparative analysis of UK and US MNCs' financial measures used as indicators of internal performance evaluation of operations

After translation (%)		Before translation (%)		
(a)	(b)	(a)	(b)	*Financial measures*
UK MNCs	US MNCs	UK MNCs	US MNCs	
41.0	(81.4)	60.0	(70.0)	Absolute amount of profit in monetary units
47.6	(80.0)	77.2	(52.9)	Return on investment (assets)
52.4	78.6)	84.8	(72.9)	Budget compared with actual profits
45.7	(72.9)	78.1	(72.9)	Budget compared with actual sales
42.8	(65.7)	44.7	(35.7)	Cash flow potential from foreign subsidiary to (US and UK) operations
22.8	(48.6)	33.3	(31.4)	Return on equity
42.9	(45.7)	64.8	(38.6)	Budget compared with actual return on investment
23.8	(34.3)	41.9	(30.0)	Ratios
5.8	(21.4)	10.5	(18.6)	Residual income
10.5	(12.9)	19.1	(11.4)	Others

(a) These figures represent the percentage of the total 105 UK MNCs that report using each particular measure, as found in the author's present study.

(b) The figures in brackets represent the percentage of the total 70 US MNCs that report using each particular measure as found by Morsicato (1978).

Source: Istemi Demirag, 'Assessing foreign subsidiary performance: the currency choice of UK MNCs', *Journal of International Business Studies*, Summer 1988, p. 271

Kirsch and Johnson (1991) found that of the 15 US MNC managers interviewed, eight indicated that their companies used both the US dollar and local currency, four the US dollar only, and three the local currency only.

Empirical studies carried out among US-based MNCs indicates that US MNCs appeared to be dollar-oriented in the mid-1960s and split between US dollar and local currency orientation in the early 1970s. By the late 1970s US MNCs were moving more towards an overall preference for local currency information; however, from the beginning of the 1980s until the early 1990s they still appeared to be parent currency-oriented. By the early 1990s they appear to be using once again both local and parent company currencies in their internal performance measures.

The evidence on UK MNCs' choice of currency for internal management evaluation is more scarce, but Demirag's findings (1986, 1988, 1990) suggest that UK MNCs appear to be more local currency-oriented than their US counterparts.

Currency orientation of US and UK MNCs Tables 15.5 and 15.6 illustrate the differences

Table 15.6 A comparative analysis of UK and US MNCs measures used as a basis of comparison for internal performance evaluation of operations

After translation (%)		Before translation (%)		Does not apply (%)		Comparative measures
(a) UK MNCs	(b) US MNCs	(a) UK MNCs	(b) US MNCs	(a) UK MNCs	(b) US MNCs	
11.4	(14.3)	12.4	(21.4)	39.0	(17.4)	Other similar manufacturing units of your corporation in the same country
30.5	(48.6)	24.8	(25.7)	19.0	(31.4)	Other similar manufacturing units of your corporation in different countries
30.5	(54.3)	21.0	(30.0)	18.1	(25.7)	Other similar manufacturing units of your corporation in the United States/United Kingdom
44.8	(65.7)	76.2	(72.9)	2.9	(2.9)	Historical data of the subsidiary (i.e. prior period balance sheets and income statements)
6.7	(4.3)	5.7	(7.1)	2.9	(4.3)	Others

(a) These figures represent the percentage of the total 105 UK MNCs that report using each particular comparison, as found in the author's present study.
(b) The figures in brackets represent the percentage of the total 70 US MNCs that report using each particular comparison, as found by Morsicato (1978).

Source: Istemi Demirag, 'Assessing foreign subsidiary performance: the currency choice of UK MNCs', *Journal of International Business Studies*, Summer 1988, p. 272

between financial and comparative measures used by UK and US multinational companies in evaluating their foreign subsidiary operations.

Table 15.5 indicates that US MNCs use financial measures more after translation than before. The use of after-translation measures by US MNCs is also greater than that of UK MNCs.

Table 15.6 shows that US MNCs also made more after-translation comparisons than UK MNCs. It is interesting, however, to note that both UK and US MNCs made more before-translation comparisons with similar manufacturing units in the same country and historical data of the subsidiaries.

Although US MNCs appeared to be more parent company currency-oriented than UK ones in their use of formal performance evaluation measures, when asked which currency they would prefer to use in internal performance evaluations, 46 (65.7 per cent) of Morsicato's sample companies stated a preference for local currency measures.

Profit related measures Return on investment, residual income, ratio analysis, comparisons of performance measures, and cash flow potential are all possible profit related measures. In general, profit related measures only provide useful information if they are used when evaluating truly divisionalized sub-units, such as profit centres and investment centres. A profit centre may be defined as any sub-unit of an organization that is assigned both revenues and expenses. For an investment centre the comparison is between income and capital.

There are problems in designing an investment centre, which add to the difficulties associated with a truly divisionalized sub-unit, and therefore the reliability and accuracy of using profit related measures for the purposes of evaluation must be questioned.

Hongren (1977) states that the ultimate test of profitability is the relationship of profit and invested capital. The most popular way of expressing this relationship is by means of a rate of return on investment. Rate of return may not be a relevant measure of performance, however, if a unit's objective is not to make profit by itself but to contribute to the profitability of the organization as a whole.

Past studies (Mauriel (1969), McInnes (1971), Robbins and Stobaugh (1973), Morsicato (1978), Persen and Lessig (1979), Choi and Czechowicz (1983), Demirag (1988)) indicate that although return on investment is one of the most popular single measures of performance used by multinational corporations, other profit related measures were shown to be used as well. Return on investment does, however, have several advantages over other performance measures. First, it is a single comprehensive figure influenced by everything that has happened which affects the financial position. Secondly, it measures how well a manager uses the assets to generate profits. Finally, it is claimed that rate of return provides a common denominator that can be directly used for comparisons.

On the other hand, return on investment does have its disadvantages. For instance, Hongren (1977) indicates the following implications of return on investment as a performance measure: it emphasizes short-term results and over-emphasizes profit; while under-emphasizing quality, employee relations, discovery of new products, etc.; because of accounting policies regarding measures of investment and other policies, it may lead to incongruent decisions being made; and finally, comparisons among divisional results can be unjustifiable, as there are usually economic and accounting differences.

Return on investment and profit related measures raise several more difficulties. First, the information received from profit related measures may lead to incorrect decisions and motivate managers in ways which are not in the best interests of the organization as a whole. In addition, top management may use the measures to conceive false pictures of a subsidiary's performance (see Henderson and Dearden (1966), Robbins and Stobaugh (1973)). These faults are inherent in profit related measures because the latter are generally used on subsidiaries which are not truly divisionalized.

BUDGETING FOR GLOBAL OPERATIONS

Robbins and Stobaugh (1973) believed that multinational headquarters prefer to use a simple measurement of performance, like return on investment. Scott (1972) also believed that return on investment was superior to budgets and that budgets may be used by multinational corporations for supplementary information concerning a subsidiary and its manager. However, more recent studies (Morsicato (1978), Persen and Lessig (1979), Choi and Czechowicz (1983), Demirag (1988)) indicate that operating budget comparisons are more frequently used by multinational corporations for evaluation purposes.

The purposes of budgeting

A budget may be defined as a quantitative expression of a plan of action and an aid to coordination and implementation. Often a budget provides a forecast and a means of comparing the actual results of operations to the budget. This comparison produces variances which can be analysed for the purpose of evaluating operating and management performance. This then leads to taking corrective actions in order to improve the effectiveness of managers and the efficiency of future operations.

Budgets are, however, used for several purposes other than evaluation; these include planning, motivation, coordination, and education.

In planning, a budget shows what management aim to achieve and how they may achieve it. One main advantage of a budget over other performance measures is that it forces management to examine in detail the general economic situation of which the company is part and the economic interrelationships among the company's activities. Therefore, budgets help managers to explore how costs and revenues will behave under a certain set of operating assumptions.

Motivation is aided by the commitment to a predetermined plan through a budget. The personnel of an organization can in this way be motivated to achieve the organization's overall objectives. Managers should also be motivated to achieve overall goals: when a manager's performance is compared against the organization's incentive scheme, it should follow that his or her commitment to organizational objectives increases.

Budgets can also assist in the coordination of an organization in two ways: first, managers of an organization's sub-units prepare budgets, and these progress to higher levels in the organization and are received and enhanced so as to harmonize the entire organization; and secondly, the usefulness of the budget may continue by providing performance yardsticks after the operations have begun. If the environmental factors change, then the interrelationship knowledge previously gained can be used effectively in developing revised budgets and plans.

As for the education aspect, the process by which this is implemented will educate managers of a particular sub-unit as to the position and role of their unit in the organization as a whole and the interrelationship of the unit with others.

Without budgets, management would compare present performance with past performance when evaluating subsidiaries' and managers' performance, whereas budgets can be used as a standard against which actual results can be compared. However, this type of comparison may be meaningless if the operating environment has changed within the period of setting the budget and comparing it. If, as is usually the case, the purpose of evaluation is to measure the manager's operating abilities rather than his or her forecasting skills, then it would be sensible to remove the effect of the uncontrollable and unforeseeable events that have occurred in the budgeting period.

Problems of budgeting

Several problems exist in budgeting, some of which stem from conflicts between the various purposes of budgeting. The conflict between evaluation and motivation creates one of these difficulties. Generally, an ex-post facto budget is effective for evaluation purposes; however, if an ex-post facto budget is used and results in a change of the standards against which managers are to be evaluated, then it is unlikely that managers will fully commit themselves to the budget objectives. Similarly, rigid application and 'fixed' standards will cause managers to lose enthusiasm when faced with large negative variances from uncontrollable and unforeseeable events. This conflict can be reduced by the use of adjustable budgets, whose objectives can be changed under predetermined conditions. Thus, the budgets maintain their motivation factors and are still possible to achieve.

Further conflict may arise between evaluation and planning. When a budget is set it will not provide an accurate forecast for planning because of uncontrollable and unforeseeable events which may occur. However, two separate budgets would seem to overcome this problem.

In order for fair evaluation of the performance of foreign subsidiaries and their managers, they must be evaluated on those variables over which they have control, not on those variables over which they have no control. We have already discussed the five main factors which affect performance evaluation, i.e. exchange rates, inflation rates, transfer prices, cost allocation, and translation; we are now interested in how, when setting and tracking budgets for comparisons in order to evaluate, the effects of the uncontrollable events can be dealt with, so as to facilitate a fair evaluation of performance.

When MNCs make plans they almost always involve making assumptions about exchange rates and how these will affect the MNC. Exchange rates are incorporated into the control process at two stages: first, when the budget is set; and secondly, when tracking the performance relative to the budget. Lessard and Lorange (1977) suggest a 3 by 3 matrix approach to determining the operating budget and tracking the performance relative to the budget. This original model was later developed further by Lessard and Sharp (1983).

The Lessard and Lorange model   Lessard and Lorange (1977) suggest three possible rates for setting budgets. They point out that when a budget is drawn up, two possible exchange rates may be used, either the spot rate or a rate that can be predicted for the end of the period. Further to this, a budget can be updated by the exchange rate prevailing at the end of the period.

When combining all these possible exchange rates, it is possible to have nine combinations for a budget and comparisons (see Table 15.7).

Table 15.7   Possible combinations of exchange rates in the control process

	Rate used to track performance relative to budget		
Rate used for determining budget	Actual at time of budget	Projected at time of budget	Actual at end of period
Actual at time of budget	A1	A2	A3
Projected at time of budget	P1	P2	P3
Actual at end of period (through updating)	E1	E2	E3

Source: Donald R. Lessard and Peter Lorange, 'Currency changes and management control: resolving the centralization/decentralization dilemma', *The Accounting Review*, **52**, July 1977, p. 630

From Table 15.7, P1, E1 and E2 are all illogical combinations. This is because they involve either forecasting exchange rates or updating the budget based on changing rates, but ignore this when evaluating performance. A2 is also illogical, as it tracks at forecasted rates but does not use this rate when setting the budget.

The other combinations are all logical and can be appraised as follows:

A1 sets and tracks the budget on the initial spot rate. This assumes that there is a constant exchange rate, resulting in the performance probably being acceptable.

In A3, the budget is set at the initial rate and tracks it on the end rate. This combination will tend to make the manager risk-averse, as there is a chance that any profits created could be lost due to exchange rate fluctuations. Thus, projects that look good on paper may be rejected because of the fact that exchange rates may fluctuate unfavourably.

P3 sets the budget at projected rates and tracks at an end-of-period rate. This combination is similar to that of A3, but if projected rates are thought to be close to the end rates, then its impact on managers' willingness to take risks will be less severe.

In P2, the budget is set and tracked at a projected rate. Under this combination the manager is not held responsible for any exchange rate fluctuations, but is judged only on his operating capabilities.

E3 sets and tracks the budget at the end-of-period rate.

Exchange rate changes will not be of direct concern to managers, thus resulting in a more relaxed manager who is less anxious about the impact of exchange rate fluctuations.

Lessard and Lorange (1977) make one basic assumption for the performance of their model: namely, that the local operating results expressed in local currency are unaffected by exchange rate fluctuations. This means that a subsidiary carries out all its transactions in its local currency (if transactions were made in different currencies, operating performances might be affected by the exchange rate fluctuations). However, even if the foreign subsidiary does not engage in any other currency while trading, it is almost inevitable that those companies with which it has traded will have dealt with other currencies; therefore, the foreign subsidiary's operating results will be indirectly affected by exchange rate fluctuations.

Exchange rates have two major effects on operating results used for evaluation: the translated profit and loss effect (translation effect), and the local currency profit and loss effect (dependence effect).

In order for an efficient evaluation system of foreign subsidiaries and their managers to be designed, a distinction must be drawn between these two effects. The argument that Lessard and Sharp (1983) bring to our attention is that, while the Lessard and Lorange (1977) model covers the translation effect, it ignores the dependence effect resulting from exchange rate fluctuations.

Demirag (1986) examined combinations of exchange rates used by 105 UK-based MNCs in determining budgets and then comparing their budget with their actual results. The study found that all the combinations suggested by Lessard and Lorange (1977) in Table 15.7 were used. However, as can be seen from Table 15.8, more combinations have been formed, these arise as the projected exchange rates for determining budgets and translating the actual performance from Table 15.7 have been split up into more possible forecasts or, rather, Table 15.8 is more precise as to which exchange rates are being used: the forecasted average exchange rate for the period, or the forecasted exchange rate for the end of the period. Both of these forecasts can be used in setting the budget and in translating the actual performance. Table

Table 15.8 Combinations of exchange rates for performance evaluation
*These figures represent the number and the percentage of the total 85 MNCs which report using each combination of exchange rates for determining the budget and comparing the realized performance relative to the budget.

Rates used for determining budget	Initial	Forecast (average)	Forecast (end of period)	Actual (average)	Actual (ending)	Others	Total number of MNCs
Initial	A1 30* MNCs (35.3%)*	A2 —	A3 1 MNC (1.1%)	A4 1 MNC (1.1%)	A5 7 MNCs (8.2%)	A6 —	39 (46.0%)
Forecast (average)	B1 —	B2 17 MNCs (20.0%)	B3 —	B4 5 MNCs (5.8%)	B5 8 MNCs (8.4%)	B6 2 MNCs (2.3%)	32 (37.6%)
Forecast (end of period)	C1 —	C2 1 MNC (1.1%)	C3 10 MNCs (11.7%)	C4 —	C5 2 MNCs (2.3%)	C6 —	13 (15.3%)
Actual (continuously updated)	D1 —	D2 —	D3 —	D4 —	D5 1 MNC (1.1%)	D6 —	1 (1.1%)
Total number of MNCs	30* (35.3%)*	18 (21.2%)	11 (21.9%)	6 (7.0%)	18 (21.2%)	2 (2.3%)	85 (100%)

Rates used for evaluating actual performance.

Source: Demirag, I. S. (1986) 'The treatment of exchange rates in internal performance evaluation', *Accounting and Business Research*, No. 62, Spring, p. 159

15.8 also shows another exchange rate used in translating the actual performance in order to compare with the budget: this is the actual average exchange rate for the period. Demirag (1986) found that 'other' exchange rates were also used when translating the actual performance in order to compare with the budget; however, this was found to be used by only 2.3 per cent of the MNCs, and they only used it when comparing actual performance with budgets set at a forecasted average exchange rate.

The combinations in Table 15.8 work in exactly the same way as described by Lessard and Lorange (1977). The shaded areas are those which are not possible to achieve, and the unshaded are those which are possible to achieve. (For a numerical example see Appendix, Table 1.)

It can be seen that the most common combination is that in A1 (this is the same combination as in A1 in Table 15.7).

The second most common combination is B2; this is comparable to P2 in Table 15.7, but forecasted average exchange rates are used for setting the budget and comparing the budget to actual results.

The third most common combination is C3; this is comparable to P2 in Table 15.7, but in C3 forecasted end-of-period exchange rates are used in setting the budget and comparing it with the realized performance results.

The fourth most common combination is B5, (this is comparable to P3 in Table 15.7).

The fifth most common combination is A5 (this is the same as combination A3).

In conclusion, a majority (52 per cent) of companies in the UK employ forecast rates in determining budgets. The same set of exchange rates in determining budgets and in comparing actual results are used by 69.4 per cent of UK MNCs. The use of the same exchange rates avoids exchange rate effects on operations, and may reduce the currency awareness of foreign subsidiary managers.

However, when translating foreign subsidiary actual operating results, the use of the opening budget forward rate does not solve the problem created by fluctuations of real exchange rates on the competitiveness of operations.

Nowadays, more foreign subsidiaries operate under global competition, so fluctuations in real exchange rates affect their costs and revenues to a great extent. These effects will cause changes in a subsidiary's operating margins, whether measured in parent or local currencies. Therefore, the creditability of any management evaluation measure, which ignores the impact of real exchange rates on operating results on which managers' performance is based, must be doubted.

The Lessard and Sharp model: contingent budgeting From this flaw in the Lessard and Lorange (1977) model, Lessard and Sharp (1983) have developed a method called 'contingent budgeting'. The purpose of this method is to take into account both the translation and dependence effects (described below).

Fluctuating exchange rates have a major impact on reported net income; this can be split into the translation effect and the dependence effect.

The translation effect occurs when local currency statements are translated into the parent currency there is a difference in inflation movements and exchange rate fluctuations in the short term.

The dependence effect occurs when net income measured in local currency depends on the exchange rates. This is because fluctuations in the exchange rate alter the competitive position of a unit and thus its profitability. Lessard and Sharp (1983) note that the Lessard and Lorange (1977) model accounts for the translation effect, but ignores the dependence effect. The reason for this is that the translation effect is fairly visible and measurable, and that foreign exchange exposure management is often identified with contractual treasury items, rather than with operating cash flows.

A further point raised by Lessard and Sharp (1983) is that fluctuations in real exchange rates result in changes in the relative prices of both local and imported goods, and this in turn gives rise to changes in operating margins, whether measured in local or parent currency. It is with this point that they suggest that serious questions must be asked about evaluation systems that do not account for the effect of real exchange rate fluctuations. Through contingent budgeting Lessard and Sharp try to create an evaluation system that does account for the effects of real exchange rate fluctuations.

Contingent budgeting is, in essence, a refinement of flexible budgeting, in which the effects of the exchange rate fluctuations are the responsibility of those who are thought best to manage exchange rate risks, leaving performance measures to incite incentives to increase the value of the organization. Managers should not then be held responsible for the effects of exchange rate fluctuations, but should have some responsibility for the effect of exchange rates on real operating items.

A contingent budget process comprises of three stages.

1. The budget is prepared in local currency depicting the most likely outcomes.
2. An audit is undertaken to demonstrate the effects of a change in exchange rates, in terms of the effect on costs and prices. This is in order to find some kind of predictability of the relationship between exchange rates, subsidiary management's best efforts, and operating cash flows.
3. When exchange rates are known at the year end, the audit can be used to prepare a set of standards using the actual exchange rates. The actual results can then be compared with these standards for a more adequate evaluation of the subsidiary and its manager.

This process should result in the manager being evaluated on his or her own actual operating capabilities. It is able to achieve this because it can exclude or account for the exchange rate fluctuations, depending on the degree of responsibility the manager is given for the effect of exchange rates.

Non-financial measures   Both financial and non-financial measures are recommended in evaluating the performance of foreign subsidiaries; this is related to the increasing preference of multinational corporations for the use of multiple methods of performance measure.

Profit measures on their own are thought inappropriate for the evaluation of foreign subsidiaries and their managers. Beyond the single divisional profit-based indices and budgeting, there should be a number of measures which account for a broader range of success criteria (see Parker (1979)). A single factor such as return on investment can lead managers to concentrate on that measure instead of making decisions that benefit the organisation as a whole (see Caplan (1971)). Similarly, the use of profit as a performance measure does not, for example, account for a subsidiary manager's ability to build good customer relations or to secure employee loyalty (see Moore and Jeadick (1976)).

Non-financial performance measures used by multinational corporations include productivity improvement, increasing market share, quality control, relationship with the host government, and employee training. These are just a few of the measures that can be used in order to indicate a range of possible goals, criteria and related activities which single profit-based index measures fail to reflect.

Performance appraisal is a form of measuring a manager's ability and efficiency which has encouraged debate over the years. Performance appraisal techniques include management by objectives approaches, essay appraisals, assessment centres, reviews, behavioural-based performance appraisal, and rating scales.

It must be noted that each of the above measures has its own strengths and weaknesses. As with productivity, quality, etc., the success of performance measures depends on how they are used relative to goals: in other words, they must be set against the right objectives.

An element that distinguishes non-financial from financial measures was brought to light by Levinson (1976). He noted that 'It may be stretching it a bit to argue that the epigram it's not the winning or losing that counts, but how you play the game' ought to be strictly followed in designing performance appraisal systems. In business, results are important, and few would disagree with that. What the epigram points out, however, is that some results are not worth the means some take to achieve them. Expanding on this, it can be pointed out that if financial results are poor, it does not necessarily mean that the manager has performed badly; it may be that, owing to certain problems associated with control and evaluation of foreign subsidiaries that we have highlighted, the financial performance measures, especially profit related measures, had in fact given the wrong impression. It should therefore be the responsibility of performance appraisal techniques to indicate how a manager has performed, so that the manager may be fairly evaluated.

REFERENCES

Bennett Stewart, G. (1983) 'A proposal for measuring international performance', *Midland Corporate Finance Journal*, Summer, pp. 56–71.

Bodinat, H. (1974) 'Multinational decentralisation', *European Business*, Summer, pp. 64–70.

Bursk, E. C. (1971) 'Financial control of multinational operations', Financial Executives Research Foundation, New York.

Business International Money Report (1979) 'Evaluating overseas performance I: what are the problems and how do MNCs deal with them?', 16 November, pp. 385–87.

Choi, F. D. S. and Czechowicz, I. J. (1983) 'Assessing foreign subsidiary performance: a multinational comparison', *Management International Review*, Vol. 4, No. 83, pp. 14–25.

Czechowicz, I. J., Choi, F. D. S. and Bavishi, V. (1982) *Assessing Foreign Subsidiary Performance Systems and Practices of Leading Multinational Companies*, Business International Corporation NY.

Daniels, J. D., Ogram, E. W. and Radebaugh, L. H. (1979) *International Business: Environment and Operations*, 2nd edition, Addison-Wesley, USA.

Demirag. I. S. (1986) 'The treatment of exchange rates in internal performance evaluaton', *Accounting and Business Research*, Vol. 16, No. 62, Spring, pp. 157–164.

Demirag, I. S. (1987) 'How U. K. companies measure overseas performance', *Accountancy*, Vol. 99, No. 1123, March, pp. 101–103.

Demirag, I. S. (1988) 'Assessing foreign subsidiary performance: the currency choice of UK MNCs', *Journal of International Business Studies*, Vol. XIX, No. 2, Summer, pp. 257–275.

Demirag, I. S. (1990) 'Multinational performance measures and their association with contextual variables', *Accounting and Business Research*, Vol. 20, No. 80, Autumn, pp. 275–85.

Demirag, I. S. (1992) 'The state of the art in assessing foreign currency operations', *Managerial Finance*, Vol. 18, Nos. 3/4, pp. 24–40.

Eiteman, D. K. and Stonehill, A. I. (1989) *Multinational Business Finance*, 5th edition, Chapter 20, Addison-Wesley, USA.

Goold, N. C. and Campbell A. (1987) *Strategies and styles: the role of the centre in managing diversified corporations*, Blackwell, Oxford and New York.

Hawkins, D. F. (1965) 'Controlling foreign operations', *Financial Executive*, February, pp. 25–32, 56.

Henderson, B. D. and Dearden, J. (1966) 'New system for divisional control', *Harvard Business Review*, September–October, pp. 144–60.

Hongren, C. (1977) *Cost Accounting: A Managerial Emphasis*, Prentice-Hall, Englewood Cliffs, NJ.

Hopwood, A. G. (1972) 'Empirical study of the role of accounting data in performance evaluation', *Journal of Accounting Research, Empirical Research in Accounting*, Selected Studies, pp. 156–93.

Ijiri, Y. (1983) 'Foreign currency accounting and its transition in management of foreign exchange risk', *Managing Foreign Exchange Risk*, ed. Herring, R. J., Cambridge University Press, Cambridge, England.

Kirsch, R. J. and Johnson, W. (1991) 'The impact of fluctuating exchange rates on US multinational corporate budgeting for, and performance evaluation of, foreign subsidiaries', *The International Journal of Accounting*, Vol. 26, pp. 149–73.

Kollaritish, F. P. (1984) 'Managerial accounting problems of multinational corporations', *International Accounting* (ed. Holzer, H. P.), Harper and Row, New York.

Lessard, D. R. and Lorange, P. (1977) 'Currency changes and management control: resolving the centralisation/decentralisation dilemma', *The Accounting Review*, Vol. III, No. 3, July, pp. 628–37.

Lessard, D. R. and Sharp, D. (1983) 'Measuring the performance of operations subject to fluctuating exchange rates', *Midland Corporate Finance Journal*, Summer, pp. 56–71

McInnes, J. M. (1971) 'Financial control systems for multinational operations: an empirical investigation', *Journal of International Business Studies*, Fall, pp. 11–28.

Mauriel, I. J. (1969) 'Evaluation and control of overseas operations', *Management Accounting*, March.

Meister, I. W. (1970) 'Managing the international finance function', The Conference Board.

Miller, E. L. (1979) *Accounting Problems of the Multinational Enterprise*, D. C. Heath and Company, Lexington Books.

Moore, C. L. and Jeadick, R. K. (1976) *Managerial Accounting*, South Western Publishing Company, 4th edition, pp. 517–20.

Morsicato, H. G. (1978) 'An investigation of the interaction of financial statement translation and multinational enterprise performance', PhD dissertation, Pennsylvania State University.

National Association of Accountants (1960) *Management Accounting Problems in Foreign Operations*, NAA Research Report 36, New York.

Parker, L. D. (1979) 'Divisional performance measurement: beyond an exclusive profit test', *Accounting and Business Research*, Autumn, pp. 309–19.

Persen, W. and Lessig, V. (1979) 'Evaluating the financial performance of overseas operations', Financial Executives Research Foundation, New York.

Robbins, S. and Stobaugh, R. (1973) 'Growth of the financial function', *Financial Executive*, July.

Scott, G. M. (1972) 'Financial control in multinational enterprises: the new challenge to accountants', *The International Journal of Accounting, Education and Research*, Vol. 7, No. 2, Spring, pp. 55–68.

Shapiro, A. C. (1989) *Multinational Financial Management*, 3rd edition, Allyn and Bacon, Newton, MA.

Solomons, D. (1965) 'Divisional performance: management and control', Financial Executives Research Foundation, New York.

ADDITIONAL READING

Appleyard, A. R. (1990) *Multi-Currency Budgeting: Some Empirical Evidence from UK Multinationals*, Pilot Study, The Chartered Institute of Management Accountants.

Business International Corporation (1982) *Solving International Accounting Problems*, January, New York.

Choi, F. D. S. and Mueller, G. G. (1984) *International Accounting*, Prentice-Hall, Englewood Cliffs, NJ.

Conference Board, The (1969) *Organising and Managing the Corporate Financial Function*, Studies in Business Policy No. 129, National Industrial Conference Board, New York.

Demirag, I. S. (1984) 'Overseas profits: can we find a happy medium?', *Accountancy*, Vol. 95, No. 1092, August, pp. 80–81.

Demirag, I. S. (1987) 'A review of the objectives of foreign currency translation', *International Journal of Accounting*, Vol. 22, No. 2, Spring, pp. 69–85.

Demirag, I. S. (1987a) 'How UK companies measure overseas performance', *Accountancy*, Vol. 99, No. 1123, March, pp. 101–103.

Demirag, I. S. (1987b) 'How UK companies account for foreign exchange', *Accountancy*, Vol. 99, No. 1124, April, pp. 87–88, 90.

Demirag, I. S. (1988) 'A review of the objectives of foreign currency translation', *International Journal of Accounting*, Vol. 2, No. 3, pp. 69–85.

Demirag, I. S. and Woodward, D. (1989) 'Wish you were here', *Career Accountant*, September, pp. 20–22.

Demirag, I. S. and Tylecote, A. (1992) The Effects of Organisational Culture, Structure and Market Expectations on Technological Innovation: A Hypothesis, *British Journal of Management*, Vol. 3, No. 1, pp. 7–20.

Eckl, S. and Robinson J. N. (1990) 'Some issues in corporate hedging policy', *Accounting and Business Research*, Autumn, Vol. 20, No. 80, pp. 287–98.

Evans, T. G., Folks W. R. and Jilling, M. (1978) *The Impact of Statement of Financial Accounting Standards No. 8 on the Foreign Exchange Risk Management Practices of American Multinationals: An Economic Impact Study*, Financial Accounting Standards Board.

Hosseini, A. and Aggarwal, R. (1983) 'Evaluating foreign affiliates: the impact of alternative foreign currency translation methods', *The International Journal of Accounting*, 19, Fall, pp. 65–87.

Kim, S. and Kuzdrall, P. (1977) 'The simulation of financial strategy under fluctuating exchange rates conditions'. *The International Journal of Accounting*, Vol. 12, No. 2, Spring, pp. 93–107.

Lessard, D. R., and Sharp, D. (1984) 'Measuring the performance of operations subject to fluctuating exchange rates', *Midland Corporate Finance Journal*, Fall, pp. 18–30.

MacRae, T. W. and Walker D. P. (1980) *Foreign Exchange Management*, Prentice-Hall, NJ.

Mauriel, J. J. (1969) 'Evaluation and control of overseas operations', *Management Accounting*, **50**, May, pp. 35–39, 52.

Morsicato, H. G. and Radebaugh, L. H. (1979) 'Internal performance evaluation of multinational enterprise operations', *International Journal of Accounting*, Fall, p. 77–94.

Morsicato, H. G. (1983) 'The effect of translation on multinational corporations' internal performance evaluation', *Journal of International Business Studies*, Spring/Summer, pp. 103–12.

Radebaugh, L. H. (1974) 'Accounting for price-level and exchange rate changes for U. S. international firms: an empirical study', *Journal of International Business Studies*, **5**, Fall, pp. 41–56.

Robbins, S. M. and Stobaugh, R. B. (1973) 'The bent measuring stick for foreign subsidiaries', *Harvard Business Review*, **51**, September–October, pp. 80–88.

Scott, G. M. (1973) *An Introduction to Financial Controls and Reporting in Multinational Enterprises*, Bureau of Business Research, Graduate School of Business, The University of Texas at Austin, Studies in International Business, 1, August.

Shank, J. K., Dillard, J. F. and Murdock, R. J. (1979) *Assessing the Economic Impact of F. A. S. B. 8*, Financial Executives Research Foundation, New York.

Tearney, M. G. and Baridwan, Z. (1989) 'The effects of translation accounting requirements and exchange rates on foreign operations' financial performance—the case of Indonesia', *The International Journal of Accounting*, Vol. 24, No. 3, pp. 251–65.

Verlage, H. C. (1975) *Transfer Pricing for Multinational Enterprises*, University of Rotterdam Press, Rotterdam.

CASE STUDY

Multikorp Inc.

Multikorp Inc. uses a number of performance criteria to evaluate its overseas operations, including return on investment. Lafitte et fils, its French subsidiary, submits the following performance report shown for the current fiscal year (translated to US dollar equivalents).

Lafitte et fils performance report

		$	$
Sales		3,100,000	
Other income		60,000	
Costs and expenses		———	3,160,000
Cost of sales	2,600,000		
Selling and administrative	165,000		
Depreciation	80,000		
Interest	81,000		
Exchange gains and losses	184,000		
			3,110,000
Income before taxes			50,000
Income taxes			21,000
Net income			29,000
Purchasing power gains			1,000
			30,000

Included in sales are $250,000 worth of components sold by Lafitte to its sister subsidiary in Brussels at a transfer price set by corporate headquarters at 40 per cent above an arm's length price. Cost of sales includes extra labour costs of US$75,000 caused by local labour laws. Administrative expenses include US$25,000 of headquarters' expenses which are allocated by

Multikorp to its French subsidiary. The parent company holds all of its subsidiaries responsible for their 'fair share' of corporate expenses.

Local financing decisions are centralized at the group's corporate treasury in the USA, as are all matters related to tax planning. At the same time, Multikorp feels that all subsidiaries should be able to cover reasonable financing costs. Moreover, it feels that foreign managers should be motivated to use local resources as efficiently as possible. Hence, Lafitte et fils is assessed a capital charge based on its net assets at the parent company's average cost of capital. This figure, which amounts to US$60,000, is included in the US$81,000 interest expense figure. One-half of the exchange gains and losses figure is attributed to transactions losses resulting from the French subsidiary's export activities. The balance arises from translating the French accounts to US dollars for consolidation purposes. Exchange risk management is also centralized at corporate treasury.

Required:

(a) On the basis of the foregoing information, prepare a performance report which isolates those elements which should be included in the evaluation of the manager of the French subsidiary.
(b) Examine the implications for managerial responsibility of measuring a foreign manager's performance by comparing:
  (i) actual and budgeted results translated at current exchange rates (i.e. at year end and year beginning respectively)
  (ii) actual and budgeted results translated at projected exchange rates (i.e. projected at year beginning)

Suggested solution:

(a) *Performance report for the manager of the French subsidiary*

	$	$
Sales (1)	3,028,571	
Other income	60,000	
		3,088,571
Costs and expenses		
Cost of sales (2)	2,525,000	
Selling and administrative (3)	140,000	
Depreciation	80,000	
Interest (4)	60,000	
Exchange gains and losses (5)	92,000	
		2,897,000
Income before taxes		191,571
Income taxes		0
Net income		191,571
Purchasing power gains		0
Adjusted income		191,571

Notes to the accounts

(1) Sales

$250,000 of sales is sold at 40 per cent above the normal price. Therefore, fair sales price for these goods should be:

$$250,000 \times 100/140 = \$178,571$$

Therefore, actual sales figure to evaluate manager from is:

$$3,100,000 - 250,000 + 178,571 = \$3,088,571$$

(2) Cost of sales

US$75,000 of cost of sales is due to local labour laws, so deemed out of manager's control. Therefore, actual cost of sales figure to evaluate manager from is:

$$2,600,000 - 75,000 = \$2,525,000$$

(3) Selling and administration

US$25,000 of selling and administration is headquarters' expenses, so is deducted as not being part of the subsidiary's expenses. Therefore, actual selling and administration figure to evaluate manager from is:

$$165,000 - 25,000 = \$140,000$$

(4) Interest

Only US$60,000 of the US$81,000 is attributable to Lafitte.

(5) Exchange gains and losses

Exactly half of the gains and losses in the Lafitte report is due to transactions of export activities. The other half is due to the method of translation used. Therefore, actual exchange gains and losses to evaluate manager from is:

$$1/2 \times 184,000 = 92,000$$

(b) (i) Budgeted and actual results at current exchange (i.e. at year beginning and year end translated rates respectively).

Under this comparison, the full impact of currency fluctuations falls on the overseas subsidiary manager. If his or her ability to hedge is constrained the manager may justifiably regard the variance as non-controllable.

Develop budget	*Track budget*
Expected volume at expected local currency prices and at current exchange rates.	Actual volume at actual local currency prices and at current exchange rates.
Variance:	
Changes in local environment	
Fluctuating currencies	

(b) (ii) Budgeted and actual results translated at projected exchange rates (i.e. projected at year beginning). In this instance, the subsidiary manager is responsible for the impact of changes in the local environment only. The evaluation of performance excludes unanticipated exchange fluctuations, while budget preparation acknowledges anticipated fluctuations. However, complications arise in budget preparation if the inter-group trading with other foreign based subsidiaries is significant. Exchange rate fluctuations between the local and other national currencies must be anticipated, as well as between the local and home-based currencies.

Develop budget	*Track budget*
Expected volume at expected local currency prices and at projected exchange rates.	Actual volume at actual local currency prices and at projected exchange rates.

Variance:
Changes in local environment

Using the projected exchange rates is equivalent to holding the subsidiary manager responsible for performance in terms of comparing local currency budgeted and actual results.

The degree of responsibility reflected by the performance measure should be geared to the overseas manager's ability to take decisions which affect transactional efficiency with or without influencing translation gains or losses.

APPENDIX

Table A1.1 shows Demirag's (1986) combination of exchange rates which may be used in performance evaluations and indicate the amount of budget variances for each type of combination used. The combinations shown here are based on Lessard and Lorange's 1977 work (see page 342).

Table A1.1   Demirag's logical combinations of foreign exchange rates (FXRs) and variance analysis example

Facts

Expected volume	1,000 units	Actual volume	800 units
Expected LC price	1 LC	Actual LC price	1 LC
Initial exchange rate	1 LC = $0.50	Actual exchange rates	
Forecast exchange rates:		Average	1 LC = $0.35
Average	1 LC = $0.40	End of period	1 LC − $0.20
End of period	1 LC = $0.25		

Budget   Actual

(1) Initial by initial

Expected volume	×	Expected LC price	×	Initial FXR	= Budget	Actual volume	×	Actual LC price	×	Initial FXR	= Performance
1,000	×	1	×	$0.50	= $500	800	×	1	×	$0.50	= $400

Total variance = Volume variance + FXR variance

[$500–400] = [200 units × ($0.50)] + 0

$100 = $100 + 0

Table A1.1 *continued*

(2) Forecast (avg.) by forecast (avg.)

Expected volume	× Expected LC price	× Forecast (avg.) FXR	= Budget	Actual volume	× Actual LC price	× Forecast (avg.) FXR	= Performance
1,000	× 1	× $0.40	= $400	800	× 1	× $0.40	= $320

Total variance = Volume variance + FXR variance
[$400–320] = [200 units × ($0.40)] + [1,000 × ($0.40 − 0.40)]
$80 = $80 + 0

(3) Forecast (End of period (EOP)) by forecast (end of period)

Expected volume	× Expected LC price	× Forecast EOP FXR	= Budget	Actual volume	× Actual LC price	× Forecast EOP FXR	= Performance
1,000	× 1	× $0.25	= $250	800	× 1	× $0.25	= $200

Total variance = Volume variance + FXR variance
[$250–200] = [200 units × ($0.25)] + 0
$50 = $50 + 0

(4) Initial by actual (avg.)

Expected volume	× Expected LC price	× Initial FXR FXR	= Budget	Actual volume	× Actual LC price	× Actual (avg.) FXR	= Performance
1,000	× 1	× $0.50	= $500	800	× 1	× $0.35	= $280

Total variance = Volume variance + FXR variance
[$500–280] = [200 units × ($0.35)] + [1,000 × ($0.50 − 0.35)]
$220 = $70 + $150

(5) Forecast (avg.) by actual (avg.)

Expected volume	× Expected LC price	× Forecast (avg.) FXR	= Budget	Actual volume	× Actual LC price	× Actual (avg.) FXR	= Performance
1,000	× 1	× $0.40	= $400	800	× 1	× $0.35	= $280

Total variance = Volume variance + FXR variance
[$400–280] = [200 units × ($0.35)] + [1,000 × ($0.40 − 0.35)]
$120 = $70 + $50

(6) Initial by actual (ending)

Expected volume	× Expected LC price	× Initial FXR	= Budget	Actual volume	× Actual LC price	× Actual (ending) FXR	= Performance
1,000	× 1	× $0.50	= $500	800	× 1	× $0.20	= $160

Total variance = Volume variance + FXR variance
[$500–160] = [200 units × ($0.20)] + [1,000 × ($0.50 − 0.20)]
$340 = $40 + $300

Table A1.1   *continued*

(7) Forecast (avg.) by actual (EOP)

Expected volume	×	Expected LC price	×	Forecast (avg.) FXR	= Budget		Actual volume	×	Actual LC price	×	Actual (EOP) FXR	= Performance
1,000	× 1			× $0.40	= $400		800	× 1			× $0.20	= $160

$$\begin{aligned} \text{Total variance} &= \text{Volume variance} &&+ \text{FXR variance} \\ [\$400\text{--}160] &= [200 \text{ units} \times (\$0.20)] &&+ [1{,}000 \times (\$0.40 - 0.20)] \\ \$240 &= \$40 &&+ \$200 \end{aligned}$$

(8) Forecast (EOP) by actual (EOP)

Expected volume	×	Expected LC price	×	Forecast (avg.) FXR	= Budget		Actual volume	×	Actual LC price	×	Actual (avg.) FXR	= Performance
1,000	× 1			× $0.25	= $250		800	× 1			× $0.20	= $160

$$\begin{aligned} \text{Total variance} &= \text{Volume variance} &&+ \text{FXR variance} \\ [\$250\text{--}160] &= [200 \text{ units} \times (\$0.20)] &&+ [1{,}000 \times (\$0.25 - 0.20)] \\ \$90 &= \$40 &&+ \$50 \end{aligned}$$

(9) Actual (updated continuously) by actual (EOP)

Expected volume	×	Expected LC price	×	Actual (updated continuously)	= Budget		Actual volume	×	Actual LC price	×	Actual (EOP)	= Performance
1,000	× 1			× $0.20	= $200		800	× 1			× $0.20	= $160

$$\begin{aligned} \text{Total variance} &= \text{Volume variance} &&+ \text{FXR variance} \\ [\$200\text{--}160] &= [200 \text{ units} \times (\$0.20)] &&+ [1{,}000 \times (\$0.20 - 0.20)] \\ \$40 &= \$40 &&+ 0 \end{aligned}$$

SHORT-TERM FINANCIAL PERFORMANCE PRESSURES ON MULTINATIONAL COMPANIES

This chapter examines the external and internal factors which influence the decision-making and control process in UK-based multinational corporations, and compare these factors with those influencing decision-making in other countries.

INTRODUCTION

Recently there have been renewed discussions and concern over claims that 'short-termism' in UK industry is distorting decision-making and adding to its difficulties in international competition. While the arguments for the benefits of short-termism on corporate performance are waning, the recent debate has moved on to the causes of such pressures. Supporters of industry argue that the financial markets place excessive weight on the short term, and managers are therefore acting under duress from the City. These arguments are supported by the recent contested takeovers in UK industry and suggestions that the capital markets do not understand or ignore the technological information given out by companies. Those who speak in defence of the City point out that the stock market's short-termism is at best not proven, and at worst not true, and argue that the real culprits are the managers who favour short-term decisions quite independently of any spur from the financial markets. Accordingly, the debate seems to focus on the 'external' and 'internal' sources of short-term pressures.

While there have been several recent empirical studies looking at these arguments, they tend to take either the City or the industry point of view. Furthermore, most of these studies have been of an *ad hoc* nature, dealing specifically with one aspect of the whole web of issues, and fail to develop a consistent framework within which the arguments from both sides can be evaluated. The purpose of this chapter is to develop such a framework by incorporating all the recent relevant studies and debates.

Empirical evidence on the incidence of short-termism over time is examined, both across countries and industries, and a conceptual framework developed for causes of short-termism. Some recommendations are made which we believe would offer a significant improvement in the international competitiveness of UK industry.

What are 'short-term' pressures? Short-term pressures (S-TP) are defined as 'factors tending to raise the discount rate applied (explicitly or implicitly) and/or to foreshorten the time horizon of investments' (Demirag and Tylecote (1992)). This definition also allows S-TP to include factors like high interest rates and low profitability which increase the opportunity cost of capital. The effect of these pressures would be to reduce investment in R&D and in other intangible assets, with their attendant uncertainty and long-term nature, and increase the bias towards projects with short-term pay-back periods.

THE INCIDENCE OF SHORT-TERM PRESSURES

In the 1950s and 1960s UK spending on R&D, mostly for new product development, was high by international standards. Although a relatively high proportion was government-funded and concentrated in the defence/aerospace areas, industry-funded R&D as a proportion of industrial output was respectable: in 1967 it was 1.33 against 1.07 in West Germany, for example. Since then, the UK's industry has fallen towards the bottom of the league of major Western countries in its own spending on R&D, 1.22 against 1.86 in West Germany in 1983 (Patel and Pavitt, 1988). Table 16.1 shows how the UK's balance of trade on manufactures, deteriorating overall, has moved at different rates and even in different directions in different industries depending on their 'relative technological advantage', that is, their share of patents taken out in the USA in their sector, compared to the UK's industry's average share of patents taken out in the USA. Similar, but more recent, evidence is also presented in a report prepared by Sciteb (1991). The report points out the following statistical evidence on UK companies' R&D-related activities: industry-funded R&D in the UK is only 1.3 per cent of domestic product industry, compared to 2.3 per cent for Germany and Japan; the UK-owned large R&D spenders invested in aggregate 2.8 per cent of their sales in R&D, compared to 4.5 per cent for the rest of the world; and the percentage of US patents granted to UK residents has been steadily declining, whereas the percentage granted to Japanese, German and French residents has increased, and this is now true in all major sectors.

It would appear that most of the UK's industry has, in the last decade or so, been performing rather as one might expect if it was subject to short-term performance pressures. But is it subject to such pressures and, if so, where do they arise?

A conceptual framework of external short-term pressures

A priori one might expect the following factors to influence the extent of short-term pressures upon firms:

1. *Economic factors* These include level of inflation, availability and cost of capital, interest rates, government subsidies, size of home market, and lack of profitable investment opportunities.

It is argued that high inflation pushes up the required returns on investment to the point where projects with long pay-back are not financially viable. However, inflation could enable companies to increase their nominal returns by increasing their prices, provided that the markets in which they operate are not price-sensitive. In internationally competitive markets, this argument depends on the competitors' ability to control their price increases and produce the same quality of goods and services. A related argument is that, as inflation causes uncertainty, investors require a premium to compensate them for uncertainty and this pushes up the real interest rates. Furthermore, this uncertainty creates a general climate of reluctance about the long term, which adversely influences investments such as R&D. Of course, there is no reason to believe that companies are unable to raise finance from countries with lower cost of capital, provided that they can hedge their currency exposure in

Table 16.1 The UK's technological competitiveness

Revealed technological advantage in 1981–84	Sector	Trade performance* 1981–84 (1963–68)
High		
(Rising)	Manufacturing of food, beverages	−0.26 (−0.62)
(Rising)	Drugs and medicines	0.40 (0.69)
(Stable)	Aircraft	0.22 (0.30)
(Stable)	Non-electrical machinery	0.20 (0.43)
Medium		
(Rising)	Fertilizers and pesticides	0.14 (−0.04)
(Stable)	Instruments	0.05 (0.12)
(Stable)	Other chemicals	0.11 (0.17)
(Falling)	Motor vehicles	−0.17 (0.79)
Low		
(Stable)	Textiles, wearing apparel and leather	−0.28 (0.07)
(Stable)	Radio, TV and communications equipment	−0.22 (0.26)
(Falling)	Electrical machinery	0.03 (0.55)

$$*\text{Trade performance} = \frac{\text{Exports–Imports}}{\text{Exports + Imports}}$$

Source: Adapted from Tables 4 and 8 in: Patel and Pavitt (1987) 'The elements of British technological competitiveness', *National Institute Economic Review*, No. 122, pp. 72–83

the international money markets. Therefore, much depends on the availability and cost of capital.

There is some evidence that Japanese and German firms have benefited from a lower and more stable cost of capital throughout the 1980s than companies in the UK or the USA (House of Lords (1991), p. 19). Marsh (1990, p. 43) argues that where there is free movement of capital internationally, real interest rates would be the same in all countries in equilibrium, as monies would flow to where the returns were greatest. While accepting that equilibrium may not be reached owing to governments' restrictive investment policies, as was the case in Japan from 1945 to 1975, he points out that from the beginning of 1971 many controls were relaxed, and therefore there should not be any significant differences in real interest rates between countries in more recent years. But is there any difference in the equity risk premia across countries? Given well integrated global markets, 'price' per unit of risk should be the same, although different markets may have different levels of risk. Baldwin (1987) has shown that, for example, the additional risk premium achieved on Japanese, as compared with US, equities, was precisely in line with the higher risk level of the Japanese market.

A more common argument relevant to the cost of capital focuses on the capital structure of companies and gearing ratios. Debt capital cost is tax-allowable, and therefore increasing gearing lowers the cost of capital. As the gearing ratio increases, the weighted average cost of capital is reduced. However, this argument ignores the Modigliani and Miller (1963) arguments that, in the absence of taxes, shareholders in companies with high debt to equity ratios require higher rate of return, as gearing increases risk, leaving the overall weighted average cost of capital unchanged. If we relax the assumption of the absence of taxation, the reduction in the cost of capital can only lead to a small reduction in the new cost of capital which is unlikely to make much difference to a company's investment decisions.

It is also argued that lack of government subsidies and tax incentives have hindered R&D investment in UK industry. In particular, it is argued that 100 per cent or more of R&D expenditure should be written off before calculating taxable profits. (Withdrawal of 100 per cent first year capital allowances in the 1980s adversely affected cash flow.) There is therefore a need for a return to a more generous system of capital allowances, with accelerated amortization at a rate chosen by the individual company. This would increase cash flow and lessen the inhibiting effects of the high cost of capital. However, while accepting the claims that more government support may encourage more investment in R&D, at least in the short term, there appears to be no strong evidence to support the argument that lack of direct government subsidies or tax incentive schemes have been the real cause of the relative poor performance of UK industry.

Much may depend on the size of the home market. Most innovations require success in the domestic market before they can be commercialized effectively on the international market. Given the small size of the UK market, a large number of product and process innovations are simply uneconomic to develop and launch in the UK, even though they would be commercialized in the US, Germany and Japanese markets. The arguments for the size of the home market seem to emphasize the role of 'economies of scale'. However, there is no relationship between the size of home market and the intellectual effort required in R&D activities. Product development decisions may well be affected by the size of home market, but with the access to the EC's large markets, this should not be a problem for UK industry. Perhaps the problems lie not with the size of the home market, but with the traditional over-dependence of UK companies on the home market. The development of an EC market might reduce this problem.

2. *Usefulness of published financial information to shareholders*   To the extent that shareholders lack or do not understand information relevant to the longer-term performance of companies (e.g. on technological progress 'in the pipeline') they will over-react to current profit, dividend announcements, earnings per share, the share's current price earnings ratio (PE), and similar easily available financial data based on historical performance or other short-term performance measures. It is therefore argued that this short-term emphasis by analysts and fund managers will create a corresponding short-term bias in stock prices.

It would seem that the key issues with the use of such short-term measures are 'dividend relevance' and 'market efficiency'. It is generally argued that increasing the dividends will reduce the expected return on a company's shares. But there is some economic evidence which is not consistent with this view. Indeed, much of the controversy surrounding dividend policy has focused on whether or not increasing the dividend increases the expected return on a company's share: for example, Litzenberger and Ramaswamy (1982) and Poterba and Summers (1984) claim that dividends will reduce the expected return on a company's shares, while Miller and Scholes (1982) and Nickell and Wadhwani (1987) argue for the irrelevance of dividend yield on expected returns.

Supporters of market efficiency argue that, in an efficient market, a company's share price, at any given moment, will reflect all the relevant information which is available about its future prospects. Dividend and earnings announcements convey significant information about the future. Management, in setting the current year's dividend, take into account their own judgements about future profitability and cash flows, and set a dividend which is consistent with this, and with sustaining a steady growth rate of future dividends. Hence, dividend announcements are an important signal of management's own knowledge and judgement about the longer-term future of the companies they manage.

Similarly, to the extent that current value accounting is used in company accounts, accounting earnings announcements may also take into account information about future prospects and convey information on current results. However, under the historical cost accounting conventions, current accounting earnings ability to provide us with a reliable indication of future earnings becomes more questionable. Accounting standards are dictated by objectivity and prudence concepts, and based on these principles any unrealized gains are not recognized in the company accounts until they are realized. Given the nature of R&D investment in the pharmaceutical sector, with typical pay-back periods of 10 to 15 years, from initial spending in research into a possible drug to a positive cash flow, it is very unlikely that current earnings and dividends will be able to signal these future pay-offs. But a more significant objection to these arguments lies in the fact that analysts and fund managers lack technological knowledge of the products in the 'pipeline'. The market efficiency claimed is purely technical: it is in the use of the information available. It remains possible that information required for a correct valuation of future cash flows is not being gathered. Moreover, it is not enough that such information be available to a minority. Arbitrage based on superior information about long-term potential will be much less lucrative than that based on information today which the rest will have tomorrow. It does, in fact, appear that the London stock market has only limited information about companies' prospects.

The rules against insider dealing may also be inhibiting, and the qualifications of the investment analysts in most sectors seem inadequate to provide an informed view of 'technology in the pipeline'. Indeed, the Innovation Advisory Board (1990, p. 7) found that while 16 out of 18 pharmaceutical analysts were science graduates, the same was true of only 8 out of 25 electronics analysts, despite that industry's research intensity. The pharmaceutical analysts may have learnt over the years from the experience of the industry: in 'ethical' pharmaceuticals, companies live or die by product innovation on an international market where there is little or no protection through tariffs or otherwise. Only those companies which have spent heavily (and wisely) on innovation have prospered. Unfortunately, this understanding and cosy relationship between the analysts and the industry (with the exception of the pharmaceutical industry) does not appear to exist in the UK. It can hardly be coincidence that 'chemistry-based' industries, of which chemicals and pharmaceuticals form the greater part, have stock market valuations such that their price earnings ratios are positively correlated with their R&D intensity. This is not true for the other main high-technology grouping, the 'physics-based' industries.

3. *Investment objectives of fund managers* In a recent study of the performance evaluation of fund managers, Ashton *et al.* (1991) observed that the principal reward that the managers seemed to receive from their work was the feeling of satisfaction at having performed better than average on their quarterly evaluations. Based on such evidence, it is often argued that fund managers' objectives are short term because they operate under intense short-term pressures owing to the fact that their portfolio performance is measured on a short-term, quarterly basis. These pressures are then transmitted to company managers and force them to increase their attention on dividend growth and the short-term performance of share prices at the expense of abandoning otherwise profitable long-term investment projects. Non-compliance with the financial institutions' demands for current increases on earnings per share means that these companies become vulnerable to takeovers.

However, the opponents of these arguments claim that although performance measurers collect their data on a quarterly cycle, the comparative performance figures which they publish are typically for periods of one year or longer. This view seems to contradict the findings of Ashton *et al.* (1991) whose findings indicate that in all cases the fund was valued at least four times per annum and the fund managers were evaluated on a slightly longer time-scale.

Another argument put forward in support of the short-term pressures on fund managers relates to their frequent changes. While it can be accepted that fund managers are changed frequently, if they perform worse than average, the responsibility for this should lie with the pension fund trustees, in the final analysis this does not change the fact that short-term pressures are exerted upon them.

4. *Importance of the market value of shares to the company* To the extent that share prices reflect shareholders' views of the company's future performance and prospects, management will be sensitive to the share price. The extent of management's concern over the market value of the share price will be influenced by:

(a) The likelihood of being subject to a contested takeover bid.

(b) The need to raise new equity capital, which may be for organic growth or for acquisitions.

A large majority of shares in quoted UK companies are now held by financial institutions, in which pension funds and insurance companies predominate. It is claimed that the institutions which own shares in UK companies are too ready to 'sell out' in a takeover situation, either in the market, or by accepting the bid, in order to make a quick short-term profit. There is therefore little loyalty to companies among the institutions.

Moreover, shareholdings in UK companies are highly fragmented, which induces the holders towards 'Exit' rather than 'Voice': shareholders who are not satisfied with companies' perform-ance and/or policies are likely to sell their holdings in those companies rather than working with them and seek to change them by putting pressure on and ultimately voting against them. Such attitudes will contribute to defensive increases in dividends and cutting back on R&D expenditure. Hence, in the event of a bid or discontented shareholders, companies cannot rely on their shareholders' 'loyalty' or 'advice'; they may enter into activities in order to deter potential predators or maximize current profits at the expense of long-term gains.

Supporters of the City point out that by selling out, either in the market or by accepting the bid, institutions can harm their long-term relationships with companies and destroy any chance of building valuable long-term dialogue with them. This seems, however, a rather feeble defence, and in the absence of any empirical evidence to the contrary there is no reason to accept that the institutions would not exert short-term pressures on companies in cases of hostile bids.

5. *Accounting regulations of R&D* Investment in tangible assets does not reduce current profit, as it is capitalized in the balance sheet. As for intangible assets, such as R&D,

accounting regulations will dictate the amount to be capitalized and expensed. To the extent that it is permitted to capitalize R&D spending, the company will be able to reduce its impact on current declared profits. Even the capitalization of expenditure would, in the long term, affect the profits of the company, as this would increase the capital base which reduces the measured return on capital next year, and, from the same time, depreciation would reduce reported profits. The protection from short-term pressures is itself only short-term. Moreover, if at some point in the future it becomes clear that money spent has been wasted, it will have to be written off. Thus, if R&D on such a project has been capitalized—as with the Rolls Royce RB211—profits will lurch suddenly downwards. This will make the company more vulnerable to a takeover bid than if the R&D had never been capitalized.

However, Goodacre *et al.* (1990) found that analysts were able to 'see through' the essentially cosmetic difference between the two reporting methods and reacted to the underlying economic reality rather than the reported earnings. Moreover, the analysts did not exhibit data fixation, and appeared to place value on what they perceived to be an appropriate level of R&D expenditure. The company which spent less on R&D, investing in plant and equipment instead, was valued significantly less highly than the company investing in R&D at an industry-average level. These results tend to support the view that short-termism in the market does not seem to extend to analysts' views on R&D.

We have outlined here external factors which may influence the extent of short-term pressures upon the company. The evidence for and against external pressures on companies remains too fragmented, relying on anecdotal evidence or on studies which isolate and support pressures either from the financial or industrial communities. We have examined all these claims and counterclaims in the hope of clearing some of the fog around the 'short-termism' debate. We shall now examine internal performance pressures and show how cultures, organizational structures and management styles can cause short-term pressures to be transmitted, and even generated, or alternatively resisted, within the company.

Internal short-term pressures

Internal factors which may give rise to short-termism include the time horizons of managers, organizational structures, management control styles, and remuneration and promotion systems and cultures.

In large and diversified companies, divisions are often divided into subsidiaries. Decisions on technological innovation and progress—on the strategies chosen, and their implementation—will to a greater or lesser extent be taken or shared by middle and lower management. In these companies, although top management would wish those below them to share their goals and objectives for the company, how far this is the case will depend, again, on culture and structure. Let us begin with structure, which is (by and large) under top management's conscious control. The familiar distinction between M-form and U-form organization has considerable relevance to performance pressures. M-form (multidivisional) organization is designed to decentralize responsibility for profit-making to middle management, but by doing so it risks destroying within the company harmonious relationships between the company and its shareholders; wherein those above know only the current financial performance of those below, while the latter, under the pressures which arise from this partial ignorance, take the decisions which count. Such a relationship between top and lower management is described by Goold and Campbell (1987) as the 'financial control' style, and it is not the only one possible, even in an M-form company, as we shall see.

Under the financial control style the company's headquarters has few staff, supported only by a strong finance function. Underneath, there are layers of general management, but prime profit responsibility is pushed right down to the lowest level. These companies focus on annual profit targets; there are no long-term planning systems and no strategy documents. The centre limits its role to approving investment and budgets, and monitoring performance. Targets are expected to be stretching and once they are agreed they become part of a contract between the business unit and the centre. Failure to deliver the promised figures can lead to management changes. The businesses which make up the financially controlled company are likely to have few linkages with each other, operate in relatively stable competitive environments, and do not involve large or long-term investment decisions.

In addition to financial control, other management styles also exist; these include strategic planning and strategic control.

In **strategic planning** companies, while divisionalization is consistent up to a point, the centre participates in and influences the development of divisional strategies. This influence takes two forms: establishing demanding planning processes, and making contributions of substance to strategic thinking. In general, by comparison with financially controlled companies, they place less emphasis on corporate control. Performance targets are set flexible, and are reviewed within the context of long-term strategic progress. The pay-off to strategic decisions is sought in the long term, and it is accepted that there may be problems along the route to building up the core businesses.

Strategic control companies are also concerned with divisional planning, but they are more diverse than strategic planning companies, and are accordingly 'chunked' into strong and largely independent divisions. The centre thus focuses more on establishing demanding planning processes, and on reviewing and criticizing divisional proposals, than on advocating particular ways forward. The role of the centre is seen to be a sympathetic and knowledgeable 100 per cent shareholder.

Companies may use a combination of strategies, and it may be difficult to find a 'correct formula' for success. This is because all styles must cope with basic conflicts or tensions which exist in the role of central management. Clear responsibilities are highly desirable as they enable a tight control to be kept on the business unit, which in turn leads to greater motivation to perform well. Broad responsibility and autonomy at the business unit level leads to a greater sense of responsibility and support efforts to meet long-term objectives, but at the same time strong leadership produces purpose and direction. However, the dilemma exists because the benefits of each style are polar opposites.

Both strategic control and planning may be consistent with M-form companies. However, if a profit centre is adopted with clear responsibilities in an organization, it is difficult to have a matrix form of organizational structure designed to bring people together over major decisions. Development of an organizational strategy may be carried out by managers closest to the business, but at the same time imposing strong leadership from the centre is not consistent with the profit centre approach in an organization. Similarly, tight controls cannot be combined with a softer response to performance evaluations. A strict financial control regime may therefore be inappropriate with strategic planning. It is likely that, in practice, most organizations will strike a balance between an extreme profit centre approach and strategic planning. Nevertheless, some organizations will adopt a strict financial control style. Why is such a management style used?

One must hope that it is because it is actually suited to their business. Goold and Campbell again:

... this means that the businesses [which make up the financially controlled firm] should have few linkages with each other, should be in relatively stable competitive environments, and should not involve large or long-term investment decisions.

Hanson Trust and BTR are typical examples studied by Goold and Campbell:

We were told about a Hanson business that made turbochargers which had come up with an investment plan, indicating several years of negative cash flow to get established in a new and developing field of technology. 'This worried us a lot. We sold the business shortly afterwards' (Goold and Campbell, p. 45).

The businesses which fit well with this style are likely to be in declining, low-technology industries with little prospect of organic growth. Goold and Campbell's sample showed organic shrinkage in 1981–5, though with acquisitions their overall growth was well above average. It seems doubtful whether, in the middle of the microelectronics revolution and the associated rapid changes in processes and products, there is any large area of manufacturing industry to which this style of management is truly suitable. The second possible reason for a company's choice of financial control style is that it is under such acute external short-term pressure that its top management has really no choice but to pass this pressure down the line to its subordinates: unless they can be induced to squeeze the maximum profit out of their activities the company will go bankrupt, be taken over, or be unable to find the necessary resources for investment.

Typically, one might expect a company's management to cling to such a structure and style where it followed a regime in which inattention to profits and cash flow had brought the company to the brink of disaster (GEC is an obvious case in point; see Jones and Marriott (1970), and Williams *et al.* (1983). We readily concede that the impact of short-term pressures need not be all bad; it is better in many ways for a company to be under acute short-term pressures than to be under little or no pressure at all, and will certainly ensure that Leibensteinian 'x-inefficiency' or 'corporate slack' is squeezed out. Moreover, where pressure is not extremely short-term, e.g. where the management feel able to wait, say, two or three years to get visible results, it will provide a strong incentive to make changes which can yield results over that time-scale. The elements of technological progress which are likely to be least vulnerable to such pressures are:

1. Research and development (R&D) expenditure, in an industry where long-term growth and profits are known to require it. Even if all R&D spending has to be (or is) subtracted from profits, it can be disclosed in the accounts, and even less knowledgeable investors may be expected to respect it. If the pay-back from such R&D is relatively predictable and rapid, so much the better.
2. Investment in 'hardware', which offers a reasonably predictable and quick return.

It can easily be shown that the type of technological change likely to be favoured in such circumstances is process change, that is, improved methods of manufacturing an existing product, particularly where the improvement involves reductions in costs (where the improvement is in quality we are dealing, in a sense, with a change in product). The outlook for such process change is particularly favourable where:

1. Worker and union resistance to required changes in manning and working practices is likely to be modest.

2. The change required is not strictly an innovation, merely the introduction of technology already introduced elsewhere.

Equally, the elements of technological progress least favoured by short-term pressures are:

1. Long-range and speculative R&D; R&D in an industry where it is not accepted that such activity is indispensable.
2. Spending on 'hardware' where the payback is uncertain and at best likely to be long-term.
3. Training.
4. Other spending which cannot be capitalized, such as market research, promotional spending, and all that is required to build up a new product's market share and overcome its early 'teething troubles'.

It follows from this that the type of technological change which will be most inhibited by short-term pressures is product innovation, particularly where the new product marks a radical departure from the existing range.

It is important to note that the 'financial control style' not only generates or transmits short-term pressures, that is, pressures which foreshorten the time horizons of decision-makers, it also 'segmentalizes' the company, i.e. it generates pressures which narrow the perspective. Those managing a given profit centre tend to concern themselves with whatever will improve *their* results: cooperation with other parts of the company will be given a low priority. Any form of technological progress which requires, or is facilitated by, such cooperation will therefore be inhibited. In practice, this usually, but not exclusively, means product change, particularly radical product change: if the company is to branch out in an altogether new direction it will probably need to call on the expertise of a number of different divisions.

If we know enough about the pressures acting upon and within companies we should be able to make some predictions about the relative speed of the different types of technological progress. There is evidence that British industry has experienced during the 1980s a definite intensification of short-term pressures. High interest rates throughout the decade, and severe recession and overvaluation at the beginning of it, were external factors accentuating short-term pressures; there also appears to have been an increase in the threat from takeovers and other examples of shareholder impatience with poor financial performance. Privatization, deregulation, and the liberalization of procurement in the defence and telecommunications industry have advanced in the same direction. Within large companies, the financial control style, or some approximation to it, appears to have become more common. (This may, of course, be partly a response to the external changes.) We would therefore expect the speed of process change to have accelerated, particularly since our two further conditions appear to have been met:

1. Worker resistance appears to have been very weak, by comparison with the 1970s and even compared to, for example, France and Germany (see Daniel (1987), and Batstone (1986)). This is partly the result of the trade union legislation of the Conservative government (see Mayhew (1985)).
2. British industry is (or at least was, at the beginning of the decade) in general so far behind some of its competitors in productivity (Prais 1981) that great advances could be made simply by technology transfer. What is more, the growing penetration of Britain and its more advanced rivals by foreign and British multinationals has meant that much of this transfer could take place within companies—the easiest way. (It was noted by Daniel (1987)

that much more process change was reported from foreign-owned than from UK-owned companies.)

On the other hand, the same logic would lead us to expect some falling off in product innovation, to a rate far below those of our rivals less affected by short-term pressures.

The evidence available tends strongly to confirm this prediction. Muellbauer (1986) and others show the remarkably rapid growth of productivity in British manufacturing since 1980. The rate of product innovation, on the other hand, is not at all impressive: this can be inferred, for example, from Patel and Pavitt's (1988) Anglo–German comparisons of patenting rates for the late 1960s and the early 1980s, and (at the other end of the chain from R&D to output) to the alarming deterioration in the UK balance of trade on manufactures. (For the connection between patenting rates and subsequent trade performance, see, for example, Fagerberg (1988).) One very recent and valuable piece of evidence is provided by a PA survey of 'Attitudes to R&D and the Application of Technology' (PA Consulting Group 1989) which found that UK companies, compared with their rivals in Japan, France, Germany and the Netherlands, put at least as much emphasis on investment in new technology as a source of new processes, but markedly less on it as a source of new products. (The country showing the most similarities was the Netherlands, which also happens to be most similar in the role of the stock market.) The PA survey also found that responsibility for R&D strategy tended to be at relatively low levels in UK companies: in only 21 per cent did it lie with a main board director (57 per cent in Japan) and in 22 per cent with middle management (1 per cent in Japan). This finding is clearly consistent with our impression that UK industry has a relatively high proportion of companies with a segmentalized structure and financial control.

There are also those who argue that managerial remuneration and reward systems also contribute to the short-termism in UK industry; it is claimed that in the UK executive incentive systems are often linked to short-term measures of accounting profit, rather than to long-term measures of value. While such rewards for achievement may enhance motivation, this short-term focus discourages managers from undertaking R&D, new capital projects, and investment in long-term market position. If the performance related element of the compensation is deferred until the end of a longer term planning period, managers would have much longer time horizons within a company and they would be encouraged to spend their entire careers within the same company.

But do all sectors of British industry suffer from short-termism? There is some evidence that the British pharmaceutical industry lacks the innovative weaknesses so apparent in other sectors of UK industry—that it can proudly boast, 'we're no worse than anybody else'. In fact, Patel and Pavitt's (1991) patent evidence, and its growth rates relative to the international competition, suggest strongly that it is doing a great deal better than that: it is arguably the most successful pharmaceutical industry of all the major countries, with two out of the world's top three companies (we can count Beecham/Smith Kline as British as well as Glaxo, since it is its British component which has had by far the stronger research record). There are two positive factors, too, which tend to confer a distinct advantage on British companies.

1. The National Health Service (NHS) The NHS has long been noted for its economy in drug purchase, both in volume and price, which makes the British market much less lucrative than population or even income figures would suggest. British companies have latterly been able to overcome this handicap by becoming multinationals. Meanwhile, they have continued to exploit the advantages of the NHS on the research side, in that they have been able to find collaborators within it, in the major teaching hospitals, who were themselves not under short-term profit pressures but able to formulate, and advance towards, long-term goals to a greater extent than might be expected in private medicine. (Whether this situation can continue in the face of the recent decline, by international standards, in NHS funding, or the planned moves towards market disciplines, is an open question.) The doctor–company relationship is a special case of the user–supplier relationship which Lundvall (1988) finds to be of great importance in innovation.

2. *British culture*   The British educational tradition has emphasized pure science over applied science and research, i.e. research for the sake of knowledge rather than for the sake of efficient production. Specifically, this means more and better physicists and chemists, and fewer engineers. The adverse consequences of this for the engineering industries are clear. For chemicals and pharmaceuticals, on the other hand, their key sources of innovative manpower are two of the prestigious pure sciences—chemistry and biochemistry—allied with the equally prestigious medicine.

Another peculiarity of British culture concerns motivation more generally. Recent international comparisons have been made (NEDC Long Term Perspectives Group 1987) of the relative intensity in the labour force of expressed desires for:

1. Material affluence and security
2. The respect and acceptance of other members of one's organization or group
3. Self-fulfilment

Britain came second only to the Netherlands in emphasis on self-fulfilment.

In the next section, a brief review of short-term pressures and their possible causes in some European countries and in Japan will be discussed.

COMPARISON OF EUROPEAN AND JAPANESE SHORT-TERM PRESSURES

Germany

Contrasts between the UK and Germany may be identified in several areas.

1. *Education*   For well over a century Germany has been widely believed to be superior to the UK in technical education at all levels: it has, for example, produced far more engineers at university level and through the day-release type of route. The disparity is even greater at lower levels of education, (technicians and skilled workers), since the vast majority of German school leavers receive some sort of continuing training. Sweden, Switzerland, Austria and the Netherlands are similar in this respect, and the French have traditionally given emphasis to science.

2. *Use of skilled manpower*   Over any long period of time you must expect the supply of education to respond to the demand for it, and this is clearly true for German technical education. The German *Unternehmer* (entrepreneur) families were very different from their British counterparts in (a) wanting their children to stay in science and management, rather than 'rising' into politics, diplomacy and other professions favoured in the UK, and (b) educating them accordingly, in the appropriate technical subjects. This ensured that these subjects were both prestigious and taught in a relevant way for industry.

3. *'Strong line, lean staff'*   There is a very sharp contrast between Germany on the one hand and both Britain and France on the other hand, in the scope of the responsibilities given to line management and those below them on the shop floor, and accordingly in the numbers

employed directly under line control, as compared to those in 'staff' functions such as quality control, finance, marketing, maintenance, etc. The Germans assign much more responsibility to the line managers, forepersons, and skilled, even semi-skilled, workers (for example, a machine operator is expected to carry out the maintenance on his or her own machine) which they are well able to cope with because of their high level of training and because they can delegate their more routine responsibilities to the next level down. A German departmental manager, therefore, can and does leave much of the day-to-day business of management to his or her foreperson. Japan resembles Germany in this way, as in others, whereas the USA is more like France and Britain.

4. *Relationships between owners, managers and the providers of capital* These have traditionally been much stronger in Germany than in the UK.

All of these factors lead to long-term pressure for growth of assets and profits, which can be compared with the short-term pressure for high cash flow and profits now felt strongly by British companies. This leads to long-term policies for product development. Production has always been a highly regarded function with well coordinated input as to how new ideas can best be brought to the market.

Since the focus on short-term pressures the function has become dominant in most British companies, and this is an even more effective drag on R&D and marketing's innovative propensities: indeed, it largely accounts for the sharp drop in British R&D spending since 1965, while in other countries, including Germany, it has been tending to rise. (Incidentally, in a 'strong line' country like Germany, effective R&D spending is likely to be understated, since much of the contribution to product and process development will be made by line employees and probably not charged as R&D spending.)

There is another important effect of the strength of German owners in general, and the banks in particular: what might be called solidarity among companies. The influence of banks is enormous and, since they have a direct ownership stake in most segments of industry, they do not want companies to cut each other's throats. Solidarity does not necessarily mean collusion among rivals; what it does mean is:

1. Cohesion in strong and disciplined employers' associations which have no modern counterpart in the UK (in the latter, individual unions are now weak and play little direct role in the pay bargaining of large companies, and there is no national-level equivalent of the Bund der deutschen Arbeitgeber (Employer's Association), the BdA).
2. Cooperative behaviour within an industry on education and training: most companies are actively involved in training (apprenticeships, etc.) even when there is no immediate payback, and there is no tactic of saving money on training and spending a proportion of it to poach other companies' skilled labour (as documented in the UK in a key industry like electronics). This is facilitated by the cooperation of the trade unions, who accept far lower relative wages for apprentices than their UK counterparts have done, and of the state, which does much to finance and supervise training.

France

The French state has become heavily involved in encouraging and guiding industrial development. Another, less visible, factor shaping French industry has been the wholesale adoption of US techniques and management methods, especially since the 1960s. This major factor made

French management very different from German, since the US model they copied placed emphasis on strong staff and a relatively weak line, with high efficiency achieved by subdividing complex tasks into a number of simpler ones which could be carried out by semi-skilled workers. This offered the additional advantage that relatively cheap unskilled immigrant workers could be employed, which French industry has done in large numbers.

The economic success of France has been variable. It has been very successful in sectors like electricity which were amenable to centralized control and large-scale investment; also in consumer durables, particularly cars, where the US model was ideally applicable (until recently). The consumer durables sector was helped by a large influx of 'Mediterranean' immigrants who provided cheap labour and helped to keep manual wage rates in manufacturing and construction well below those in Germany. But cheap labour and centralized investment planning are not the answer in high-technology industry, where the German combination of 'strong line, lean staff' and intelligent owner/bank control is much more appropriate, and France was quite unable to catch up with the Germans, Swiss and Swedes in the 'old' high-technology sectors like machine tools, or take a leading position in the new high-technology sectors like telecommunications or computers. However, one high-technology area in which France is successful (like Britain, and for the same reasons) is aerospace; both countries spend heavily on maintaining independent defences and defence industries.

Forty years after the end of the Second World War France's 'catching-up' programme can still not be called a real success (although it has passed the UK!). It does, however, have a definite advantage in the state's willingness to pump large sums of money into 'sunrise' industries. This was exemplified at the end of 1988 by the sale of the microprocessor maker INMOS by Thorn/EMI (which under the usual short-term pressures suffered by British business could not survive short-term cash flow problems and their effect on its accounts) to Thomson/SGS, which is effectively owned 50/50 by the French and Italian governments.

Italy

By the early 1970s the Italian union movement had gained such strength in the larger plants in the north that it was a major constraint on management decision-taking. In precisely those mass-production industries where it had been doing particularly well, Italian management now found itself severely restricted. It reacted in various ways. Companies like Fiat became ever more capital-intensive, and replaced workers who went on strike by machines, while the more general reaction has been to keep plants small and to subcontract as far as possible to even smaller ones—including home-based outworkers. Whole districts flourished (even before 1970) through the development of particular industries based on small companies which together enjoyed external economies of scale, e.g. the Bresciani, the producers of steel and steel products in small electric-arc furnaces in the Brescia area; or the ceramic tile manufacturers a little further south, in Emilia.

Owners, management and education in northern industry There are some important similarities between Italy and Germany. As in Germany, the education system is well suited to industrial needs: generations of northern manufacturing families have gained a good, relevant education at the local university and then gone into the family business, or into a company where other relatives have been employed.

The present situation Apart from the great handicap of the poorer south, Italian industry looks to be healthier than French, in some important ways: it has, for example, succeeded in making good progress in the machine tool industry, where the French have failed; and flourishes in all kinds of areas where design is important. Even the constraint on much of Italian industry of keeping plant size down is becoming less of a problem, as new technology increases the productive capacity per person. Small firms clustered together in particular regions (like Emilia and Venezia) in such a way as to provide each other with 'external economies' have prospered and gone upmarket to a considerable extent through 'flexible specialization' (see Piore and Sable (1984)).

Japan

Historical background   Modern Japanese history dates from the mid-nineteenth century when the country strove to catch up technologically with the West. Even at that time Japan had sophisticated organizations in government and in commerce, and high standards of education and of artisan technology, and it was able to build very quickly on these foundations.

Two organizational traditions are extremely important in Japan:

1. *Vertical relationships*   These are based on the feudal tradition of reciprocal loyalty between lord and vassal. There is a very strong sense of hierarchy associated with this tradition.
2. *Horizontal relationships*   These include relationships within work groups, such as existed in the rice-growing villages and depended on very close cooperation among the workers. This promoted the attitude that 'the group is more important than the individual'. This view still exists, and may even be applied to the country as a whole with the individuals, the workforce, striving for the success of 'Japan Ltd'.

Early Japanese industry was broadly split into many small businesses, developed from craftspeople and shopkeepers, and a few *zaibatsu* or 'money cliques', financial–industrial conglomerates each owned by one or two families which had the capital and connections to establish themselves in the higher-technology sectors of the day (e.g. steel, shipbuilding, chemicals, banking, insurance, foreign trade). In the 1920s there was a wave of strikes, and in the face of this and the shortages of skilled labour the *zaibatsu* and other large companies began the practice of 'life-time employment' for skilled workers, to attach them to the company.

The *zaibatsu* also developed what is called 'relational subcontracting', based on the economic fact that outside the large companies wage rates were very low indeed and so was the availability of modern machinery. The way for a big company to prosper and grow quickly was to restrict itself to those activities for which modern equipment was essential. The task of supplying all those services and components for which it was not essential was subcontracted to small firms—many set up with the big company's encouragement by its skilled workers or lower managers. Within this 'dual economy', there was and still is a very feudal relationship between large companies and their small subcontractors (see Kuniyasu (1990)). The subcontractors are supposed to be permanently tied to the big company, and although feudal traditions emphasize reciprocity it is always the lord who has the best of the bargain.

The post-war crisis and reforms   All of this changed in the decade after 1945. The Japanese defeat in the Second World War threw all their hierarchies into question, as the American occupiers insisted on largely breaking up the powerful *zaibatsu* economic groups. The new Japanese big company was much more egalitarian: pay relativities between top managers and the shopfloor were drastically narrowed, to a ratio rather lower than in most Western countries, and the principle of lifetime employment was extended to the whole 'core' labour force. The core workers were now treated with far more respect—the 'horizontal' tradition was now in the ascendant. The 'enterprise unions', although expected to be committed to the prosperity of the company, were also expected to contribute brainpower as well as labour: thus they were henceforth fully involved in suggestion schemes and in quality circles.

The *zaibatsu* effectively reformed as *keiretsu* or *kigyo shudan*, but not in exactly the same format since they were no longer dominated by family shareholders. Instead they were linked together by reciprocal shareholdings which gave each a commitment to, and protection by, all the others. Reciprocal shareholdings in fact became accepted as links between any two companies which bought or sold from each other.

The pattern of stakeholding Companies have a number of stakeholders. Internally there are managers and employees at various levels and in various functions; externally there are shareholders (whose status is privileged in law), creditors (including banks), suppliers, customers, even rivals, and government at various levels. All these could be described as stakeholders in every market economy, but their relationships to the company vary, and are very different in Japan from the pattern in the USA or the UK.

Internal stakeholders In a big Japanese company the core workforce—including most employees and all managers—are permanent staff members. The longer they have been with the company the greater the gap between what they earn and can hope to earn in future within the company, and what they could hope to earn elsewhere. In a sense they have risk capital tied up in the company: if it were to fail, that capital would be lost. What return they make on their capital over their lifetimes depends on the profitability of the company—since, with the exception of senior management, pay is tied quite closely to profits—and its rate of growth. The bigger the company the better it will pay, in general, and above all the faster it grows the greater the opportunity for promotion. Almost all vacant senior posts are filled internally; in this way all the 'core employees' are treated as important stakeholders. Senior managers are usually shareholders, with shareholdings in proportion to their status. Unlike the typical US system, their pay is not tied to profits as that would be regarded as offering too much temptation to follow short-term strategies, nor are share option schemes common. Managers are not expected to sell their shares while employed in the company. Senior managers have a lot of authority within the company, but this is exercised in the context of the company as a community, or family; they feel an obligation to hand on to junior managers a prosperous and growing organization. As the workforce is, in a sense, 'permanent', it makes sense to invest heavily in training its human capital to develop skills to the highest levels.

The total effect of these relationships is to induce top management to pursue long-term organic growth—of sales, employees, and profit—without having to worry overmuch in the short term about profitability, since hostile takeovers are almost unknown. Internal growth not only allows promotion, it also helps the company to keep down costs since junior employees are paid less. External growth runs counter to the ethos of the Japanese company since it does nothing in itself to promote the organic growth the organization needs and it may lead to problems post-acquisition as the cultures of two separate companies need to be integrated.

Kester (1990) identifies four elements in Japanese corporate governance: implicit contracting founded on trust; extensive reciprocal shareholdings and implicit reciprocal trade agreements with a few key stakeholders; managerial incentives aligned to growth; and early selective intervention by key stakeholders, especially banks. In such a system the need for takeovers aimed at correcting managerial failure is minimized as there is extensive information-sharing among companies, bonded by reciprocal shareholdings, and the close monitoring by banks. His description of the rescue of Akai, a consumer electronics company, in the mid-1980s, is a good example of this. Part of the Mitsubishi group of companies, Akai ran into difficulties in the aftermath of the yen's appreciation in 1985. Mitsubishi Bank provided the finance and three senior executives; Mitsubishi Electric increased its direct ownership of the company and sent seven of its top engineers to help Akai develop digital audio tape recorders.

The fundamental thrust of the restructuring was less one of generating cash in the short run to satisfy creditor demands than one of preserving Akai's role in the Mitsubishi group's global network of trading relationships.

Kester does not present this method of governance as static or culturally dependent; he sees the seeds of Japanese industrial success undermining some key stakeholder relationships. Companies are cash-rich and hence less dependent on their banks; while banks are facing competition, made all the more keen by international agreements requiring them to have larger capital bases.

Japanese companies as global competitors: strategic intent versus strategic fit   Hamel and Prahalad (1989) consider that Western and Japanese managers tend to have radically differing 'implicit strategy models', with divergent views of competitive advantage and the role of top management. The most common Western model centred on the problem of maintaining strategic fit, which implies trimming ambitions to match available resources. It seeks to reduce financial risk by building a balanced portfolio of cash-generating and cash-consuming businesses. Faced by larger competitors it tends to lead to a search for niches—or to not challenging an entrenched competitor.

The Japanese model centres on strategic intent, the aim of arranging resources to realize seemingly unattainable goals. It emphasizes the need to accelerate organizational learning to outpace competitors in building new advantages (while strategic fit looks rather at the advantages which are already there), and seeks to reduce competitive risk by ensuring a well balanced and sufficiently broad portfolio of advantages. Faced with a large entrenched competitor it looks for new advantages which will devalue the competitor's existing ones.

The way the organization is disaggregated in the top managers' minds and in practice differs crucially. The Western model disaggregates into product market strategic business units (SBUs) defined by common products, channels and customers; each SBU is seen as independent in terms of the critical skills it needs, whereas the Japanese model takes in core competencies (e.g. microprocessor controls, electronic imaging, etc.) always seeking synergies across SBUs. Thus the Western model sees the relationship between corporate and business strategies in terms of financial objectives imposed by the corporate level on the business level, and between business and financial levels in terms of tight rules as to how to operate. The Japanese model, on the other hand, sees corporate and business strategies as all parts of a particular strategic intent; and functional strategies fit into that, too, by the careful setting of intermediate goals, or challenges, with lower level employees encouraged to explore how these goals can be achieved.

Strategic intent envisages a desired leadership position and establishes the criterion the organization will use to judge progress towards it. In the case of Komatsu and Canon the intent involved replacing an established leader—'Encircle Caterpillar' and 'Beat Xerox' respectively. Honda and NEC, on the other hand, did not have specific competitors in their sights; Honda aimed to be a 'second Ford'—an automotive pioneer—largely through a distinctive core competence in engines, while NEC aimed to rise to prominence in information technology by exploiting the convergence of computing and telecommunications. These strategic intents cannot be given detailed formulation in strategic planning; the end is clear, but the meaning may require great flexibility. Since the end is known by all in the company they can all join in the search for the means; what is more, they can identify with the end in a way they never could with a Western company's search for, say, high return on capital and (perhaps) some vague mission statement.

To attack stronger competitors Japanese companies aim for competitive innovation, not imitation, via:

1. *Seeking distinct advantage*   Colour television is a good example of this. The first Japanese advantage was in labour costs, then in quality and reliability, followed by channels and brands. They then enlarged the scope of products and businesses to increase the return on these investments. The latest advantage has come from regional manufacturing and design centres to tailor products more closely to national markets; for example, Sony in the UK. Note that flexible manufacturing systems combined with good marketing intelligence now allow cost leadership *and* differentiation.

2. *Searching for new market opportunities*   Japanese companies often base a competitive attack on a market that is just outside the main market territory currently occupied by industry leaders (for example, a particular product segment ('low end' in motor cycles) and/or slice of value chain (computer components) or geographical market (Eastern Europe)). From the perspective of a UK multinational, the implication is that more effort in an area may be justified than the immediate returns would suggest, to prevent a competitor using it as a base of attack.

3. *Changing the traditional ways of operating within a market*   Kodak and IBM in the 1970s tried to meet Xerox head-on and failed; Canon, however, standardized machines and components to reduce costs, in contrast to Xerox's wide range. Canon decided to distribute via office-product dealers and not via a huge sales force such as that used by Xerox, and dispensed with a national service network by designing in reliability and serviceability and leaving servicing to the dealers. Canon also sold its products rather than leased them, in order to reduce financing costs. These measures reduced the barriers to entry and also reduced Xerox's ability to retaliate.

4. *Competing through collaboration*   'My enemy's enemy is my friend.' Smaller rivals of the main rival are obvious allies for joint ventures. Japanese companies have even undercut the long-term strength of rivals by manufacturing for them as original equipment manufacturers (OEM) to sell under their own brand name, thus impeding the rivals' development efforts. Collaboration also offers the opportunity to closely examine rivals' strengths.

An important feature of strategic intent, therefore, is the need for lower levels of management to share in the discussion of strategy and the problems of the company.

Should shareholders in the UK be blamed for short-termism and for the unwillingness of UK top managers to commit their companies to the ambitious goals associated with 'strategic intent'? Possibly, but according to Hamel and Prahalad (1989): 'Investors aren't hopelessly short-term, they're justifiably sceptical.'

CONCLUSIONS AND RECOMMENDATIONS

Clearly, improved education, training and communication at all levels is required and will do much to improve the return on innovation. Changes in company law are required to involve shareholders more closely in corporate governance and improve the flow of information to them, and there is also a case for direct government involvement to provide greater tax incentives to companies engaged in long-term investments. Companies can also do much to help themselves; top management cannot expect shareholders to understand and support their strategy for long-term investment and innovation if they do not have one, or fail to clearly inform shareholders of their strategy. The existing system of performance evaluation and performance-based remuneration should be broadened by the use of 'leading indicators' like market share, new products in the pipeline, customer satisfaction, and quality improvements. Crude short-term accounting measures of profitability which discourage investment should not be given a high profile in company assessments, and should be replaced by performance indicators which measure long-term market share, employment stability, and long-term profits which are in accordance with the company's strategic plans. It seems that the extent of short-term pressures may depend on national and organizational culture and historical events. The relationships between industry and government, extent of family ownership of businesses, and education can all play a significant role in the fight against short-term pressures. These pressures appear to be better managed in Germany and in Japan than in Britain, which may suggest that we can learn from the experiences of these nations.

REFERENCES

Ashton, D. Crossland, M. and Moizer, P. (1991) 'The performance evaluation of fund managers', paper presented at the British Accounting Association Annual Conference, April, University of Salford, Salford, UK.

Baldwin, C. Y. (1987) 'Competing for capital in a global environment', *Midland Corporate Finance Journal*, **5**, pp. 43–64.

Batstone, E. V. (1986) 'Labour and productivity', *Oxford Review of Economic Policy*, **2** (3), pp. 32–43.

Daniel, W. W. (1987) *Workplace Industrial Relationships and Technical Change*, PSI/Frances Pinter, London.

Fagerberg, J. (1988) 'International competitiveness', *Economic Journal*, **98** (391), December, pp. 20–21.

Goold, M. C. and Campbell, A. (1987) *Strategies and Styles: The Role of the Centre in Managing Diversified Corporations*, Basil Blackwell, Oxford and New York.

Hamel, G. and Prahalad, C. K. (1989) 'Strategic intent', *Harvard Business Review*, May–June, pp. 63–76.

House of Lords (1991) 'Innovation in manufacturing industry', Select Committee on Science and Technology, Vol. 1 Report, HL Paper 18–1, HMSO, London.

Innovation Advisory Board (1990) *Innovation: City Attitudes and Practices*, Department of Trade and Industry, London.

Jones, R. and Marriott, O. (1970) *The anatomy of a merger: the history of GEC, AEI and English Electric*, Cape, London.

Kester, W. C. (1990) *Japanese Takeovers*, Harvard Business School Press, pp. 298.

Kuniyasu, S. (1990) 'The feudal world of Japanese manufacturing', *Harvard Business Review*, November–December, pp. 38–49.

Litzenberger, R. H. and Ramaswamy, K. (1982) 'The effects of dividends on common stock prices: tax effects or information effects', *Journal of Finance*, **37**, pp. 429–43.

Lundvall, B. A. (1988) 'Innovation as an interactive process: user–producer relations', in *Technical Change and Economic Theory* (eds. Dosi, G., *et al.*) Pinter, London.

Mayhew, Ken (1985) 'Reforming the labour market', *Oxford Review of Economic Policy*, **1**, Summer, pp. 60–79.

Miller, M. H. and Scholes, M. S. (1982) 'Dividends and taxes: some empirical evidence', *Journal of Political Economy*, Vol. 90, No. 6, pp. 1118–41.

Modigliani, F. and Miller, M. H. (1963) 'Corporate income taxes and the cost of capital: a correction', *American Economic Review*, Vol. 53, pp. 433–43.

Muellbauer, J. (1986) 'The assessment: productivity and competitiveness in British manufacturing', *Oxford Review of Economic Policy*, **2** (3), pp. 1–25.

NEDC, Long-Term Perspectives Group (1987) 'IT futures—it can work', National-Economical Development Council, London.

Nickell, S. J. and Wadhwani S. B. (1987) 'Myopia, the "dividend puzzle", and share prices', Centre for Labour Economics, Discussion Paper No. 272, London School of Economics and Political Science.

PA Consulting Group (1989) *Attitudes to R&D and the Application of Technology*, PA Consulting Group, Cambridge.

Patel, P. and Pavitt, K. (1987) 'The elements of British technological competitiveness', *National Institute Economic Review*, 122, pp. 72–83.

Patel, P. and Pavitt, K. (1988) 'Technological activities in FR Germany and the UK: differences and determinants', Science Policy Research Unit, University of Sussex, Working Paper, March.

Patel, P. and Pavitt, K. (1991) 'Europe's technological performance', Chapter 3 in Freeman, C., Sharp, M. and Walker, W. (eds) *Technology and The Future of Europe*, Pinter, London.

Piore, M. J. and Sable, C. S. (1984) *The New Industrial Divide*, Basic Books, New York.

Poterba, J. and Summers, L. (1984) 'New evidence that taxes affect the valuation of dividends', *Journal of Finance*, Vol. 34, No. 5, pp. 1397–41.

Prais, S. J. (1981) *Productivity and Industrial Structure: a Statistical Study of Manufacturing Industry in Britain, Germany and the United States*, Cambridge University Press, Cambridge.

Sciteb (1991) *R&D Short-termism? Enhancing the Performance of the UK Team*, ORBIC for Sciteb, Faversham.

Williams, K., Williams, J. and Thomas, D. (1983) *Why are the British bad at manufacturing?*, Routledge, Keegan and Paul, London.

ADDITIONAL READING

Abegglen, J. C. and Stalk, Jnr., G. (1985) *Kaisha, The Japanese Corporation*, Basic Books, New York.

Barton, H., Brown, D., Cound, J. and Willey, K. (1989) 'Decision processes for strategic capital investment within UK-based diversified industry', MBA Project Report, London Business School, May.

Baysinger, B. and Hoskisson, R. E. (1989) 'Diversification strategy and R&D intensity in multi-product firms', *Academy of Management Journal*, **32**, pp. 310–32.

Chaney, P. K. and Devinney, T. M. (1992) 'New product innovations and stock price performance', *Journal of Business Finance and Accounting*, **19** (5), September, pp. 677–95.

Clark, R. (1979) *The Japanese Company*, Yale University Press, Newhaven and London.

Confederation of British Industry (1987) *Investing for Britain's future: Report of the City Industry Task Force*, CBI, London.

Cosh, A. D. and Hughes, A. (1987) 'The anatomy of corporate control: directors, shareholders and executive remuneration in giant US and UK corporations', *Cambridge Journal of Economics*, **11**, pp. 401–22.

Demirag, I. and Tonkin, D. (1991) 'The UK research and development scoreboard', *The Independent*, 10 June, pp. 20–21.

Demirag, I. and Tonkin, D. (1992) 'The UK research and development scoreboard', *The Independent*, 9 June, pp. 18–19.

Demirag, I. and Tylecote, A. (1992) 'The effects of oganizational culture, structure and market expectations on technological innovation: a hypothesis', *British Journal of Management*, Vol. 3, pp. 7–20.

Doyle, P. (1987) 'Marketing and the British chief executive', *Journal of Marketing Management*, Winter, pp. 121–32.

The Economist (1991) 'What makes Yoshio invent', 12 January, p. 75.

Fama, E. F. (1970) 'Efficient capital markets: a review of theory and empirical work', *Journal of Finance*, Vol. 25, pp. 383–417.

Goodacre, A. (1991) 'R&D expenditure and the analysts' view', *Accountancy*, April, pp. 78–79.

Guerrieri, P. and Tylecote, A. (1992) 'National competitive advantages and microeconomic behaviour', paper presented at the Fourth Annual Conference, European Association for Evolutionary Political Economy, Paris, 4–6 November.

Hitt, M. A., Hoskisson, R. E., Ireland R. D. and Harrison, J. S. (1991) 'Effects of acquisitions on R&D inputs and outputs', *Academy of Management Journal*, Vol. 34, No. 3, pp. 693–703.

Hodder, J. E. (1986) 'Evaluation of manufacturing investments: a comparison of U.S. and Japanese practices', *Financial Management*, Spring, pp. 17–24.

Hoskisson, R. E. and Hitt, M. A. (1988) 'Strategic control systems and relative R&D investment in large multiproduct firms', *Strategic Management Journal*, Vol. 9, pp. 605–21.

Kamin, J. Y., Bijaoui, I. and Horesh, R. (1982) 'Some determinants of the cost distributions in the process of technological innovation', *Research Policy*, **11**, pp. 83–94.

Kono, T. (1982) *Strategy and Structure of Japanese Enterprises*, Macmillan, London.

Marsh, P. (1990) *Short-termism on Trial*, Institutional Fund Managers Association, London.

Mayhew, K. (1991) 'Training—the problem for employers', *Employment Institute Economic Report*, Vol. 5, No. 10, March/April.

McKinsey and Company Inc. (1988) *Performance and Competitive Success: Strengthening Competitiveness in UK Electronics: A report prepared for the NEDC Electronics Industry Sector Group*, National Economic Development Office, London.

Miller, M. H. and Modigliani, F. (1961) 'Dividend policy, growth and the valuation of shares', *Journal of Business*, Vol. 34, pp. 411–33.

Moody, J. (1989) *How the City Appraises Technology Investments*, Scientific Resources Ltd., Cambridge.

Myers, S. C. (1984) 'Finance theory and financial strategy', *Interfaces*, Vol. 14, pp. 126–37.

Nakatani, I. (1987) 'The lure of low U.S. taxes', *Economic Eye*, March, pp. 4–6.

National Association of Pension Funds (1990) *Creative Tension?*, NAPF, London.

Odagiri, H. (1988) 'Japanese management: an "economic" view', Working Paper 60, Centre for Business Strategy, London Business School.

Odagiri, H. (1989) 'Industrial innovation in Japan: a view on policy and management', Working Paper 70, Centre for Business Strategy, London Business School.

O'Hanlon, J., Poon, S. and Yaansah, R. A. (1992) 'Market recognition of differences in earnings persistence: UK Evidence', *Journal of Business Finance and Accounting*, **19**(4), June, pp. 625–39.

Ouchi, W. (1981) *Theory Z*, Addison-Wesley, Reading, MA.

Rockley, L. E. (1973) *Investment for Profitability*, Business Books, London.

Schleifer, A. and Vishny, R. (1990) 'Equilibrium short horizons of investors and firms', *American Economic Association Papers and Proceedings*, 80:2, May, pp. 148–53.

Sasaki, N. (1981) *Management and Industrial Structure in Japan*, Pergamon, Oxford.

Securities and Exchange Commission Office of Economic Analysis (1985) 'Institutional ownership, tender offers, and long-term investments', 19 April.

Thompson, S. (1988) 'Agency costs of internal organisation', Ch.4 in Thompson, S. and M. Wright (eds), *Internal Organisation, Efficiency and Profit*, Philip Allan, Oxford.

SEVENTEEN

INTERNATIONAL TAXATION

INTRODUCTION

The purpose of this chapter is to provide an overview of some of the main issues that are usually considered under the subject of international taxation.

WHAT IS INTERNATIONAL TAX?

International tax basically involves the taxation of a cross-border transaction. Such transactions invariably give rise to tax problems because consideration will have to be given to two or more competing tax systems.

Double taxation

If a payment is made from one country to another, the source country may want to tax the payment before the monies leave the state while the country where the monies are received (e.g. where the recipient individual or company is resident) may also claim taxing rights under its domestic laws. Thus, two countries are seeking to tax the same payment. Double taxation of the same funds would invariably have a detrimental effect on international trade and therefore world economy.

In order to mitigate this double taxation, many states have incorporated into their domestic legislation some form of double taxation relief. Basically, there are two methods by which this may be given:

1. Some countries give relief by exempting income which has already been taxed in another country. Thus, regardless of the rate of tax incurred in the source country, no further tax will be payable in the recipient's country of residence.
2. The second method is where the recipient country taxes the income but gives a credit for the taxes incurred in the source country. (This is the method adopted by the UK.) The overall effect of the credit method is that the recipient incurs the higher of the two tax rates.

Example A UK company receives interest of £100 which has been subject to tax in the source country of £40. UK tax on the £100 is £33. As £40 has already been deducted, there is no additional UK tax. However, the £7 additional tax is not repaid and the UK company therefore incurs 40 per cent on that income. On the other hand, if the overseas tax incurred had been £30, there would have been an additional UK tax liability of £3.

It is not only the rate of tax which affects the overall tax charge, but also the amount of any deductions which are offsettable against the income. For example, a jurisdiction may tax gross income at a rate of 20 per cent, while such income is taxed in the UK on a net basis. The effective rate of foreign tax is thus increased.

International tax rates: a summary

Listed below are the corporate tax rates for a selection of countries.

Australia	39%
Belgium	Sliding scale to 41%: excess profit over certain limit is at 39%
Canada	38%
Denmark	34%
France	33.3%
Germany	50% or 36% on distributed profits
Ireland	40%
Italy	36%
Japan	28%/37.5%[1]
Luxembourg	Sliding scale: effective rate 39.4%
The Netherlands	40% on first DFL250,000, 35% on excess
Portugal	36%
Spain	35%
UK	33%

[1] Rate depends upon share capital and level of income.

Double taxation treaties

In order to minimize the possibility of double taxation occurring, most countries in the world have entered into double taxation treaties with each other. The UK, along with most Western European countries, the USA, Canada, Australia and New Zealand, is a member of the Organization for Economic Cooperation and Development (OECD). In an attempt to achieve uniformity in the treaties concluded by member states, Model Conventions have been drafted by the Committee on Fiscal Affairs of the OECD (the most recent Model was adopted in 1992). Treaties concluded bilaterally between two countries invariably follow the OECD Model. However, since each treaty has to take into account variations in the tax systems and fiscal policies, deviations from the Model will result.

Each treaty must be looked at individually. A specific article may not appear, or the type of relief may vary. Broadly, however, the majority of treaties will have common articles, as follows:

Article 1	Personal scope
Article 2	Taxes covered
Article 3	General definitions
Article 4	Residence
Article 5	Permanent establishment

Article 6	Income from immovable property
Article 7	Business profits
Article 8	Shipping, inland waterways transport and air transport
Article 9	Associate enterprises
Article 10	Dividends
Article 11	Interest
Article 12	Royalties
Article 13	Capital gains
Article 14	Independent personal services
Article 15	Dependent personal services
Article 16	Directors' fees
Article 17	Artistes and athletes
Article 18	Pensions
Article 19	Government services
Article 20	Students
Article 21	Other income
Article 22	Capital
Article 23	Avoidance of double taxation
Article 24	Non-discrimination
Article 25	Mutual agreement procedure
Article 26	Exchange of information (and administrative assistance)
Article 27	Diplomatic agents and consular officers
Article 28	Territorial extension
Article 29	Entry into force
Article 30	Termination

The articles of the treaty which refer to specific sources of income may provide one or a combination of the following:

1. Exemption or reduced rate of taxation in one of the states.
2. Taxing rights for both states, with credit relief or exemption relief being available.

Where an enterprise of one of the states is entitled to a reduced rate of withholding tax by the other state, a claim invariably needs to be submitted by the payer to the tax authorities in advance of any payments being made, in order for the reduced rate to apply. Where such a claim is not made, the payer may have to deduct the full rate of withholding tax and the payee will have to make a claim for repayment of the excess amount.

Taxation of trading income

When a company decides to enter another country to further its trade it may do so in a number of ways: it may establish a representative office to market the business, with all actual sales being conducted in the country where the company is actually located; or it may establish a sales office, a branch or subsidiary company. The way a company decides to conduct its business in the second country will affect its taxability there.

The first step in deciding whether an enterprise has a tax exposure in another jurisdiction is to consider whether that company is 'trading with' or 'trading in' that territory. The tax laws of most countries will not regard a foreign enterprise as having a taxable presence nor will its activities be regarded as giving rise to taxable income where the enterprise is merely selling goods or providing services to local residents without having some form of presence there.

The majority of treaties provide that the trading profits of an enterprise will not be subject to taxation in a particular state unless the enterprise is trading in that state through a 'permanent establishment'. The term 'permanent establishment' is defined in Article 5 of the OECD Model Convention and is reproduced with some modifications in individual treaties. Broadly, the term means a fixed place of business through which the trade of the enterprise is partly or wholly carried on.

Article 5 specifically mentions several types of business which will not amount to a permanent establishment; for example, where stock is held in a country solely for the purpose of storage, display or delivery, or where an office is opened purely for purchasing or gathering information. A construction site which exists for less than a specific period (usually but not always 12 months) will also not cause a permanent establishment to exist.

A person who has and habitually exercises authority to conclude contracts in the name of the enterprise (an agent) will often amount to a permanent establishment unless he or she acts for a number of third parties as agent in the ordinary course of his or her business.

Branch versus subsidiary

When an enterprise has decided that it must establish a clear presence in another jurisdiction, the choice will be between a branch and a subsidiary. The final choice will be determined by a number of factors, but here we will address only the taxation considerations.

It will be necessary to carefully compare the tax treatment in the host country of a branch of a foreign entity and of a locally incorporated and resident subsidiary in the light of both local law and any relevant double tax treaty. Depending upon precise local laws, a subsidiary will invariably produce a higher tax liability on remitted profits than a branch. This is because generally, although the profits themselves will be taxed at the same rates, branch profits will not normally incur any further tax charge on remittance to the head office, whereas dividends paid by a subsidiary to a foreign parent will be subject to a withholding tax (albeit at a reduced rate where a double tax treaty or EC directive applies).

It is also necessary, however, to consider whether the host country taxes the profits of a branch of a foreign company at a higher than normal rate and whether, if it does so, treaty protection is available, e.g. under the non-discrimination article.

Invariably, companies looking to establish a presence in the overseas jurisdiction will establish a branch initially in order to utilize the branch losses against the head office profits for home country tax purposes, and then establish a subsidiary at a later date when the entity becomes profitable. One point to note where this policy is suggested, however, is that on incorporation of the branch, the parent company may find itself with a tax charge on the disposal of the branch assets to the subsidiary.

Other considerations when deciding whether to trade through a branch or a subsidiary include:

1. The local audit and accounting requirements for a branch are generally less tedious than for a subsidiary.
2. A subsidiary may be able to take advantage of local incentives and grants which may not be available to a branch.

3. A subsidiary takes longer to form and is less flexible in its formation and closure than a branch.
4. There may be commercial advantages in trading through a subsidiary as opposed to a branch, for example, local profile.

Dividend income

When a company is considering setting up an operation in another jurisdiction and the subsidiary route is an option, one question will invariably be: What is the tax cost of repatriating those profits back to the parent company in the form of a dividend?

Assuming the subsidiary has been established in a jurisdiction which is not a tax haven, its profits will have been subject to corporate taxes in that state. On payment of the dividend from the net profits, the subsidiary will invariably be required to deduct withholding tax under the domestic laws of the state of which it is a resident.

The parent receiving the dividend will generally be entitled to relief for this withholding tax against its eventual tax liability on the dividend. However, there may, of course, be no liability in the hands of the parent, either because the dividend is not treated as taxable income under the domestic laws of the parent company's jurisdiction, or because the parent has available deductions which reduce the taxable amount.

The withholding tax could therefore be another disincentive for companies considering establishing a subsidiary in another jurisdiction. For this reason, the dividend article of most tax treaties provides for a reduced rate of withholding from dividends paid to shareholders who satisfy certain conditions. Invariably, there will be one rate for individual shareholders resident in the other state and another rate for companies which are resident in the other state and hold a specified percentage of the shares.

The UK operates what is known as the 'imputation' system. When a dividend is paid, advance corporation tax (ACT) at the appropriate rate is accounted for to the Inland Revenue. This is not a withholding tax, but an advance payment of the company's liability to corporation tax for the accounting period in which the dividend is paid. As such, the UK's domestic law does permit non-resident individuals or companies to claim relief for this tax. However, many of the treaties which have been negotiated by the UK do permit at least a partial refund of ACT to shareholders who satisfy the specified conditions.

In addition, the UK tax authorities have introduced a number of 'plans', e.g. the 'H Plan' and the 'P Plan'. The basis of these plans is that 'qualifying companies' can pay dividends plus a proportion of the ACT directly to 'qualifying shareholders', and only pay the reduced ACT to the Inland Revenue. Once a plan has been accepted for a particular company, it is simple to operate from an administrative point of view and provides an immediate cash flow benefit to the shareholders.

HOLDING COMPANIES

So far we have considered whether a company should establish a presence in another jurisdiction in the form of a branch or subsidiary. Assuming a subsidiary is required, it is also necessary to consider the ownership of the subsidiary. There are basically three options:

1. The parent company holds the subsidiary company directly or through a subsidiary resident in the same jurisdiction as the parent.

2. A 'local' holding company is interposed, i.e. a holding company which is resident in the same jurisdiction as the subsidiary for taxation purposes.
3. An 'offshore' holding company is interposed, i.e. a holding company which is resident in a third state.

There are potential benefits to be obtained from both the second and third options which are not available with the first option.

If external financing is required to fund the acquisition of the subsidiary, a local holding company may allow efficient utilization of interest against the profits of the subsidiary, particularly if the host jurisdiction pools profits and losses of companies within a group. The use of a local holding company also provides flexibility in any future sale: a disposal can be made either of the shares in the local holding company or of the shares in the trading subsidiary by the local holding company. In the first case the gain will arise in the state where the parent company is resident, but in the second the gain transfers to the other state.

An offshore holding company offers three potential benefits:

1. Capital gains protection: if established in an appropriate jurisdiction, gains realized by the holding company on a sale of the subsidiary can escape tax altogether.
2. Withholding tax minimization: in certain cases the judicious use of an offshore holding company can reduce the aggregate withholding tax burden when profits are repatriated from the subsidiary to the parent.
3. Double tax credit relief: in the case of UK parent companies, an offshore holding company can increase double tax relief on dividends from high and low taxed subsidiaries.

Taxation of foreign exchange gains and losses

Where cross-border transactions are present, exchange gains and losses will invariably also be present. The tax treatment of these gains and losses is very complex, and varies from country to country. In many countries exchange differences arising from normal trading will be taken into account in the overall trading profit. Where the exchange difference relates to a capital transaction, the difference may be recognized in some countries but not in others.

The UK is at present undergoing a major rehaul of its treatment of foreign exchange gains and losses. Under the present system, gains and losses arising from currency fluctuations are not always taken into account for tax purposes in the same way and, in some cases they are not taken into account at all. For example, some may be treated as trading profits or losses and some as capital gains, while others fall outside the tax system altogether so that gains are not taxed nor losses relieved.

From a date yet to be announced, the UK is to introduce comprehensive rules for the taxation of companies' exchange gains and losses. The broad concept is that exchange gains and losses will be calculated by converting the value of an asset or liability into sterling at the end of the company's current and preceding accounting periods and taking the difference. The specific rules, however, are very complex.

TAX HAVENS

Tax havens are jurisdictions which offer a reduced or nil rate of taxation. Generally speaking, they fall into two specific categories:

1. Pure tax havens which generally impose a nil or low rate of tax
2. Hybrid tax havens which offer specific tax incentives

In international tax planning there is obviously a clear theoretical advantage in arranging for profits to accrue to a company or trust located in a tax haven because the tax imposed may be less than would otherwise accrue to an entity in a high-tax jurisdiction.

Clearly, widespread use of tax havens results in a major loss of revenue to those jurisdictions where taxation is being avoided, and many countries have, over the years, legislated domestic measures to try to curb the abuse of tax havens. These measures exist in many forms; the most usual is legislation which permits the tax authorities to tax certain unremitted income of tax haven companies, where the company is controlled by residents. In the UK, this is the 'controlled foreign company' (CFC) legislation.

Broadly, a CFC is a company which is resident outside the UK, controlled by persons resident in the UK, and subject to a low level of taxation in the territory in which it is resident. A 'low level of taxation' is defined as being less than three-quarters of the prevailing UK rate (for accounting periods beginning prior to 16 March 1993 the proportion was half).

In addition, the Inland Revenue has produced a list of countries which are to be excluded from the CFC provisions, even though the rate of corporation tax would be considered to be low.

The effect of the UK CFC provisions is that UK corporation tax is chargeable on the profits of a company, as calculated under UK tax principles, by apportioning such profits among the persons who have or had an interest in the company at some time during the relevant period.

It is possible to escape a tax charge under the CFC provisions by satisfying one of the four tests set out below:

1. The 'acceptable distribution' test
2. The 'exempt activities' test
3. The 'public quotation' test
4. The 'motive' test

The most common escape route is the 'acceptable distribution' policy. This entails, in the case of trading companies, the distribution of at least 50 per cent (90 per cent for non-trading companies) of available profits within 18 months of the relevant period.

Broadly, the 'exempt activities' test requires that the foreign subsidiary is a company of substance and is involved in normal trading activities, although the exact rules are somewhat complex.

The 'motive' test is very difficult, if not almost impossible, to satisfy and is therefore generally avoided.

The comparable legislation in the USA is the Subpart F provisions, which provide for the taxation of US shareholders of controlled foreign corporations on their pro rata share of certain categories of undistributed profits from tax haven activities and certain other activities of the foreign corporation.

Tax havens can vary, from those that are free from most or all forms of tax including corporation tax, inheritance tax, income tax, capital gains tax, withholding tax, securities turnover tax (or their local equivalents) to centres that specialize in the reduction of tax for selected purposes or even industries. Centres that are free from tax for overseas companies include the Bahamas, Bermuda and the Cayman Islands. Centres such as the Isle of Man, the Channel Islands and Gibraltar offer low rates of tax (generally less than 20 per cent), while others such as Luxembourg specialize in facilities for holding companies. Tax haven business in some of the smaller centres plays a significant role in the overall well-being of the economy, with, for example, more than 40 per cent of Jersey's GNP being derived from tax haven business. The centres create local income by levying various fees upon incorporation of a tax haven company, and annual registration fees. Tax havens attract foreign banks, accountants and lawyers to invest, resulting in office and other ancillary developments, the creation of local employment, and often an improvement in communications facilities.

In recent years there has been a significant increase in the number of centres offering tax haven facilities, by no means all of which could be described as offshore operations. Relatively new tax havens include the islands of Malta, part of the island of Madeira, and the International Financial Services Centre in Dublin. Some have benefited from political changes; for example, the uncertainty of Hong Kong's future as a financial centre after 1997 has led to large sums moving from there into tax havens, while others are taking advantage of traditional tax haven centres experiencing capacity constraints, especially Luxembourg (holding company business) and the Isle of Man (population restrictions).

The recent spate of financial scandals, especially the BCCI and Maxwell affairs, have somewhat tarnished the reputations of tax havens. Nevertheless, the havens themselves are very keen to demonstrate their financial respectability and integrity. Key factors are the degree of investor protection that a haven can offer, and a willingness to prevent the investment or laundering of money obtained by criminal means, particularly drug money. Other factors that are likely to be important in the selection of a tax haven include:

1. The political and economic stability of the country
2. The taxes (if any) that exist
3. Tax treaties between the tax haven and other countries
4. Exchange controls (most tax havens have none)
5. The nature of the legal, banking and accounting systems
6. Transportation and communications facilities
7. The cost of forming a company, the length of time this takes and the annual cost of maintaining a company

The nature of tax havens varies considerably; the following brief examples illustrate some of the differences that exist.

Bahamas

An independent country within the British Commonwealth, with a well developed legal system based primarily upon UK law.

Main features
- No taxation
- A long-established tax haven (over 40 years)
- Secrecy of information is guaranteed, especially within the banking system
- Excellent communications facilities
- Well developed trust business, shipping business and offshore insurance activities

Non-financial tax haven companies
Since the Companies Act of 1990 these are organized in the form of 'International Business

Companies'. An International Business Company is one which does not carry on business with residents of the Bahamas, does not own property and does not engage in financial business (banking, insurance, etc.).

Summarized corporate details
- No share capital is necessary for companies in the Bahamas, although some usually exists.
- Companies can be formed very quickly (in less than one hour, it is said).
- A minimum of two shareholders and one director is required.
- No annual accounts need to be produced.

Cost of tax haven companies
Registration fees:
Between B$100 and B$1000
Annual fees:
Incorporation: between B$100 and B$1000
Licence: between B$100 and B$350

Cayman Islands

A British dependent territory where the economy is largely reliant on tourism and tax haven business. The legal system is based upon UK law.

Main features
- Excellent confidentiality. It is a criminal offence for bank employees to divulge information
- No taxation
- No exchange controls
- Politically stable
- Specializes in banking and trust companies, mutual funds, shipping and captive insurance

Corporate forms
Ordinary non-resident companies
These must have at least one shareholder, one director and a company secretary. A brief annual return must be filed each year detailing the company's shareholders and capital structure. No audit is required (regulations differ for banks and other financial companies).
Exempted companies
This is the most common form for offshore operations. Such companies are required to divulge even less information, and the register of members of the company is not available for public inspection.

Costs of tax haven companies
Incorporation fee:
Ordinary non-resident companies: US$610–1, 585
Exempted companies: US$1,037–2,341
Annual fee:
Ordinary companies
Without share capital: US$305
With share capital: US$427–915

Exempted companies
Without share capital: US$579
With share capital: US$701–1,707

Isle of Man

A highly stable offshore centre in a convenient location with excellent legal and other services. A crown dependency with considerable political autonomy.

Main features
- Political stability: an independent parliament for more than 1,000 years
- Highly qualified workforce
- Good financial, regulatory and supervisory framework, through the Financial Supervision Commission
- Low taxation
- Fast formation of companies
- Very attractive for investment and fund management, deposit-taking by banks and other financial institutions and trusts
- Long-established shipping register and life assurance activities

Corporate forms
Companies may be public or private. Private companies do not have to file audited accounts, but are prohibited from offering their shares to the general public.

Corporate fees
Initial fee and annual filing fee: £35
Capital duty: £95–5,000 payable upon incorporation

Taxation
Profits are taxed at a rate of 20 per cent of the net profit after dividend distributions. High levels of capital allowances are available.

Non-resident companies and exempt companies are free from tax on profits, which makes the Isle of Man attractive for offshore financial institutions.

Malta

An independent republic in the Mediterranean which is currently an associate member of the European Community, but is seeking full membership.

Main features
- Good standards of law, accountancy and education, with significantly lower costs than exist on most of mainland Europe
- Good international communications facilities
- Encouragement of offshore business through the Malta International Business Activities Act
- Strict confidentiality laws
- All applicants for offshore company status are strictly vetted to prevent criminal or other undesirable activities
- Double taxation treaties exist with more than 20 countries
- Specializes in shipping

Corporate forms

Non-trading companies, e.g. corporate holding companies. These are tax exempt.

Trading companies, which is interpreted widely to include banking, insurance and other financial services. Trading companies pay 5 per cent tax on income and are not subject to indirect taxes.

Both forms of company are exempt from any exchange controls, stamp duties, withholding tax, social security payments or customs duties.

Costs of tax haven companies

Registration fee:
Trading companies: £M1,100
Non-trading companies: £M600
Annual fee:
Trading companies: £M1,025
Non-trading companies: £M525

SUMMARY

This chapter has sought to illustrate some of the basic features of international taxation. The topic is highly complex and dynamic, with tax rules and tax rates subject to frequent change. Companies which engage in significant international operations are strongly advised to seek expert advice to enable them to fully understand the tax implications of their activities and to take full advantage of any opportunities that exist to minimize their global tax liability.

ADDITIONAL READING

Euromoney (1992) 'The 1992 guide to offshore financial centres', May, Euromoney Publications, London.
Hughes, T. (1990) 'International tax planning for UK companies', Coopers and Lybrand Deloitte, UK.
OECD (1987) *Taxation in Developed Countries.*
Price Waterhouse (1991) 'Corporate taxes—a worldwide summary', New York.

INDEX